QUEEN OF THE NIGHT

QUEEN OF THE NIGHT

Rediscovering the Celtic Moon Goddess

SHARYNNE MACLEOD NICMHACHA

WEISER BOOKS
Boston, MA/York Beach, ME

FIRST PUBLISHED IN 2005 BY
RED WHEEL/WEISER, LLC
York Beach, ME
With offices at:
368 Congress Street
Boston, MA 02210
www.redwheelweiser.com

Library of Congress Cataloging-in-Publication Data
NicMhacha, Sharynne MacLeod.
Queen of the Night : rediscovering the Celtic moon goddess /
Sharynne MacLeod NicMhacha.
p. cm.
Includes bibliographical references.
ISBN 1-57863-284-6
1. Moon worship--British Isles. 2. Goddesses, Celtic--British Isles.
3. Celts--British Isles--Religion. 4. British Isles--Religious life and customs. I. Title.
BL915.M65N53 2005
299'.161212--dc22   2004019053

Typeset in Minion by Sky Peck Design

PRINTED IN CANADA
TCP
12 11 10 09 08 07 06 05
8 7 6 5 4 3 2 1

This book is dedicated to three special goddesses—
Diane, Sharon G., and my Mother—
Without whose unfailing love and support
It could never have been written.

Thou art the star of the ocean,
The jewel of the clouds,
The flower garland of branches,
And the Queen of the Heavens.

CONTENTS

ACKNOWLEDGMENTS

I would like to thank and bless Rich Taylor, Ben Bruch, Christopher Penczak, James Mobius, Carin Roberge, Kevin Gregg, Kathleen Callahan, Scott Dakota, Kate Chadbourne, Michael Newton, Charlene Shipman, Bart Mallio, The Barnas, The Rowan Grove, Andy Krueger, Dan, Anne, Joe, Brian and Lau, my family, friends, and students, and the welcoming and supportive students and faculty of the Harvard University Celtic Department.

FOREWORD

The cyclical movement of the Moon across the great ballroom of space and time is one of the oldest dances there is, and one to which people down the ages have responded with wonder, creativity, and even a sense of gratitude. The Moon, after all, is our nearest celestial neighbor, and it is no surprise that her regular exits and entrances from the night sky have inspired a kind of neighborly interest and friendly solicitude. How comforting to see that silver face above us and to know that each time she leaves us, she will soon return. It is in this spirit that the people of Scotland once hailed the new Moon as they might greet a cherished friend: "Hail to thee, thou new Moon . . . /I am bending to thee my knee/I am offering thee my love."[1]

That elemental friendship we feel when we gaze upon the Moon is what has inspired such a host of symbols, stories, images, sayings, customs, beliefs, myths, and traditions all over the world. This book is our map to that treasure trove, and we are lucky to have Sharynne NicMhacha as our learned guide. She has scoured the glossaries, the annals, the ancient tales, the place lore, the archaeological record, the ethnographies, and the mythologies in order to bring to us an accurate and complete picture of Moon imagery and veneration in the British Isles. Like the ancient Irish poets whose task it was to synthesize and harmonize all the stories, Sharynne has the ability to make sense of this vast corpus and to see it in its fullest context. It is her gift to seek and to find meaning in material, which other scholars have dismissed as impenetrable or tangential, and the meaning she finds pertains not only to the originators of these traditions but extends also to us today. She firmly believes, as do I, that tradition is not a dead thing to be catalogued and forgotten, but a living being that offers us fresh ways of imagining the past and the present. She offers this wonderful store of tradition to us in the hopes that we will make use of it and reshape what is ancient according to our contemporary and changing needs.

So often we find books that are either rigorously academic (and dry as bone) or intuitive and popular (and wildly inattentive to fact). Sharynne's work combines the best of each approach, delivering meticulous research from the best sources and remembering all the while that her intelligent, nonspecialist reader wishes not only to know but to *understand*. She has given us, in a sense, both sides of the Moon, so that we have everything we need to join in the *seanrince*, the "old dance," and to perceive our own pulse music while dancing under the Moon.

—Dr. Kate Chadbourne
Harvard University

ROOT OF THE OAK, BLOSSOM OF THE APPLE

ANCIENT DISCOVERY AND MODERN SYNTHESIS

Often the most seemingly ordinary occurrences lead to the most extraordinary journeys. Such has been the case with the writing of this book. Years ago, my students (most of whom could rightly be called my teachers) asked if I was aware of any evidence for the worship of the Moon in early Celtic culture. While it is clear that the Celts venerated the natural world and held some of their religious rituals in outdoor settings, other than scattered hints of lunar calendars, the veneration of sky gods, and a few references to folklore practices pertaining to the new Moon, I could not in good faith tell the group that a coherent system of lunar-related beliefs existed, at least not to the best of my knowledge.

Celtic Studies is less than a century old. There is much that we can know, much that we don't know, and even more that has yet to be collated, compared, and interpreted. It is an exciting time to be involved in research of these traditions, as a great deal of quality, groundbreaking work has been accomplished in the last few decades, much of which eclipses the writings of earlier pioneers in the field. There is still so much we can learn and discover, supporting our particular fields of expertise with the wisdom of others—cultural anthropology, linguistics, comparative mythology, archaeology, etc. We are truly at play in the fields of the past, and yet our work is a serious and reverent exploration of what has been and what could be.

I must confess that I originally thought any research into Celtic Moon worship would result, at best, in the creation of a small booklet or pamphlet. However, as I considered the many aspects or angles from which I might approach such a topic, I began to see a world of possibility. My task was doubly challenging in that I was committed to bridging the gap between academia and the general reader, the scientist and the spiritual seeker. While the research presented in this book is at the same level as my professional work, I endeavored to write in a style that would perhaps be more accessible than that found in many academic journals.

Thus, this book is for every person who wants to know more about the Celts, whether fueled by Celtic ancestry, the love of Celtic music or art, a book or novel, a movie, an unexplained natural or spiritual experience, or a love of ancient history or mythology. My colleagues may refer to the information presented here with confidence, and I have (perhaps quite heretically) provided a series of exercises and meditations at the end of each chapter to assist the motivated reader or student in further exploring and understanding the material. It is my premise that in order to show respect for these traditions we must use good resources, understand what the sources represent, and not impose our modern beliefs (cultural, historical, or spiritual) on a culture that to some degree cannot defend itself or appear before us to explain "what once was."

And so, let our journey of exploration begin! In attempting to understand what role the Moon played in the lives of early Celtic peoples (societies defined by the use of Celtic languages and certain similarities in culture), we will look at the primal symbolism of the Moon in a number of ancient societies, including Indo-European cultures and those that practice shamanic traditions. While the stone circles and burial mounds of Ireland and the British Isles are decidedly pre-Celtic, it seems that some of the beliefs of the people who inhabited these lands prior to the Celts were incorporated into Celtic tradition (the legends associated with Newgrange, for example). We will explore the ancient Celtic religion and the Druids, both interesting topics, which have attracted a plethora of fantastical and patently unhistorical "facts." Happily, there is much we can and do know, in a grounded *and* inspiring fashion, about both. We'll also learn about Celtic lunar time reckoning and calendars, Irish and British myths and legends, sacred plants and animals, gods and goddesses, and many other topics, which I must confess, I find fascinating!

In true Celtic fashion, I hope to honor my ancestors (who, in addition to dancers, artists, peasants, and fishwives, include such figures as Lady MacBeth, Fergus of Galloway, Uther Pendragon, King Arthur's sister Anna Morgawse, a panoply of Pictish princesses, and Leod, progenitor of the fabled "Fairy Clan MacLeod") as well as the Old Gods or *síd*-dwellers (who were in some cases considered the mythical ancestors of certain Goidelic or Brythonic families) with this work. My colleagues may (or may not) be surprised to realize that there are academically minded and fully realistic practitioners of ancient Celtic spirituality (such as can be known and practiced in this day and age) among their ranks. Perhaps such an interest should inspire no more wonder or reaction than an interest in Buddhism or a fascination with rugby or stamp collecting. The sources and the work speak for themselves.

I would also like to say that I sincerely hope that the popular reader, perhaps accustomed to the abundance of poorly researched and ill-founded writings about the Celts, will be assisted and inspired by the material presented here. It is a wholehearted attempt to provide roots for the tradition, rather than just blossoms, as both are necessary. I hope you enjoy reading this book as much as I enjoyed creating it. A blessing on those who helped the strands of the tradition appear before my eyes, as well as on those who helped weave them together.

Bendachtan dée ocus an-dée fort!

THE MOON THROUGH HISTORY

FROM PERFECT SPHERE TO POWERFUL GODDESS

Muses, speak to us of the wide-winged Moon . . .
The light from her immortal head flows downwards from the skies
And bathes all of the earth . . .
Her rays fill the air whenever bright Selene arises from the Sea
And puts on her garments which gleam from afar . . .
At the time of waxing light, her beams shine brightest from the heavens
And she is revealed as a sign and an omen to mortals.

—FROM THE HOMERIC HYMN TO SELENE, GREEK, 7TH CENTURY B.C.E.

Since the beginning of time, the Moon has been an object of wonder, beauty, power, and guidance to those of us on Earth. Its great brilliance and the regularity of its phases can be viewed around the world, from rainforests to deserts, from tundras to heavily forested mountains. The brightest object in the sky other than the Sun, the Moon's light shines on all places, creatures, and cultures, affecting the tides and other elements of nature, and showering its blessings upon the Earth as it has done for ages.

Some of the most important (and basic) information relating to the observation of the Moon is often obscured by the artificial illumination of streetlights and modern indoor lighting. Most people are aware of the changing shape of the crescent and full Moon and have heard indistinct rumors pertaining to the effect of the full Moon. Beyond this, the phases of the Moon are only observed by the most diligent in our society. All of us have noted and enjoyed the magic of a particularly brilliant moonlit night, and, despite our knowledge of its rocky exterior, we are still struck by its beauty.

What can we learn about the Moon, our only natural satellite? We know that it orbits the Earth once each month. During this time, the angle between the Earth, the Sun, and the Moon changes, creating varying illuminated shapes that we perceive as the cycle of its phases. The light of the Moon is actually the light of the Sun reflected off its own surface. The visible phase of the Moon is a result of the position it has reached in its orbit around the Earth. When the Moon lies exactly between the Earth and the Sun, its phase is "new"; a crescent Moon (with its back to the right and its open points or "horns" to the left) is seen shortly thereafter. As the Moon moves further along in its orbital path, the size of the crescent increases, and the Moon is said to be "waxing." It reaches its first quarter and "gibbous" positions as it approaches fullness. After the full Moon, it begins to wane, becoming gibbous again and reaching its third quarter. Then a crescent Moon reappears, this time, with its back to the left and horns to the right.[1]

The Moon completes one revolution around the Earth in 27.32 days, a time period known as the *sidereal* month. The *synodic* month (the time from one new Moon to the next) is 29.5 days. This is slightly different from the Moon's orbital period or revolution (as measured against the stars), because the Earth itself moves a significant distance in its own orbit around the Sun during that time. This synodic month is sometimes referred to as a lunar month or *lunation*.[3] In addition, the rising of the Moon varies over time. The Moon moves eastward (against the stellar background) by about thirteen degrees each day, rising later on each successive day. The time difference between one moonrise and the next is usually about fifty minutes (although this time period changes throughout the year). In the Northern Hemisphere, the time difference between moonrises is greatest around March and shortest around September.[3]

The Earth and the Moon both cast long conical shadows out into space. An eclipse of the Sun occurs when the Earth passes through the shadow cone of the Moon. This occurs only when the Moon is new. A lunar eclipse (which may be total or partial) is seen when the Moon passes through the Earth's shadow cone; this occurs only when the Moon is full. Unlike a solar eclipse, a lunar eclipse may be seen from an entire hemisphere of the Earth.[4] Eclipses tend to occur in groups of two or three; a lunar eclipse is always preceded or followed by a solar eclipse. In addition, an eclipse of the Sun or Moon recurs at the same place each 6,585 days (approximately eighteen years, plus ten or eleven days).

The appearance and timing of lunar eclipses was of extreme significance to early humans. Their cyclical pattern was known to the Babylonians and the Chaldeans, and was described by the Greeks as *saros*. The Greek philosopher Thales of Miletus utilized this time period to predict the eclipse of May 28, 585 B.C.E.[5]

The Moon also affects the tides, causing the ebb and flow of the waters that are the source of life on our planet. It exerts a gravitational pull upon the Earth, which is strongest on the side of the Earth closest to the Moon. This pull causes the Earth to bulge toward the Moon on the side nearest to the Moon and away from it on the opposite side. The effect is much stronger in the ocean than on the Earth's crust; hence, we perceive a marked difference between low and high tides. Since the Earth moves much faster than the Moon in its orbit, these bulges move around the Earth once a day, causing two high tides daily. These natural patterns were utilized by early cultures to assist with fishing, sailing, and crossing tidal land bridges.[6]

Ancient people observed the changes in the Moon's appearance and noticed their regular pattern, a comforting cycle in a world filled with uncertainty and change. Eventually, they realized that plants grew and could be gathered according to the Moon's phases and that the timing or performance of other activities could be regulated or enhanced by these cycles as well. Because of its brilliance, its ability to transform itself, its perceived beneficence and assistance with important earthly considerations, concepts of great spiritual significance became associated with the Moon and its remarkable transformations. Hence, the Moon was often regarded as the abode of a deity or thought of as a deity in and of itself.

The sacred cycles and patterns of the moon's orbit were utilized by the Celts in measuring time and determining when important events and rituals took place. The new moon was particularly important in terms of celebrating religious occasions. The druids, who were guardians of sacred lore, were said to have studied the movement of the stars and the heavens. Therefore, it is reasonable to suppose that they were aware of the approach of lunar eclipses and other celestial phenomenon. And, as we shall see, the moon was believed to be the home, or personification, of a great goddess.

The Perfect Face of the Moon

Various theories pertaining to the nature of the Moon and its relationship with the Earth have existed throughout the ages. The natural features of its surface have been variously interpreted as a human face, an animal, or other images, lending credence to perceptions of the Moon's sacred nature.

Eventually, observers realized that the Moon moved around the Earth, a discovery that had a profound effect on the earliest lunar theories. In 270 B.C.E. Aristarchus of Samos made a remarkably accurate estimate of the Moon's distance from Earth. Aspects of his work also suggest that he believed the Earth moved around the Sun (anticipating Copernicus by 1,900 years).[7] In the 4th century B.C.E., Aristotle maintained that the heavens (beginning with the Moon) were the realm of perfection, while the sublunary region was a realm of change and corruption. The problem was, that if the Moon existed in a realm of perfection, it must be a perfect (i.e., perfectly smooth) sphere. How, then, to explain the obvious markings and patterns on the Moon's face? To solve this dilemna, Aristotle mused that the Moon may have suffered some contamination from the lower realm. His theory remained popular for many centuries, and later medieval theorists tried to explain the lunar markings in Aristotelian terms, suggesting that the Moon was a mirror that reflected the Earth's markings, or that vapors existed between the Sun and Moon. Eventually, a standard explanation evolved that claimed there were variations of "density" in the lunar orb. This theory preserved the perfection of the Moon and, therefore, of the heavens themselves.[8]

Around 80 C.E., Plutarch wrote an essay entitled *On the Face of the Orb of the Moon*, in which he theorized that the Moon must be "earthy," with mountains and ravines. In spite of this theory (and due to continued doubt and speculation as to the nature of the markings), most people continued to represent the Moon without its markings. In medieval and Renaissance art, the Moon was often depicted as a crescent, both to clarify its identity and to avoid issues about the nature of its surface. Not surprisingly, Leonardo da Vinci was one of the few who did make an attempt to realistically portray the Moon's surface and appearance.[9]

The invention of the telescope allowed a more accurate perception and representation of the lunar surface. Galileo's observations led him to the conclusion that the changing dark lines on the Moon were shadows, which illustrated that the Moon had both mountains and valleys. Sadly for the followers of Aristotle, this meant that the Moon was not a smooth sphere and, therefore, not perfect as their system claimed. Other observers produced more accurate depictions of the Moon, its phases, and its markings. Eventually, the science of *selenography* (named after Selene, the Greek goddess of the Moon) developed, demonstrating to astronomers how to properly represent heavenly bodies.[10]

Ancient Highlands and Lunar Crystals

Modern science has led to discoveries unimaginable to these lunar pioneers. We have made great progress in lunar research, culminating in the physical exploration of the Moon itself. From these journeys, we know that most of the Moon's surface is covered with a mixture of fine dust and rocky debris produced by meteor impacts. We now know that the Moon has no atmosphere and no magnetic field, and is exposed directly to solar winds. Over the 4 billion years of its existence, hydrogen ions from these winds have become embedded in the surface materials. We also know that the Moon's crust is about 68 km thick (42.2 miles) and covers a partially molten mantle and probably a small core.[11]

Modern instrumentation shows that the Moon is ornamented with a variety of topographical features, including terraced craters (with sunken floors and protruding central peaks), concentric craters (nested, concentric multiple rings), ghost craters (whose walls are barely traceable), ray craters (surrounded by markings of bright rays that may extend for great distances), rills (whose crater floors are marked with complicated systems of narrow furrows), lunar bays (with only partial crater walls), crater chains, and isolated mountain peaks (either domelike or of irregular shape).[12]

The lunar surface consists of two main types of terrain—the ancient highlands, which are heavily cratered, and the much younger and smoother *maria* or grey plains, sometimes referred to as the Moon's "seas." The maria, huge impact craters that were later flooded by molten lava, make up about 16 percent of the Moon's exterior.[13] Many of the rocks found in the maria are dark, fine-grained igneous rocks known as basalts that are composed mainly of plagioclase feldspar and pyroxene, a calcium-magnesium-iron silicate that forms yellowish-brown crystals. These may be found with or without olivine, a magnesium-iron silicate with pale green crystals. The rocks of the highlands are predominantly plagioclase-rich rocks and crystals. In addition, the Moon's surface contains tiny rock fragments held in a matrix of glass. Naturally formed glass beads of various colors have also been found, including orange glass (formed by an impact into a lava lake) and emerald-green glass (found during the Apollo 15 mission).[14]

Rocks collected from the surface of the Moon have been shown to be between 3 and 4.6 billion years old. By comparison, the oldest rocks found on Earth are rarely more than 3 billion years old. The dating of these rocks has helped focus speculations about the age and origin of the Moon. One popular theory holds that the Earth collided with a very large object (as large or larger than Mars), and that the Moon formed from materials ejected from this collision. Interestingly, the mass of the Moon is not much larger than the minimum necessary for a solid body to assume spherical form.[15] Its formation and existence (and perhaps our own as well) may be a fortuitous event—perhaps one that was divinely guided or inspired.

She Who Measures Time

The modern English word "moon" is derived from Old English *mona*, which comes from the Indo-European root-word *mé*, from which we also get the words "month" and "measure."[16] This reflects the ancient tradition of measuring time according to the revolutions of the Moon. Fairly early in the current era, however, the Moon became associated with another unit of time measurement—the days of the seven-day week.

This lunar association appears in the English "Monday," as well as in a number of Germanic languages: German *Montag*, Dutch *Maandag*, and Danish *Mandag*, for example. It also occurs in various Romance languages, in which the word for "moon" derives from Latin *luna*: French *lundi*, Italian *lunedi*, Spanish *lunes*, and Romanian *luni*. The other days of the week were named after additional planets—Saturn (Saturday) and the Sun (Sunday)—and a variety of deities in Roman or Germanic form (see Table 1).[17]

Table 1. Linguistic Roots of Germanic and Romance Day Names

Day	Germanic Deity	Romance Deity
Tuesday	*Tiu*, Germanic god of war and the sky	*Mardi*, Mars' Day (French)
Wednesday	*Woden*, chief of the Germanic gods	*Mercredi*, Mercury's Day (French)
Thursday	*Thor*, god of thunder and lightning	*dies Iovis*, Jupiter's Day (Roman)
Friday	*Frigg*, wife of Odin, goddess of love and the hearth	*Veneris dies*, Venus' Day (Roman), and Vendredi (French)

The full Moon, long associated with supernatural power and magical occurrences in many traditions, was considered a welcome friend and guide in the night. Its appearance was connected with various practical and earthly considerations, and the appearance of the seasonal Moons helped farmers know when to plant or harvest crops, or when to perform other activities in harmony with the phases of the Moon. Table 2 gives one version of the traditional names for these lunar phases.[18]

Table 2. Seasonal Phases of the Moon

MONTH	MOON	MONTH	MOON
January	Wolf Moon	July	Buck Moon
February	Snow Moon	August	Sturgeon Moon
March	Worm Moon	September	Harvest Moon
April	Pink Moon	October	Hunter's Moon
May	Flower Moon	November	Beaver Moon
June	Strawberry Moon	December	Cold Moon

The full Moon that occurs closest to the time of the Autumnal Equinox (September 21) is called the Harvest Moon and rises just after sunset. Its brightness is legendary, lighting up the fields and enabling work to continue late into the night. The next full Moon, which also rises early in the evening, is known as the Hunter's Moon. In the Southern Hemisphere, of course, there is a six-month shift in these dates.

Most of our modern calendar months have thirty or thirty-one days, making it possible for two full Moons to occur in one month (except February). If two full Moons do occur in one month, the second of these is referred to as a Blue Moon—hence, the saying that describes something that occurs only very infrequently as happening "once in a Blue Moon." Actually, Blue Moons can occur more frequently than the saying indicates—once every two and a half years, or seven times every nineteen years.[19]

The measurement of time, the celebration of the seasons, and the sacred cycles and passages of people's lives have been associated with the divine in many cultures since earliest times. This was certainly true even before the advent of recorded history, which represents only a small fraction of the time we have been watching the Moon's passages and marveling at her mysteries.

☽   ☽   ☽

Meditations and Exercises

Following is a list of simple practices to put you more closely in touch with the cycles and phases of the Moon and allow you to tap into its powers.

1) Keep a journal in which you mark and record the passing of time in lunar months. Notice if you are able to perceive any natural energies, patterns, or rhythms that appear in or correspond to this system. Watch for subtle changes in the plant world, in bodies of water, in the activities of animals (or people), and in your own life.

2) Think about the traditional names of the full Moons (Wolf Moon, Snow Moon, Harvest Moon, etc.). Are these names appropriate or meaningful for you? What images, associations, or energies are associated with each? You may want to create your own annual system of full-Moon names and lore.

3) Spend time at the ocean during both low and high tide. Meditate and see what images arise. Also notice if the Moon's energy is stronger or different during each tidal phase. Make an offering to the Moon at the ocean's edge—perhaps a crystal or a silver or blue stone—and consider spending some time cleaning up the beach in her honor.

4) Think about the pattern formed by the Moon's transit through its various shapes: crescent, first quarter, gibbous, full, gibbous, third quarter, crescent, and void Moon (including the alternation of the Moon's horns from side to side). What images or energy patterns are evident? How do these relate to the universe, creation, the cycles of nature, or the energies in your own life?

5) During the next lunar month, use a sketchbook to draw or record the shape of the Moon's changing phases. Also record the markings of the full Moon, and see if these differ from month to month. Look at photographs of the Moon's surface. Notice the wonderful variety of features and shapes, and see if any of these particularly appeal to you. Using either a photograph or your own drawings, meditate on these features. What do they say about the age and history of the Moon?

6) Think about the names of the days of the week, and the planets and deities for which they are named. Meditate on the weekly progression of images in this cycle, and see if any patterns emerge. Keep track of this for several months, and notice if there are any cycles of activity or energy that seem to correspond with these associations: Sunday/the Sun, Monday/the Moon, Tuesday/god of war or sky, Wednesday/chief god/messenger deity, Thursday/sky or thunder god, Friday/goddess of love or beauty, Saturday/saturn.

7) Create an altar to the Moon to use for full- or new-Moon observances. Use a
silver, white, or silver-blue altar cloth and include a silver bowl filled with
water, sea salt, and a moonstone, pearl, or opal (alternatively, yellow-brown or
pale green crystals, or orange or emerald-green glass, as found on the Moon's
surface). Make an offering of an object that represents the crescent Moon
(horns, for example) and the full Moon (a quartz or glass sphere). Consecrate
these items using the smoke from herbs sacred to the Moon. In selecting herbs
for this rite, you may decide to follow the tradition of a particular ancient culture or use the associations found in modern eclectic spiritual traditions,
which draw on a wide range of sources, both ancient and modern. These latter
traditions, as well as certain folkloric sources, suggest the following herbs:
moonwort, violet, willow, jasmine, sweet flag, iris, clary sage, lily of the valley,
orris root, anise, ginger, rowan, coriander, sea holly, wintergreen, and white or
wild roses.[20]

THE DARKNESS OF REBIRTH

MEASURING THE CIRCLE OF LIFE

I will tell you another thing.
There is no "origin" of all Mortals,
nor is there any end in death.

—EMPEDOKLES

In order to understand the many layers of significance humankind has drawn from the appearance of the Moon and its phases, we must delve into the primal symbolism that forms an integral part of many of the world's religious and mythological systems. In spite of cultural and temporal differences, certain patterns and concepts emerge that are common to many systems of belief. For instance, in many spiritual traditions, the concepts of birth, death, and rebirth form a fundamental and highly significant aspect of doctrine and practice. These concepts, which affect many aspects of our worldly and spiritual lives, find an important parallel in the forms and transformations of the lunar cycle, which can be seen to reflect the certainty of birth, death, and rebirth of life—all life.

The fact that the Moon regularly appeared ("was born"), existed for some time in a state of beauty, toil, change, and growth, and then seemed to disappear ("die"), only to be born once more, appeared as a symbolic representation of the patterns of human existence. It also implied the naturalness and certainty of each person's immortal existence. This metaphysical truth was reflected in everything in the cosmos that had a life essence, no matter how large or small the being, no matter how short or long its life cycle. The Moon's transformations were echoed in the cyclical patterns of the lives of plants, animals, and humans, as well as in the soil, rocks, landscapes, seasons, and elements. The ancients realized that, from the delicate butterfly to the solid stone it rests upon, life arose, waned, and was transformed into new life. This pattern demonstrated to them that death was not final, but was always followed by new life in a wondrous variety of forms and possibilities.

The wisdom and symbolism inherent in the Moon's cycle enabled people to compare patterns and energies that existed in the rhythms and incarnations of their own lives and integrate these facts and experiences into a sophisticated system of religious thought and spiritual understanding. Mircea Eliade, the great scholar of world religion, theorized that it was lunar symbolism that enabled humankind to relate and interpret a number of extremely important concepts, including the cycle of birth, becoming, death, and rebirth; cosmic darkness, prenatal existence, and life after death; fate, temporality, death, and immortality; concepts of fertility and fecundity; and symbols associated with spinning, weaving, and the Thread of Life. Let us explore each of these concepts in turn.[1]

Birth, Becoming, Death, and Rebirth

The birth of the Moon is a sacred event experienced with the first sighting of the new Moon. The crescent then changes and transforms, gaining power (in many traditions) as it grows.[2] The death of the Moon occurs at the end of its waning period, after which it is reborn out of the blackness of the void Moon. The appearance of the new Moon after three nights of relative darkness, its growth and transformation as it approaches the radiance of the full Moon, its eventual waning and disappearance, and subsequent reappearance or "rebirth" presented ancient people with an obvious and powerful metaphor of their own experience of birth, death, and renewal. An additional concept, "becoming," arose from watching the changing forms of the Moon, changes that led to speculation about the patterns and transitions of human lives as well.[3]

This cycle revealed to people the pattern of their own lives and also illustrated the interconnectedness of all life. All things that come into existence grow and become, and then wane and return from whence they once emerged. All share common experiences, suffer similar difficulties, and enjoy the blessings of transformation and rebirth.[4]

The association of the Moon with the idea of change, and with natural processes of transformation and becoming, provides a key to understanding what the Moon meant to ancient people, and how it supported and enriched their lives. The idea of becoming is important because it provides a basis for understanding the challenging periods of growth and change that occur in our own lives. These events may be unbidden and painful, or welcome and joyful. The process of transformation may begin in a difficult fashion, and yet result in something wonderful and unexpected. Changes are necessary and natural; they are also inevitable. Many spiritual traditions maintain that change is the only certain thing in life. Clinging to old patterns or incarnations creates suffering and makes change more frightening and painful than it needs to be. Remaining open to the guidance of the divine helps us welcome new possibilities, releases us from pain, and brings us more expediently to a positive outcome.

It has also been said that change is the one constant in the universe. Systems of belief that honor and embrace change provide the flexibility and understanding necessary to experience joy and contentment in this earthly incarnation. Resistance to or fear of change is understandable, but without a proper explanation or theological framework for dealing with change, we risk unnecessary suffering.

This is one of the many reasons for the Moon's reemergence in New Age and neopagan spiritualities. In these religious systems, the numinous world of nature is honored, the divine considered immanent (as well as outside of us), the cosmos perceived as a balanced harmony of male and female, and light and dark energies acknowledged, embraced, and resacralized. Change and transformation are accepted, sanctified, and celebrated at a variety of seasonal rites and are reflected in the daily lives of the participants.

The Moon can serve as a powerful guide and inspiration during times of difficulty, uncertainty, or change. We need only think of its graceful and noble manifestations and draw strength from the steady and methodical progress it displays as it changes form and experiences its own transformations. In this place, there is no fear, no judgment, no resistance. As the Moon traverses the sky and follows its own path, all its forms are wonderful, each full of integrity and appropriate to the place in which it finds itself.

The Cosmic Darkness and Life after Death

Lunar connections to concepts of cosmic darkness and life after death probably evolved from associations related to life, rebirth, and the cycles of the Moon. These concepts are related to the mysteries of the void Moon and the natural quest to understand what happens after the death of (and before the rebirth of) the Moon and all other life-forms. Early people must have wondered where the Moon was during its absence, and from whence it was reborn. Similarly, they must have wondered where and how humans existed after their waning period or death.[5]

"Cosmic darkness" is a religious concept that describes or explains this mystery. The term refers to a specialized place or state of being that can be accessed and validated through meditation, prayer, or other spiritual exercises or experiences. A great deal of philosophical and theological speculation concerning this state of being is found in numerous religious systems, both ancient and modern.[6] The cosmic darkness is the mysterious Otherworld, sometimes represented as a temple, dwelling, or region located in the sky realm or the Underworld. It is frequently described as a cave or primordial ocean that symbolizes the other planes of existence.[7]

This place of primal darkness is analogous to the cosmic womb from which the universe arose, or the cosmic ocean from which life emerged. This is where we were, in some form, before our worldly birth, and whence we will return (at least temporarily) before our next transformation and emergence. These events are often associated with what Eliade refers to as a lunar type of rebirth, one in which light or life emerges from darkness.[8] Although various types of creation myths are found around the world, this symbolism exists in many cosmologies. The mysterious reappearance of the luminous lunar crescent out of the velvety darkness is a perfect metaphor for the mysteries of death and rebirth. The Moon evokes and embodies these spiritual concepts effortlessly, powerfully, and most beautifully.

Fate, Death, and Immortality

The concepts of fate, death, and immortality are associated with passages of a sacred nature—including the Moon's inevitable disappearance and its promised return. Death is the ultimate fate or destiny of living things. Its arrival is certain, and its appearance of finality, terrifying. None can deny its power or existence. Some cultures acknowledge these truths yet do not fear death. They may even find comfort in its reliability, knowing that death is just one step along the path of existence. It is considered to be a hallowed step that leads to the next incarnation, whether in a mortal form or a joyful existence in the Otherworld. Whatever lies on the other side of the door, it is a wonder.

In addition, the finality of death is both a construct and an illusion. The rebirth that follows it is as certain as the death that precedes and creates it. The state of death is temporary, and our existence in the other plane often considered impermanent.[9] This is the place where our souls heal and grow, where they incorporate new life energies and wisdom, and where they will transform into a new forms with a new existence to explore. While some may be skeptical of the certainty of this process, it is interesting to note that, in the annals of recorded religious thought, the vast majority of spiritual and cultural traditions embrace a belief in death and rebirth.

Immortality and concepts of time are also strands of this interwoven web of ideas. The cyclical phases of the Moon reinforced the idea of time as a cyclical phenomenon. This is in opposition to the modern Western perception and expression of time as linear. In primal cultures (ancient and modern), it is considered to be self-evident that all things exist in a sacred circle or hoop, and that all are reborn. Patterns of existence ebb and flow; they change, and yet they are reliable and regular. What once was, will be again. What dies, is reborn. Hence, all life is immortal.

The Waters, Fertility, and Fecundity

In many cultures, the Moon was associated on both a spiritual and mundane level with the concept of "The Waters," an association no doubt rooted in the Moon's profound effect on bodies of water and the creatures living within them. The power of this luminous being to affect and move the great waters of the Earth would have afforded it great respect and devotion. We have seen that the primordial ocean was considered one of the traditional sites of the cosmic darkness, the very source of life. Thus, as the Moon dipped below the horizon, it would have journeyed into this sacred realm (a place from where it would emerge rejuvenated). These important concepts helped define the widespread tradition that the Moon was the realm or personification of a deity.

Another theme associated with the Moon's influence on liquids, fertility, and creation relates to the reproductive cycle of women. Early on, women noticed the connection between their menstrual cycles and the cycles of the Moon, both of which are in the vicinity of twenty-eight days. This sacred time was connected with fertility and fecundity, resulting in the connection of the Moon with these attributes as well. Its primal association with the waters of creation and themes of birth and rebirth strengthened this connection.

In a number of cultural traditions, plants were planted and grown in accordance with the phases of the Moon, with sowing taking place at the new Moon and harvesting during the waning Moon. This reflected a perception that certain energies were more abundant during specific lunar phases and could be brought to bear on the growth patterns of the plant kingdom. The death and rebirth of plants is easy to observe, as their life cycles are relatively short. The annual patterns that plants undergo during their seasonal cycles of growth, death, and replanting (or rebirth) were seen by ancient people as sacred and highly symbolic. Thus, in addition to a connection with the waters and marine life, the Moon was perceived to have a deep association with the fecundity of the plant realm as well.

Plants, crops, trees, and vegetation often serve as symbols of universal renewal (something which the Moon also symbolizes). There are many ways of expressing this cosmogony, which reflects the passage from virtual to formal, from conceptual to tangible. In looking at the world around us, it is impossible not to notice the great variety of life-forms that reflect these principles. Everywhere there is evidence of the richly varied manifestations of these cycles of existence, including the rebirth of life, the sacrality of transformation, the immortality of the soul and all life-forms, and the emergence of life from death, the darkness, or the unseen.[10] This observation may have led to the widespread belief that energy precedes matter, that the spiritual world is the source of the mundane or earthly realm, constantly affecting its forms and events. Systems of thought as diverse as quantum physics, magic and witchcraft, certain forms of monotheism, and numerous polytheist and/or animistic traditions all recognize (and operate in accordance with) this underlying principle.

Spinning, Weaving, and the Thread of Life

The ritual symbolism of weaving and the concept of the thread of life may be familiar to many readers from the Greek myths concerning a group of supernatural figures known as the Fates. The origin of these concepts is much older than these tales, however, and its existence more widespread (attested by the wide variety of associated beliefs found around the globe).

Fate was represented in Greek mythology as a group of three goddesses called the *Moirai*, who were said to be children of Night (The goddess Nyx). The Moirai—Klotho, the Spinner; Lachesis, the Apportioner; and Atropos, the Inevitable[11]—spun a thread whose length determined the length of a person's life. Dressed in white garments, they dwelt in a heavenly cave near a pool from which "white water" was said to emanate.[12] A number of lunar concepts surface in this description: otherworldly women dressed in white who live in the sky realm, a cave, a body of white or luminous water, and associations with life, death, and destiny. The name of these divine beings (moira) has in one case been translated as "part" and, according to the Orphists, their number corresponded to the three parts of the Moon (presumably the crescent, full, and void Moons).[13]

We have seen that lunar symbolism is associated with the cyclical nature of time, cyclical patterns of death and rebirth, and concepts of fate or destiny. In Greek mythology (as well as other cultural or mythological systems), destiny, time, and fate are sometimes represented as being connected with female figures who weave or spin. In many societies, women traditionally perform the work of spinning. This is due in part to a common cultural arrangement in which women perform most kinds of domestic work. It may also be due to the cyclical nature of the work itself (or some other obscure or symbolic aspect of it). Spinning had a mystical, even taboo, significance in many societies, and in many cases, had to be performed away from the light of the Sun and almost in secret. Men were often forbidden to perform or even watch this work.[14]

In addition, spinning was considered a difficult or perilous craft. Women gathered in groups (often at night or in darkness) to meet and spin. In some cases, spinning could only be performed in specific houses, during designated periods of times, and until certain hours. Beliefs pertaining to the dangers or powers associated with spinning were still in existence in parts of Europe during the early part of the 20th century (such as those connected with the Germanic fairies Perchta, Holda, and Frau Holle). In Japan, this mythological memory was expressed through tension or conflict between groups of spinning girls and men's secret societies. At night, the men and their god sometimes attacked the spinning girls, destroying their work and their equipment.[15]

It is possible that some of these traditions may have led to the legendary connection between women and nocturnal gatherings of witches, even though in many cultures, witches were both male and female. Witches met at night, gathering at unknown or restricted locations, to perform activities not accessible or even visible to other members of society. Spinning (which has magical connotations) was performed under the light of and perhaps the guidance or power of the Moon. It often took place in darkness, in some cases behind a veil of secrecy or fear. It is easy to imagine how rumors, fear, or misunderstandings might have arisen under these circumstances. However the legends associated with witchcraft came about, the connection between women and spinning and their association with lunar concepts and symbolism is clearly an ancient one.

Sun and Moon: Being and Becoming

The symbolism that arose from the Moon's phases forms a complex and sophisticated system of perception, belief, and experience. It has been postulated that concepts as diverse as cyclism, dualism, and polarity, as well as the reconciliation or balance of apparently contradictory or opposing forms or energies, were either discovered or clarified by virtue of lunar symbolism.[16] We have already explored the concept of cyclism. What about dualism, polarity, and the reconciliation of opposites? These may, perhaps, be best understood by examining attributes associated with the Moon and those of its partner (or antagonist), the Sun.

The Sun and Moon share a number of common aspects. Both rise in the east and set in the west; both move through the heavens, experience changes and cycles, and shine their light upon the Earth during that portion of the daily cycle over which they preside. The symbolism associated with the Sun, however, contrasts greatly with that of the Moon. Mircea Eliade describes these differences in *The Sacred and the Profane:*

> The moon confers a religious valorization on cosmic becoming and reconciles man to death. The sun, on the contrary, reveals a different mode of existence. The sun does not share in becoming; although always in motion, the sun remains unchangeable; its form is always the same.[17]

These observations are not meant to diminish the obvious importance of the Sun in our lives. We cannot exist without the Sun, whose rays shower light, warmth, energy, comfort, and blessings upon us. The Sun makes possible the growth of plants and animals, the movement of rivers and streams, and the passage of the seasons.

Like the Moon, the Sun also has its cycles. These are longer and, in some ways, more grand in scope than those of the Moon, discernible at various points during the solar year. Most cultural or religious traditions embrace a Theology of the Sun, expressing awe and gratitude for its existence (as well as its power and beneficence), giving thanks for its many gifts, and invoking its return when the days are short. The Sun has long been associated with power, healing, fertility, and other life-promoting concepts.[18]

What of the opposition of solar and lunar attributes—the idea of Becoming, as opposed to (or differing from) that of Being? The Moon is constantly changing. It is always in flux, in progress, in motion. The concept of change, which may have seemed threatening to those in the mortal realm, became less symbolically charged when people observed that the Moon changed but always returned, following a predictable and reliable pattern of growth and transformation. While the Sun changes in its own way, its long cycles providing stability, support, and its own brand of constancy, the Moon is always in a very obvious process of transforming, of becoming something else. Both the Sun and Moon experience passages, moving from darkness to light to darkness again (just as humans emerge from darkness, experience light and life, and return to the place of origin). Passage is an important part of cosmic existence, and the idea of passage (especially as it relates to transitions into new states of being) is particularly relevant to lunar symbolism. While the Sun always exists, the Moon is the symbol and archetype of cosmic Becoming.[19]

Solar-based systems have sometimes embraced and glorified religious and cultural values such as power, autonomy, sovereignty, and intelligence. These are, of course, important and beneficial attributes and may be why some cultures associate their supreme religious being(s) with the Sun. While early Christian perceptions of the "simple, Sun-worshipping heathens" still float about in modern times, some of the societies that maintained a strong solar religious focus are now realized to have been quite sophisticated and well-developed, often exerting a strong influence on the course of history.[20] However, while these solar/celestial gods maintained their prestige and power in some cultures, in other places, they diminished in importance (sometimes even disappearing altogether) as the deities of the Underworld, associated with fertility, creation, and abundance, were perceived to be more accessible to humans.[21]

These attributes played a role in another set of solar/lunar oppositions, one that resulted in a new kind of myth, as well as a change of attitude toward the concept of darkness. Lunar myths explain and sanctify the origins of life, the wonders of rebirth, and the ability of all creatures to grow, adapt, transform, and experience profound changes of state and condition. These myths almost always involve a passage to and/or from a place of cosmic darkness. A very different sort of story is expressed in the many heroic myths that are solar in nature. In these tales, the hero is compared with the Sun and is renowned for fighting "darkness," descending into the dark realms of danger and death and usually (but not always) emerging victorious.[22]

At first glance, this familiar theme seems quite innocuous. However, it represents a notable shift in perception concerning the concept of darkness. In lunar mythology, darkness is one of the natural and necessary modes of the divine (which is comprised of a polarized, yet complementary, set of opposites—male/female, dark/light, etc.). In solar mythology, darkness symbolizes that which the cultural or spiritual hero opposes. In the lunar system, life (and the Moon) are born and reborn out of darkness. In the solar-based system, darkness is something to be feared, conquered, or destroyed, a perception that can lead to an imbalance of energies.[23]

Another example of celestial polarity is the perceived opposition between intelligence and intuition (an opposition that reflects a polarity of gender). In some schools of thought, the Moon was associated with intuition, feeling, and creativity, while the Sun was equated with intelligence, logic, and rationality. Likewise, the Moon's reign over the night sky, its changeability, and its association with water, menstrual cycles, and creation often resulted in its perception as a female figure. The solar figure, on the other hand (whether king, warrior, or hero), was almost invariably male. The Moon was associated with feeling, internal knowing, intuition, becoming, and growth; the Sun represented rationality, a state of being, and a sense of power and authority.[24]

One result of this solar connection with logic and science was that, after a long process of rationalization, religious feeling diminished or disappeared.[25] Religious belief (including the belief in the processes of religion, which include a certain amount of feeling, intuition, and openness to growth) suffered due to these associations. In societies where the solar hero became a primary focus in religious or cultural thought, "Darkness was no longer valorized as a necessary phase in cosmic life; in the perspective of solar religion, it is opposed to life, to forms, and to intelligence."[26] This process of solar rationalization also resulted in the desanctification of nature, including the Moon. As Eliade puts it:

This desacralization of solar hierophanies is only one among many other similar processes through whose operation the entire cosmos is finally emptied of its religious content. But . . . the complete secularization of nature is a fact for only a limited number of moderns—those devoid of all religious feeling . . .[27]

The Sun, in some cases, represented authority, stability, rationality, and the constancy and centralization of power. It was also associated with sovereignty, which in various cultures was conceived of as male or female, human or divine.[28] It often represents the male hero or king who fears, fights, and attempts to conquer or diminish the power of darkness (embodied in a place of unknown power or essence). While the Sun was revered as the bringer of light, warmth, joy, and life, it was also associated with logic and science (as well as the reliance upon these as a countermeasure to the less stable or predictable energies associated with emotion, intuition, and transformation). The Sun is light, life, action, and warmth; it is the essence of Being.

The Moon, on the other hand, is the quintessential symbol of change, transformation, and growth, and symbolizes the inevitability of death and rebirth. The Moon's phases demonstrate its masterful ability to live and move in harmony with the processes and energies of time and nature, to adapt and grow, and to pass from one form to the next. Its place of origin is the place of darkness where souls heal and transform and from where life originates. It is often associated with sovereignty of the self (rather than authority over others). The Moon symbolizes and embodies that which flows, that which is changeable and yet predictable, that which rejuvenates. The Moon is darkness and rest, reflection and intuition; it is the very essence of Becoming.

Initiation and Transformation

Many societies enact rites of initiation to commemorate and facilitate the passage from childhood to adulthood, with its attendant privileges and responsibilities. These rites vary from culture to culture and have only recently disappeared from Western life, where they had already lost most of their significance and no longer provided the transformational experience necessary (Sweet 16 parties, etc.). In primal cultures (as in Western culture), separate ceremonies exist for young men and women.

The process of a young girl's initiation frequently begins with her segregation from society at the first signs of menstruation. This contrasts with the initiation of young boys who are often initiated in a collective group. The length of the girl's segregation varies widely (from three days in Australia to twenty months in New Zealand, for example).[29] The symbolism of darkness is often emphasized in this segregation, as the girls may be isolated in a dark corner of the house or forbidden to see the Sun. This custom may derive from or lend support to the mystical connection between women and the Moon. The symbolism and ceremonies associated with these rites of passage also support the idea that people grow in perfection through a second birth, suggesting that the Moon serves as an excellent symbol or guide for the initiate.[30]

During their initiation, the young women are generally placed under the supervision of older women or female relatives. They are instructed in the secrets of sexuality and fertility, the customs of the tribe, and some of its religious traditions (those which are accessible to women). Some of this education is general and pertains to the girl's responsibilities in society and the cosmos. Much of it is religious in nature, revealing to the young girl the sacrality of women and ritually preparing her to become a creator of life. In most primal cultures, the power of creation and its attendant responsibilities are perceived as religious in nature. This mystery begins with the appearance of a woman's menstrual cycle and culminates at the moment of childbirth. The revelation to a young woman that she is a creator is a religious experience that cannot be translated into masculine terms.[31]

Once again spinning enters the scene. During seclusion, the young girls are taught ritual songs and dances, as well as specifically feminine skills such as weaving and spinning. In some cultures, after the seclusion of the young women is over, they continue to meet in the house of an old woman to spin together. There even seems to be a connection between spinning, female initiation, and sexuality.

In some societies (including early 20th-century Russia), girls enjoy some degree of sexual freedom prior to marriage. Sometimes their meetings with boys take place in the house where they gather to spin. Even in societies where virginity is highly valued, these meetings are not only tolerated by the parents, but sometimes even encouraged. These sexual freedoms are not considered profane or erotic, but rather ritualistic in nature. It is reasonable to assume that these traditions embody fragments of a forgotten mystery whose meaning was once more clearly woven into the cultural memory of the society. The antiquity and profound nature of these beliefs is referred to in Eliade's *Rites and Symbols of Initiation:*

> The fact that cases of such ritual behavior have been preserved down to the 20th century among peoples long since Christianized proves, I believe, that we are here dealing with an extremely archaic religious experience, a basic experience of women's soul.[32]

The Creation of the Year

Another rite of passage that reflects the symbolism of the lunar cycle is the rebirth of the year at the time of the New Year's festivities. Most societies hold New Year celebrations at some significant point in the solar or lunar calendar; these are experienced by society as a whole, rather than individually, as with initiation rites.[33] Rituals associated with the New Year are often connected with the renewal of food and provisions, the continuity of life in the community, seasonal changes, and other religious or symbolic events. Great significance and ceremony are attached to the New Year, which is the end of one grand annual cycle as well as the beginning of the next.[34]

The timing of New Year's celebrations are often calculated based on the observation of natural or cosmological rhythms and cycles. As with individual initiation ceremonies, rituals of purification often take place in order to properly prepare for the symbolic regeneration of life. In many cultures, this regeneration is symbolized by a ritualized recitation, enactment, or commemoration of the events that led to the creation of the world. Time is often temporarily suspended during the New Year's rites in order to accommodate the process of re-creation, which is invoked during these ritualized repetitions, a rite that takes place every year in order to reenact "that which has been done before."[35]

Many New Year's mythologies include great spiritual or symbolic endings that are believed to have preceded creation. Floods, destruction, or the ending of a race of men or other beings often results in the birth of a new humanity, world, or cosmos. The continuation of human life often occurs as a result of the survival or activities of a mythical ancestor who escapes the catastrophe. Such was the case in early Irish tradition, where the figure of Fintan escaped a flood and survived in various animal forms to witness the subsequent incoming waves of humanity.[36] Interestingly, in some cases, this primal ancestor is said to have escaped from a lunar animal of some kind. Here we can see a possible connection between the lunar and yearly cycles. The disappearance of the Moon, the chaos or darkness that follows, and the reappearance of the Moon are symbolically equivalent to the suspension of time, the reenactment of creation, and the symbolic rebirth of time commemorated during the New Year's ritual.[37]

In early cultures, nature was considered a religious system in and of itself, and the laws of nature revealed to people the various modes of existence of the sacred realms. For early hunter-gatherers, the patterns inherent in the seasons, the movement of animals, and the availability and growth of wild vegetation influenced spiritual concepts related to the passage of sacred time. After farming was introduced, the patterns connected with the growth of crops and the timing and success of the harvest affected these concepts, along with their related symbolism. The natural world provided food and encouraged or destroyed life. The forces of nature were, therefore, vital, sacred, and deserving of reverence and propitiation.[38] It is only in modern times that people perceive themselves as separate from nature and not entirely dependent upon it for survival. This is, of course, an illusion, as illustrated in this Native American proverb:

Only after the last tree has been cut down,
Only after the last river has been poisoned,
Only after the last fish has been caught,
Only then will you find that money cannot be eaten.[39]

The dependence of humans on the natural world finds expression in New Year's rituals, which are often held at an important point in time. Many cultures celebrate the New Year near the Spring Equinox to mark the important agricultural practices that take place at this time of year. In some cases, seeds are symbolically sown during the ritual.[40] Even in societies that do not practice farming, cyclical patterns in the growth of wild vegetation and the movement of herds are observed and commemorated. Early Celtic society, for example, supported itself primarily through herding. Therefore, their New Year occured in autumn when the herds were brought back from summer pasture to provide food supplies for the winter or receive shelter until the next warm season.[41] The primordial idea of regeneration is what is important here, and this is a primary focus in New Year's ceremonies in which rituals of purification and creation take place.

Since time is suspended during the New Year, this is often considered a very liminal period. Things that are out of the ordinary may take place; special rituals and prayers are made; purification, regeneration, and creation (all events of a mystical nature) are celebrated. During this potent and magical time, divination frequently takes place. This was evidently the case in ancient Babylon, and it is still true in many countries today. A great deal of folklore relating to Samain divination (the old Celtic New Year) has been recorded in the various Celtic countries. Since time is dissolved or suspended, the veil between the worlds is thin. Therefore, it is considered a potent time to connect with the Otherworld, the source of life and wisdom. The New Year was considered a time of great potential, as society, the year, and the world were about to be reborn. As such, it was a powerful time for progress and transformation. Divination rites are most powerful at this time of year and help ascertain what energies or events can be foreseen or avoided.[42] The powerful and reliable rebirth of the Moon and its association with creation and rejuvenation are the symbolic equivalent of the birth of the New Year, a magical time when society and a symbolic new world arise from a point outside of space and time.

The Circle of Eternal Return

We have seen how, in numerous primal cultures (as well as some modern religious systems), time is perceived as cyclical, rather than linear. People exist in a continual present that progresses in a circular or cyclical pattern.[43] In earliest times, the Moon was used to measure cyclical time, as its forms and patterns were visceral, predictable, and frequently repeated. These patterns of cyclical existence occurred everywhere in the natural world.

The observation of the Moon's reappearance after three nights of relative darkness also seems to have resulted in the sanctification of this specific time period in many spiritual traditions. Three days and nights is a sacred period of time in a number of cultures and is often associated with rites of initiation, healing ceremonies, and other passages or transformations. In Celtic myth and legend, many significant changes or events take place during or after a period of three days and nights. These events include healings, adventures, sacred journeys, and encounters with the Otherworld.

Early people were necessarily observant of the laws and patterns that existed in nature, and noticed that all life-forms undergo a period of existence and endurance, followed by a period during which the life force weakens and ebbs. To recover this vitality (i.e., to gain a new life), all creatures and forms are reabsorbed back into the void from where they originated. While the nature of this transformation and the length of time it takes varies, it is a reality experienced by all. For example: A small insect is eaten by a bird. The bird is then eaten by a predator. The predator dies, and its body decays and is absorbed into the ground. The soil is enriched and produces a number of green plants. A small insect flies by and feeds off the leaves of the green plant. The cycle is repeated endlessly, giving rise to innumerable events, life-forms, and possibilities. These natural events represent and explain the cyclical structure of time.

The past, then, is connected to and may reflect the future, which helps explain the popularity of divination rites at the time of the New Year. Because time continues in a circle, no event is irreversible, no transformation final, and no ending a true death. The repetition of this pattern, which is reflected so magnificently in the Moon's phases, is also ceremonially reenacted on a grand scale at the time of the great rebirth. All life is transformed and reborn at the New Year, which is the end of one year as well as the beginning of the next. It is the hallowed point of connection within the circle of time.

$$\text{☽} \qquad \text{☽} \qquad \text{☽}$$

Meditations and Exercises

Following are a few simple methods for reinforcing the cyclical metaphors of the Moon in your life.

1) Observe the Moon every night for a lunar month, starting at the new Moon. Pay special attention to its absence during the three nights of the void Moon. What is different? What energies are apparent or absent? What does its disappearance each month say about death? What does its reappearance reveal about the certainty of rebirth and transformation? How does this affect your prior notions about death, life after death, or reincarnation? Do some journal exercises or compose a poem in honor of the Moon's return as a result of your reflections.

2) Meditate on the concept of cosmic darkness. What symbolism or attributes have you associated with darkness in the past? Is it frightening, mysterious, inspiring? Explore your previous conceptions (as well as new possibilities) by creating a ritual in which you fully experience the primal darkness. During the void Moon (and/or in a very dark place), meditate on the essence of darkness to see what it represents or contains. Try to become fully connected with this concept; let yourself be embraced by it to see what it feels like, using all of your senses. Concentrate on your breath, your sensations, and the feeling of the sacred void all around you. Utilize this quiet time for healing, reflection, or prayer. Or chant a short invocation of the Moon that you compose spontaneously in the darkness. Connecting with the spirit of inspiration and composing poetry in the dark is a time-honored tradition of the Celtic poet and seer. See if any images or words come to you, or any solutions to problems or queries. Incorporate a ritualized ending to the exercise to help you experience rebirth from darkness into light. This can be as simple as lighting a candle or as profound as going out into the sunshine after reemerging from a cave or other natural location. Record your experience in the primal darkness, as well as how it felt to come back from that state. Notice if any transformation occurs

at this time or afterward as a result of having been completely conscious of and open to the sacred energies inherent in the primordial void, the place of origin.

3) Over the course of several lunar months or seasons, keep a journal in which you record your observations and discoveries of the cycles of the plant world. Notice the plants that grow in your area (whether urban or rural). Beginning in early spring, note the order in which plants, buds, and greenery appear. Which plants live for a short while, which for many months? Notice the interweaving of their appearance and existence. Also, take time to discover how the lives and cycles of plants intersect with the Moon's phases. Pay special attention to plants associated with the Moon to see if any special energies or connections exist. These plants include willow, violets, lilies, roses, iris, and rowan.

4) Read about spinning, and perhaps learn how to do it. You can do this with an inexpensive drop spindle, or, if you end up getting hooked, by purchasing a wheel. I have found spinning with a spindle to be quite challenging at first, but once you get the hang of it, it is very enjoyable and quite trance inducing. See what images and energies are apparent when performing this activity. Over time, words, poems, or chants may arise from the rhythm of the spinning. In Irish and Scottish Gaelic traditions, songs, which imitated the rhythm of the wheel, were sung to accompany the work. Experience this activity during different phases of the Moon.

5) Think about the mythological attributes of the Sun and Moon. How do these resonate with you? Have you generally been more partial to or resonant with one of these over the others? If so, take the time to connect with the energies of both, reflecting on their important aspects. What about lunar intuition versus solar intellect? Which is easier for you? Take time to explore and develop your potential in both areas. Reflect upon the concepts of Being and Becoming. Do these mirror energies or patterns in your own life or changes you'd like to encourage? In this work, read about specific cultural mythologies you have not previously explored. See if there are any solar or lunar heroes or heroines who inspire you. Write a poem or invocation to these entities, perhaps to use in a ceremony.

6) Have you ever thought about the premise that energy precedes matter? It is a radical and powerful shift away from modern thought and attitudes that glorify power, force, and the material world. It is important to consider the energy we give to thoughts, actions, language, and beliefs, noting that these can profoundly alter our manifest reality. This is expressed in a Hindu saying: "Prana (life energy) follows your attention." Notice if you habitually engage in limiting or forcing thoughts or activities. Make a long-term plan to alter the way you consciously think about or view the connection between intent and

visualization, with physical reality or effect. Write about this in your journal over a period of several months. Keep in mind the symbolism of the cosmic darkness, the symbolic attributes connected with liminal points of time and space, and the creative aspects of the void.

7) Design a New Year's ritual for yourself that includes the following traditional elements: acknowledgment of seasonal changes, purification, gratitude for renewal of food, mythical or spiritual ancestors or animals, lunar symbolism and renewal, creation and/or rebirth, encouraging the continuity of life for the individual and the community, divination, and regeneration/rejuvenation. Use a white or green altar cloth and candles (symbolic of renewal and purification), a vessel of water sprinkled with herbs to be used in purification, lunar herbs to burn as incense for purification or propitiation, plants and other items symbolic of the season, offerings of food you have prepared yourself, plants that symbolize regeneration, items for divination, a symbol of the ancestors, and objects that symbolize that which you wish to see manifest in the coming year. Write a poem, invocation, or story, which reflects your perceptions of creation to recite or enact during the ritual. Remember to give thanks, thinking of community, family, or tribe as well as yourself. Take time to notice how lunar symbolism fits into and reflects the New Year's ceremony and its ancient religious concepts.

8) Think about the concept of cyclical time, an idea quite foreign to most people. It is challenging to comprehend how the past is perhaps not the past, and the future no different from what is happening right now. Reread the section about the New Year and the circle of eternal time. If you have already performed a New Year's ceremony and recited a poem or story having to do with creation, you may find that helpful. Sit in a quiet place where you can read through the following guided visualization and reflect on the concepts and experiences it describes:

> Take three slow, deep breaths. Visualize your energy slowly moving toward the ground, from head to feet, releasing all tension and worries. Connect with the energy of the Earth and the ancestors for a few minutes, until you are ready to begin. Envision yourself as a member of an ancient primal or tribal society, where traditions are maintained carefully over many centuries. The Elders have experienced a great deal and are keepers of powerful traditions, which have enabled the people to survive for a very long time. They deserve respect, as it is their wisdom that maintains the tribe. In this society, tribal customs are enforced and personal responsibility is expected. This may seem restrictive to those accustomed to modern freedoms, but along with these regulations and restrictions comes guidance, protection within

the group, and the privilege and benefits of time-honored wisdom. Think about the remarkable amount of knowledge that has been passed along for centuries.

It is the time of the New Year. Picture yourself in ceremonial dress after having engaged in a purifying bath of some kind. You have come to watch the elders perform the traditional ceremony. One of them tells a story about the oldest animals; another recites a traditional poem about the creation of the world. As it has been done, so it will be done. Several others sing a song of praise to the ancestors, and the primary male and female elders chant an invocation to the gods, asking for blessings and rebirth. The year is a circle, and time is a circle. The ancient traditions are carried out each year, until the new cycle is reached once again. The New Year is a point outside of time when the spirits are close at hand and divination is fruitful. Once this point passes, the cycle begins again. Time is a circle.

How does the concept of cyclical time change how you currently experience life? How might it enhance your emotional, spiritual, or personal growth? In working toward an understanding and experience of this concept, you may find it helpful to read authentic ancient texts or hymns, meditate, spend time in nature, and connect with, honor, and learn from helpful spirits, deities, or ancestors. It may also be useful to do some of these things in accordance with the lunar phases (particularly the void and new Moons). See if you are able to open yourself to new ideas and experiences, as well as to the possibilities of cyclical growth, expansion, and transformation.

THE HARE OF THE SIXTH HEAVEN

Shamans, Seers, and Druids

Mogh Ruith then descended from the sky
And got into his beautifully ornamented chariot
Drawn by fast and furious oxen
Having the speed of the wind of March and the agility of birds.

—Forbhais Droma Dámhgháire, 15th-century Irish text

Shamanism has been called the oldest religion. Indeed, shamanism may be the most ancient spiritual system whose beliefs and rituals are known to us. The rites and techniques associated with shamanism are remarkably widespread and exist in almost every corner of the globe. Striking similarities of symbolism, belief, and practice are found in shamanic cultures far removed from one another in both space and time. One explanation for these similarities is that the beliefs and techniques of shamanic practice have arisen as a result of shared human experience, or from a learned or innate ability to connect with the realms of the divine. Since these cosmologies and rituals have arisen from and reflect encounters with deities and spirits in parallel planes of existence, their constituent symbolic elements may be seen as a mirror of the Otherworld itself.

Before exploring the significance of the Moon in shamanic tradition, let's consider what shamanism is. The shaman is a powerful spiritual figure whose rituals and beliefs have existed on every continent of the globe for millennia. In recent years, however, the word "shamanism" has been used to refer to a number of spiritual experiences or meditative techniques that are not necessarily shamanic. This has sometimes blurred the distinction between shamanic and nonshamanic practices, to the point where almost any meditative or spiritual experience may be labeled shamanic.[1] At the other end of the spectrum, we encounter academics who are wary of the term, sometimes due to the aforementioned confusion, and sometimes due to a lack of professional expertise or information on the topic.

Shamanism, in its strictest definition, is a religious phenomenon that originated in Siberia and Central Asia; the word "shaman" has its origin in these regions. However, the same magical and spiritual system is found all over the world, from North America to Indonesia, from Africa to Australia, and from Europe to the

Middle East.[2] Shamanic cosmology almost invariably involves the perception of three sacred realms: the Sky Realm (or Upper World), the Middle Realm (or Earth), and the Lower Realm (or Underworld). A central tree, pillar, or mountain connects the three worlds and is often utilized to travel between the realms.[3] The shaman specializes in an altered or ecstatic state in which his or her soul is perceived to leave the body and either ascend to the Sky Realm or descend to the Underworld. Through the shamanic trance or meditative experience (which I will refer to as the "shamanic journey"), the shaman cures illness, accompanies the spirits of the dead to the Underworld, and serves as a mediator between the people and their gods, who reside in the Upper and Lower Worlds. Shamans are also credited with magical abilities, including mastery over fire and magical flight.[4]

Masters and Mistresses of Magical Flight

The shaman's spiritual experiences are often involved with the mystical aspects of religion and exert a powerful influence over a society's religious ideology, mythology, and rituals. Shamans may coexist with other magical and religious practitioners, but, in many cases, the magical and religious life of the culture often centers around them, particularly in cultures where the ecstatic journey is considered the supreme religious experience.[5] In these cultures, the shamans often constitute a small mystical elite who direct the community's religious life. Since the shamans are of the elect, they have access to areas of the sacred that may be inaccessible to other members of the community. It is said that the shaman alone can "see the soul" or know its form or destiny. Indeed, shamans are specialists in those areas of religious life involving the soul, including illness (which is equated with loss of the soul), death or misfortune (which may require spiritual guidance or intervention), and sacrificial rites involving a mystical journey of the soul to the Otherworld.[6]

Spirits, Guides, and Elders

In many cases, the future shaman is selected by one of two methods: hereditary transmission of the shamanic vocation or spontaneous vocation—a spiritual "call" or "election." There are instances in which individuals become shamans by their own will or the will of the clan, but they are considered less powerful than those who inherit the profession or who obey the call of the gods and the spirits.[7] Future shamans are not recognized as shamans until they have received two kinds of teaching: ecstatic (dreams or trances) and traditional. This training is provided by the spirits and the old master shamans and is equivalent to an initiation. Ecstatic training occurs during dreams, religious ecstasies, or a physical or spiritual illness. While these may constitute an initiation, they are always followed by theoretical and practical instruction. This traditional instruction includes shamanic techniques, the names and functions of the spirits, the mythology and genealogy of the clan, and secret languages.[8]

Whether shamanic initiation takes place in an ecstatic dream, religious trance, illness, unusual event, or public ritual, it almost invariably includes the traditional pattern of spiritual ordeal, death, and rebirth. As we have seen, this pattern is widely associated with the lunar cycle. Ceremonial initiatory rites may include a period of seclusion in the wilderness, marking the face and body with ashes (associated with the dead), symbolic burial, difficult ordeals, hypnotic sleep (drinks that make the candidate unconscious), and a symbolic descent to the Underworld. All initiatory rituals, however, must involve a deliberate quest for shamanic powers on the part of the initiate.[9]

Frequently, initiation involves an encounter with a divine or semidivine being. This spirit appears to the candidate in a dream (or during an illness or other situation), indicating that the candidate has been chosen and urging him or her to pursue a new life. Many times, the spirits are the souls of the initiates' shaman ancestors, but they may also be the souls of more general ancestors or of animal or plant spirits. Familiarity with spirits is extremely common—indeed, they are known as "familiars," or as helping, assistant, or guardian spirits.[10] The frequent appearance of animal spirits explains the widespread phenomenon in which shamans imitate animal cries or behavior. The shaman "becomes" the animal, transforming into the animal's form to partake of its power and wisdom.[11]

Seeing spirits, or having spirit visions, is extremely important during shamanic initiation. The ability to see spirits (whether in dreams or in a waking state) is a sure sign that someone has attained a spiritual condition and transcended the normal condition of consciousness. Shamans have direct and concrete experiences with gods and spirits (with whom they often have a very personal relationship). They see spirits face to face, talk with them, and pray to them (but usually do not control them).[12] In some cases, they must learn a secret language that is used during rituals and that will enable them to communicate with the spirits. This language may be learned from a human teacher or from the spirits themselves. Shamans also frequently possess a special song they sing or chant to invoke the spirits during journeys or rituals. And, in addition to invoking the great gods of the people, they may work with deities that are unique to them. These personal deities are often unknown to the rest of the people, and the shaman alone makes offerings to these divinities.[13]

The Drum, The Horse, and Three Worlds

One item usually considered indispensable during the shamanic journey or ritual is the shaman's drum. It plays an important role both physically and symbolically and has a number of magical functions. The sound of the drum is used to assist shamans in their ascent or descent to the sacred realms, and it is sometimes referred to as the "horse," which they ride to the other worlds.[14] In addition, drums may be used for divination. In many cases, shamans go out into the wilderness to select a sacred tree for use in making the wooden shell of the drum. This tree is considered to represent the World Tree, and the wood may be selected based upon the type of trees considered sacred in that culture (birch, oak, ash, etc.).[15]

Once shamans have created their drums, they often decorate them with religious symbols. This decoration often includes a tree or an inverted tree (with its roots in the air and its branches facing downward, symbolizing the descent to the Lower Worlds). This is one of the most archaic symbols known for the World Tree. The artwork on the drum may illustrate methods used by the shaman to accomplish the breakthrough between spiritual planes, as well as symbols of the sacred realms, plants, animals, and deities. As an example, the drums of Lapp shamans may depict the three worlds, gods and goddesses, shamans, sacrificial animals, snakes, birds, horsemen, the World Tree, the god of the chase, Underworld gods, the dead, boats, and mythical persons.[16]

Allowing for cultural diversity in shamanic ceremony and nomenclature, the similarities of practice and belief that exist in shamanic cultures around the world are reflected in the inclusion of these important elements:

- Shamanic call or vocation

- Earthly and spiritual training and initiation

- Bestowal of shamanic powers by the elders and the gods or spirits

- Relationship with spirits and deities (including ancestors and animals)

- Work with the soul (curing illness, escorting the souls of the dead) through the shamanic journey

- Role as mediator between the people and their gods

- Use of chanting, drumming, and other methods to travel spiritually to the Upper or Lower Worlds to perform work (often assisted by spirits) that benefits the community

The Three Worlds and the Celtic Tradition

The sacred shamanic triad of Sky, Earth, and Underworld/Ocean formed an important part of the Celtic perception of the cosmos.[17] While there does not appear to be any Celtic reference to the World Tree (using that specific name), a number of sacred trees, or *bile* (a word that also means "pillar"), were venerated in early Irish tradition.

As in a great number of shamanic cultures, Celtic religious ceremonies or tribal assemblies often took place in the presence of a sacred tree or pillar.[18] These trees may have served as a sort of localized World Tree in the various tribal territories. They were venerated due to their antiquity, wisdom, healing properties, or other special characteristics (attributes associated with the World Tree in many other cultures),[19] and it was forbidden to harm these trees in any way. Fairly recent accounts in which Irish workmen refused to cut down "fairy trees" (thorns or other trees associated with fairy hills) to make way for roads or buildings may be a reflection of this tradition.

Many sacred trees were associated with healing wells or wells of wisdom in Celtic tradition. Similarly, the Norse World Tree Ygdrassil was associated with a well of wisdom and another well of destiny.[20] One of the most beautiful descriptions of a sacred tree associated with an Otherworld well comes from the tale *Cormac's Adventures in the Land of Promise*. The presence of hazel trees/nuts and salmon (which were associated with divine wisdom) highlight the sanctity of this scene:

> . . . Then he [Cormac] saw in the enclosure a shining fountain, with five streams flowing out of it, and the hosts in turn drinking its water. Nine hazels of *Buan* grew over the well. The purple hazels dropped their nuts into the fountain, and the five salmon which were in the fountain severed them and sent their husks floating down the streams. Now the sound of those streams was more melodious than any music that men sing . . . [21]

The god Manannán mac Lir later appears to Cormac to explain the vision he has seen:

> The fountain which thou sawest, with the five streams out of it, is the Fountain of Knowledge, and the streams are the five senses through which knowledge is obtained. And no one will have knowledge who drinks not a draught out of the fountain itself and out of the streams. The folk of many arts are those who drink of them both.[22]

In a variety of shamanic traditions, deities and spirits are said to inhabit both the Upper and Lower Worlds. However, while the celestial gods are generally benevolent, they are also quite passive and of little assistance in mortal affairs. The deities of the Lower World may be more vindictive, but they are closer to the Earth (facilitating communication and interaction between the two worlds). Among the Yakut, they are allied with men by ties of blood and an organization into clans.[23] This is highly reminiscent of Celtic folk traditions pertaining to the fairies or subterranean inhabitants of the fairy mounds.

The fairies can be mischievous or even dangerous, but if shown respect, they can also be of assistance to mortals. Their society mirrored many aspects of traditional Celtic society; in some cases, they interbred with humans.[24] In addition, while archaeological evidence attests to the existence of what may be called celestial deities in Celtic tradition (Lug/Lugus, Belenus, Taranis, and others), evidence garnered from a variety of sources supports the widespread and long-lasting veneration of deities or spirits of a chthonic nature (in terms of where the deities lived and how they were propitiated).[25]

There are, however, several interesting references to celestial deities in Celtic tradition, the realm in which the Moon plays an important role. In various shamanic rituals, one of the most widely invoked celestial deities was a god of storms or thunder. The shaman may imitate the sound of thunder during ritual and, in some cases, the sky god was said to speak "through the voice of the thunder."[26] Some ancient Celts worshipped a deity called Taranis (The Thunderer), who was associated with the eagle and the wheel (both symbols of the sky realm).[27] In addition, a prayer collected last century in the Scottish Highlands was called "The Voice of Thunder." While this title may reflect the celestial attributes of the Christian deity to whom it was offered at the time of its collection, many charms and prayers in circulation during the same period show clear evidence of their pagan origins. The prayer in question begins with the following invocation: "O God of the elements, O God of the mysteries, O God of the fountains." It goes on to invoke the protection of this celestial god.[28] The god Taranis was also invoked for victory and protection, and, in at least one shamanic culture, thunder was considered to be a specific protector of shamans as well as warriors.[29]

Druids, Bards, and Seers

Shamans are members of a religious elite who communicate with the gods and spirits, cure illness, and care for the souls of the people. They exert a great deal of influence over the ideology, rituals, and mythology of their culture and, in many cases, are responsible for offering sacrifices to the gods. They provide training for young initiates, teaching them shamanic techniques, the names and functions of the spirits and gods, secret languages, and the mythology and genealogy of the clan. They are often credited with mastery over fire, the power of magical flight, and the ability to transform into the shape of animals. And while the magical and religious life of the community frequently revolves around the shaman, in many cases, they coexist with other religious or magical practitioners.

Classical accounts by Greek and Roman writers provide quite a bit of information about the religious leaders of the Celts. Writers like Diodorus Siculus, Strabo, Pomponius Mela, and Caesar (writing between the 1st century B.C.E. and

1st century C.E.) mention that, in Gaul, there were three kinds of venerated persons—Druids, bards, and seers (*vates*)—who were counted among the elite. The Druids are described as highly respected theologians who engaged in natural and moral philosophy. They are called "teachers of wisdom" and were reputed to know the size and shape of the world, the motion of the stars and the heavens, and the will of the gods. Several accounts state that no sacrifices were made or blessings sought without the presence of a Druid, "for they say that thank-offerings should be given to the gods by means of those who are experts in the nature of the divine, and, as it were, in communion with it." The Druids evidently taught that the soul was immortal and provided lengthy and intensive training to Druidic students in secret locations.[30] Myths, legends, and other texts credit the Druids with mastery over fire and other elements, healing, secret languages, maintaining genealogies, knowledge of the Otherworld realms, the power of magical flight, and the ability to shape-shift.[31]

We can see that the Druid, like the shaman, was a member of a religious elite that exerted a great influence on the ideology, theology, and mythology of the people. They appear to have been the preeminent members of a magico-religious class that also included other types of specialists. Like the shaman, the Druids were considered experts in the nature of the divine and matters pertaining to the soul. They were associated with magic, healing, and the acquisition of divine wisdom. They were also responsible for communicating with the gods (to whom they alone could offer sacrifices) and the training of initiates.

In later times, some of the roles originally attributed to the Druids were taken over by the poetic grade of society. More than mere entertainers, poetics were highly respected (and in some cases, feared) and were often gifted with the ability to prophesy or "see into" the other worlds.[32] The poetic student underwent vigorous training for many years. In his 1695 account, *A Description of the Western Islands of Scotland,* Martin Martin writes about the poets of the Scottish Highlands (who were still held in great esteem). He mentions that, after the Druids were extinct, the bards took over the traditional task of preserving genealogies, and then relates their unusual method of poetic training:

> I must not omit to relate their way of study, which is very singular: they shut their doors and windows for a day's time, and lie on their backs, with a stone upon their belly, and plaids about their heads, and their eyes being covered, they pump their brains for rhetorical encomium or panegyric; and indeed they furnish such a style from the dark cell, as is understood by very few . . .[33]

The image of young poetic candidates lying in a dark place with their plaid garments wrapped about their heads is highly suggestive of the darkness considered necessary for the shaman's journey to and connection with the powers and wisdom of the Otherworld. While the reference to the stone placed on the belly has been interpreted as an "ordeal" of some kind, it is equally plausible that this was to promote a deep and regular breathing pattern to facilitate an altered state of consciousness. It is not hard to imagine that, in their darkened rooms, with all other stimuli blocked out for an entire day, poetic candidates would have entered into an altered state and connected with the inspiration of the Otherworld. A similar method was reported in a 1722 account pertaining to the Irish bardic schools. Celtic scholar Osborn Bergin felt that this practice of composing in the dark looked like "a relic of some rite or ceremony of divination handed down from pagan times, long after its original purpose had been forgotten."[34]

An intriguing description of Welsh mantic practices associated with the acquisition of divine knowledge was preserved by Giraldus Cambrensis (Gerald of Wales) in his late 12th-century work entitled *The Description of Wales*:

> There are certain men among the people of Wales . . . called *Awenyddion*, who are led by their innate understanding. When consulted about some uncertainty or another, they immediately roar out as if seized from without by some spirit, and, as it were, taken over. They do not set forth coherently that which is requested, rather they speak through many evasions and riddles, and in meaningless and empty words, disjointed rather than cohering—but sounding splendid! The one who listens attentively will have an answer to the information that is sought. In the wake of this ecstacy, they are roused by others as if from a deep sleep, and are thus forced to come to themselves.[35]

Numerous reports state that the language of shamanic songs, utterances, and prophecies may often be difficult to understand and that, in some cases, returning from the shamanic journey could be difficult, much like waking after a deep sleep.[36]

The Sacred White Horse

The horse is one of the most important symbols in numerous shamanic traditions. To "ride a horse" spiritually is one of the most characteristic methods in Central and Northern Asia (and many other areas) of accomplishing the shamanic journey. The horse was able to produce a breakthrough in plane and was therefore associated with a change of state (including initiations, shamanic journeys, and death). For this reason, the horse was associated with funerary symbolism and seen as a *psychopomp*, a spirit that guided or accompanied the souls of the dead to the next realm. The importance of the horse was such that, in many shamanic cultures, horses were sacrificed and offered to the gods. The offering often consisted of a white horse or mare. This custom also existed among many Indo-European peoples and others.[37]

Shamanic drums and costumes are often adorned with images of horses, illustrating the shaman's ability to "ride" the spirit horse/drum to the divine realms. In addition, in numerous shamanic cultures from India to South America, wooden stick-horses are used in shamanic rituals. In these contexts, the shamanic trance may be induced by drumming or by dancing astride a horse-headed stick. After initiation, the Buryat shamaness wore a cap of iron with three points resembling the horns of a deer and carried a stick-horse made of wood or iron and two horse-headed sticks encircled with bells.[38]

Horses figure prominently in the shamanic trances of the Yakut, which take place in the evening. After staring into the fire, shamans don their shamanic costumes, and begin to smoke. Their heads fall to their chests and their eyes close. A white mare's hide is spread in the middle of the yurt. The shamans drink cold water and then genuflect to the four points of the compass. Horsehair is thrown on the fire and covered over with ashes. In the darkness, the shamans sit on the mare's hide and dream, while those in attendance wait and listen. They drum and chant a beautiful song like this one:

> The strong bull of the earth, the horse of the steppe,
> The strong bull has bellowed! The horse of the steppe has trembled!
> I am above you all . . . I am the man who has all gifts! . . .
> Come, then, O horse of the steppe, and teach!
> Appear, then, marvelous bull of the Universe, and answer!
> O Lord of Power, command! . . .
> O Lady my Mother, show me my faults
> and the road that I must follow!
> Fly before me . . . Prepare my way for me! . . .
> O Spirits of the Sun who dwell in the South on the nine wooded hills,
> O Mothers of Light . . . I implore you . . . may your three shadows
>   remain high! . . .
> And thou in the West, on thy mountain, O Lord my Ancestor
> Of fearful powers . . . be with me![39]

The horse also plays a very important role in Celtic religious symbolism. Horses seem to have been used as sacrificial offerings, as horse skulls are frequently found in Celtic offering pits. They were also used until fairly recent times as foundation deposits to ensure luck and stability for new buildings.[40] Horses are often associated with journeys to and from the Otherworld, sometimes enticing, carrying, or accompanying travelers on their journey. The widely worshiped Celtic goddess, Epona (Divine Horse Goddess), was depicted with horses and symbols of abundance, but she was also associated with funerary symbolism, as in shamanic tradition. The Welsh goddess Rhiannon (Divine Queen) was also associated with horses, as well as with sovereignty, and owned magical Otherworld birds whose songs had healing properties.[41] In addition, various folk rites and processions, which often take place at liminal points of the year, have been recorded in which white, grey, or light-colored horses or mares are featured. One of the best known is the Welsh tradition known as the *Mari Lwyd* (perhaps "Grey Mare"?). The ceremony takes place during the liminal period between Yule and the Gregorian New Year and involves a procession with the decorated skull of a mare.[42]

As the horse was considered extremely sacred, its sacrifice would have been a serious and potent offering to the gods. The complex ceremony associated with the Altaic horse sacrifice records some of this reverence and symbolism:

> In a specially chosen meadow, a young birch is provided with nine notches and placed inside a new yurt. A small palisade of birch sticks is set up around the yurt, and a birch stick with a knot of horsehair set at the entrance. A light-coloured horse is chosen, and it is ascertained in some manner that the horse is pleasing to the divinity involved. The shaman shakes a birch branch over the horse's back to prepare its soul for flight to the sky realm. Later, after throwing branches on the fire and fumigating his drum, he invokes spirits and spirit helpers, and engages in symbolic activity associated with capturing the horse's soul. The horse is blessed, and finally sacrificed and offered to the gods or spirits.[43]

Interestingly, a sacrificial ritual from early Ireland also featured a white horse (in this case, a mare). In Ulster, during the king's inauguration rite, the candidate, who seeks a change of state or status, is ritually united with the Goddess of Sovereignty, symbolized by the white horse. Gerald of Wales, in his 12th-century account, *The History and Topography of Ireland,* describes this ceremony in the north of Ireland:

> When the whole people of that land has been gathered together in one place, a white mare is brought forward into the middle of the assembly. He who is to be inaugurated . . . has bestial intercourse with her before all [symbolically, one would assume]. The mare is then killed, cut up in pieces, and boiled in water. A bath is prepared for the man afterwards in the same water. He sits in the bath surrounded by all his people, and all eat of the meat of the mare.[44]

While medieval historians do not always accurately or objectively describe the people, events, and traditions of other cultures, certain elements of this account do seem to reflect native tradition. The Goddess of Sovereignty was associated with horses in a number of tales, and horses were associated with transformation and passages to the Otherworld in both Celtic and shamanic tradition. The king's ceremonial alliance with the mare reflects his sacred union with the representative of the Sovereignty Goddess, without whose blessing he could not reign successfully.

In particular, it is the white horse that seems to play an especially important part in both Celtic and shamanic traditions. In addition to the white mare, which serves as a representative of the Goddess of Sovereignty, and the Welsh Grey Mare (the *Mari Lwyd*), a number of other supernatural or divine white or grey horses figure prominently in Irish and Welsh tales and legends. In Celtic legends, a variety of animals—most often the horse, deer, bird, or dog—emerge from the Otherworld to entice or guide mortals toward a particular place, person, or event. Frequently distinguished by their great size or beauty, these animals are often described as white, red, or white with red ears or other markings.

Horses of a similar description also exist in shamanic contexts. For example, in Sudan, one future shaman dreamt of a white horse with a red belly. White horses and mares are also specifically associated with the rituals of Yakut shamans, in which they address the deities of their people who reside in both the Upper and Lower worlds. During these rituals, white or roan-colored animals are offered to the deities of the Underworld. While most divinities are offered dapple-gray mares or roan mares with white hocks or heads, the Yakut goddess called The Lady of the White Colt receives just that. A white horse is also associated with Mongol shamanic rites. Mongol shamans utilize mirrors in ceremonies associated with the souls of the dead. They gaze into the mirror (a receptacle for the "soul-shade") to see the dead person's soul. Sometimes, when looking into the mirror, the shaman will see what is called "the white horse of the shamans."[45]

Shamanic Illness and Fairy Wives

In some cases, shamanic initiation is preceded by an initiatory illness. A possible example of shamanic illness in a Celtic context comes from the early Irish tale *Serglige Con Culainn* (The Wasting Sickness of Cú Chulainn).[46] After encountering a group of Otherworld birds, the great Irish hero, Cú Chulainn, sits down to rest with his back against a stone pillar (perhaps symbolizing the World Tree or pillar).[47] His soul was "angry within him, and sleep fell upon him." Two Otherworld women dressed in green and purple mantles appear to Cú in a vision and whip him until he is all but dead. When the men of Ulster find him, they seek to wake him. However, his friend Fergus warns against it: "Nay, you shall not move him, for he is seeing a vision." This same warning is found in many shamanic cultures.

Cú later regains consciousness, but does not speak of his experience. For a year, he is unwell and cared for by his wife, Emer. A year later, near the Feast of

Samain, Cú's friend and charioteer, Loeg, is sent to the Otherworld to make inquiries about his master's condition. He encounters one of the fairy women and returns to Cú Chulainn, praising her beauty and the wonders of the Otherworld. Upon hearing this report, Cú rises up. "[He] passed his hand over his face . . . his mind was strengthened." He bids Loeg to go and ask the fairy women to return his strength. Cú's wife urges Loeg to bring back healing for her husband and sings a song in which the healing of Druids is mentioned. She sings a second song, encouraging her husband to rise from his illness, which he does.

Loeg returns to the Otherworld, where it is revealed to him that Cú Chulainn is needed to assist with a battle (a test or ordeal, perhaps).[48] Cú arrives and helps an Otherworld king gain a victory over his opponent. He lingers for a while in the Otherworld, for he has fallen in love with Fand, the wife of the god Manannán mac Lir. Cú's mortal wife, Emer, becomes jealous, and eventually the Druids give him a "drink of forgetfulness" so he will not remember Fand or the Otherworld and is able to return home. Cú had been close to death for almost a year, but, as a result of his successful interaction with the inhabitants of the Otherworld (and the assistance of friends, family, and Druids), he is healed.

A number of shamanic elements are present in this tale, including the presence of Otherworld birds, visions of spirits, ordeals (whipping, illness, battle), and journeys to the Otherworld to acquire information, obtain healing, and perform beneficial tasks. Perhaps this story records faintly remembered elements of traditional initiation rites that may have included an initiatory illness or ordeal, as well as a symbolic death and rebirth.

One particularly interesting feature of this story is a love affair between mortal and divine figures. This element is widespread in shamanic cultures, and many shamans are reported to have relationships with celestial or Otherworldly wives or female spirits. Similarly, numerous Celtic stories exist in which mortal men fall in love with divine or supernatural women, or in which mortal women fall in love with divine men, although this is less common.[49] The Teleut shaman often has a celestial wife who entices him to stay with her by offering him an elaborate banquet. In order to continue with his journey, however, the shaman must not taste any of it. This theme is extremely common in Celtic folk tradition. Mortals who enter the Otherworld realms are offered enticing items of fairy food and drink. However, if they partake of any, they may never return home.[50] Autobiographies of Saora shamans and shamanesses include descriptions of their marriages to spirits of the subterranean realms and contain striking parallels to Central Asian shamanic accounts, as well as to European tales of fairy lovers who inhabit the lower regions.[51]

During their spiritual ascent, when they reach the fourteenth heaven, Teleut shamans come upon the nine daughters of the great deity Ulgan, a group of divine women who confer magical powers upon them. Celtic legends also feature groups of three or nine divine women (goddesses, priestesses, and witches) who are credited with a variety of magical abilities. In addition, in shamanic accounts, divine women are sometimes regarded as the mothers, wives, or teachers of heroes.[52] Similarly, a great number of Celtic tales mention divine women, individually or in groups, who assist heroes or other people during their earthly or Otherworldly journeys or adventures.

Otherworld women also figure in an Uriankhai legend in which an Otherworldly wife leaves her mortal husband after giving him a son. This motif is common around the world and is well known in Celtic tradition.[53] Celtic myths and legends record a number of important or semidivine figures, many of whom are skilled or blessed in some way, who are the offspring of a mortal man and divine woman (or vice versa). The Scottish clan MacLeod is said to descend from just such an Otherworldly union. Clan tradition maintains that an early MacLeod king fell in love with a fairy woman. The couple lived happily together for many years, and the fairy wife bore the king a son. Eventually, she had to return to her own world, however, and was exceedingly sad to leave her husband and son behind. The king and his beloved fairy wife parted tearfully at the Fairy Bridge (which can still be seen on the Isle of Skye). The fairy woman left the boy in the care of the king and his clan, wrapping him in a piece of known as The Fairy Flag, which is on display at Dunvegan Castle. The cloth was imbued with magical powers and has been used successfully by the clan several times to protect against disease and ensure victory in battle.[54]

Fairy Hills and Crystals

One of the most important aspects of Celtic mythology is the reverence and lore associated with fairy mounds or hills. Many of these are actually Neolithic burial mounds to which legends were attached by the incoming Celts. The gods and goddesses of the Irish (the *Tuatha Dé Danann*) are said to inhabit these sacred mounds, and a great deal of complex lore is associated with the hills. Interactions between mortals and those who inhabit the mounds may be dangerous or beneficial; in many cases, humans who enter the mounds may or may not be able to return to their own world. The powers attributed to these hills are evident from tales in which people sleeping on or near fairy mounds are abducted into the hill, have an Otherworld encounter, experience a vision, go mad, or acquire Otherworld gifts and blessings. Dreams and visions are said to be a consequence of sleeping on or near a fairy hill. In a number of shamanic cultures, it is believed that the souls of the dead or ancestral shamans are involved in choosing future shamans. For this reason, initiates may lie or sleep on top of graves to obtain shamanic powers.[55]

One of the most revered of all the Celtic mounds or fairy hills is Brug na Boinne (modern Newgrange), which was the home of several Celtic deities.

Originally constructed by pre-Celtic peoples, it was used as a religious site for thousands of years. Stones of white quartz uncovered during its excavation are thought to have decorated the outer façade of the site. Crystal objects of a sacred nature are mentioned in a number of Celtic tales, and quartz crystals and white quartz pebbles were considered to have magical, protective, and healing properties in Celtic folklore tradition well into the 20th century. Not surprisingly, quartz stones and crystals are featured in numerous shamanic rites on several continents. In some cultures, when shamans undergo initiation, they may experience a sort of spiritual or visionary dismemberment. Later, when being put back together in preparation for transformation or rebirth, they may see their bodies being filled with crystals or similar stones. Perhaps this is one possible origin for the widespread connection between quartz/crystals and healing.[56]

The Divine Madness of the Forest

Shamans are often said to be able to fly like birds; in their wanderings or ordeals, they sometimes perch in the branches of trees. A Hungarian shaman was described as being able to "jump up in a willow tree and sit on a branch that would have been too weak for a bird."[57] The flight of the bird is a universal symbol, which represents the journey of the soul, and this concept is sometimes associated with initiatory illness or divine madness. In Sumatra, initiates are reported to have "disappeared," to have been carried off by the spirits into the sky. They are usually returned to their village three or four days later. However, if candidates don't return, a search is instigated, and they are usually found in the top of a tree conversing with spirits. They will appear to have lost their minds, and a sacrificial rite must be performed to restore their wits.

A Celtic myth containing similar imagery comes from a group of Welsh tales known as *The Mabinogi*. In one story, the divine figure Lleu is pierced with a magical spear, which causes him to fly off in the form of an eagle. His uncle, Gwydion (a powerful magician), finds him perched in the top of a tree in a debilitated state. He sings three magical verses, or *englynion*, to lure his nephew down from the tree. Lleu comes down and is healed, his power having been restored.[58]

Another famous example of divine madness is connected with a figure known as Suibne Geilt (Mad Sweeney), a prince of northeastern Ulster or Scotland. He was reported to have gone mad during battle in the year 637 C.E. and wandered off to live in the woods. A number of shamanic images appear in 12th-century poems attributed to Suibne.

I wander restlessly from place to place
It has fallen upon me to be without sense or reason . . .
Shunning people, racing a red deer over the moor.
Sleeping in the woods at night with no feathers

In the top of a dense, bushy tree . . .
I run wildly to the mountains
Few have surpassed me in speed . . .[59]

In another poem, Suibne addresses a number of trees (many of which were considered to have sacred or magical attributes) and praises the beauty and goodness of his domain:

Leafy oak of many branches
You are high above the trees . . .
Little hazel, small branching one
Chest of hazelnuts . . .
Rowan tree, little one of berries
Your blossoms are lovely . . .
Gentle and blessed birch
High spirited harmonious one . . .

If I were to wander alone
Searching the mountains of the dark earth
I would prefer the shelter of a single hut
In mighty Glen Bolcán.
Good is its pure, blue-green water
Good its clean, rough wind . . .
Good its bright pleasant willow,
Better its melodious birch.[60]

Suibne mentions the birch several times, offering it more praise than the other trees and even referring to it as "blessed." The birch is the first tree (or letter) of the early Irish writing system known as *ogam*. In Central Asia (as well as regions of Europe adjacent to Celtic territories), the birch was often singled out as the most sacred of trees and considered a symbolic representative of the World Tree.[61]

The Power of Magical Flight

One of the most important and universal of the powers credited to shamans and other magical practitioners around the world is the power of magical flight. This attribute indicates that these individuals have attained the ability to behave like spirits and function in both this world and the Otherworld. In medieval Europe, witches and wizards were also believed to be able to fly through the air. While this power was attributed to the fairies (perhaps contributing to the Victorian image of the tiny winged fairy), in actual Celtic folk tradition, these beings did not have wings. Those fairies that were able to fly or levitate did so through the use of magical plants, which they rode like a horse, imbuing them with magical powers by reciting charms or incantations. This may be a folk memory of the use of ritual hallucinogens (a common shamanic tradition), or of the widespread concept of the shaman "riding" or flying to the Otherworld. In addition, it may be one origin of the image of the witch riding her broomstick. In all of these cases, however, the power of flight expresses a spiritual intelligence or power, as well as the ability to understand secret or metaphysical truths.

Images pertaining to magical flight and transformation are mentioned in another poem attributed to Suibne Geilt:

> Last night I was in Benn Boirche
> Raindrops beat upon me in cold Echtga . . .
> Tonight my body has been shattered
> In the fork of a tree in bright Gáille . . .
> I have endured many hardships
> Since feathers grew on my body. . . .
> I am Suibne the Wandering One.
> Swiftly I run across the glen
> Suibne is no fit name for me;
> Better than I should be called "Antlered One."[62]

Suibne runs or "flies" with the assistance of feathers he perceives to have grown on his body (perhaps a memory of a shamanic cloak). He is a wanderer (the wanderings of the mad initiate?), but says that this is no proper name for him; Horn Head would be better. This epithet brings to mind the deer symbolism of shamanic costumes, the horned cap of the Buryat shaman, and the widely revered antlered god of the early Celts.[63]

The drums and costumes of shamans often feature images of sacred animals the shaman uses to fly to the Otherworld realms. The most frequently occurring animal images are the stag/reindeer, the bear, and the bird. Ornithomorphic costumes are very widespread; these are found in various Asian, Siberian, Indonesian, and North American settings. Manchu shamanic headgear was made of feathers and imitated the form of a bird, and the Tungus felt that a bird costume was indispensable for flight to the Otherworld. Mongol shamans had "wings" on their shoulders that made them feel as though they had changed into birds upon donning this sacred apparel. A comparison has been made between these shamanic costumes and the *tuige*, or mantle, traditionally worn by the Celtic poet or *fili*, which is described in Cormac's Glossary:

> A covering of birds, for it is of skins of birds white and many-coloured that the poet's *tuige* is made from the girdle downwards, and of mallard's necks and of their crests from the girdle upwards to their neck.[64]

This cloak transformed the mortal poet into a figure of power and must have been a wondrous thing to see. Its two-fold design (white and many-colored on the lower half, with luminescent green and blue mallard feathers on the upper half) would have been stunning and an object of wonder to those who saw the poet in ceremonial garb. The fili is adorned with symbolism associated with magic, flight, and Otherworld birds, whose feathers are described in Celtic myths as blue, white, purple, yellow, and multicolored and who possessed the ability to pass between the worlds. Perhaps the two halves of the tuige symbolized the poet's ability to "see" or function in both worlds.

Another fascinating description of shamanic apparel is associated with a great Druidic figure known as Mug Roith, whose name means "Devotee of the Wheel," perhaps a symbol of the celestial realms, since Mug Roith was said to be able to fly through the skies. He also displayed a number of other magical powers, including mastery over fire, water, and other elements, all well-known shamanic motifs. In *Forbhais Droma Dámhgháire* (The Siege of Knocklong), Mug Roith is described in his splendor, exhibiting fantastical powers and garments worthy of an arch-Druid or shaman:

> The bull-hide from a hornless brown bull belonging to Mogh Roith was now brought to him, along with his speckled bird-mask with its billowing wings and the rest of his druidic gear. He proceeded to fly up into the sky and the firmament along with the fire, and he continued to turn and beat the fire towards the north as he chanted a rhetoric, "I fashion druid's arrows . . ."

> Mogh Roith then descended from the sky and got into his beautifully ornamented chariot drawn by fast and furious oxen with the speed of the March wind and the agility of birds.[65]

This passage appears to be a description of a shaman. Animal hides are used in many shamanic (and Celtic) rituals, including those associated with divination and prophecy. The speckled bird mask appears to be an exact parallel to bird-feather headgear used by shamans. Like the shaman, Mug Roith flies up into the sky and exhibits his mastery over fire. He owns a chariot drawn by oxen, reminiscent of solar and lunar chariots associated with Indo-European sky gods. These animals possessed the agility of birds, symbolizing the power of magical flight and the journey of the soul.

The Language of Birds, The Wisdom of Animals

Around the world, it is believed that to learn the language of animals (particularly the language of birds) is to demonstrate the ability to discern the secrets of nature, to prophesy or "walk between the worlds." This power is attributed to shamans in some cultures. Early textual sources indicate that, in some cases, the Druids were said to understand the language of birds. Birds travel between this world and the other world, both literally and symbolically. As with the horse, they often represent the journey of the soul to the next plane, as well as transformations and changes of state. To transform oneself into a bird (or to be accompanied by a bird) symbolizes the undertaking of a spiritual journey to the sacred realms. Birds also figure prominently in Celtic mythology as messengers between the worlds, a role associated with transformation and sacred journeys. A number of Celtic tales describe mortals and divine figures who are transformed into bird form for various reasons (a change of state often associated with ordeals, healing, shape-shifting, and journeys to the Otherworld).

Shamans use certain words in their rituals believed to have their origin in the cries of birds and animals. In addition to their customary spirit songs and songs that arise spontaneously from shamanic experiences (journeys, visions, and prophetic revelations), they may also sing or recite magical texts. In fact, magic and song (especially songs similar to those of birds) are frequently expressed by the same word. In a number of Celtic languages, there was a similar analogy between verbs signifying "to sing" and "to recite poetry." In early times, poems and songs were probably chanted, rather than melodically sung. Chanting is a wide-spread technique used to induce an altered state and connect both the performer and the listener with the divine. In medieval times, the bard played on the harp while a reciter chanted or recited the poet's song or poetic creation. Poets were often credited with the gift of prophecy, as well as the ability to gain inspiration and wisdom directly from the Otherworld.[66]

Transformation into animal form is another key element of the shamanic experience and its related symbolism. By experiencing the nature and essence of another being—a plant, animal, or other natural form—shamans learn the secrets of nature and the sacred realms, which are usually perceived as intertwined or connected. These were also important elements in Celtic mythological tradition. The numinous or sacred was perceived as immanent in nature and the landscape; the Otherworld was elsewhere, but also all around us. Animal transformations abound in Celtic myth and legends, and mortals and divinities were frequently transformed into birds.

A number of poems attributed to certain early Celtic poets, seers, or magicians have been analyzed by scholars, and it is believed that these may reflect elements of early Celtic mystical or spiritual belief. These poems describe magical or spiritual transformations into various shapes or forms (including animals and elements of nature or the cosmos) and allude to the power and wisdom attained by experiencing these other forms.

Some of the most intriguing poems were attributed to the Welsh poet Taliesin. He is said to have flourished in the 6th century and is well known for the poems he composed in praise of his patrons and benefactors, which was the historical custom. However, a group of more mystical poems, of a very different nature and style from poems we know to have been written by the historically attested figure, have also been attributed to Taliesin.

Taliesin, whose name means "Radiant Brow," was enlisted to aid the sorceress Cerridwen in preparing a magical brew. The boiling of this brew would eventually produce three drops of liquid capable of conferring upon their recipient the gift of prophecy and wisdom. Cerridwen brews the potion for her son, but, at the crucial moment, the three drops fall upon Taliesin, who is, at that point, known as Gwion Bach, Little Poisonous One. A magical chase ensues, during which the angry sorceress and Gwion Bach transform themselves into a variety of animal forms. Near the end of the chase, Taliesin changes himself into a grain of wheat to hide from Cerridwen, but she turns herself into a hen and eats him. He is later "born" (or "reborn") from this supernatural female in human form and becomes the shining poet, seer, and magician, Taliesin.[67]

An excerpt from one of Taliesin's more mystical or cryptic works describes the various forms he experienced before being reborn. He alludes to his ability to "sing" since he was very young. In many spiritual traditions, "naming" or "singing" things brings them to fruition and causes their physical manifestation. Whether these poems were written by the 6th-century praise-poet Taliesin or were attributed to an archetypal poet and seer called Taliesin, it is possible that they express elements of native beliefs associated with magical or spiritual transformations and experiences.

I was in many shapes before I was released:
I was a slender enchanted sword—I believe that it was done.
I was rain-drops in the air, I was stars' beam;
I was a word in letters, I was a book in origin;
I was lanterns of light for a year and a half;
I was a bridge that stretched over sixty estuaries;
I was a path, I was an eagle, I was a coracle in seas;
I was a bubble in beer, I was a drop in a shower;
I was a sword in hand, I was a shield in battle;
I was a string in a harp enchanted nine years, in the water as foam;
I was a spark in fire, I was wood in a bonfire;
I am not one who does not sing; I have sung since I was small.[68]

In *Lebor Gabála Érenn* (The Book of Invasions), a similar set of experiences is intoned by the poet Amairgen. He chants a magical poem to overcome the Druidic magic of the Tuatha Dé Danann in order to facilitate a change of state for his people (to enable the Gaels to take possession of the land of Ireland). Birds, animals, and various elements of the natural world (including the Moon) are mentioned in this beautiful poem:

I am a wind in the sea (for depth).
I am a sea-wave upon the land (for heaviness).
I am the sound of the sea (for fearsomeness).
I am a stag of seven combats (for strength).
I am a hawk on a cliff (for agility).
I am a tear-drop of the sun (for purity).
I am fair (i.e. there is no plant fairer than I).
I am a boar for valour (for harshness)
I am a salmon in a pool (for swiftness).
I am a lake in a plain (for size).
I am the excellence of arts (for beauty) . . .
Who explains the stones of the mountains?
Who invokes the ages of the moon? [69]

The Moon and the Sky Realm

The Sun, Moon, stars, and lunar crescent play an important role as symbolic representatives of the celestial realms. For this reason (among others), the Moon often figures prominently in artwork associated with the drums, costumes, and other ritual objects in shamanic tradition.[70]

In considering the characteristics or significance of the Upper and Lower Worlds, it is important to note that, contrary to Western perception, the Lower World is not associated with negative energies or beings (nor is the Upper World considered superior). Both realms are important, although the particulars of their nature or character vary from culture to culture. In some cases, the Lower Realm is considered the more important and powerful of the two; in these instances, the shaman invokes and prays to the deities, spirits, ancestors, or animals of the Underworld for healing, power, and assistance.

In Yakut tradition, there are two classes of gods—those above and those below. There is no opposition between them (they are regarded in terms of specialization), and Yakut shamans may invoke the deities of both the Upper and Lower Realms. However, their primary shamanic rituals take place at night, and these are focused on the Lower World. Sacrifice is not made to the celestial deities whose rites are performed during the day.[71] Indeed, there appears to be a preference for darkness and night in a number of shamanic traditions, as darkness is often deemed necessary for the shamanic journey. Whether the ritual takes place in a cave or darkened hut, at night or with the eyes covered, darkness does seem to assist with the shamanic process.[72] This connection with darkness and night may be one reason for the Moon's symbolic significance in shamanic contexts.

The Moon plays an important role in numerous shamanic rites around the world, including those connected with healing, initiation, soul work, and the quest for power. In North and South American shamanic healing ceremonies, when a soul is perceived to have been carried off by spirits (or the dead are sought), the shaman enters the Otherworld realm where the abductor is thought to be hiding. In one such account, the soul of a child had been carried off by the Moon and hidden under a pot. The shaman went to the Moon and, after many adventures, found the pot and freed the child's soul.[73]

In Inuit tradition, after invoking their familiars, shamans travel spiritually to various regions of the cosmos, including the depths of the Earth, the ocean, and the Moon.[74] Inuit shamans traditionally engage in a spiritual quest to obtain *qaumaneq*, loosely translated as "shamanic power or enlightenment." This is a mystical faculty that the master shaman sometimes obtains for the young shaman from the spirit of the Moon.[75]

An Inuit shaman from Baffinland reported that, during a shamanic journey, he was carried to the Moon by his helping spirit (a bear). Once there, he came upon a house whose door was made from the jaw of a walrus. At the doorway to the house, he was threatened by someone inside. Considered an intruder, he was told that he would be torn to pieces if he attempted to come in. (This is a well-known motif in shamanic experiences or ordeals: the "difficult entrance.") The shaman was, however, able to enter the house and, once inside, he encountered the Man in the Moon and his wife, who is the Sun. After various experiences, the shaman returned to his body and the realm of Earth.[76]

Among the shamans of Central and Northern Asia (particularly the Altai), the Moon is frequently associated with the shamanic ascent to the Sky Realm. During this journey, they ascend through various celestial levels or realms—usually up to nine of them (or, if they are extremely powerful, through twelve or even more). The sixth of these heavens is traditionally associated with the Moon. Once the shamans have reached this level, they encounter the Moon and bow to it reverently. Sometimes, while in the sixth heaven, they insert a comic episode involving a hunt for a hare into the retelling to enliven the performance. Since the hare is considered a lunar animal, it is natural that this encounter should take place in the sixth heaven.[77]

The Moon also plays a significant role in an Altai ritual that features a spiritual ascent to the Upper World. During the shaman's journey, a white or light-colored horse is blessed and sacrificed as an offering to the gods. Family ceremonies and celebrations take place, followed by a shamanic ceremony that lasts for two or three evenings. This ritual focuses on a young birch tree with nine steps notched into its trunk. This is a symbol of the World Tree and is known as a *tapty*. When the time comes for the ascent, the shaman enters into an altered state of consciousness and, while in ecstasy, circles the birch tree, imitating the sound of thunder (symbolizing a celestial deity). He or she then sits upon a bench covered with horsehide (which represents the soul of the horse) and recites a chant:

> *I have climbed a step . . .*
> *I have reached a plane . . .*
> *I have climbed to the tapty's head . . .*
> *I have risen to the full moon.*[78]

The shaman continues to climb the birch tree and enters the upper celestial realms, stopping at a certain point in the ascent to bow to the Moon in the sixth heaven. He or she then climbs as high as strength permits and addresses Bai Ulgan, one of the sky gods:

> *Prince, to whom three ladders lead . . .*
> *Father Ulgan, thrice exalted,*
> *Whom the moon's axe-edge spares,*
> *Who uses the horse's hoof! . . .*[79]

There is one more aspect of shamanic belief in which the Moon plays an important role—the tradition of the spirit or fairy lover. The folklore of the Yakut mentions young celestial spirits who descend to the Earth and marry mortal women. These spirits are the children of the Sun, the Moon, the Pleaides, and other divine beings. Teleut shamans (among others) are reported to have celestial wives who live in the seventh heaven. In a typical encounter between shamans and their Otherworldly wives, the woman asks the shaman to remain with her, enticing him with a special banquet she has prepared for him. She may lure the shaman to stay with her by assuring him that the road to the sky realm has been blocked. However, the shaman will refuse to believe her. To demonstrate his determination to continue his ascent, he repeats the following words (alluding to the stop the shaman makes on his celestial journey to venerate the Sun and Moon):

> *We shall go up the spiral groove*
> *cut in the shaman tree*
> *and give praise to the full moon . . .*[80]

We have seen that lunar symbolism is associated with death, transformation, renewal, and rebirth. This symbolism also forms an important part of the shamanic initiation. Once shamans have experienced initiation (which often includes death and rebirth), they are transformed into a powerful magical and religious practitioner with new spiritual abilities and a unique connection to the Otherworld. Lunar or spiritual death and rebirth appear in many contexts as the pivotal experience that leads to this new identity.

Shamanism in Celtic Culture

How does this exploration of shamanism bring us closer to an understanding of the Celtic veneration for the Moon? We now know that the Moon plays an important role in the symbolism and rites associated with shamanism, and that shamanism played a role in the spiritual beliefs and practices of the Celts. That being the case, the significance of the Moon in shamanic traditions, its role in rituals associated with the Sky Realm, and its potent spiritual symbolism connected with initiation, transformation, and magical flight may also have formed part of early Celtic tradition. We will examine these questions in the next chapter.[81]

As our quest will ultimately focus on the sanctity of the Moon in Celtic tradition, we will explore whether shamanism formed some part of Celtic religion. Shamanism is an area of cultural research which has, until fairly recently, been somewhat overlooked, especially as it pertains to European traditions. Most scholars will readily admit to the existence of shamanism in Norse, Lapp, and even Scythian cultures, yet seem to have trouble "crossing the bridge" to consider the possibility of such practices among the near neighbors of these people. Mircea Eliade notes that:

> The wide area inhabited by the ancient Celts brought them in contact with other peoples, some of whom are certainly known to have practiced shamanism to a greater or lesser degree, including Scythians, Central Asians and even the Norse. . . . Given the economic, social and religious parallels between the ancient Indo-Europeans and the ancient Proto-Turks, we must determine to what extent the various historical Indo-European peoples still preserve shamanic survivals comparable to Turko-Tatar shamanism.[82]

I close our journey to the Moon of the shamanic realms with this beautiful poem, which was recited during their ascent to the sky by Altaic shamans as they invoked the birds of the celestial realms and described their connection with the Sun and Moon:

> *Birds of Heaven, five* Markut,
> *Ye with mighty copper talons,*
> *Copper is the moon's talon,*
> *And of ice the moon's beak.*
> *Broad thy wings, of mighty sweep,*
> *Like a fan thy long tail,*
> *Hides the moon thy left wing,*
> *And the sun thy right wing.*
> *Thou, the mother of the nine eagles . . . who weariest not . . .*
> *Come to me, singing!* [83]

ANCIENT SYMBOLS, ANCIENT STORIES

A HYMN TO THE MOON GODDESS

Fire, having become speech, entered into the mouth.
Wind, having become the breath, entered into the nostrils.
The sun, having become vision, entered into the eyes.
The four quarters, having become hearing, entered into the ears . . .
The moon, having become the mind, entered into the heart.

—THE UPANISHADS

The Celts belonged to the larger Indo-European family of cultures. To gain a deeper understanding of the role of the Moon goddess in Celtic culture, therefore, we must first understand the role played by the Moon in other Indo-European traditions—Roman, Greek, and Hindu.

The Horns of Artemis

The Indo-European lunar deity most familiar to us is probably Diana, a Roman goddess associated with the Moon, hunting, the woodlands, fertility, and child-birth. Her identity owes much to the Greek goddess Artemis, as many of the major gods and goddesses of the Roman pantheon were adapted from Greek traditions. Artemis was an extremely popular deity with a wide range of functions and attributes. According to Greek sources, she was widely worshipped even in the earliest times. She was a virgin goddess of the hunt who ran through the wilderness with female attendants whose chastity she guarded as fiercely as her own. One of Artemis' titles was Agrotera (She of the Wild). She was widely associated with hills, mountains, and trees (including willow, chestnut, and cedar), as well as with groves, rivers, and areas well nourished by water. In these places, she upheld and preserved the sanctity of nature and promoted fertility—specifically, natural fertility, which does not depend upon the efforts of man.[1]

Artemis' brother and twin was the deity Apollo, associated with the Sun, healing, music, and the arts. Like Apollo, Artemis was often represented with a bow (illustrating her connection with hunting and wild animals). Her bow was also used to carry out vengeance against those who crossed her, interfered with her pursuit of chastity, or did not show her respect. As a goddess associated with the outdoors, Artemis presided over "the wild," that which exists beyond the hearth or outside of society. The natural world, which was her domain, was beautiful and beneficent, a provider of life. It could also be harsh and terrifying, bringing about death or destruction. This dual aspect was also reflected in the attributes of the goddess herself: she both guarded and hunted wild beasts, and while she was invoked to protect women in childbirth, she could also cause misfortune or death.

Artemis was often portrayed in art as a young woman arrayed in hunting garb. In some cases, she is accompanied by young animals and frequently wears horns on her head or a headdress in the shape of a crescent Moon. Many of her religious cults were connected with pivotal periods of time in women's lives—specifically, those associated with passages such as birth, puberty and initiation, and death. Artemis' affiliation with women is, to some degree, tied in to the lunar concept of transformation, and the relationship between these transitions and the phases of the Moon should by now be clear. Other associations with the Moon are suggested by the description of Artemis' bow as being "all of silver" (in the Homeric Hymn to Artemis), as well as by a title ascribed to her, Hegemone, which means The Precursor. This may refer to the second half of the lunar month, in which the Moon precedes the Sun.

Further underscoring Artemis' link with life passages and transitions are the female initiation rites associated with her. When noble Athenian girls reached puberty, they participated in an initiation ritual involving special ceremonies, processions, and ritual dances. The girls were called "bears," as the she-bear was one of the goddess' symbols. This is probably due to the tale of Callisto, a beloved follower of Artemis (or Diana, as Ovid calls her in his *Metamorphoses*), who was raped and defiled by Zeus and thus excluded from Artemis' train. The jealous Hera transformed Callisto into a bear, but, to save her from death by a hunter (Callisto's own son once he had grown to adulthood), Zeus transformed them both into stars. Callisto became the Great Bear (Arctus, or Ursa Major) and her son, Arcas, became the Bear Warden (Arctophylax, or Arcturus).

In addition, dances and masquerades of a fairly erotic nature (involving men and women) seem to have been associated with the worship of Artemis. Cymbals have been found in one of her temples, as well as terracotta masks representing the grotesque faces of women and men (items that may have been used by the dancers). These ritual dances may be linked with the popular image of Artemis dancing with her nymphs. Even in relatively modern times, Greek peasants maintained a belief in the nymphs or *Nereids*.[2] The Nereids frequent the same places as the nymphs who attend Artemis, have similar occupations, and appear in similar tales. They also have a queen who is known to them as The Great Lady, The Fair Lady, or The Queen of the Mountains.

In Sparta, the cult of Artemis Korythalia included the offering of suckling pigs in the goddess' temple and the performance of "lascivious" dances. This epithet was derived from one of the names of the May Bough (*korythale*), a laurel branch that was set up in front of a house when boys came of age or when girls got married. In modern times, it is still erected in front of a house for a wedding. Here again, we can perceive an expression of Artemis' connection with pivotal points in women's lives.

Not surprisingly, the divine huntress plays a prominent role in a number of tales that feature hunters and deer. One of the best known is the story of Iphigenia, daughter of the famous Greek leader, Agamemnon. Agamemnon had provoked the anger of Artemis by killing a stag in one of her sacred groves (or, in another version, by boasting that he was a superior hunter).[3] Artemis demanded the sacrifice of Agememnon's daughter, Iphigenia, before she would allow his fleet to sail, to which her father reluctantly agreed. At the last moment, a stag was substituted for his daughter in the sacrificial rite and Iphigenia was whisked away to become a priestess of Artemis. The replacement (or transmutation) of a woman with a deer may correspond with the custom of men wearing stag's antlers on their heads at one of Artemis' festivals. It is thought that animal horns or antlers may have, in some cases, symbolized the crescent Moon.

The stag also figures in the story of Artemis and the hunter Actaeon. One day, while out hunting, Actaeon became very thirsty. He entered a small grotto where a little stream widened into a pool and decided to cool himself in the water. Unbeknownst to Actaeon, this was the favorite bathing place of Artemis. He accidentally came upon her just as she let her garments fall to the ground, and he saw her standing in naked beauty at the water's edge. Artemis flung a few drops of water into his face and transformed him into a stag.

As in the tale of Callisto, the stars of the night sky are featured in another story of Artemis' vengeance. Like Actaeon, Orion was a great hunter. He attempted to ravish Artemis (or one of her companions), and in revenge, she killed him and his dog with a scorpion. Orion became a constellation, and his dog became Sirius, the Dog Star. In one variant of the story, Artemis killed Orion out of jealousy because Aurora, The Dawn, had fallen in love with him. In another version, Orion was pursuing the Pleiades, daughters of Atlas, who were all subsequently turned into stars.

Another connection with the night sky is suggested by the tale of Artemis' birth. Artemis' mother, Leto, one of the Titans, became pregnant by Zeus. When the time came for her to bear the twins, Apollo and Artemis, she could find no land in which to have her children. Everywhere she inquired, she was turned away with fear, for jealous Hera had decreed that Leto should not bring forth her children in any place where the Sun shone. Leto had a sister called Asteria, whose name means Star Goddess. Zeus had attempted to seduce her as well, but she fled from him, turning herself into a quail. Zeus tried to overtake her (in the form of an eagle), but she then turned herself into a stone, falling into the sea and remaining hidden beneath the waves. Asteria became the small rocky island on which Leto was able to bear her children, for, as she had just emerged from beneath the waves, the Sun had not yet shone upon her.[4]

Because Artemis came into the world first, she was able to help her mother give birth to Apollo (suggesting the belief that the Moon was created before the Sun). This may also be the origin of Artemis' traditional role as an assistant to women in childbirth. In addition, because of the order of their birth, Artemis' birthday was celebrated on the sixth day of the month and Apollo's on the seventh. This is particularly interesting in light of the many shamanic traditions in which the Moon is associated with the sixth heaven and the Sun with the seventh.

The Chariot of the Moon

The Greek pantheon also included a goddess who was not only associated with the Moon, but who personified it. This was Selene, whose name is connected with the word *selas*, meaning "light."[5] Her mother was the Titan Theia (The Divine) and her father the Titan Hyperion. Theia gave birth to the Sun (Helios, or *Sol* in Latin), as well as the Moon (Selene, or *Luna* in Latin). In one version of the story, the mother of Helios and Selene was Euryphaessa (She Who Shines Far and Wide), perhaps an epithet of Theia.

Only a small amount of evidence has survived concerning the worship of Helios and Selene. We know that Helios (the Unwearying Eye) was commonly invoked in oaths and that he had a daughter called Helia (whose name also means Sun). Both Helios and Selene were depicted as charioteers driving a pair of horses or oxen. Their sister, Eos, The Dawn (Latin *Aurora*), also drove a pair of animals in front of a chariot. In some cases, Selene is shown simply riding a horse, mule, or steer.[6] Her identity with the lunar orb is illustrated by one of her epithets, Mene, a word that refers to both the Moon and the lunar month. While Selene is described as being of great importance in terms of magic, she does not appear to have played an extensive role in Greek mythology. Instead, Helios and Selene lent their solar and lunar attributes to other deities who appeared in human, rather than celestial, form.

A number of tales have survived pertaining to Selene's amorous encounters. In one story, she is wedded to the Sun, while in another, she is chased by the woodland nymph Pan. In yet a third tale, Selene is pursued by Zeus and subsequently bears a him a daughter called Pandia, The Entirely Shining or The Entirely Bright (probably referring to the brightness of the full Moon). Perhaps her best-known affair, however, involved the youth Endymion, a young shepherd of great beauty. Selene saw him and fell in love with him, traveling down from the heavens to kiss him and lay by him. As a result of Selene's visit, the youth fell into an eternal slumber. Endymion never awoke to see the shining, silvery form bending over him, but remained asleep—immortal, but never again to be in a conscious state. He was motionless, as if in death, yet warm and living. Night after night, Selene visited him and covered him with her kisses. It was said that she lulled him into this sleep so that she could always find him and caress him as she wished. This story seems to reflect the perceived connection between the Moon, night, the dream state, and the desires of the unconscious mind, exemplified by the name of Selene's beloved: Endymion means He Who Finds Himself Within.

The Homeric *Hymn to Selene* praises the beauty of Selene's form and her sacred pathway. The poem tells of the great beauty that emerges when the dark sky grows bright from the glow of Selene's golden crown. She is envisioned as yoking together a pair of shining colts with high-arching necks and driving her Moon chariot on the evening of the full Moon. Her great pathway is then completed, and she is hailed as a great Queen, a snowy-armed goddess, the shining Moon goddess Selene.[7]

The Double Life of Hecate

Artemis was also associated with another ancient Greek goddess, Hecate, whose name means *Worker from Afar*.[8] Hecate and Artemis share several titles, attributes, and functions, and, in some cases, Hecate served as an attendant or temple guardian for Artemis. In one account, Hecate's mother is said to be Asteria, the Star Goddess (sister of Artemis' mother, Leto), which would make Hecate cousin to Artemis and Apollo. The tiny island next to Delos (the island where Artemis and Apollo were born) was at one point named after Hecate.

The goddess Hecate has two distinct incarnations: one derived from early sources (both literary and archaeological) and one from later sources. The early evidence represents Hecate as a beneficent goddess, a specialized deity of gateways and divine attendantship associated with birth, death, and personal interaction between humans and deities. The *Theogony* of Hesiod mentions that Hecate was honored by Zeus above all others and granted rights by him in the realms of Earth, Sea, and Sky (as she is the direct descendant of Gaia, Okeanos, and Ouranos, the personified Earth, Sea, and Sky).[9] Hecate is also described as a nurse to all living things and credited with bestowing victory in battle, granting fishermen a bountiful catch, protecting horsemen, stables, and herds of cattle, goats, and sheep, and attending and helping with a variety of sports and games.

Statues of Hecate (in single or triple form) were commonly placed in front of houses, and women often prayed to her as they left the home. Her triple-faced or triple-formed image was also displayed in front of doorways and temples. In addition, images of Hecate were set up at crossroads (potent places of potential benefit or misfortune), as it was believed that she could both produce and avert ghosts and other magical evils. In many instances, Hecate was depicted as a youthful woman carrying two torches. Her main symbols were the torch, the snake, the dog, the whip, and the key. The "procession of the key" was a major element in the Hekatesia festival, in which the key bearer was the high priestess of Hecate. The key may symbolize the guardianship of the land of the dead, the ability to pass between the worlds, or the ritualized opening of a sanctuary to reveal the deity to worshippers (all concepts associated with the goddess).

Hecate had a number of illustrious epithets, including Antaia (To Whom One Makes Supplication), Anassa (Lady or Queen), Enodia (In The Road), Propylaia (Before the Gate), Apotropaios (One Who Banishes or Turns Away), and Phosphoros (Light Bringer). Many of these illustrate Hecate's role as a companion and guide, a goddess of transitions, and a guardian of doorways, houses, temples, and other entranceways. In this guise, Hecate served as an assistant to Demeter, as well as a guide and protectress to Persephone upon her return from the Underworld. Artwork portraying Hecate in this role shows her carrying two torches, looking back on Persephone whom she leads back to this world. These titles and images indicate that Hecate (like Artemis) was involved with transitions and passages, concepts also associated with the Moon.

Hecate was worshipped during the Classical period in Ionia and the Aegean Isles, and was also involved with the mysteries that took place at the sanctuary of the great gods on the island of Samothrace.[10] Religious calendars found at Erythia from the 4th or 3rd century B.C.E. mention that she received sacrifices on certain days (especially the first, second, and seventh days of the month). A major sanctuary dedicated to Hecate existed at Lagina that drew great festal assemblies annually; at Aigina the people were said to honor Hecate above all, faithfully celebrating her mystery every year. However, while Hecate enjoyed great popularity in certain areas, evidence for her worship as a great goddess overall is sparse, and she is often seen as an attendant to deities like Artemis, Demeter, Cybele, Apollo, and Helios. Through her connection with Artemis, she was closely associated with young women who became beneficial or guardian spirits after their sacrificial death. These women became immortal attendants to Artemis and were often specifically renamed Hecate.[11]

As a goddess of transitions, Hecate was also connected with ceremonies of death, whose associated rites and customs were traditionally the domain of women in ancient Greece. After a person passed away, offerings were made to Hecate and other chthonic deities consisting of "house sweepings." These were left at a crossroads at the new Moon after thirty days of mourning. Hecate was also associated with women in her role as *kourotrophos* or nurse, a role that connected her with childbirth (another parallel with the goddess of the hunt). Hecate was, in fact, the oldest known kourotrophos in Greek religious tradition and was therefore called the "nurse to all living things."

Hecate's early attributes contrast quite sharply with her better-known image from later eras. In subsequent evidence, she is portrayed as a goddess of witchcraft and sorcery who frequented crossroads on moonless nights accompanied by evil ghosts and barking dogs. If a person had bad dreams, saw frightening figures, or leapt from his or her bed, Hecate was said to be the cause. She was also associated with restless spirits and phantasms that attacked people, either through their own volition or under the command of spiteful persons. This quote from Plutarch describes the associated phenomena:

> [the superstitious] go to the beggar priests and sorcerers who say: If you fear phantasms in your sleep or hear the procession of *Hekate Chthonia*, call on the old woman who performs purifications, dip yourself in the ocean, and sit down on the ground for the whole day.[12]

In Greek mythological tradition, Hecate was one of the chthonic deities who dwelt beneath the Earth's surface and who were mainly concerned with matters of basic living: fertility, childbirth, crops, fate, and death.[13] Sacrificial rites involving chthonic deities were characterized by the use of low altars on which offerings were made "into the earth" rather than "into the air," as with celestial deities. Hecate shares a number of attributes with other chthonic deities, including multiple faces or forms, an association with crossroads, monthly sacrificial meals, symbolic dogs, snakes, and keys, dealings with the dead, and dangerous magic. Offerings of food in the form of scraps or specially prepared loaves were left at a crossroad every new Moon for Hecate Chthonia. These may have been intended to placate or bind the dangerous spirits that were thought to lurk at the crossroad or to solicit the aid of the deities for the same purpose.

Two chthonic deities, Hecate and Hermes, were often invoked in cursing magic utilized to bind the soul, intellect, tongue, or limbs of the accursed individual symbolically or literally. In later times (primarily through literary sources rather than folk or popular religious traditions), Hecate, here associated with magical workings of a chthonic nature, also became associated with the figure of Medea. Medea was an extremely popular character in about a dozen Greek and Latin plays and other literary works. She usually appears as an evil magician and herbalist who is a descendant of Helios and a priestess and student of Hecate.

In a number of plays, Medea performs a variety of magical rites, summoning spirits and invoking Hecate. Outside of these created works, no text or artwork exists that supports these magical practices and there is no evidence of a living or mortal woman actually invoking Hecate in the manner of Medea. The sorceress utilizes a system of magic associated with women (in these written sources, at least), but which may not represent actual traditions or practices. These supernatural portrayals of women may, in fact, be misogynistic fantasies or literary creations of the rigid patriarchal system of Classical Greece. This may be one reason why certain types of literary evidence pertaining to Hecate either did not survive or did so in altered form. Nevertheless, it is clear that, in later times, Hecate was associated with magic and witchcraft, and, as a goddess of witchcraft, she was particularly associated with women, whose area of concern or expertise witchcraft was considered to be.

The symbolism that became associated with Hecate in later times probably came about because of her earlier connection with liminal places and points in time, which had the potential for benefit as well as danger or misfortune. Her association with liminal places such as doorways and crossroads, initiations and difficult transitions, and the Underworld may have created a darker reputation over time. Her connection with women's passages and liminal experiences (including childbirth, death, and journeys to the Underworld) could conceivably have resulted in an accumulation of speculation, fear, and superstition.

What about the popular image of Hecate as a Moon goddess? We have seen that several of her rites are connected with the lunar cycle. Offerings associated with death rites were made at a crossroad at the new Moon, as were general sacrifices to the chthonic deities (including Hecate Chthonia). Like the New Year, the new Moon was considered a time of transition frequently associated with uncertainty and fear of the unknown. Hecate's protection may have been most needed at potentially dangerous points of the month or year, as well as at liminal places like doorways and crossroads. While there seems to be a common perception that Hecate was always a Moon goddess, most of the evidence for this association comes from the later period. No artwork exists before the Roman period connecting Hecate with the Moon. Sometimes her torches are said to be symbols of the Moon, although this is not their usual role. Aristophanes mentions the torches, saying that they "show the way at night." While this could refer to moonlight, it could also imply a "light in the darkness." This may be a man-made light (like a torch) or an allegory of Hecate's role as a guide and protectress in general.

Another possible link with the Moon arises from other scattered references. One of Bacchylides' works refers to an unnamed daughter of Nux (Night), who was a benefactor of footracers at the Olympiad of 452. Another of his works contains the following passage: "Hecate, torch-bearing holy daughter of great-bosomed Night."[14] Interestingly, the four-year Olympic cycle was measured as one-half of a "great year" of 100 months or lunar cycles, and the final ceremonies were held at the full Moon. In addition, the Greek word for 100 is *hekaton*. If Hecate is the goddess involved (in the *Theogony*, she is said to assist athletes), this would help support an earlier lunar aspect.

Hecate's association with Helios, the Sun god, in literary sources (and their connection with cursing magic) has also been cited as evidence for her role as a Moon goddess, but this evidence is quite late. However, in the *Hymn to Demeter*, Hecate and Helios witness Persephone's kidnapping and inform Demeter of her daughter's abduction.[15] A common theme found in many parts of the world is one in which the Sun and Moon (due to their perceived ability to observe everything that happens) are questioned concerning events that take place on Earth. In the tale of Demeter, Helios is directly called a "watcher," but Hecate is said to be able only to hear Persephone from her cave.[16] Some suggest that this illustrates the abduction of Persephone during the day, when Hecate (as a goddess of the Moon) would have been hidden from sight. If this is the case, these events (recorded in an early text) may lend support to Hecate's early aspect as a Moon deity.

One additional example may support a connection between Hecate and the Moon. Two major sanctuaries were located in Caria, one dedicated to Hecate (at Lagina) and another dedicated to Zeus Chrysaoreus nearby. Strabo refers to these sanctuaries and mentions the great assemblies that flocked to Hecate's temple each year. The two temples were closely linked, and the priesthood of Zeus was seen as a prerequisite for that of Hecate. The *Theogony* of Hesiod (the earliest literary text that provides us with information about Hecate) mentions the high status she was afforded by Zeus and her equal rights or shares in the realms of Earth, Ocean, and Sky. Zeus's title at Caria means "Of the Golden Sword" or "Of Golden Brilliance," which suggests an emphasis on his aspect as a sky or Sun god. Perhaps Hecate was seen in some fashion as a complementary Moon goddess. In the accounts that state that Hecate's father was Zeus, the sky god, her mother is said to be Asteria, the star goddess. This union could reasonably have produced a goddess associated with the Moon who received offerings at the time of the new Moon and was connected with transformation, passages, initiations, and liminal places and times. Hecate was clearly a guiding light who assisted with transitions and passages, a nurse who cared for living things, and a powerful and beneficent goddess who was honored and revered in the three realms of Earth, Sea, and Sky.

Lunar Dynasties and the Elixir of Immortality

Numerous parallels exist between elements of Hindu and Celtic society and religion. Many of these underline the shared Indo-European heritage of these two cultures and, in some cases, demonstrate the great antiquity of these common elements. While Hindu mythology is a complex system that cannot be outlined in a work of this length, we will briefly examine the ways in which the Moon is portrayed in Hindu tradition and try to identify parallels between it and Celtic lore.[17]

Shared cultural and religious elements between the two cultures include:[18]

- Three-fold division of the religious class (and of society)

- Existence of a privileged class of religious specialists (Brahmans/Druids)

- Importance placed on the bardic class, similarities in methods of learning, composition, and transmission, and their power and status in society

- A significant oral tradition that preserved traditional knowledge pertaining to society, religion, and poetry (including history, law, genealogy, and the origins of important persons, places, customs, and traditions)

- An epic form of great antiquity consisting of a prose narrative interspersed with occasional passages of verse

- The belief that blessings were bestowed upon those who listened to certain important or sacred stories

- Motif of the "fairy" or Otherworld lover

- Laws pertaining to marriage and the legal degrees of kinship

- Importance and magical power of the concept of Truth, especially as it relates to a king's just and successful reign

- Sacred taboos or prohibitions, often imposed upon heroes or kings

Hindu mythology mentions a group of eight deities known as the *Vasus*, whose chief was originally Indra, and later, Vishnu. The eight original Vasus were the deities of day, water, the Moon, the Pole Star, wind, fire, dawn, and light. These were born from the navel of Brahma, the Creator.[19] In certain variants of the story in which the Vasus originate from Vishnu (a deity who was born in the very middle of the night when the "Moon was victorious"), the moment of their creation is described in this way:

> In the beginning this universe was the waters, the ocean. Prajapati became the wind and moved in the ocean. He saw the earth and became a boar and seized her . . .[20]

Here, the deity, in the form of a wind moving in the ocean (and later as a sacred animal), unites with the Earth to give rise to the Moon and the other features listed above. These elements are also mentioned in the magical incantation of the Irish poet Amairgen, which was quoted in full in the previous chapter, and which begins:

> *I am a wind in the sea . . . I am a sea-wave upon the land . . .*
> *I am the sound of the sea . . . (and later) I am a boar for valour . . .*[21]

In another tale, the Vasus travel to visit Shiva and Parvati on Mount Meru. This sacred peak was adorned with gems and called "Luminary," famed "throughout the triple world." It was said to be immeasurable and unapproachable by all people. Pleasant, clear winds blew there, wafting various perfumes, and great trees blossomed, bearing flowers of all seasons.[22] This scene probably depicts the World Tree or Mountain, the center of the three worlds. It is also reminiscent of passages from Celtic legends in which the beauty of the Celtic Otherworld is praised. These frequently describe a wondrous land whose trees bore leaf, fruit, and blossom at the same time.

The Moon is featured in another Hindu account of creation known as The Churning of the Ocean. The story focuses on the winning of the *amrita* ("immortal"), an elixir of immortality. The gods are assembled on Mount Meru, pondering how to go about obtaining the amrita, when the god Vishnu makes a suggestion:

> Let the Devas and the Asuras churn the pail of the ocean, and then the elixir
> will emerge as the ocean is churned, along with all herbs and jewels.[23]

They proceed to Mount Mandara, uproot it, and set it on the back of a tortoise as a paddle. Using the snake Vasuki as a rope, they begin to churn the ocean. The Asuras and Danavas (two groups of divine beings) hold onto one end of the snake and the Devas (another group) hold onto the other, twirling Mount Mandara about so that its trees fall over and the friction sets them on fire. Indra puts out the fire with water from his clouds, but the heat causes the sap of the plants to flow into the ocean. The ocean is turned to milk and then to butter.[24] With one final effort, the gods churn the ocean and a number of divine elements appear: the Sun, the Moon, the Goddess of Fortune ("and other treasures"), and finally, the divine physician Dhanvantari bearing the magical elixir. Vishnu tricks the Asuras into surrendering the elixir and gives it to the Devas to drink. The figure Rahu tries to snatch a drop but, before he can swallow it, he is decapitated by Vishnu. Since that time, there has been a feud between Rahu and the Moon (with which amrita, the elixir of immortality, is identified). This explains the waxing and waning of the Moon, which disappears and reappears from Rahu's throat.

A beautiful passage pertaining to the Sun and Moon comes from a story concerning the god Shiva and his wife, Parvati. After their marrriage, Shiva was intent on his worship of Sandhya (Twilight), and Parvati became upset. She determined to leave him and practice asceticism in order to ensure her marital happiness. Shiva comes to her and says:

> "Why do you torment yourself like this, when you could obtain whatever
> you want merely by asking me? You are the oblation and I am the fire; I am
> the sun and you are the moon. Therefore you should not make a separa-
> tion between us, as if we were distinct people. . . ." Thereafter . . . their
> paired bodies became one, because of their love.[25]

In Hindu tradition, there is also a group of myths concerned with cosmic creation and destruction that sets forth the histories of what are known as the solar and lunar dynasties. Lunar dynasties figure in the story of King Ila, a perplexing tale full of androgynous beings and sex changes. Ila was originally the eldest daughter of Manu, but, through the grace and will of the gods Mitra and Varuna, became a man called Sudyumna. However, Shiva commanded Sudyumna to become a woman again, "in order to increase the dynasty of the Moon." Later, through a horse sacrifice, Sudyumna became an androgyne and, in this state, was called both Ila and Sudyumna, for s/he was a man for one month and a woman for one month.

As time went on and his/her shape changed and alternated cyclically, various sexual unions occurred, and children were produced. In the form of Ila, she lived in the palace of the son of the Moon and bore him a son. As Sudyumna, he had three additional sons who ruled the land during the periods of time when their father's female form prevented him from doing so. Eventually, Ila/Sudyumna was installed as king. Over time, however, he passed the rule on to the son of Ila (himself in female form) and the son of the Moon. While this may seem confusing, there is method to the madness. The change of state to female form was said to be for the sake of the dynasty of the Moon, in order to increase it through procreation and establish it as a lunar entity. While there appear to have been initial objections to the female gender of the ruling entity, it is interesting to note that it is the offspring of Ila's female incarnation (rather than of the male half) who, in this lunar myth, finally inherits the throne.[26]

Night Weavers and the Morning Star

We can see that, in Hindu mythology, the Moon is associated with a number of divine elements or concepts that appear in other cultural or religious contexts, including creation and the cosmic origin of things, the ocean, plants, and the birth of divine figures. In most of these examples, however, the Moon is associated with male divinities in some fashion, and none (other than amrita, the elixir of immortality) expressly personifies the Moon. But Hindu goddesses or female divine figures who display lunar attributes do exist. While a number of divine figures in Hindu tradition are in some way likened to or connected with the Sun, other divinities appear to be associated with the Moon, the stars, and the night sky. The goddess Arundhati was the Morning Star, for example, and the divine female figure Rohini ("red" or "red cow") was a constellation (as well as the wife of the Moon). She was described as a female deer, perhaps expressing the aforementioned connection between deer antlers or horns and the Moon.[27]

In early Vedic literature, the goddess Ratri was associated with night; in some cases, she was said to be the night itself. She especially personified a power or presence that people petitioned for comfort and security in the dark hours before sunrise. Ratri is often described as a beautiful maiden (as is her sister, Usas, who is the dawn). She is praised as being glorious and immortal as well as for providing light in the darkness, "for she is arrayed with countless stars." A benign deity who gave rest to all creatures, Ratri was also credited with bestowing the life-sustaining dew. Her relationship with Usas is often mentioned, and the two sisters are referred to as lovely maidens (and sometimes as twins). They are described as strengtheners of vital power, weavers of time, and mothers of eternal law. In their alternating and endless manifestations, they represent the rhythmic patterns of the cosmos in which light and dark (and periods of rest and activity) alternate in the sacred flow of time.[28]

In early sources, Ratri was invoked to protect people from dangers particular to the night, including wolves, thieves, and creatures of the night that can do harm. In other texts, however, Ratri is described in less positive terms and is sometimes associated with things that are harmful or injurious to people. In the Rig Veda, she is chased away by Agni, the god of fire, as well as by her sister, Usas. She is called "barren and gloomy," in comparison with her bright sister of the dawn. Sometimes Ratri is associated with the very creatures or dangers of the night from which she is elsewhere petitioned for protection. As the guardian of night and protectress of the people during their rest, she is the night itself and all things, benign and hostile, which inhabit the night.[29] The nocturnal symbolism associated with Ratri reflects universal elements of the lunar symbolism we have encountered in other contexts: light or creation emerging from darkness, female weavers or spinners of time or destiny, the eternal order of space, time, and creation, the ebb and flow of energies, water, and periods of light and darkness. Her role as a protectress against the unknown dangers of the darkness and her subsequent association with these dangers is reminiscent of the dual aspects of Artemis and Hecate.

The Dark Side of Life

The Moon makes a symbolic appearance in passages describing the dark aspects of other goddesses who also figure in the Hindu pantheon. One of these is the *Mahadevi*, whose name may be translated as "Great Goddess." Texts celebrating this powerful female divinity express a theology in which the ultimate reality in the universe is a powerful, creative, and transcendent female being. She is a creator figure, the root of the world and queen of the cosmos. In various sources, she is known as "She Who Pervades All," "She Whose Womb Contains the Universe," "Mother of All," "Root of the Tree of the Universe," and "She Who Is Supreme Knowledge." In addition to these beneficent attributes, the Mahadevi also has a fierce and terrifying aspect associated with death and destruction.[30]

In exploring and ascertaining the power and importance of the Mahadevi (also called the Devi, The Goddess), it is important to remember that Hindu religion is polytheistic, with numerous powerful male and female deities.[31] The *yoni* ("womb" or "source") was the sacred image of the goddess' organ of generation and was worshipped together with the *linga* (phallic symbol). While in later sources the Mahadevi reflects or incorporates the identities or characteristics of a number of Hindu goddesses, in the earliest religious texts, these goddesses were considered to be separate entities. Sadly, the powerful female divinities of Hindu tradition do not reflect the reality of the human condition, for Hindu society was rigidly patriarchal. Societies do not always reflect the gender roles or attributes of their deities, whether that spirituality is perceived or transmitted through written records or through archaeological artifacts.

In any case, in later times, the Mahadevi was indeed a very popular and powerful deity who combined the powers of life and death into one mighty goddess. She is said to be very attentive to the world and to her devotees in particular. Described as the embodiment of female beauty and the exciter of desire, the Mahadevi could grant wisdom, learning, and liberation, but was also fond of violence and quarreling. She shows concern (much like a mother) for her children, but her favorite guise is a traditionally male role: a warrior or protector of the cosmos. Her ability to assume various forms, which are benign and terrible or auspicious and dangerous, is evident from the wide range of descriptive passages in which she appears as a surpassingly beautiful woman or a great devourer, wrathful and drenched in blood. In one hymn, she is associated with life, victory, mercy, and nourishment, as well as with the night of death. These contradictions only form a dichotomy in a modern Western mindset, in which ideas and elements are separated and categorized, and where time is perceived as linear rather than cyclical. In primal cultures, life is seen as part of death and death as part of life. Life arises from death and both exist cyclically and simultaneously.[32]

Interestingly, as a deity associated with creation and the promotion of life, the Mahadevi was generally not a goddess revealed in nature. In most cases, she appears to have been connected with practical knowledge, civilization, and culture. However, in certain guises in which she is associated with nourishment and food, the Devi may sometimes be identified with the earth. In particular, she is connected with the mysterious power through which apparently lifeless seeds grow after being put into the earth. This power is seen as a potent energy or presence associated with the earth, often perceived as a specifically female force or essence. The Mahadevi possesses a reservoir of life energy, which can produce crops and nourish the living things that grow on the Earth's surface, as well as revitalize declining life force.

In her equally powerful bloodthirsty aspect, the Mahadevi demands to be renourished by blood, and ultimately by the lives of all living creatures. She embodies the fierce and terrible forms associated with war—blood, destruction, death, and hunger. These forms exhibit qualities that threaten the world and illustrate the dangerous and uncontrollable side of the Mahadevi's character. While the goddess demands blood to replenish her, she also gives life unstintingly. Both aspects are necessary and interconnected. Each side exists because of the other, feeds off the other, and demands the existence of the other. Life and death, summer and winter, light and dark, Sun and Moon—all are part of the integral and very sacred whole.

In light of this fact, it is not surprising that the Moon was symbolically associated with the terrifying forms or aspects of the Mahadevi, which were in some cases associated or identified with other powerful and terrifying goddesses. These female figures were connected with death, hunger, and destruction and were feared because their wild behavior threatened cosmic stability. Again, this is just one aspect of the whole, as chaos or destruction alternated with and balanced sacred order, stability, and existence.

One of these terrifying deities was known as Candamari. Descriptions of her appearance are vivid and alarming, and her movements were said to be so impetuous that the waters of the ocean were embroiled by the heavy impact of her feet. Mountains were laid low by her huge hands as she waved them in a joyous display while destroying demons. She carried a club with ringing bells, and human skulls swayed to and fro at her side. On top of her forehead, the Moon was ritualistically and dramatically displayed, although it was said to be terrified by her matted hair, which was entwined with madly excited serpents.

The Moon is also mentioned in relation to another intimidating goddess called Camunda. Her appearance is described in a hymn praising the goddess and her powers. She was evidently surrounded by demons and wore a garland of skulls, which laughed and terrified the beings of the Earth. She was covered with snakes and showered flames from her eyes, which destroyed the world. In one text, Camunda herself performs a dance that destroys the world, an activity also attributed to other deities. As she danced, she played a musical instrument whose neck was Mount Meru, whose string was the cosmic serpent, and whose gourd was the crescent Moon. She played this instrument during the flood, which destroyed the world and during the last night at the end of the world.[33]

In both of these instances, the Moon is associated with a powerful female entity in turn associated with darkness, death, and destruction. These beings are the counterparts and predecessors of the female forms that balance and emerge from them, and that create and sustain life. The two aspects, light and dark, life-promoting and death-producing, are clearly reflected in the alternating light and dark aspects of the lunar cycle, whose symbol appears here in connection with the dark side of life. These associations are interesting in light of other cultural contexts in which women are associated with darkness and the powers of night, magic and witchcraft, shape-shifting and destruction, female power and sexuality, the powers of life and death, and the Moon and its phases.

Hindu mythology abounds with symbolism of this kind, which at first glance appears opposing or conflicting, but which, in reality, is balanced and holistic, forming a sacred and integral unity. Hindu goddesses in particular are associated with these attributes and this positive and empowered integration. While the power and autonomy of these female deities is not manifest in the lives of Hindu women, these goddesses are, nonetheless, extremely popular. They embody the promise and essence of the potential contained in female energies, as well as the threatening force of their independence and power. The figure of the Mahadevi (and her terrifying destructive and lunar aspects) incorporated the power of creation, the patterns of life, death, and rebirth, and the cycles of life that feed and support each other into powerful female images that ultimately support and maintain life, creating, destroying, and renewing the life force as needed, while personifying and sustaining the Earth, a living being and sacred cosmic organism.

The Horse of the Sun and the Mare of the Moon

In numerous religious traditions, the Sun and Moon are perceived as shining chariots drawn by sacred animals. We have already encountered the horse-drawn chariot of Helios and the horse- or oxen-led chariot of Selene in tales from Greek mythology. In Hindu tradition, there are also two different sets of associations pertaining to the Sun and Moon. In one set, the stallion (connected with the Sun and day) is contrasted with the mare (connected with the Moon and night). In another model, the stallion of the Sun is contrasted with the bull of the Moon.[34] The relationship between oxen or cattle and the Moon may have arisen from the image of the "horned" or crescent Moon.

It should be noted that, in classical Hinduism, both the Moon and the Sun are generally masculine. This is an exception to the fairly prevalent Indo-European model, which features a masculine Sun or Sun god and a feminine Moon or Moon deity.[35] Another notable variation comes from Norse tradition, where the Sun is female and the Moon male.[36] This is also the case with a Baltic variant of the swan-maiden/swan-god myth, where we encounter atypical symbolism of female fire/Sun and male water/Moon.[37]

Prior to the composition of the Rig Veda (c. 1200 B.C.E.), in the earlier Indo-European period, an important goddess appeared in myth and ritual who was associated with the Moon and with mares. She was said to choose a royal human consort on whom she bestowed various powers for a limited period of time.[38] She survives in the Rig Veda in the figures of Urvasi, Saranyu, and Yami, each of whom appears in a single, obscure hymn. By the time these hymns were recorded, however, no worship was being offered to these female deities, as they were, at the time, portrayed as immoral, dangerous, or cruel.[39]

The connection between mares and powerful or dangerous female figures or energies also appears in other Hindu sources. In addition to being associated with the Moon, the mare is also connected with "the fire of lust." The positive image of the yogi (a respected figure whose powers are held in and controlled) was contrasted with the "evil goddess," the woman who holds back her milk. It was implied that a man may voluntarily hold in his powers (although this may have destructive results when they break out against his will), but a woman may only hold in her powers under compulsion. For this reason, yoginis (who practice voluntary self-control) are assimilated to a herd of mares. These women are servants of the goddess Kali and are considered to be, not only highly erotic, but dangerous, because they act like men.[40]

Yogis, Soma, and Female Seed

Lunar symbolism is also found in connection with the sexual meditations and theories of Tantrism. A specialized meditation known as the "interior androgynization" of the yogi is described as the union of the male Sun and female Moon within the yogi's body. These traditional associations are reversed in another Tantric exercise, in which the Moon in the head is perceived as cool semen and the devouring fire in the stomach the red female Sun (menstrual blood). Symbols associated with this meditation are the thunderbolt phallus (which is white) and the female genitalia (a red lotus). Reversal of the traditional Sun/Moon associations are also found in a text that describes how, during intercourse, the man's linga draws out the female flux or flow and absorbs it into his own body. In this case, the male semen also represents the Moon and the female flux the Sun.[41]

The association of the Moon with semen also occurs in Iranian myths pertaining to the sacred primordial ox. The seed of this creature (which is ejaculated at death) was carried up to the Moon, where it was purified and sent back to Earth in order to cause the birth of all species of domestic animals. There is also a large body of Indo-Iranian work that speculates on the nature of semen as a universal life-sap with a luminous essence, thought to be connected to the celestial bodies.[42]

An interesting example of the traditional solar/lunar sexual associations comes from the southern region of modern India, where women are thought to have a kind of white seed of their own. In this region, the Sun is masculine and the Moon feminine. This is also the case in the *Puranas*, where *tejas* ("fiery energy") is used as a euphemism for semen. In *Sasruta*, however, semen is characterized as moonlike (due to its pale color), and female "seed" (menstrual blood) is red and fiery. Examples of both sets of symbolism are found throughout the world, although the standard Indo-European model usually contains a masculine Sun and feminine Moon.[43]

In a number of mythological systems, the Sun and Moon are seen as contrasting elements that personify or reflect male and female energies or properties. The Sun is frequently perceived as constant/male and the Moon as inconstant/female. This connection is reflected in the *Upanishads*, where the path to the Sun is a release, while the path to the Moon is rebirth.[44] In addition, the Moon is associated with reproductive seed through its connection with *soma*, an ambrosial offering to the gods through which they sustain their immortality.[45] Soma is also used as a name for the Moon, the place where the ambrosia is stored and where it is sometimes incarnate as a god.[46] All of these concepts are found in this description of the rebirth of the soul from the *Upanishads:*

> The soul of the man who is to be reborn goes to the moon, and pours down onto the earth as rain (a metaphor for seed shed by the celestial gods). This rain goes into the plants (of which Soma is king), is eaten by a man and transformed into semen which then impregnates a woman. Hence the soul is reborn.[47]

Prior to rebirth, some souls enter the path of flame that leads to the Sun and to ultimate release or spiritual achievement. Those who are not released enter the Moon (identified with soma) and are nourishment for the gods. After this, they rain down and are reborn. This system of belief corresponds with the common perception of the Sun as constant, expressing a state of being, and the Moon as inconstant, symbolizing change, growth, transformation, and rebirth.

The Body of the Universe

The Moon plays a major role in a fascinating system of symbolic analogies found in a number of Indo-European contexts. In this system, the parts of the human body are compared or identified with elements of the Earth or the cosmos. In many cases, these appear in connection with descriptions of the original act of creation.[48] While there are some variations, in general the nine-fold analogy runs as shown in Table 3 below.

The mind was also associated with the Moon in the pseudo-Hippokratic Greek text *Peri Hebdomadon,* which dates to the 5th century B.C.E. In this text, the mind (the "organ of consciousness") was envisioned as residing in the physical

Table 3. Indo-European Associations of Elements and the Human Body

ELEMENT	BODY
Earth	Flesh
Stone	Bone
Plants	Hair
Water	Blood
Wind	Breath
Sun	Eyes
Moon	Mind
Clouds	Brain
Heavens	Head

area of the lungs and the diaphragm. This may suggest the Moon's central position in the system, as it was associated with the center of the body. It may also be that the popular connection between mental or emotional states and the phases of the Moon derive, in part, from this ancient homology of the Moon and the mind.[49]

One example of this system is found in the "Song of Purusa" (the primordial or original man), found in the Rig Veda and composed around 900 B.C.E. The song begins by asking what elemental pieces were created from the cosmogonic division of Purusa. His mouth is equated with the sacred class, his arms with the warrior class, his thighs with the common classes, and his feet with the serving classes. In addition, the song describes the birth of various sacred elements of the cosmos from the parts of his body: the Moon was born of his mind, the Sun from his eye, fire and the god Indra from his mouth, the wind from his breath, the atmosphere from his navel, heaven from his head, Earth from his feet, and the four cardinal directions from his ears.[50]

The cosmic elements that occur in this traditional set of associations are mentioned by Herodotus in his *History*, where he states that the gods of the Persians (who are Indo-European peoples) were not worshipped in anthropomorphic form. Instead, he presents a list of non-anthropomorphic deities including Heaven, Sun, Moon, Earth, Fire, Water, and the Winds. These primal deities are comprised of many of the same cosmic elements that appear as alloforms of the parts of the body (heaven, Sun, Moon, Earth, fire/Sun, water and wind, as well as stone, plants, and clouds).[51]

The concept of creation arising from the sacrifice or body parts of a primordial figure also occurs in Norse mythology. In an ancient Germanic poem called the *Grímnismál*, the origin of the cosmos is associated with the death and transformation of the giant Ymir (Twin), the first living being in the universe. This ancient tradition states that the Earth was made from Ymir's flesh, the sea from his sweat (or blood), the mountains from his bones, the trees from his hair, the clouds from his brain, and the heavens from his skull. Then, from his brows the "gentle gods" made Midgard (the human realm) for the sons of men.[52]

Similar imagery is found in Greek tradition, where the transformation of Atlas is set forth by Ovid in his *Metamorphoses*. Here Atlas was said to have been made into a mountain, his beard and hair changed into forests, and his hands and arms transformed into mountain ridges. His head became the summit of the mountain and his bones became stone. He then grew to an immense size and the sky and stars rested upon him.[53]

The primordial man of Christian tradition (Adam) was also created from these elements, although here, the associations are somewhat altered. In this system, the elements are divided into eight parts, rather than nine. The first part is the Earth, which is described as "the lowliest of all parts" (a major difference between Christian theology and most primal cultures). The second part is the sea, which is equated with blood and wisdom. The third is the Sun, associated with beauty and the eyes. The fourth part is the celestial clouds, connected with thoughts and weakness. The fifth part is the wind (or the air), associated with breath and envy. The sixth part is stones, equated with firmness. The seventh part is the light of this world, which is "made into flesh" and associated with humility and sweetness. Finally, the eighth part is the Holy Spirit, that which is placed into humans "for all that is good and full of zeal"; this is considered the foremost part.[54]

While only eight elements are listed in this analogy, most traditional religious systems include the nine-fold analogy listed above. Where variants occur, it is frequently the Moon whose associations are different, or who is absent. Indeed, the Moon does not appear in many Christian versions of the system. However, a Christian (or perhaps Christianized) Slavic version of the analogies from the Old Russian "Poem on the Dove King," does include the Moon. While the poem was collected from oral tradition early in the 19th century, literary references to it are found in texts that date from 600 years earlier. Perhaps the inclusion of the Moon reflects the preservation of earlier Slavic (Indo-European) folk traditions prior to the arrival or influence of Christianity. In this system, light is said to have come from the Lord, the Sun from the face of God, the "young shining moon" from his breast, the dawn from his eyes, the "sparkling stars" from his garments, the wild winds from the Holy Spirit, strong bones from the stones, and "our bodies from the damp earth."[55]

A Romanian variant that probably draws on earlier Slavic, Greek, or Latin traditions occurs in a text called *Questions and Answers*, dated to around 1800. In this variant, there are only eight parts, but here the Moon is once again included. In this text, our bodies are said to have been created from soil, our bones from stones, our blood from the dew, our eyes from the Sun, our thoughts from the clouds, our breath from the wind, our intellect from the Moon, and the gift of prophecy from the Holy Spirit.[56]

The power of the full nine-fold system, in which the Moon plays an important and integral part, is evident from its many creative manifestations over a large region, as well as its preservation for a period of over 3,000 years.

In some cases, instead of being associated with the mind, the Sun and Moon were associated with the eyes. In the 9th-century rescension of the Iranian *Greater Bundahisn* (which contains elements likely dating to a much earlier period, 3rd to 7th century C.E.), the common Indo-European set of correspondences is expressed, along with the Sun/Moon and eye correspondence, or perhaps, innovation. The text states that each person has skin like the sky, flesh like the Earth, bones like the mountains, veins like rivers, blood like the water in the seas, a belly like the ocean, hair like plants, and breath drawn in and out as the wind. The top of the head and the brain are likened to a realm of endless light, the head to the heavens, and the two eyes to the Sun and the Moon.[57]

In later Hindu tradition, these symbolic concepts were associated with idea of the cosmos as a living being and the Earth as a personified goddess. Texts praising the Mahadevi contain many passages in which she is identified with the world or the cosmos. She is also identified with *prakruti* (primordial matter or nature), that which is the basic substance of creation and the world, and which is considered a living being. The world is said to be filled by the Devi, who constitutes every living thing. She is present everywhere in the universe, from Brahma to each blade of grass. She even proclaims to Vishnu that everything that is seen is herself. Her connection with the Earth is expressed through identification of parts of the world with parts of her body. In this lovely poem, the Earth is said to be the goddess' loins, the ocean her bowels, the mountains her bones, the rivers her veins, the trees her hair, the Sun and Moon her eyes, and the lower worlds her hips, feet, and legs.[58]

The same system was described centuries later by Sir Walter Raleigh in his *History of the World*. He wrote that the bodies of humans were created from earth and dust and compared the bones of our bodies to rocks and stones. Our blood resembled the waters which were carried by brooks and rivers all over the Earth. Breath was associated with the air, hair with the grass of the Earth, and our generative power with Nature, "which produceth all things." In addition, he compares our "determinations" with the clouds and our eyes with "the light of the Sunne and Moone."[59]

It may be that other versions also included this correspondence of the two eyes with the Sun and the Moon. The "lunar eye" may have been subsumed by the "solar eye or eyes," as some texts indicate, accounting for the Moon's varying characteristics. Interestingly, the Sun, once again, is stable, while the Moon is variable and changing. In addition, this particular correspondence almost seems to suggest the scientific connection of the right side of the brain with the left eye/left side of the body (and with intuition and creativity), and the left side of the brain with the right eye/side of the body (and with logic and reasoning). Perhaps this was one of the original concepts expressed by this system.

In this chapter we have explored lunar symbolism found in various Indo-European religious traditions, including a connection with gods and goddesses of the Moon and the night sky, darkness, transformation and passages, liminal places and events, the Sea, the Sky Realm, and the Underworld. Many of these deities were concerned with the creation and promotion of life, as well as its destruction and its reemergence out of the void—elements also reflected in the luminous cycle of the Moon's phases. In many of these spiritual traditions, the Moon is also associated with sacred animals (deer, cattle, and horses), the ambrosial food of the gods, and the elixir of immortality, as well as the mind or intuition of the universe itself. These sacred symbols will undoubtedly illuminate the rest of our search, as we explore another Indo-European tradition, that of the Celts.

☽   ☽   ☽

Meditations and Exercises

Experiment with these inspirational techniques for making the Moon goddess a part of your life.

1) Write a poem or journal exercise in which you explore the powers and characteristics of the goddess Artemis, including wild animals and nature, deer and their antlers, the promotion and protection of life, fertility and chastity, initiation rites, pivotal or liminal points in time, the night sky, and themes of sanctity, transformation, and respect. Think about how these attributes relate to the Moon, its cyclical phases, and the wide range of lunar symbols and attributes we have discussed. Create a piece of artwork that explores the goddess' various aspects and attributes. Or create an altar to honor Artemis, utilizing a green cloth, a set of deer's antlers, symbols of Artemis' bow and the crescent Moon, images of wild animals (including the bear), a wand or other object made of willow, chestnut, or cedar, cymbals or masks, and a laurel bough.

2) Create a poem or hymn in honor of Selene, She Who Shines Far and Wide. Begin by honoring her divine parents and her brother Helios, the Sun. Reflect on Selene's connection with creation and cosmology, light and illumination, passages and rebirth, magic, the measurement or passing of time, and her sacred animals and chariot. Phrases or images from the Homeric *Hymn to Selene* may suggest a good starting point or provide inspiration.

3) Compile a list of the attributes associated with both aspects of Hecate's dual incarnation. Try to form an image of her in your mind that includes both aspects. Once you are clear on her composite form, sit and meditate on Hecate's divine powers and attributes, including her festivals and temples, her rights in the three realms, her role as a guardian and guide at liminal places and times, her symbolic torches and key, and the beneficial role she plays in people's lives (victory in battle, fishing, stables and herds, sports and games). Remember that Hecate's "dark" or mysterious aspects are complementary to the attributes listed above. Therefore, it is important to include in your meditation Hecate's association with passages and transformation, the cosmic darkness, doorways and crossroads, women's mysteries and magic, and the new Moon. Deepen your experience by chanting Hecate's various names and titles during an invocation.

> *Anassa, Antaia, Enodia, Propylaia,*
> *Hecate Phosphoros, Hecate Chthonia.*

You may wish to include the names or titles of other divine figures associated with the Moon or the night sky in this invocation: Nux (Night), Asteria (The

Star goddess), Eos (The Dawn), Neaira (The New One), Kleta (The Invoked), Phaenna (The Brilliant), Auxo (The Waxing), and Hegemone (The Precursor).

4) Ritually create a painting, drawing, piece of needlework, song, or story that includes the following images from Hindu mythological tradition: The great heights of Mount Meru (which was descended from the Sun and called "Luminary") adorned with gems and blossoming trees and surrounded by perfumed breezes. The mountain is located at the center of the three worlds, and, in the heavens above, you can see the faint outline of the constellation of the sacred female deer (Rohini). A mysterious yet beneficent goddess spreads her midnight-blue mantle over the skies. This is Ratri, the divine presence who provides comfort and light during the night. She is arrayed with countless stars and is responsible for the morning dew. She is also known as a "weaver of time." In front of the mountain is the cosmic ocean, which has been stirred or churned until it forms a spiral. Out of the center of the spiral arise the Sun and Moon, herbs, jewels, various deities, and amrita, the elixir of immortality.

5) Create and enact a ceremony to celebrate the power of and propitiate the Mahadevi, creator and queen of the cosmos, mother of warriors and goddess of sacrifice, death, and life. Create a poem or chant to invoke her dual aspect (including those attributes you find challenging). Invoke and honor the Devi's beauty and skill, her many blessings, the protection of the cosmos, her role as a nurturing mother to her devotees, the female power or essence that gives life to seeds in the dark earth, and the esoteric meaning behind ritualized images of anger, violence, destruction, death, and the replenishment of her life force with offerings of life. Draw a picture of the Mahadevi as a sacred unified divinity who is both beautiful and terrible, demanding, devouring, transforming, creating, and producing life. She may wear a crescent Moon on her forehead, symbolic of her connection with female power and the concept of destruction that precedes and is necessary for transformation and rebirth.

6) Create a ritual item such as a wand, bowl, rattle, talisman, sculpture, cloth, or garment that is decorated with the stallion (Sun/day imagery) and the mare or white ox (Moon/night imagery). The inclusion of both aspects or images will make the sacred item energetically complete and more powerful in terms of its inherent and potential energies. Consecrate the item by censing it in the smoke from solar herbs (rosemary, chamomile, marigold, saffron, frankincense, sunflower, ash, etc.) and leave it out in the sunlight to absorb the power of the Sun for three full days just prior to the full Moon. Then, set the item out under the moonlight the night before the full Moon, the night of the full Moon, and the night after. Wrap the item in a sacred cloth and put it in a dark place during the waning and void Moon. On the night of the new Moon, purify the object with water and the

smoke from lunar herbs at the first appearance of the lunar crescent. When this has been done, the object is ready for use.

7) Meditate on the ancient system of sacred correspondences described above, in which the Moon is associated with the mind (the emotions and intuition in particular). Take a few minutes to become grounded and centered. Allow the stress to drain out of your body and focus on the breath as it enters your lungs and exits your mouth in a gentle, unforced cycle. When you are ready, take the time to open yourself to the experience described in each phrase of the following guided meditation:

Imagine that your body is of the same essence as the Earth. You are rooted in the sacred land and derive your nature from the dark, moist soil. Feel what it is like to "be" and "be comprised of" the rich, brown earth. Inside this sacred substance are your bones, which now contain the sacred energies of the rocks and stones—ancient, strong, and steadfast. Coursing through your veins is pure, clear water, which purifies and nourishes you. See if you can ascertain the source of this water (the cosmic ocean, or a sacred river, lake, stream, or well). Your hair is now made of the green plants, grasses, flowers, and trees. Your head feels expansive, lofty as the heavens, a place of wonder and possibility. Inside your head, you can feel the wonder of the clouds, ancient and eternal, filled with sacred knowledge, concepts, and forms. Your mind is the pale Moon, cool and radiant, and exudes a luminous essence that promotes growth, change, and transformation. Your ears are the four cardinal directions. They listen, absorb, and process all manner of knowledge and information, bringing into your mind and soul the songs of birds, the rushing of water, the language of the trees and the grass-covered fields, and the words of the ancestors. Your eyes are like the Sun, the fiery light of the heavens, sparkling jewels of radiant fire. They shine forth with power and brilliance. Finally, focus upon your breath. It is the wind—the wind of time, the wind that dances upon the surface of the cosmic ocean, and the wind of respiration, inspiration, and spirit. Let yourself exist for some time in this sacred state, at one with the body, wisdom, and soul of the universe.

HENGES, BARROWS, AND CAIRNS

THE MOON IN BRITISH AND IRISH PREHISTORY

Here oft, when Evening sheds her twilight ray,
And gilds with fainter beam departing day,
With breathless gaze, and cheek with terror pale,
The lingering shepherd startles at the tale,
How, at deep midnight, by the moon's chill glance,
Unearthly forms prolong the viewless dance;
While on each whisp'ring breeze that murmurs by,
His busied fancy hears the hollow sigh.

—THOMAS STOKES SALMON, *STONEHENGE*, 1823

The mysterious and omnipresent stone circles and spiral-embellished passage graves of Britain and Ireland have fascinated people for centuries. When were they built, and what was their purpose? Is it possible that these remarkable monuments were connected with the worship of the Sun and Moon in ancient times? The answers to these and other questions lie in the culture and society of these ancient people. In this chapter, we will examine the times in which these sacred sites were built.

There were many significant cultural and spiritual developments and variations in early Britain and Ireland. Therefore, referring to these "ancient people" in a general or generic sense can be somewhat misleading. Indeed, we must remain sensitive to the differences between the prehistoric societies of these regions in order to better understand how each lived their lives and interacted with the world of the divine.

The Abundance of the Land

Although early archaeological records are sparse, enough evidence has survived to show that people have been living in the British Isles since about 450,000 B.C.E.[1] For more than 99 percent of that time, these inhabitants supported themselves by hunting and gathering. The early peoples of Britain were quite mobile, with few possessions and very basic shelters. They tended to live within the limitations of the environment—a combination of forest and grasslands—rather than modify it.

These early people used flint tools and hunted a wide variety of animals, including wild ox, deer, bear, wolf, wild horse, jaguar, elephant, lion, and rhinoceros. They lived in caves or simple wooden structures—probably small and easy to construct to ensure optimal mobility for following the movement of the herds. They settled in river valleys, by lakes, or in areas near the confluence of rivers. They used stone tools and weapons, including hand axes and short spears. Evidence from modern hunter-gatherer societies suggests that these ancient people would have possessed sophisticated and well-coordinated hunting strategies, as well as an in-depth knowledge of their environment and the behavior of the animals they hunted for survival. Sadly, however, for the first 400,000 years of human settlement, we have no evidence of burials or other religious activity that can help us in our inquiry into the religious and spiritual lives of these people.[2]

Modern man was present in Europe starting around 40,000 B.C.E. A number of important changes and developments took place during the early eras. Tools became more specialized, and there is clearer evidence of the use of spears. The first burial site in Britain, which dates to between 25,000 and 16,000 B.C.E., was discovered in 1823. The remains were called the Red Lady of Paviland, but they are actually from the body of an adult male. Buried inside a cave, the body was sprinkled with red ochre and placed near a mammoth skull, perforated shells, and ivory rods and bracelets.[3] Since the ice cap had advanced into Northern Europe by about 18,000 B.C.E., there are no further traces of settlement in Britain from that point until around 12,000 B.C.E. The south of Britain became suitable for habitation at that time, and large numbers of elk, reindeer, red deer, horses, and other smaller mammals returned to the area.[4]

Around 8000 B.C.E., the woodlands of Britain (as well as the soil) began to grow and mature, with pine and birch trees the predominant species. Wild ox, red and roe deer, and wild pig were the most commonly hunted creatures, along with smaller animals and birds. These were pursued with spears or with bows and arrows.[5] Bone tools have been discovered that may have been used for digging up roots and tubers. Most habitations were in the open rather than in caves; they were often located near the banks of rivers.[6] Beads of shale and amber have been found at a number of sites, as well as iron pyrites, probably for making fires. People moved into the north of Britain (northern England and Scotland) between 8000 to 7000 B.C.E. As most of these settlements were coastal, fish and shellfish (as well as land resources) were important food sources.[7]

There are only a few surviving burials from this period, some accompanied by animal bones and teeth, and fossils. We don't have much evidence pertaining to the religious beliefs of this time period, but it is interesting to note that the earliest known artwork in Britain comes from this era. These include the decorated jaw of a horse, an ivory point decorated with a fish, a rib bone on which the image of a horse is engraved, and a reindeer rib on which a masked figure is depicted. One most remarkable find dates from this time period: twenty-one stag frontlets, complete with antlers, some of which have perforations around the edge. These may have been attached to a headdress of some kind, perhaps worn during a hunting ritual or used as a disguise for hunting.[8]

By 6000 B.C.E., Britain was no longer physically connected to the mainland of Europe and had become an island. The woodlands became denser, with oak, alder, elm, and lime the most common types of trees.[9] Settlements sprung up in river valleys and along the coast, and there is evidence for population growth. As water levels rose due to melting ice, there was less and less land available for settlement. Red deer and other animals were hunted, and plant foods must also have been eaten, including the abundant hazelnut. On the coast, crabs, limpets, periwinkles, whelks, oysters, lobsters, and fish (salmon, cod, and sturgeon) were gathered. Some settlements seem to have become more permanent, and off-site seasonal hunting camps were used during the summer months. This settled approach resulted in the advent of trade, as areas rich in tool-making materials (flint, chert, sandstone) could provide goods to groups living in other regions.[10]

Ireland may have been inhabited prior to about 7000 B.C.E., but there is no surviving evidence of human habitation prior to that date, primarily due to destruction of evidence by Ice Age glaciers.[11] The remains that have survived show that the island was heavily forested with hazel, pine, oak, elm, and ash. There was abundant game and fish (salmon, trout, eels, shellfish, deer, pigs, small mammals, and game birds) as well as edible plants (nuts, wild fruits, and berries). Hazelnuts were particularly abundant and easily stored, and seem to have formed an important part of the diet, especially in winter and early spring, prior to the widespread availability of salmon.[12] People used stone tools (axes, scrapers, arrows, spears, loom weights, and spindle whorls) made of flint, chert, porcellanite, felsite, basalt, quartzite, and sandstone. The climate was warm and wet, yet quite stable, and the expansion of the peat bogs had not yet occurred.[13]

No Irish monuments exist from this era, and only scant evidence pertaining to the construction of dwellings, which could have been made from skin, reeds, or sod. We do not know much about the religious beliefs or the organization of society in this early period, but the few surviving burial sites that can be attributed to early hunter-gatherers seem to demonstrate that respect was paid to the dead and that certain objects took on a symbolic (and possibly religious) character. The introduction of agriculture, which took place at the end of this era, resulted in many significant changes, including an increased concern with showing respect for ancestors.

The Sickle and the Bull

Agriculture was introduced in Britain around 3500 B.C.E. This was probably the result of acculturation—the adoption of ideas, tools, or resources that often accompanies trade or other human movement or contact—rather than invasions or large incoming population groups. The first farmers the early Britons encountered may have been incoming colonists from Brittany or the lower Rhine Valley who brought seed and animals with them in order to start small farms, thus providing inspiration and impetus for the indigenous population to adopt these new ways.[14] Environmental conditions were excellent for the introduction of farming, as the climate was more moderate than it is today, with longer growing seasons, less risk of drought, higher elevation limits for cultivation, good soil (in general), and less need to provide shelter for animals during the winter. Most of the landscape was still wooded, so river valleys and coastal areas were selected to start the first small farmsteads.[15]

Farming spread rapidly after its introduction, reaching Ireland and remote parts of Britain and Scotland soon thereafter. In the far north and west, however, hunter-gatherers continued their way of life and were not much affected by the introduction of farming.[16] The first people to adopt farming methods raised cattle, pigs, and sheep (from which they obtained meat, milk, and hides) and grew wheat and barley. Cattle were the most common animals, and their hides were used to make a variety of products. Sheep were raised in numbers equal to cattle in Scotland because of the preponderance of open grassland, and in some parts of England, both pigs and cattle were popular, especially in regions where they could be left alone to browse the woodlands for food.[17]

Fields were cross-ploughed with a simple plough pulled by one or more oxen. Flint sickles were used to harvest the grain, and quernstones were used to grind it. Open areas were utilized for farming, but land was cleared as well. Fields were created for growing grain and keeping animals, which resulted in huge changes in the landscape.[18] Animals were probably still hunted to some degree in order to supplement the food supply. Game included red deer, wild horse, wild boar, hare, wildcat, badger, beaver, bear, wolf, and smaller animals. Fish and shellfish were gathered, as well as plant products such as hazelnuts, crab apples, haws, sloes, and blackberries.[19]

There is very little evidence relating to settlements from the early part of this period, although later evidence of small farms and villages has survived. These included houses made of timber or stone, often located on low hills or in river valleys.[20] Fairly good-sized hilltop enclosures surrounded by ditches also existed, and some were used for settlement. Others may have been used at regular or varied periods of time, perhaps for festivals when the population gathered from outlying farmsteads to meet at a central location. There are few burials from this era, and no information about the social organization or religious beliefs of the early farmers.[21]

Farming was introduced in Ireland around the same time as in Britain. Small groups of pioneering farmers probably sailed to Ireland (perhaps from northern or eastern Britain) with the necessary grain, tools, and domesticated animals.[22] Society became even more settled, although some members of the community would have been away at times hunting, fishing, trading, or taking cattle to the summer pastures. Sturdy timber houses suitable for single or extended families of four to ten people were built, often of oak, with hazel or willow used for wattle.[23] Early farming settlements in Ireland were often located near lakes, rivers, or even adjacent communities.[24] Pottery is first evident around this time, and trade took place between Ireland and Britain—primarily for high-quality flint for arrowheads, knives, and scrapers, and dark, blue-grey speckled porcellanite for axes, adzes, and chisels. The introduction of agriculture created a more reliable food supply, but also the need for more people to perform the necessary work. This, in turn, resulted in population growth, and the attendant need for land and territory.[25]

The Seeds of Change

The introduction of agriculture brought about many changes, as well as new pressures in various aspects of society. These were the result of the new ways of living, changes in values, an increasing demand for land, and the need to manage group labor—something quite different from the focus on individual skill in a society that primarily hunts for a living. It is thought that these pressures and changes may have led to the construction of new types of monuments that appear at this time—structures different from anything that had previously been constructed. These were built from stone or from wood and turf. Although there was a great deal of regional variation in the style of these ritual monuments, in Britain, there seem to have been four main types:

1) Rotunda graves: Round stone mounds or cairns with a central cist or grave.

2) Portal dolmens: Monuments comprised of four or more large upright stones supporting a central roof or capstone. Some were associated with cremation burials. The front of these distinctive monuments looks like an "h" or a doorway of some kind.

3) Simple passage graves: Circular mounds or cairns inside which is a short passageway leading to a small rectangular or polygonal chamber.

4) Façade monuments: A variety of tomb made of wood or stone, often used for family burials. These were square or rectangular in shape, with a forecourt in the front. The forecourts frequently contain fire pits or hearths, potholes, and bones, suggesting that rituals may have been carried out in front of them prior to depositing the burials inside. Wayland's Smithy in Oxfordshire is a good example of this type of monument.[26]

Around 2800 B.C.E., even larger tombs were constructed in many areas. These were primarily rectangular- or trapezoidal-shaped mounds, although some were round. Typically, they covered one or more earlier burial sites of the types described above. The West Kennet Long Barrow in Wiltshire typifies this new development in monument construction. These sites required a great deal of manpower to construct—between 7,000 to 16,000 man-hours—much more than earlier types of monuments. Thousands of these tombs are known, and their locations reflect the expansion of farming settlements between the years 3200 and 2500 B.C.E. It is thought that the size of the monuments may reflect the size and relative prosperity of the communities that built them, as smaller tombs are found in areas containing poorer-quality farming land.[27]

It is estimated that about 200,000 people inhabited the island of Britain during this era, living in small groups as well as in slightly larger communities. Most of the large tombs contain multiple burials, although these represent only a small fraction of the population. This may mean that these are the burial places of kings or queens, priests or priestesses, leaders or heroes, or some other special category of person. Grave goods are sparse in these tombs, and in general, only personal items such as beads, pendants, necklaces, and pottery cups or bowls were buried with the dead. These do not seem to imply provision for an afterlife, but may have been placed there simply to show respect for the deceased.[28]

It is hard to say exactly what religious ideas lay behind the building of these remarkable tombs. Because of their cost in manpower, the beliefs associated with them were undoubtedly significant. The tombs would have had great symbolic value, as they enabled the group to show a direct connection with the past and, through this, demonstrate their ownership and connection with the land. Perhaps the ancestors provided magical assistance with fertility, abundance, stability, and protection.

These remarkable monuments may also have been symbols of power or prestige, as well as territory markers.[29] Land was becoming more and more valuable, and establishing rights to a specific area would have been very important. If one's ancestors had rights to the land, this helped support any current claims to the territory. Establishing such a right was important when there may have been competing claims for the inheritance of resources. Indeed, early farming societies were probably not as peaceful as people imagine, and warfare was likely to have been quite common. Weapons and arrowheads have been found at a number of sites (sometimes imbedded in humans), and defended sites and enclosures were first constructed during this time period.[30]

A somewhat similar situation existed in Ireland during this era, where more than 1,500 megalithic tombs are known from the Neolithic period. Four types are found in Ireland, some of which are similar to those found in Britain:

1) Court tombs: Probably the earliest megalithic monuments built in Ireland. About 400 are known, mostly from the northern part of the country. They have distinctive oval or U-shaped courtyards, usually set into the eastern end of a

long wedge-shaped cairn. It is believed that rituals took place in the courtyard prior to depositing the cremated remains of the deceased into the tomb itself. Knives, scrapers, polished stone axeheads, pottery, bone beads, animal-tooth pendants, and stone beads and necklaces (often made of serpentine) were buried with the dead. Bones of ox, sheep, goat, and pig have also been found; these may constitute the remains of funeral feasts.[31]

2) Portal tombs: These are perhaps the most visually impressive sites, although they are quite simple in design. They are usually comprised of two tall portal stones and a lower backstone supporting a massive stone roof. About 170 are known in Ireland (most in the north, with a few in the southeast and west), some associated with cremation burials.[32]

3) Passage tombs: Generally situated on hilltops or ridges, passage tombs are often grouped together. There are more than 200 still existing in Ireland (mostly in the northern and eastern parts of the country), and others are known to have existed. The major monuments in the Boyne Valley (County Meath) are among the finest in all of Europe. Passage graves consist of round mounds surrounded by a ring or kerb of large stones, covering a low narrow passage leading to a burial chamber (often with a corbelled stone roof). The dead were usually cremated and buried with pottery, stone beads and pendants, bone and antler pins, and small stone or chalk balls (possibly fertility symbols). Large stone basins were found in some tombs, as well as ritual objects like the ceremonial stone macehead from Knowth.[33]

Many of the Irish passage graves (like similar sites located in Brittany) are notable for the beautiful carved designs found on the stones of the tombs. The most common designs are circles, spirals, arcs, serpentine lines, lozenges, and triangles, often cleverly and harmoniously combined, adapting to the shape of the stones. Certain designs are more common at particular sites—spirals at Newgrange, concentric circles at Knowth, and rayed circles at Dowth and Loughcrew.[34] Probably the most impressive of these sites is the great monument at Newgrange, whose reconstructed mound is now decorated with white quartz stones, which some archaeologists feel may be similar to the original design. A specially constructed stone box above the entranceway allows the rays of the rising Sun to shine into the back of the chamber around the Winter Solstice (December 21).[35]

4) Wedge tombs: These constitute the largest group of tombs in Ireland. Over 460 are known, located west of a line extending from northeast Antrim to Cork Harbor. The entrance of these wedge-shaped tombs generally faces the southwest, and there is often an antechamber in front of the main chamber. Many of these sites seem to be located near copper mines or outcrops, or near good winterage lands. Both burials and cremations are found in these tombs, and

pottery, arrowheads, and evidence of bronzeworking accompany the dead. While this type of tomb is not found in Britain, they do exist in Brittany.[36]

As was most likely the case in Britain, the Irish Neolithic tombs probably served as monuments to the ancestors, as well as territory markers to establish rights over land. Fortifications of hilltop sites suggest similar social tensions due to increasing population density and stress on available farmland, which may indicate movement toward a more stratified society. The construction of these remarkable monuments would have required the marshalling of many resources (people, materials, labor), and some sort of regal or sacral authority must have been in place to organize the monumental tasks. It is difficult, however, to construct specific theories (or generalizations) about the organization of society at this time due to the scant remains of domestic sites, the variety in size and type of the tombs, variations in burial customs, and of course, the lack of written records.

Due to similarities in cairn shape, chamber arrangements, and decorative ornamentation between Irish and British tombs and those found on the Continent and in the Mediterranean, it was once thought that these building ideas originally spread from the Mediterranean. Indeed, many books based on this supposition have been written. However, radiocarbon dating techniques show that this is not, in fact, the case. The tombs and monuments of Northern Europe actually predate those of the Mediterranean by more than 1,000 years, and thus represent the earliest known style of traditional architecture in Europe. The symbols and forms associated with these monuments probably arose from changes in society and culture brought about by the introduction of farming. Rather than forming part of a great pan-European/Middle Eastern system of belief, these sites are the unique expressions of early people who lived in Britain, Ireland, and Brittany, reflecting their creativity, their spiritual beliefs, and their connection with the land and the ancestors who preceded them.

Henges, Beakers, and Monuments

After about 2500 B.C.E., even more changes took place in Britain. While the environment was generally the same, land clearing resulted in soil erosion, and there is early evidence of the formation of peat bogs. The aurochs became extinct; red squirrels appeared; and brown bears were evidently very common. At this time, for some reason, various camps and settlements were abandoned, areas previously cleared for farming became overrun with woodland, weeds, or scrub, and there is increasing evidence of warfare.[37]

The most startling development, however, is the abandonment of the chambered tombs and long barrows. Around this time, many of these previously venerated sites were blocked up and never used again. While a few long barrows and other older sites continued to be used, new monuments were constructed. Round barrows became quite widespread. While the earlier tombs seem to have focused on the community or the ancestral group, these new sites usually contain single graves, perhaps reflecting an increasing emphasis on hierarchy.[38] These new monuments included the following types:

1) Long mounds (also called bank barrows): Hilltop mounds, very long and narrow, usually over 100 meters long [109 yards], often built over the burned remains of earlier sites.

2) Cursus monuments: Similar to long mounds, though usually much longer (up to 700 meters [765 yards]). They include a pair of linear ditches with internal banks on each side of the mound.

3) Developed passage graves: Similar to simple passage graves, but with large round mounds and a long passage leading to the central stone chamber.

4) Henges: Circular enclosures surrounded by a ditch with an outer bank. Stonehenge is the most famous example of this type of monument.

5) Clava cairns (Scotland only): Similar to passage graves, except these are usually open in the southwest sector and have a ring of upright stones set around the edge of the cairn.

6) Recumbent stone circles (Scotland only): Ring-shaped cairns with a cremation burial in the central space, around which is a ring of stones of varying heights. The two tallest stones stand in the southwest on either side of a recumbent stone, which lies flat on the ground.[39]

Grave goods in these sites are different as well as more plentiful. They include polished flint blades, flint arrowheads, shale or jet belt-sliders, stone maceheads, beads, pendants, bone pins, boar's-tusk implements or blades, and antler points or tines. A variety of presumably ritualistic objects have also been found, such as antler maceheads, large stone or flint axes, and flat copper axes, the earliest metal objects used in Britain, probably imported from Ireland. (These items seem to suggest prestige, power, or status, as they differ from the everyday objects (pottery, flint, quernstones) previously seen in connection with burials.[40]

Around 2000 B.C.E., the acquisition and trade of fine goods increased. Many ideas and styles were imported from Continental Europe, including finely finished and carefully decorated red pottery vessels referred to as "beakers." These seem to have originally been drinking vessels, which were later buried with the dead. Other imported items include triangular-shaped arrowheads, stone wristguards for archers, shale and jet buttons, stone battle-axes, and gold earrings and button caps.[41]

At some point in time, certain items apparently came to be considered appropriate for burial with men or women. Both sexes were buried with pottery, craft tools, and dress fittings and ornaments. Weapons were generally only buried with men (bronze and flint daggers, flint and stone axes, arrowheads and wristguards), although male burials could also include gold button caps, antler tools, pyrites, and amber buttons. Jet or shale beads, on the other hand, were only buried with women, who could also receive jet buttons, bone pins, gold and bronze earrings, antler picks or hoes, and bronze awls. Some women were buried with weapons, particularly bronze daggers and flint blades.[42]

Ritual and domestic building at this time seems to have been focused on a display of power. Huge henge-like enclosures were built, such as those at Durrington Walls, Avebury, and Mount Pleasant. Silbury Hill, the largest prehistoric man-made mound in Europe, was also built at this time. These sites were constructed using only antler picks, baskets, and ropes, and required enormous amounts of labor. Durrington Walls, which extends over an area of thirty acres, would have required at least 900,000 man-hours to build. A powerful ritual or societal incentive or authority must have inspired and supported the effort and organization necessary to build ritual sites of this magnitude.[43]

Circles of Stone

Around 1700 B.C.E., the evocative stone circles of the British Isles appear for the first time. These are comprised of a large ring of widely spaced stones, which seem to delineate or form the boundary of a sacred or important site. Some were built inside henge monuments and may have replaced earlier wooden structures. Stone rows and alignments were also set up, like those at Callanish in Scotland and the Merry Maidens in Cornwall.[44] We will explore the position and alignment of these circles later, especially as they relate to the observation or worship of the Moon.

Stonehenge, which was originally a simple cremation cemetery, was remodeled at this time. A ceremonial avenue was added, and a double circle of eighty-two dressed bluestones imported from South Wales was set up. Later, thirty huge upright sarsen stones were erected and capped with lintel stones to form the stone monument familiar to us.[45]

Although some burials took place, cremation seems to have been most widespread, which may suggest that land was at a premium. Round barrows were still the most common kind of burial site, although some henges were used as well. The struggle for power seems to have continued during this era, as large palisades were built in certain areas. Prestige goods that symbolized power continued to be produced, even becoming devalued in some cases due to reproductions and fakes, causing them to be viewed as common and relegated to the status of domestic items. A number of elaborate burials were discovered in Wessex and south-central

England containing a wide variety of impressive gold objects. These include gold ornaments and jewelry, as well as a shoulder-cape of beaten gold. These rich grave goods are from a specific area, however, and grave goods in other regions were generally much simpler. Gold became scarcer after 1500 B.C.E., and polished stone hammers and battle-axes, daggers, bulb-headed pins, and amber and glass beads were used instead.[46]

Trade between Britain, Ireland, and the Continent resulted in the circulation of stone and copper axes, gold lunulae, flint axes, and Baltic amber. Metalwork followed styles known on the Continent, and pins, spears, and daggers were produced using Cornish tin and Welsh copper and gold. Early metal tools were imported, but, as knowledge of metalworking spread, objects of copper, gold, and bronze were produced at home in Britain and Ireland. Flint mining was also practiced, and the small chalk figurine from Norfolk of what seems to be a pregnant female is thought to have been made to encourage the fertility of the mine, which was evidently not very productive after a certain point. There is good evidence for woodworking, boneworking, basketry, and wool production. Many types of beautiful ornaments were created as well, such as the ornate jet necklaces from the northern part of Britain.[47]

Between 1500 and 600 B.C.E. (just prior to the estimated arrival of the Celts, whose archaeology will be discussed in a later chapter), the previous interest in megalithic monuments and stone circles declined. The use of round barrows also lessened, although in some areas, old barrows were reused for a while. Cremation continued to be more widespread than burial, and grave goods became less common. Large cremation cemeteries were widely used, referred to as "Urnfields," after the large pottery vessels or urns in which the remains of the dead were placed. In some parts of western Britain, cremations were placed near standing stones. There is little differentiation of burials at these locations, unlike in previous eras.[48]

Metalworking continued to develop, producing a wide variety of tools and ornaments. Evidence suggests that early smiths generally worked within a radius of nine to twelve miles, making bronze objects for the communities in their local area. Larger items were also created (including rapiers, large spearheads, and swords), apparently on a considerable scale in certain areas. As the art of metallurgy developed further, buckets, cauldrons, shields, and horse-harness fittings were produced. Both bronze and gold were used, with iron coming onto the scene a bit later. Metalwork associated with horses is seen starting around 1000 B.C.E., which may be when horse riding was first practiced in Britain.[49]

People in Bronze Age Britain lived in settlements, some of which were enclosed, in circular houses of wood or stone. Animals and crops were raised and fields were enclosed with stone or hedges. Defended settlements known as hillforts were built on top of hills, and new kinds of weapons were developed—some practical, some ornamental. Society seems to have been organized into powerful political units by this point, units whose leaders were concerned with defending their territory to provide for the needs of their people.

Around this time, an interesting ritual custom developed. Large and sometimes elaborate metal items (as well as other objects) began to be deposited as offerings in rivers, lakes, and peat bogs. This may have been due to a variety of factors, including the onset of colder, wetter weather conditions, increasing population, the spread of peat bogs, and depletion of the soil in some areas.[50] Perhaps serious and prestigious offerings to deities associated with water or the Underworld were deemed necessary to cope with these difficulties. At the end of this period, the archaeological record displays evidence of objects associated with horsemanship, combat, and display, and traditions associated with feasting and drinking ceremonies, the first indicators of what may be identified as Celtic society in the British Isles.[51]

The Bronze Age in Ireland

The inhabitants of Bronze Age Ireland also supported themselves by means of agriculture and husbandry. Society was probably highly organized and hierarchical in nature. As in Britain, the climate had become cooler and wetter, and the impact of early farming practices led to the development and expansion of peat bogs and changes in the predominant tree species; elm and pine declined, and ash trees and yew forests increased.[52] Metalworking was introduced between 2000 and 2500 B.C.E. Vast cultural changes occurred due to the introduction of metallurgy, although stone tools were still used for some time and were only replaced gradually. Initially, copper and gold were used, followed by bronze, an alloy made from copper and tin.

Copper was used to make a variety of tools—some practical, some possibly ornamental and ceremonial—including daggers, halberds, and axes.[53] Gold occurs in Ireland at over 130 locations; it was used to make torcs, armlets, dress-fasteners, and lock-rings for the hair, as well as sheet-gold for earrings, lunulae (crescent-shaped neck ornaments), and decorated circular objects known as "Sun discs." Tin was mined in Wicklow and Avoca, and probably also imported from Cornwall. Bronze items included knives, daggers, halberds, spearheads, bronze axes (suitable for woodworking and felling trees), and a variety of other metal objects that may have had a ceremonial or ritual purpose.[54]

As in Britain, a number of changes associated with burial and ritual practices took place in Bronze Age Ireland. Although wedge tombs continued to be used for some time, megalithic tombs were generally no longer built. New types of megalithic monuments were constructed, including stone circles, stone rows, and standing stones (monoliths). Both burial mounds and cremation cemeteries were utilized.[55] Beaker-type pottery and burials are found, and associated grave goods include copper daggers, stone archer's wrist-guards, flint knives and scrapers, arrowheads and buttons, bone pins, beads, boar's tusks, stone axe heads, and bronze axes, knives, and daggers. Beads of *faience* (a glass-like substance), jet, and imported amber were used, as well as amber necklaces and bracelets made of jet and lignite.[56]

In the later part of the Bronze Age (circa 1300 B.C.E. onward), even more changes took place. Indeed, there was much unrest and change in many parts of Europe, as well as in the Mediterranean. Ireland was extensively occupied during this period (particularly in the northern and eastern regions), and society became more organized, producing metalwork on a large scale. Circular houses with thatched roofs were built of wattle and daub, although there is also evidence of stone houses and rectangular wooden houses. Settlements were often enclosed, and farmsteads (supporting one or more families) included houses, storage facilities, livestock enclosures, and field systems. Smiths' workshops have been found, as well as large outdoor cooking pits. Sites located near rivers were favored, as were hilltop locations, especially later in the period.[57]

During the latter period, wagons with wheels were introduced, harnessed horses appear in the record, and sophisticated objects were produced from wood and leather. Both metalworking and weaponry developed in sophistication and intensity, and metal shields, buckets, and cauldrons were created. Archaeological evidence suggests that people wore neckrings known as *torcs*, one or (often) two plain, twisted, or pennanular bracelets, spiral finger-rings, and tress rings (perhaps to gather the hair on either side), as well as elaborate amber necklaces, bronze pins, gold gorgets and ornaments, and cloak pins.[58]

The advent of the Iron Age (around the 7th century B.C.E.) brought sweeping changes and developments. We do not know if the introduction of iron resulted from the arrival or invasion of Iron Age Celts from the Continent, or simply from the spread of new ideas and technologies from other parts of Europe. There is no real evidence of violence accompanying this development, and some Bronze Age sites were still considered sacred into the Iron Age, which argues against the invasion theory, to some degree. Newgrange, a Bronze Age monument, became an important religious site in the Iron Age pagan religion of Ireland, as did Emain Macha.[59]

Perhaps the most common thread that runs through this prehistoric narrative is that of change and development. When we speak of "ancient people" in Ireland or Britain (or elsewhere, for that matter), we must be specific concerning when, where, and of whom we speak. It is neither accurate nor respectful to make generalizations about ancient people, whose lives, cultures, and beliefs were undoubtedly as complex and sophisticated as our own. These early societies fluidly incorporated ancient customs and new experiences into a rich tapestry of experience.

Lunar Alignments and the Land of the Dead

We have seen that the Moon itself is a great emblem of change and growth. How was it perceived or venerated during the various eras of British and Irish prehistory? As we explore the possibility of Moon worship in ancient times and search for traces of a goddess associated with the Moon, one of the challenges we face is that it is very difficult (if not impossible) to ascertain the spiritual beliefs of people when these have not been recorded in writing or clearly decipherable symbols.

Some of the earliest possible religious items in Europe are some early female figurines dating to between 25,000 and 20,000 B.C.E. Thirty-five figurines in all have been found at twelve different sites (from Siberia to southern France) that appear to symbolize pregnant female forms. Many have theorized (and others accepted as fact) that people in various ancient cultures worshipped a Great Goddess and that these figurines represent such a deity. Similar objects from modern hunter-gatherer societies were used for a variety of purposes—fertility idols, talismans to assist with pregnancy or childbirth, sympathetic magic, mourning rituals, and as children's dolls—but none represented deities. In addition, the lack of contextual evidence makes the figurines almost impossible to interpret.[60] It is interesting to note, however, that they were constructed during a relatively short period of time during the Old Stone Age, when temperatures were cooling. They may, therefore, be related to a desire for increased warmth, life, energy, and abundance.[61]

Only two female statuettes have been found in Britain, both from a much later date in the Neolithic era. These consist of roughly carved blocks of chalk that can be interpreted as female forms. One was found in connection with a pair of chalk balls and a chalk phallus, objects that have been found in abundance at a number of sites. Perhaps most interesting for our search are three reliefs from France, dating to the earlier period, that depict women holding up particular objects. In one relief, the object can be identified as a bison horn marked with thirteen lines. The woman in the picture, who is painted red (apparently the color most often associated with divine matters in the Paleolithic era) rests her left hand on her abdomen. The horn with its thirteen markings may represent or be associated with the Moon, and the woman's hand on her belly may be related to fertility or menstrual cycles (often connected with the Moon).[62]

Other artwork that may pertain to early gods or goddesses are stone carvings from Britain, Ireland, and Brittany that have been interpreted by some as representing human faces or shapes (perhaps deities of some sort). In the Barclodiad y Gawres tomb in Anglesey, Wales, one stelae is thought to represent a stylized human torso; a stone at Knowth West has been interpreted as having a human figure on it as well. Cairn U at Dowth contains stones, which may portray a female figure, and similar forms appear at Barclodiad and Seefin (along with a more angular male figure). These images are very abstract or stylized, however, and may represent something else altogether. The most convincing example comes from the late Neolithic Age in Brittany, where gallery graves are known to contain upright stones bearing a fairly obvious female figure, although these are sometimes indicated by little more than a pair of breasts. We have no way of knowing exactly what these figures are intended to represent, but it is reasonable to suggest that they may be female deities or supernatural figures associated with death, liminality, transitions, or rebirth.[63]

The shapes and symbols used to decorate the megalithic tombs have also produced a number of interesting theories. While some of these, such as circles or sets of concentric circles, can be interpreted as representations of the full Moon, the lack of crescent shapes makes it difficult to differentiate between possible Sun and Moon symbols (if these are, in fact, what is represented). The distinctive "cup-and-ring" carvings found primarily in Scotland have also been interpreted in a number of ways. Some feel these may be star charts or maps, in which case, some of the larger markings may represent the Moon. These theories are far from conclusive, however.[64] Many designs appear on pottery produced in various periods of prehistory, but no crescent or circular shapes are evident. In addition, while the crescent shape of boar's-tusk pendants and gold lunulae, and the design of mother-of-pearl disk-shaped ornaments from Central Europe are suggestive of the Moon, there is no way to know if they were thought of in this way.[65]

When the great Neolithic monuments began their decline, however, the form and layout of some of the monuments that took their place seem to contain alignments with certain celestial movements—in particular, the rising and setting of the Sun and Moon. It has been argued that they served as observatories of some kind, based on several factors: the general alignments on extreme risings and settings of the Sun and Moon; regularities in spacing and number of stones, which suggests the use of rudimentary mathematical skills; and the fact that some sites were built at high altitudes, allowing a clear line of sight over the tree cover of the time. However, it is equally (if not more) likely that they served as calendars to help ascertain the timing of rituals and seasonal events or activities.[66] Knowledge of the sky and the natural calendar is very important for communities who rely on agriculture for their survival. Thus these new sites may have had both sacred and practical significance.[67]

A great deal of speculation has taken place concerning the alignments of various Neolithic monuments—passage graves, henges, and stone circles. These theories are not always based in solid fact, nor are their creators sufficiently knowledgeable in the sciences or aware of current or updated research. We do know that several sites are aligned with the Winter Solstice. Both Newgrange and Drumbeg are focused on the midwinter sunrise, while the entrance of Maes Howe in the Orkneys is aligned on the midwinter sunset.[68] In addition, unconfirmed reports suggest that, while the entrance to Cairn G at Carrowkeel allows the Sun's rays to enter the inner chamber for a month on either side of the

Summer Solstice (an alignment not nearly as accurate as the sites mentioned above), it may be that the original intent was to allow in the light of the full Moon on either side of the Winter Solstice. The tomb evidently points to the most northerly point the setting Moon reaches on the horizon (an event that only happens every 18.6 years) and appears to be oriented toward a hill called Knocknarea (which may be translated as "Hill of the Moon").[69] At the time of writing, it was unknown if the Carrowkeel lunar alignment had yet been scientifically confirmed by an outside source.

One method that has proven quite productive is to study types of monuments rather than looking only at individual examples. A very interesting observation that has come to light from this type of research is that a number of monuments are oriented toward the southwest. This is evident in some early sites, and later was common to many of them.[70] The southwest is the direction that aligns with the midwinter sunset and (as Ronald Hutton points out) perhaps also with the rising Moon.[71]

Stonehenge itself may be aligned on a northeast/southwest axis, as its earliest phase contained a main entrance and causeway in the northeast aligned with the sunrise of Summer Solstice, and a smaller secondary entrance in the south. Later, when the sarsen stones were erected, four station stones were set up that may have marked alignments with the midwinter sunset as well as certain lunar cycles.[72] Other scholars point out that the four station stones mark a right angle to the alignment that focuses on the midsummer sunrise and therefore may also have been aligned with the midsummer full Moon, which would rise perpendicular to the rising midsummer Sun.[73]

While many authorities feel that the Heel Stone at Stonehenge was one of a pair that once stood on either side of the entrance, framing the midsummer Sun as it appeared over the horizon, archaeologist Aubrey Burl has questioned this. He suggests that the empty socket on the opposite side of the original entrance (located in the southwest) originally contained the Heel Stone, which was moved to indicate more accurately the rising of the Moon (not the Sun). He also feels that the fifty-four post holes in front of the entrance were aligned with the various points at which the Moon rose in successive months, and that the southern "secondary" entrance pointed toward the place at which it was highest in the sky. Needless to say, scholars are not in agreement about this or many other aspects of the construction of Stonehenge.[74]

Many later sites are also aligned with the southwest. The stone circle in Cumbria known as Long Meg and her Daughters has one entrance that aligns with the midwinter sunset, and Ballynoes in County Down, the Druid's Circle in Gwynedd, and the Stipple Stones on Bodmin Moor all have entrances in the general vicinity of the southwest. Several Cornish stone rings have their tallest stone at that point, as does the Beltany Ring in Donegal. The Lios Circle in County Limerick has two huge megaliths that frame this direction, opposite the entrance, which is in the northeast.[75] Of the large group of Irish stone circles in south Munster, more than one hundred contain an entrance in the northeast, flanked by the tallest stones of the circle. Directly opposite this, in the southwest quadrant, is the lowest stone (sometimes set up horizontally).[76]

Many of the stone rows in Cork and Kerry are comprised of stones of graded heights, and these often have their tallest stone at one end, mainly in the southwest. These rows share a general northeast/southwest orientation with the stone circles of the area, and seem to be aligned on the portion of the sky in which the Sun rises and sets (focusing on the Sun's position in winter, rather than summer).[77] Ronald Hutton points out that there may be some unknown relationship between the stone circles (which are ideal for gatherings) and the stone rows (which are ideal for processions).[78]

In Scotland, a group of stone circles in Perthshire are aligned with the largest stone in the southwest.[79] The recumbent stone circles of central Aberdeenshire include a flat slab flanked by the two tallest upright stones of the circle, frequently in the southwest quadrant.[80] The great stone monument at Callanish in Lewis contains an avenue of stones leading to the northeast, and there may have been a similar avenue in the south.[81] While many Scottish passage graves have an easterly alignment, the monuments of the Clava-cairn type face the southwest. In fact, two of the passage graves at Balnuaran (Clava, Inverness-shire) are aligned on exactly the same southwest axis, a line that points to the midwinter sunset.[82] Some scholars feel that the Clava cairns are also aligned with major phases of the Moon.[83] Anna and Graham Ritchie point out the precision used in the construction of the Ring of Brodgar, where the monument's astronomical layout seems to involve a number of barrows that surround it. They suggest that the builders may have been able to track lunar movements by using a number of points on the horizon as markers.[84]

Lunar alignments are possible at a number of other sites as well. Aubrey Burl's survey of the Wiltshire long barrows demonstrated that, while the alignment of many faced the span of the Sun's movement, a significant minority were aligned with points outside the Sun's span, but within that of the Moon. Burl suggested that those with possible lunar alignments may have served as a location for moonlit rituals held in the forecourt of the tomb.[85] In his survey of the later Clava cairns and recumbent stone circles of Scotland (most of which face the southwest quadrant), Burl found that the alignments suggested by these monuments are within a span that is too wide for sunsets at significant times, like solstices and equinoxes, but do in fact cover the major and minor lunar standstills.

Likewise, Burl feels that stone rings with recumbent stones in the southwest-to-southeast sector are not aligned with the midwinter sunset at all, but with points associated with the Moon's movements. He maintains that the Moon would have been framed between the two flanking stones as it passed over the recumbent stone. In light of this, he suggests that ceremonies at these sites may have been nocturnal, perhaps even performed on a monthly basis. Quartz stones are sometimes found scattered in front of the recumbent stone, which he feels may lend weight to the theory that these types of monuments were associated with lunar rituals.[86] White stones were also found outside the monuments at Newgrange and Knowth, and may have had some religious significance. They are also known to have been scattered or buried within certain stone rings in Wales and southwest Ireland.[87]

We can see that there is a good possibility that the Moon played an important role in the construction, layout, and alignment of prehistoric monuments in Britain and Ireland, and formed part of early religious beliefs and ceremonies in these areas. The Sun seems to have played an important role as well, as evidenced by the widespread focus on the directions of northeast and southwest. The northeast is associated with the midsummer sunrise, the warmest and brightest point of the year, while southwest is associated with midwinter sunset, the darkest point of the year. Many sites have entrances in the northeast (as well as ceremonial avenues), perhaps used to ritually welcome or honor the Sun. No doubt the recumbent stones and other markers located in the southwest also had their symbolic meaning, perhaps associated with death or the darkest part of year.

While we should not oversimplify the religious beliefs of early people into an easy case of Sun worship, it seems reasonable that this did form part of these prehistoric religious systems. One common early symbol is the equal-armed cross, which has been interpreted as a Sun symbol. In some cases, it is depicted as being carried in a boat, chariot, or cart, probably symbolizing the Sun's movement across the heavens. Gold disks were also created with this symbol engraved upon them.[88] Perhaps the four points of the cross symbolized the two solstices and two equinoxes of the solar year. While the Sun would have been regarded as the source of warmth, comfort, and life, the light and movement of the Moon would also have been considered important. Certainly its cycles would have been easier to view and contemplate. It regularly undergoes dramatic changes, and, being associated with night, was also possibly associated with darkness, mystery, and death. It is hard to know whether solar or lunar alignments were the predominant focus of these early rites, or if their religious beliefs included some combination of the two in a balanced and complementary fashion.[89]

The Irish Gods of the Quadrant of Death

It is possible that, in early times, the Winter Solstice, the point of the Sun's weakest power, may have also symbolized the point of the Moon's greatest power if these were perceived as opposing or even complementary bodies of light. Moreover, the darkest point of the year may reasonably have been associated with death. In Irish tradition, the southwest seems to have been associated with darkness, mystery, death, and chthonic elements, even in relatively modern folklore accounts. And, as we have seen, the Moon is associated with darkness and death in numerous symbolic and spiritual contexts.

One related example comes from Irish folk tradition, where we encounter a figure known as Donn, whose name means "brown," or perhaps simply "dark." Donn was one of the sons of Mil, the early Goidelic settlers in Ireland. He insulted the goddesses of the land and was drowned at Inbhear Scéne (Kenmare Bay in County Kerry). He is said to have thenceforth inhabited an island off the southwest coast of Ireland called Teach Duinn (The House of Donn, now known as Bull Rock). This story may echo an earlier myth in which a deity known as Donn inhabited an Otherworld island. Texts from the eighth to tenth centuries refer to Teach Duinn as the location "where the dead assemble," and describe the deceased traveling to and from the island. In the death-tale of Conaire, the hero is killed by three red-haired men who are described as "sons of Donn, king of the dead at the red tower of the dead." The three sons are quoted as saying "we ride the horses of Donn—although we are alive, we are dead!" In a 9th-century source, Donn himself is quoted as saying, "To me, to my house, you shall all come after your deaths."[90]

Traditions concerning this supernatural figure were collected well into modern times. In some cases, he is associated with certain mysterious hills, and folklore traditions tell of people who were brought into the hill to be with Donn when they died. He was evidently a formidable figure to encounter, but in some instances, could be quite congenial. In certain areas, he is considered a personification of the weather or certain celestial occurrences. The appearance of thunder and lightning meant Donn was traveling wildly in the sky, and clouds appearing over his hill were being gathered by him in preparation for rain.

It is possible that Donn was in some way associated with lunar concepts, in light of his association with death and with celestial events. He is sometimes portrayed as a night horseman who rides a white horse. One folk account describes him as an old man dressed in white who instructed a large number of students in "the mysteries of the creation since the stars began to shine" (reminiscent of the Druids, as well as the Moon's associations with creation). As late as the 1700s, Donn was poetically invoked by an Irish poet who, despairing of his situation, begged him to open his door and receive the poet in his palace "under the waves," perhaps the place where the Moon went for its repose.[91]

Another mysterious figure associated with the southwest is the Cailleach or Hag of Irish folk tradition. She was associated in particular with the Beare Peninsula in west Cork, and the island known as Inis Boi was considered to be her residence. The Cailleach was portrayed as an ancient, wise, but also somewhat sinister old woman. She may originally have had an aspect as a goddess of the land due to her connection with harvest customs, as well as her role in Scottish folk tradition where she helped create the landscape and is said to roam the hills protecting sacred wells and wild animals. She has a more chthonic character in Ireland, however, where various standing stones are said to be people or animals magically transformed by her.[92] The province of Munster, in the southwest of Ireland, is sometimes described as being associated with female supernatural figures and the world of the dead. It is represented as a "primeval world, a place of origin," which brings to mind the primal darkness of the lunar Underworld.[93]

An Ancient Irish Lunar Map

In 1999, Dr. David Whitehouse, the Science Editor of the BBC, released a report about a potentially remarkable discovery. It stated that Dr. Phillip Stooke of the University of Western Ontario had evidently discovered what may be a map of the Moon carved into a rock at the Neolithic site known as Knowth, located in County Meath. Dr. Stooke is a planetary cartographer who regularly works with NASA charting the planets of outer space. His knowledge of the Moon's surface enabled him to view an apparently meaningless or undecipherable design with a different eye and see something in it.[94]

The "map" is comprised of a series of arcs, points, and other markings, and may have originally been drawn on the stone with chalk or colored paint. When placed over a picture of the full Moon, these markings line up at more than a dozen points of correspondence with the overall pattern of known lunar features. The key to lunar identification are the thick arched lines that correspond to the Moon's vast "seas," which are clearly visible on the face of the full Moon. Crucial to verification of his initial concept, however, were certain alignments with isolated spots on the edge of the seas. Indeed, the spots on the rock carving corresponded exactly with these lunar points. If Dr. Stooke is correct, this is the oldest map of the Moon ever found, ten times older than anything previously discovered.[95]

The BBC report also mentioned that certain investigations at Knowth (which were not specified) showed that, at certain times of the year, moonlight shines down the eastern passage of the tomb and may have illuminated the lunar map. The stone onto which the map is carved forms the end wall of the eastern passage and has three sections. Each of these is similar, but each is oriented differently. This may depict the apparent rotation of the disk of the full Moon as it crosses the sky. Knowth encompasses several tombs, including several small tombs that face various points within a semicircle covering the now-familiar quadrant of northeast through southwest. Professor of Archaeology George Eogan points out that, while some of the tombs at Knowth are north of this quadrant (and therefore potentially not associated with the rising or setting of the Sun), they may be "aligned towards some other celestial body."[96] Dr. Stooke is investigating the possibility of lunar insignia carved on a stone bowl at Knowth, as well as six other carvings that may depict the movement of the Moon.[97]

While caution is advised in the interpretation of any new discovery, it is also true that ancient people looked up to see the same Moon we do, undoubtedly taking note of its markings and regarding it with wonder and awe. It seems reasonable to suggest that they would have included the Sun and Moon in their system of religious beliefs (along with various deities) and that these heavenly bodies were incorporated into their system of time measurement as well as their sacred calendar. The well-documented alignment with the direction of southwest, which is aligned with the point of the Sun's diminishing light (and perhaps that of the rising Moon) illuminates the Moon's role as mistress of darkness and death, and ultimately, of the mysteries of transformation and rebirth.

☽   ☽   ☽

Meditations and Exercises

These simple exercises can help you grow closer to your environment and connect with a primal knowledge largely lost in modern life.

1) How much do you know about the plants and animals in your area? Would you be able to identify any wild plants or foods in your environment? There are many wonderful books on edible plants to help you explore and connect with this ancient and primal knowledge, which has (to a large extent) been lost by many modern cultures. You may want to prepare ritual feasts using seasonally available wild foods, including those that might have been available in ancient times.

2) Have you ever grown your own food? Even the simple act of growing herbs and vegetables in a small garden plot can be a profound experience for modern people. Preparing the soil with your hands and dropping in the tiny seeds (which do not seem to be capable of bringing forth the bounty they usually, and miraculously, do) can be a real act of faith and illumination. Imagine if this were one of your only sources of food. How could you work with the cycles of nature to produce the best results? How might you propitiate the gods of the land and of fertility to help ensure your survival? Refer to Farmer's Almanacs (which are comprised of ancient, time-tested knowledge), as these provide a great deal of useful information, including how to plant, grow, and reap in harmony with the phases of the Moon.

3) Visit a farm near the area in which you live. Learning about domesticated farm animals in person (creatures that many of us never encounter) is an excellent way of connecting with the way our ancestors once lived and how many peo-

ple around the globe still do live. The care and feeding of animals is a sacred task, as is the ability to diagnose and treat their illnesses. Animals are sacred creatures in their own right, as they help to carry on the cycles of life. Learn about the ancient and more modern traditional lore associated with each of these animals.

4) Grains in ancient times were somewhat different from those generally available today. Take some time to learn about the ancient "staffs of life." Prepare some bread or cakes using these grains (often available at health food stores). Spelt is an ancient type of wheat eaten by the Celts. It is flavorful, healthful, and has a tough husk, therefore not always requiring the use of pesticides. Many people who are allergic to wheat can tolerate this grain. (Modern grains are chosen for high output, disregarding nutritional content and digestibility.) Make a ritual loaf of spelt, barley, and oats. Here is a simple recipe using products available in ancient times:

SHARYNNE'S FAMOUS SPELT BREAD RECIPE

3 cups wholegrain flour (all spelt is excellent; or one cup each spelt, barley, and oat flour for a heartier, but slightly crumbly, loaf)

1 cup liquid (organic cow's milk, or goat or sheep's milk. For those with dairy intolerances, oat, almond, rice, or soymilk is great. In a pinch, or when camping, water may even be used.)

1 egg (try to use natural farm-raised chicken eggs or, for the more open-minded, see if you can obtain duck, goose, or other types of fresh eggs.)

Optional: For those who don't mind "cheating" a bit and prefer a much lighter, more conventionally textured loaf of bread, add 1 tablespoon baking powder. You may want to add seasonally available berries, seeds, or bits of chopped fruit. One quarter cup melted butter is also a nice addition.

Mix ingredients in a large bowl. Place in greased loaf pan and bake at 375°F for about forty minutes, or until a bit hard and crisp on the top.

5) Why do you think early farming societies started to build monuments to their ancestors? Take some time to meditate on this, envisioning yourself living in those times, relying on the land, and perhaps also on the spirits of nature. Earlier cultures inhabited large, open hunting areas, but now land is becoming almost a "commodity." Was there rivalry or tension? Or were the monuments

built for purely spiritual reasons, to honor those who came before? Perhaps the tombs were associated with new ways of envisioning that society's connection with spirit—spirits who lived in or on the land, rather than in the forest.

6) Design your own megalithic tomb! (Have some fun with this! . . . odd as that may sound). If you were responsible for building a great stone (or timber and/or earth) monument to the dead or the ancestors, how would you construct it? Sketch some designs, or construct a small model from stones and other natural materials. Will the tomb provide a location for rituals, or will it be more of an "innerworld" site, designed to house the dead and provide space for sacred practitioners to honor them and connect with the gods and the spirits? In addition to its layout and design, consider its location and orientation in terms of the directions, the Sun, and/or the Moon. What sorts of things should be buried with the dead, and what do they signify? What sorts of symbols or designs might be incorporated into the stones of the tomb, and what will their placement, symbolism, and function be?

7) Visit a metalsmith or blacksmith's shop to learn about metallurgy and see how metal products and jewelry are made. Smiths were considered sacred in many early societies, including shamanistic cultures, and still are in many primal cultures. Their craft is unlike anything that preceded it and required mastery over the four elements: earth (ore), fire, air (to feed the fire), and water (to cool and finish).

8) Think about the relief from France in which a woman (painted red) is holding up a bison horn marked with thirteen lines. She holds her left hand on her belly. What do you think the significance of this representation is? Why do you think the color red was considered sacred in ancient times? It is still one of the most significant colors in many cultures today. Some say this is because it is the color of blood (and therefore, of life). In addition, after black and white, red is the next color that receives a name in many languages. It is also a color that stands out in natural contexts, whether the background is green, white, or brown. Meditate on this image and on the color, and see what comes to you.

9) Make your own primal artwork out of clay—perhaps based on early female figurines, stylized images of females from Breton gallery graves, chalk figures or phalluses, cup-and-ring marks, or other megalithic designs. Include the lunar crescent in your design, or use it as an offering at the new or full Moon.

10) Think about the stone circles and henges and their orientation with the northeast (midsummer sunrise) and the southwest (midwinter sunset). Do you think this southwest alignment has some association with the Moon's potency or power at the time of the waning Sun? How might the Moon's phases have

been venerated at the various sites? (Look at photos of these sites to assist you in your visualization). Do you think any nocturnal or lunar-based rituals took place? What about the white quartz pebbles? Take some time to meditate on these images and concepts, and then devise your own lunar-based ritual utilizing these elements as a basis. You may want to honor a figure similar to Donn, Irish god of the dead, or the Cailleach, a chthonic goddess associated with the land, death, and transformation.

Sixth Lunation

DRUIDS, MISTLETOE, AND WARRIOR QUEENS

CLASSICAL ACCOUNTS OF CELTIC CULTURE

*Magic undoubtedly had a hold on Gaul, even down to living memory; for it was in
the reign of Tiberius Caesar that the Druids and that type of soothsayer and healer
were abolished. But why mention this about a practice that has crossed Ocean
and penetrated to the empty vastnesses of nature? Britain today is so mesmerized
by it and practices it with so much ceremony that one might think
it was she who gave it to the Persians.*

—PLINY THE ELDER, *NATURAL HISTORY*

The lives of people who lived in ancient times often seem mysterious and alluring to us in the present, the details seemingly enshrouded in the mists of time and beyond our perception and understanding. We have three important tools, however, through which we can catch a glimpse of certain aspects of life in the past: archaeology, native records (accounts written by members of the society itself, which contain information about its culture and traditional lore), and foreign accounts (records written by outsiders, which transmit information about the people and society in question). Each of these methods has its benefits and drawbacks.

Archaeology is valuable in that it provides a contemporary record of people's material lives, showing us where and how they lived, how they sustained themselves, and sometimes (through religious art, artifacts, and ritual sites) a little about how they perceived their world and the world of the divine. Archaeological evidence allows us to see for ourselves the houses, tools, ornaments, and art of a particular culture. In many cases, however, this evidence is sketchy or incomplete. Moreover, we must remember that it can be misleading to make assumptions about religious beliefs and other aspects of culture based on material items alone—especially in the absence of written records.

The Celts did not generally commit their cultural information to writing. For this reason, we have very little written evidence from the pagan period pertaining to Celtic society or religion. The majority of what may be called Celtic mythological information was recorded by Christian monks and scribes in early Ireland and

Britain along with other cultural lore—histories (both factual and pseudo-historical), genealogies, law, poetry, stories, and legends. These records were often written or recorded by native Celts (in some cases, not long after the pagan period), but were influenced by both the new religion and Classical and medieval learned traditions imported from continental Europe. Nevertheless, we can deduce quite a bit from these sources about the cultural and religious beliefs of the pagan Celts, as well as how they perceived themselves and the world around them.

In this chapter, we will explore evidence from foreign reports and written accounts recorded by people who met or encountered the Celts in the pagan era through trade, travel, or military campaigns. The positive side to these reports is that, in many cases, they are contemporary accounts, written down during the period when the pagan Celts flourished in various parts of Europe.

These accounts have several drawbacks, however. In some cases, they are secondhand reports based on earlier accounts that may or may not be contemporary and, therefore, not always written by people who had actually met any Celts. These secondhand reports may be embellished or altered from the original source. In addition, whether recorded first- or secondhand, they often suffer from cultural bias. This means that the writer may have come from a culture that considered itself superior to the Celts and may or may not have fully or objectively understood what was seen or encountered. In any case, the fact that many of these reports are contemporary with pagan Celtic culture does imbue them with a great deal of potential value, and we should not assume that all of the information they contain is inaccurate.

The accounts we will examine were written by writers, historians, and other figures associated with Classical Greek or Roman cultures; hence, they are referred to as "Classical" accounts. They provide a great deal of fascinating information about the Celts and where and how they lived. They often refer the Celts' bravery in battle and their love of music, hunting, fighting, boasting, poetry, and personal ornament. These records provide us with information pertaining to early Celtic religion, including assemblies and rituals, the role of the Druids, and other traditional beliefs. They have also preserved information concerning the veneration of the Moon and its role in the measurement of both mundane and sacred time. To begin with, let's take a look at some Classical accounts that describe the Celts and their society, as it is important to understand a culture as a whole when attempting to study or interpret its religious beliefs and traditions.

Golden Torques, Blue Woad, and . . . Black Pearls?

In the late 1st century B.C.E., a Classical writer known as Diodorus Siculus wrote about the Celts who inhabited the island of Britain. He states that the Celts were ruled by many kings and chieftains who, for the most part, lived in peace with one another. The land was inhabited by tribes whom Diodorus describes as "aboriginal" and whose lifestyle evidently preserved "the old ways." Compared to the Roman lifestyle, he tells us, "their way of life is frugal and far different from the luxury engendered by wealth."[1] The British Celts are reported to have lived in simple dwellings made of wood or reeds, supporting themselves by growing grain, which they harvested as it was ripe, grinding it daily to make their food. The climate was evidently quite cold, "since the island lies under the Great Bear."[2]

Caesar's account of the Britons, also written in the 1st century B.C.E., confirmed Diodorus' report concerning the large population of the island of Britain, which Caesar describes as being "inhabited by people who claim on the strength of their own tradition to be indigenous to the island." He compares the homesteads of the Britons to those of the Gauls, and mentions their herds of numerous cattle. As is often the case with these reports, Caesar's accounts are a combination of the reliable and the innacurate.[3]

> Most of those inhabiting the interior do not grow corn, but live instead on milk and meat and clothe themselves in skin. All the Britons dye themselves with woad, which produces a blue colour, and as a result their appearance in battle is all the more daunting. They wear their hair long, and shave all their bodies with the exception of their heads and upper lip. Wives are shared between groups of ten or twelve men, especially between brothers and between fathers and sons. The offspring . . . are considered the children of the man with whom the woman first lived.[4]

The description of the Celts' appearance is supported elsewhere, but Caesar's comments about polygamy may reflect some amount of exaggeration, or at least an insufficient understanding of what may have been a complex system of kinship and descent. While the Britons may have sustained themselves largely with products of herding, such as meat and milk, they also grew some crops as well (as mentioned by Diodorus Siculus).

The Celts who inhabited Gaul are also described in the writings of Strabo, who records the production of cattle, grain, gold, silver, and iron, some of which were exported to other countries. Strabo compares the customs of the Gaulish Celts with those of Britain and mentions that they were in some ways similar to each other. Other aspects of British customs, however, he interprets as being "simpler and more barbaric."[5] Here is an example of cultural bias or interpretation, an element that must be taken into consideration when attempting to understand and make use of this evidence.

Tacitus claimed that these two cultures (British and Gaulish) had a similar language and that the Celts in these regions displayed "the same boldness in courting danger." He states, however, that the Britons displayed a greater ferocity, as they had not experienced a "period of peace," as had those in Gaul. Here he is referring to the *pax Romana*, the "peace" that was the by-product of enforced occupation by the Romans. Like other writers, Tacitus mentions the rainy, misty climate of Britain and the relatively short duration of summer as compared to Mediterranean regions. He states that crops germinated quickly, but were slow to ripen due to the "great moistures of earth and sky." He also reports that Britain produced gold, silver, and other metals, as well as dark or blue-black pearls from its waters.[6]

Many Classical accounts refer to the striking appearance of the Celts, whose height, build, and complexion may have seemed unusual to those more familiar with Mediterranean or other European population groups. Tacitus describes the variations of appearance found among the British Celts, and mentions the red hair and large limbs of the Caledonians. Strabo compared the appearance of the British and Gaulish Celts, commenting that those in Britain were "not so blond" as in Gaul and of "looser build." He mentions the love of personal ornament among the Gauls, some of whom wore gold torques around their necks and bracelets on their arms and wrists. In the 3rd century C.E., Herodian repeats some information included in the earlier reports of Dio Cassius, but provides additional detail about the appearance of the Caledonians. Here he refers to the tribes who inhabited the region that would one day be known as Scotland:

> They adorn their waists and necks with iron, considering this an ornament and a sign of wealth, just as other barbarians do gold. They tattoo their bodies with various designs and pictures of all kinds of animals . . . They are extremely warlike and bloodthirsty, although their armament consists simply of a narrow shield, a spear, and a sword that hangs beside their naked bodies.[7]

Dio Cassius wrote about the Caledonians, whom he describes as inhabiting the "wild and waterless mountains and desolate marshy plains" of northern Britain, claiming that these people possessed "neither walls nor cities nor farms," and that they lived on game, flocks, and certain fruits.[8] This is not entirely accurate, as archaeology shows that there were farmsteads (solitary and in small groups) and some fortified sites. Farming took place in certain parts of the north, but not everywhere to the extent it was practiced in the southern part of Britain. In certain areas of northern Britain, people still supported themselves by hunting, gathering, and fishing, as they had done since earliest times, while others engaged in farming and herding.

Dio Cassius reported that the Caledonians used chariots and small swift horses in battle and also engaged the enemy on foot, as they were "very fast runners and very resolute when they stand their ground." Caledonian warriors evidently made use of daggers, shields, and short spears with a bronze "apple" at the end of the shaft that made a loud noise when shaken to terrify the enemy. In addition, he claims that the northern Britons somehow lived without clothes or shoes, yet had a democratic form of government. He describes how they were able to endure cold, hunger, and other hardships, "for they plunge into the marshes and stay there for many days with only their heads above water; in the forests they live on bark and roots." Dio also states that, in case of emergency, the Caledonians prepared a type of food of which a small piece the size of a bean prevented them from feeling hunger or thirst.[9]

Much of this report is probably best interpreted as a description of the hardiness and resourcefulness of the Caledonians and their ability to utilize the resources of the land in which they lived, in spite of the sometimes-harsh climate and terrain. Like other indigenous peoples, they would have made use of many food sources, including wild foods, roots, and herbal preparations. An intimate knowledge of the land would have enabled them to conceal or camouflage themselves in order to observe the activities of outsiders and protect their society and autonomy. Once we remove the outer shell of these accounts, we can discern the kernel of truth contained within.

Druids, Bards, and Seers

What about Celtic religion? One common element found in a number of Classical reports is a reference to three classes of venerated persons in Celtic society, some of whom were associated with religious activities. In Gaulish society, these constitute the well-known trio of Druids, bards, and seers (*vates*). Strabo describes the bards as singers or poets, the seers as students of natural philosophy who performed "ritual ceremonies," and the Druids as judges of disputes, arbitrators in times of war, and wise men involved in the study and instruction of numerous topics, including natural philosophy.[10]

Diodorus Siculus also mentions the three classes of persons. He states that the seers foretold the future through the observation of birds or the sacrifice of animals, and that they were greatly respected. The bards he describes as singing to the accompaniment of instruments similar to lyres (probably harps), "either in praise of people or to deride them," a statement that could have been made about the poets of medieval Ireland and Wales many centuries later. At a particular time of year, the Druids evidently gathered at a consecrated spot considered to be the center of all Gaul. At this gathering, they handled legal disputes and probably held social or religious assemblies.

Diodorus mentions the Druids' ability to step between contending armies "as though they were holding some wild animal spellbound with their chanting." He describes them as philosophers and theologians, and states that the Celts in Gaul would not consider making a sacrifice or offering without their presence:

... for they say that thank-offerings should be given to the gods by means of those who are expert in the nature of the divine, and ... in communion with it. They also believe it is through these people that blessings should be sought.[11]

A little of the religious ideology of the Celts may be discerned from the reports of Diogenes Laertius, who wrote that the Druids expounded their philosophy in riddles and bid the people to "reverence the gods, do no evil, and practice valour."[12] Tacitus maintained that similar rites and religious beliefs existed in both Britain and Gaul,[13] and Caesar made this comment about the piety of the Celts in Gaul:

The Gallic nation as a whole is very much devoted to religion. For this reason those affected by more serious diseases or engaged in the dangers of battle either offer or promise to offer human [i.e., great] sacrifice, and they employ the Druids to act for them in this.[14]

Caesar mentions the esteem in which Druids and warriors were held in Gaul and describes great piles of offerings assembled in certain consecrated places. He observes that it was rare and "in defiance of religion" for anyone to hide war booty in their homes rather than offer it to the gods or to remove any of the offerings once placed in these areas.[15] Additional information preserved in Caesar's account illustrates the important role the Druids played in Celtic society and religion.[16] The Druids, he tells us, were regarded with great respect, did not usually take part in war, and were exempt from taxation and other liabilities. They officiated at religious ceremonies and supervised public and private sacrifices or offerings. They handed down decisions on most public and private disputes, deciding the outcome and penalty of various crimes, including murder and border disputes. Those who did not abide by their judgments were banned from sacrifices (i.e., religious assemblies)—the heaviest possible penalty. Large numbers of young men, he claims, came to them for instruction, some of their own volition, others sent by parents and relatives. They were expected to learn a great number of verses by heart (as it was contrary to their religious beliefs to commit these teachings to writing) and could remain under the tutelage and instruction of the Druids for up to twenty years.

Caesar also makes reference to the gods of the Gauls, although his descriptions of them are subject to what is known as *interpretatio Romana*, the interpretation of native Celtic deities through culturally colored lenses. The effect of this was that, in many cases, Celtic gods were simply equated with Roman gods of a vaguely similar description. The Romans did not require conquered or subjugated populations to stop worshipping their own deities, and so, in Britain and Gaul, for example, both Roman and Celtic deities were worshipped.

Sometimes Roman and Celtic deities were associated with one another and thus invoked or venerated together. They may have been perceived as the same deity, or as a new "hybrid" deity with the characteristics of both. This often reflected the way the Romans interpreted the attributes of Celtic deities. There are a number of inscriptions that demonstrate this custom in which the name of a Roman and a Celtic deity are linked, as in the inscriptions to Apollo Maponus, Mars Toutatis, or Sulis Minerva.

In this system of Roman interpretation, Caesar generally equates Celtic deities with the closest Roman deity. He reports that the Gauls worshipped Mercury most of all, regarding him as the inventor of all crafts, a guide on journeys, and important in matters of money and trade. The Gaulish deity in question may have been similar to the Irish god Lug, master and inventor of various crafts and skills. Next in popularity was Apollo, probably a native deity associated with healing, the Sun, poetry, or music. Some feel this may reflect the Gaulish equivalent of the widely worshipped British deity Maponus. After this came Mars (probably a native Celtic deity of war), Jupiter (a father deity, perhaps similar to the Continental deity Sucellos or the Irish god An Dagda), and Minerva, who taught the principles of arts and crafts (perhaps a goddess such as the Irish deity Bríg, later known as Bridget).[17]

In spite of a lack of historical or social objectivity, we can see that there is a great deal of relevant information in these Classical accounts. The information preserved in these records can be compared with that obtained from archaeology, native writings, and other historical sources in order to establish the reliability and usefulness of the information they contain. In spite of certain problems and limitations, some of the information about customs and beliefs preserved for us by the Classical authors is reasonably accurate, and therefore quite useful in our quest for knowledge about the religion of the ancient Celts.

The Moon and Early Celtic Society

What role did the Moon play in ancient Celtic religion, according to these accounts?

Caesar mentions that the Druids engaged in a great deal of discussion concerning "the stars and their motion, the size of the universe and the earth, the composition of the world, and the strength and power of the immortal gods."[18] It seems reasonable to assume that the phases and cycles of the Moon would have formed part of Druidic lore as well. This assumption is supported by the discovery of a lunar-based calendar (perhaps used by the Druids) that will be discussed in the next chapter.

The Moon is mentioned in an interesting report concerning the Galatians, Celts who inhabited an easterly region roughly corresponding to modern-day Turkey. The report in question mentions that an eclipse of the Moon in 218 B.C.E. brought a Galatian army to a halt. This may indicate that the Galatians worshipped the Moon, that they were apprehensive of what they may have considered a significant or disastrous omen, or that they were filled with awe at observing such a remarkable natural event.[19]

The possibility of Moon worship is suggested by the writings of Strabo, who stated that the Celtiberians worshipped an unnamed god at the full Moon. They reportedly performed their devotions with their families in front of the gates of the town and danced throughout the night.[20] This is a somewhat unusual example of the veneration of the full Moon, as the available evidence generally points to the veneration of the new Moon in Celtic contexts, although various phases of the Moon, including the full Moon, play a role in Celtic folk traditions.

In *Celts and the Classical World*, David Rankin provides a great deal of interesting and unusual information pertaining to early Celtic society and religion, including information about the Celtiberians of northern Spain. Among other gods and goddesses, the Iberian Celts venerated the water deities Ataecina and Endovellius. Offerings in wells and bodies of water were common all over the Celtic world; indeed, these may have been perceived as entrances to the Underworld. For this reason, Rankin states that Ataecina may have been a goddess of the Underworld.[21] As we shall see below, there may have been a connection between the Moon and the Underworld in Celtic systems of religious belief.

Caesar once made the observation that the Germanic tribes who lived near the Celts worshipped only "the forces of nature." Some scholars feel that his distinction between Germanic and Celtic peoples may be somewhat indistinct. We do possess evidence pertaining to the religious beliefs of the Germanic peoples, which shows that they did worship gods and goddesses. This is also the case with the Celts (whether or not Caesar's cultural observations are valid), who venerated male and female deities, both of which were considered powerful. In some cases, the gods were associated with various facets of society—wisdom, healing, skill, battle, power, magic, or learning—while others were associated with features of the land or the forces of nature.

What may have been confusing to the outside observer was the fact that the Celts did not usually represent their deities in human form, and from what we can tell, did not often make images of them at all. Early Celtic art was somewhat impressionistic or abstract, especially when compared with Greek and Roman realism. When invading Celtic tribes entered the precinct of Delphi around 279 B.C.E. and saw no gold or silver offerings, but only statues of wood and stone, they are reported to have laughed at the Greeks for making figures of the gods in human shape.[22] A similar scenario is evident in one of Strabo's accounts, where he describes one of the Celtiberian tribes as *aetheoi*, a word that refers to the worship of gods that are unrecognizable to the Greeks—probably without specific physical characteristics or perhaps not represented in anthropomorphic statues.[23]

The Celts are known to have produced artwork, symbolism, and designs of great beauty, artistry, and sophistication. The lack of lifelike idols or statuary may reflect a cultural taboo against representing deities at all (or in human form, past a certain point). It may also reflect the perception that the gods were immanent in nature, and that their powers and attributes were both physical and symbolic, perhaps operating on several different levels simultaneously.

How did the Celts honor the great forces of nature like the Sun, Moon, sea, wind, and stars? Some of these elements were deified, or formed part of the complex system of attributes assigned to various Celtic gods and goddesses. We will examine some of these deities in an upcoming chapter.

The features and elements of nature were considered powerful in their own right. There is quite a bit of evidence that the Celts swore oaths by the forces of nature. One of the most common formulas was swearing "by Earth, Sea, and Sky" to do (or not do) a particular thing. This tripartite pledge may reflect the cosmological (and possibly shamanic) perception of the existence of three worlds. Other elements are mentioned as well, as in one story where Cú Chulainn invokes the power of a particular river. The clouds and stars are also mentioned in connection with a pledge to the sky.[24]

An example of an oath that refers to the Moon comes from the *Dindshenchas* (The Lore of Places). This is an early Irish text that records native traditions pertaining to sacred or significant places, including the people, deities, and events associated with them. One example mentions an important assembly that took place on the 1st of August, and records an oath used to ensure that the gathering would be held every third year. In this oath, the people swore by "heaven, Earth, Sun, Moon, and sea" (as well as a variety of other things) to faithfully hold the assembly, as had been done for centuries.[25]

The Moon is mentioned in connection with another pledge that comes from an Irish pseudo-historical myth (a legend comprised of historical and mythological elements) fabricated by the Goidelic (Gaelic) element of early Irish society to explain the custom of matrilineal succession found among the Picts or *Cruithni* (another population group). This account claims that the Picts had no women when they arrived in Ireland, a land where the Goidels "already were" (a statement made to support Goidelic claims of supremacy or authority in early Ireland, not necessarily historically accurate). Therefore, the Goidels "gave them" three women on the condition that their kingdom in Britain should be inherited through the female line.[26] Evidently, the Picts agreed to this, and swore "by the Sun and the Moon" that their kingdom would be ruled by the female line of descent to the end of the world. This myth helps explain the Pictish custom and also supports the claims of the Goidels (the Irish of Gaelic descent) over Pictish (Cruithnic) territories in Ulster and, perhaps later, in western Scotland.[27]

The Moon also played a role in a ceremony used to procure a particular magical item which appears to be unique to the Celts. Pliny (*Natural History*) describes a type of "egg" held in great esteem by the Gaulish Celts. It was a natural item believed to be created from the saliva and bodily secretions of great numbers of entwined serpents, who then tossed the object into the air with their hissing. It was necessary to catch the object in a blanket before it touched the ground and then retreat from the snakes on horseback until one had reached a river. (It was believed that the snakes were unable to follow past this point because no pursuing supernatural or dangerous entities were able to cross running water.) The "Druid's Egg" was believed to bring power in judicial situations and provide access to royalty.[28] In his article on this tradition, French Celticist Jean Gricourt states that the Druids maintained that it was necessary to procure the "Serpent's Egg" during a certain phase of the Moon.[29]

Remarkably, a similar belief existed in 19th-century Scotland, almost two thousand years later. A dark grey egg-shaped object was said to be sometimes found among the heather. It was believed to be created from the saliva of a serpent, which traveled around and around the clump of heather, emitting a froth from its mouth. When the saliva dried, the object grew hard as a stone, but was very light in weight. It was said to have healing powers and to protect against the unwanted magic of fairy women.[30]

The Moon, Immortality, and the God of the Underworld

Lunar symbolism may also have been associated with an important tradition attributed to the Druids, that of the immortality of the soul. One of the beliefs espoused by Druids of Gaul was that the soul did not perish, "but after death passes from one person to another." This was evidently a great incentive to bravery among Celtic warriors and leaders.[31] Strabo mentions the Druidic belief concerning the immortality of the soul, stating that the Druids maintained "that the soul, like the universe, is immortal, though at some time . . . both fire and water will overwhelm them."

Because of this belief, the Celts were said to bury things with the dead that were appropriate to the living, even putting off the transaction of business affairs and the recovery of debts "until the next world."[32] Valerius Maximus, writing in the 1st century C.E., mentions this belief, which was evidently held by the Celtic inhabitants of the Greek port of Massilia in southern Gaul, now Marseilles in modern France:

> Leaving the town of Massilia one encounters that ancient usage of the Gauls. It is said that they are in the habit of lending money to be repaid in the next world. The reason for this is they are convinced that the souls of men are immortal. I should call them stupid were it not for the fact that these trouser-wearing folk have exactly the same belief as that held by the Greek Pythagoras.[33]

The Celtic belief in the immortality of the soul actually differed from Pythagorean doctrines of immortality and the transmigration of the soul, but was recognizable to the Greeks in light of their familiarity with his work.[34] One major distinction was the absence of any idea concerning punishment or retribution after death in Celtic eschatological teaching, which differs from Pythagorean concepts of death and rebirth.[35] Whatever its exact form may have been, Celtic belief in rebirth and the cyclical return of souls may be perceived as having parallels with the symbolism of the lunar cycle and the significance attached to the appearance of the new Moon.

These native concepts were described poetically by Lucan in the 1st century C.E., as he paints a gloomy and mysterious (but respectful and probably overly romantic) picture of the Druids and their belief in the cyclical rebirth of the soul in his *Pharsalia*:

> And you [Druids] set aside your arms and sought again your barbaric rites and the sinister practice of your religion. To you alone is granted knowledge of the gods and the powers of heaven, or you alone are ignorant of them. The depths of groves in far-off forests are your abode, your teaching that the shades of the dead seek not the silent home of Erebus and the pallid realms of Pluto deep below; instead the same soul controls a body in another world, and if what you sing of is true, death is but the mid-point of a long existence.[36]

Information pertaining to possible connections with lunar concepts occurs in the works of Caesar, especially in terms of lunar cycles and the creation or origin of life in the primal darkness (similar to the period of the void Moon, which precedes the appearance or birth of the new Moon). These accounts record that the Gauls stated they were descended from a figure to whom Caesar refers as Dis Pater, and that this was the tradition of the Druids. The name (which is an example of *interpretatio Romana*) refers to Father *Dis*, a divine figure associated with the Roman Underworld.

In many religious or cultural traditions found around the world, the origin of a tribe or social group is sometimes attributed to a divine founder or ancestor. This was true of certain Celtic tribes, whose members claimed descent from various noble, wise, brave, or supernaturally inclined heroes, ancestresses, or deities. This was even the case in medieval Ireland, where certain population groups claimed descent from heroes or pagan deities well into the Christian era. The Celtic deity referred to by Caesar may be similar to the Irish divine figure Donn, who was associated with the world of the dead. Another candidate is the god known as Cernunnos, whose symbolism may suggest a connection with regeneration and the Underworld among other powers and attributes.[37]

If a tribe claimed descent from (or "came from") a god of the Underworld (who in Roman tradition was associated with a shadowy, sunless place), this may have reflected a native perception of life or existence emerging from a place of primal darkness. It is possible that lunar symbolism (which reflects these concepts) may have played a role in social and religious traditions associated with the origins and cycles of life, as well as with doctrines concerned with themes of immortality and rebirth. Such a possibility is supported by this commentary of Caesar's concerning Dis Pater and the beliefs of the Gauls:

> The Gauls affirm that they are all descended from a common father, *Dis*, and say that this is the tradition of the Druids. *For that reason* they determine all periods of time by the number, not of days, but of nights, and in their observance of birthdays and the beginnings of months and years day follows night.[38]

His statement seems to indicate a direct correlation between the Gaulish Celts' belief in their origin or descent from a god of the Underworld and their measurement of time by nights rather than days.[39] It may be that this deity was associated with night, which (for the Gauls) preceded day, in much the same way as cosmic darkness precedes the creation of life. Indeed, here time is explicitly stated as being conceived in this fashion, which may support such a theory.

It may be that theological traditions of sacred time and space were conceived in a similar fashion. If so, the concept of life and creation arising out of the cosmic darkness may have formed some part of the beliefs associated with the Underworld for the Gauls and other Celtic peoples as well. While the Lower World was considered dark or frightening in Roman mythology (and evil in Christian polarity), in Celtic tradition, the darkness of the Underworld was holy, associated as it was with the regeneration of life.

The Celtic Underworld may have been perceived metaphorically as a vessel, womb, or sacred place associated with the void (and therefore with creation and rebirth), expressed in physical or mythological terms as the cauldron of rebirth or renewal.[40] Like the temporal reality of the period of darkness that precedes the rebirth of the Moon, the Underworld may have spatially (and temporally) symbolized a realm of both darkness and potential, a primal world from which creation or life forces emerged. The deity who presided over this domain (and possibly over night itself) would have been considered very powerful, regulating, blessing, and controlling the cycles and forces of both life and death.

The Gathering of Sacred Plants

In his *Natural History*, the Classical author Pliny records three ancient Celtic rituals connected with the gathering of sacred plants, one of which was associated with the phases of the Moon. In the first ritual, a plant he calls *selago* was ceremonially gathered by a person clad in white, with bare feet washed clean, without the use of any iron implement. An offering of bread and wine was made before gathering the plant, which was then carried in a fresh white cloth. The Druids of Gaul taught that the plant warded off all harm from the person who possessed it, and that the smoke of the plant was good for eye troubles.[41]

One candidate for the identity of this plant is club moss (*lycopodium*). An infusion of club moss can be used as a powerful emetic or cathartic, but it should be administered with great caution. Interestingly, like selago, fumigation with club moss was used to treat eye disease in folk medicine.[42] In addition, club moss was considered a powerful plant of protection, as illustrated in these Scottish folk charms:

> *The club-moss is on my person,*
> *No harm or mishap can befall me;*
> *No sprite shall slay me, no arrow shall wound me,*
> *No fay or dun water-nymph shall tear me.*[43]

> *Thou man who travellest blithely*
> *Nor hurt nor harm shall befall thee*
> *Nor in sunshine nor in darkness*
> *If but the club-moss be on thy pathway.*[44]

The second ritual mentioned by Pliny concerns a plant referred to as *samolus*, which evidently grew in damp areas. It was gathered with the left hand by a person who was fasting. The person was not to "look at it" (the plant), or perhaps "not look behind him" (the translation is unclear). He or she was also not supposed to put the plant down anywhere except in a drinking trough in which it was crushed for the animals (pigs and cattle) to drink. In this way, it was utilized as a charm against disease.[45] The plant in question could be *samolus valerandi*, brook weed or water pimpernel. Like Pliny's samolus, it is commonly found in damp areas, including streams and wet coastal regions.[46]

A number of fascinating customs associated with the gathering of sacred plants have been recorded in Scottish folklore traditions. For example, club moss, St. John's Wort, and the shamrock were to be gathered only if found when the person was not actively seeking them (when the plant appears "in one's path" or "makes itself known or visible to a person"). A number of other plants, including yarrow and ivy, were traditionally gathered using only one hand, although the hand is not specified.[47] One of the charms used for gathering St. John's Wort, however, states that the plant should be plucked with the right hand, but preserved with the left.[48] These practices may reflect traditions similar to those recorded in the samolus ritual, where the plant had to be gathered with the left hand and was not to be looked at (or for?) directly.

The third and best known of the rites recorded by Pliny concerns the ritual gathering of mistletoe (*viscum album*). He writes of the great respect accorded to mistletoe by the Gaulish Celts, and mentions that the Druids considered it extremely sacred, especially if found growing on an oak tree. He also states that the Druids chose groves of oak for that reason and performed no rites without its foliage. Indeed, they considered anything growing on oak to have been "sent by heaven" (i.e., the gods) and a sign that the tree had been chosen by the gods. Here, he describes the ceremony with which the sacred mistletoe was gathered:

> Mistletoe growing on an oak . . . is a rare find, and when it is found it is gathered with great reverence, above all on the 6th day of the moon (it is the moon that marks out for them the beginning of months and years and cycles of thirty years) because this day is already exercising great influence though the moon is not halfway through its course.[49]

After a sacrifice and banquet had been prepared beneath the tree with great ceremony, two bulls whose horns had been bound for the first time on that occasion were led forward. The priest (probably a Druid), dressed in a white robe, climbed the tree and reaped the mistletoe with what is described as a "golden sickle." Afterward, a sacrifice or thank-offering was made to the appropriate deity.

There are a number of interesting elements in this rite. As in the ritual used to gather selago, the plant was gathered into a white cloth or blanket.[50] While a sickle made of gold would be too soft to cut through the tough stem of the mistletoe plant, a gold-colored implement, perhaps made of bronze or some other alloy, would have sufficed. Pliny's account mentions that an offering was made to an appropriate deity. While we do not know the name or exact attributes of this god (or goddess), it is interesting to note the existence of certain images that may be associated with mistletoe. In early Celtic art, there are many representations of human heads wearing strange leaf-shaped crowns or headdresses. These images are also found on stone monuments, jewelry, and other ornaments. The lobe-shaped leaves closely resemble the distinctive shape of the leaves of European mistletoe. If this is indeed what they are intended to represent, the faces portrayed may be those of Druids or deities associated with mistletoe, and its rites and religious symbolism.[51]

In the Gaulish ritual, mistletoe was gathered on the sixth day of the Moon, which would place the ceremony around the time of the Moon's first quarter. Although it was "not yet halfway through its course," the Moon was perceived as already exercising great influence. It may be that the waxing quality of the Moon was associated with the rising potency of the plant's qualities or vital essence. This same belief is found many centuries later in Celtic folkloric tradition, where plants were gathered during the waxing Moon to preserve and make best use of their medicinal, nutritional, or magical properties.

The Leaves of Life and Death

Mistletoe is an evergreen plant that grows parasitically on a number of trees, preferably those with soft bark. It can be found growing on ash, hawthorn, lime, pear, rose, and poplar trees, but is most commonly found on old apple trees, which were very sacred in Celtic myth and legend, and most rarely, on oak, probably adding to its mystique and potential power.[52] The greenish flowers of the plant grow in threes—a sacred number in Celtic tradition—and appear sometime between March and May, the period preceding Beltaine. These develop into the characteristic white berries, which generally ripen between September and November, the time period preceding Samain.[53]

The English name for the plant, which literally means "mistletoe twig," comes from an Old English compound word, *misteltan* (from *tan*, "twig" and *mistel*, "mistletoe"). The bird known as the mistlethrush got its name because of its fondness for mistletoe berries.[54] The origin of the word *mistel* itself is unknown. One theory suggests that it comes from either Old Dutch *mist* ("birdlime," one of the folk names for mistletoe) or *mistl* ("different"), referring to the fact that the twigs are different from the tree on which they grow.[55]

Pliny mentions that the Gauls believed that, when taken in liquid form, mistletoe granted fertility to sterile animals and was an antidote for all poisons. It was evidently called "all-heal" in Gaul, and still is in Scotland and Ireland (Scottish Gaelic *uil'-ioc* and modern Irish *uile-íoc*).[56] European mistletoe is sometimes called "all-heal" even in English. The plant does indeed have a number of important medicinal applications.[57]

In early Celtic religion, various ritual actions were performed and deities invoked in order to bring protection to the tribe or individual. This included protection from illness, famine, warfare, and other disasters or difficulties. The Gaulish Celts seem to have felt that mistletoe served to alleviate or protect against poison and disease. The plant maintained its reputation as a protector into relatively modern times. In Scotland, a sprig of mistletoe was sometimes placed in babies' cradles to prevent them from being stolen by fairies and replaced by changelings. Mistletoe was one of the magical plants used on the Isle of Skye, where it was also considered to be a magical plant of protection.[58]

Scottish folklore accounts record a remarkable ceremony associated with the gathering of mistletoe. The ritual was performed at Samain, and, as in the Gaulish rite, the sacred plant was gathered from an oak tree. Mistletoe is very rare in Scotland, which may have added to its reputation and perceived power.[59] After walking around the tree three times sunwise and "pronouncing a certain spell" (whose words were not recorded), the supplicant cut the plant using a new dirk.[60] The ceremony was considered a sure charm against "glamour or witchery" (i.e., undesirable worldly or Otherworldly forces or effects), and the plant thus gathered was thought to be an infallible guard for its possessor on the day of battle. It is interesting to note that, in Scottish Gaelic, mistletoe is also called *druidhe-lus* ("Druid-herb or plant").[61]

Vikings, Valkyries, and May Day

Mistletoe is also found in connection with Norse mythology. The chief god, Odin, had a son called Balder, described as the fairest of gods, very wise and merciful, and most deserving of praise. When the young god experienced ominous dreams, the gods feared this was a sign that danger might befall him. They sent his mother, the goddess Frigg, to extract an oath from all things on Earth (whether living creatures, plants, or things made of metal, wood, or stone) that they would not harm him.

Once the oath had been secured, the gods found it amusing to throw darts and heavy objects at Balder, knowing he would suffer no harm. Loki, however, disguised himself as a woman and, while conversing with Frigg, found out that one small plant, the mistletoe, had not taken the oath (Frigg thought the plant too young to threaten her son). Loki obtained some mistletoe and persuaded Hoder, the blind god, to throw it at Balder in sport, guiding his hand as he threw it. The dart of mistletoe pierced Balder through and he fell dead.

The gods were very distraught and tried to have Balder released from the Underworld. This was only possible if every living thing on Earth wept for his death. Unfortunately, one giantess refused to weep for him (perhaps Loki in disguise), and Balder was therefore unable to return to the world of the living.[62] In this tale, mistletoe plays an important role in the life, death, and possible rebirth of a divine figure associated with youth, beauty, and vitality. Its connection with rebirth in particular brings to mind its lunar symbolism.

Mistletoe may be associated with Balder's birth as well. In one text, he is said to have "sprung secretly from celestial seed."[63] This may refer to the circumstances of his birth (he is the offspring of the "divine seed" of his parents, the deities Odin and Frigg). It may also be an allusion to mistletoe, which generates through the propagation and spreading of seeds high up in the branches of trees, rather than in the ground, like other plants. Certain modern pagan sources suggest that the sticky white berries of mistletoe represent the semen of a male divinity—perhaps a horned god like Cernunnos. While we do not know if this is true in a historical sense, in Gaulish tradition, mistletoe was believed to grant fertility (or "seed") to sterile animals.[64]

In one version of Balder's tale, he is described as being aided by a group of supernatural women (perhaps the Valkyries). They kept a special food for him, over which snakes had dropped poison, which rendered him invincible.[65] In Scottish folk tradition, protective properties were attributed to mistletoe, which rendered the owner invincible. While the plant exhibits many life-promoting properties, it can be dangerous or even poisonous. Its Gaulish association with poison (as an effective antidote) is mentioned in Pliny's account as well. Perhaps mistletoe is the "magical food" mentioned in Balder's tale.

Also, if the Valkyries are the divine females referred to in the story, it is interesting to note that, like mistletoe, they are associated with the powers of both life and death. They are perhaps best known for their journeys to the battlefields of Earth where they decided the course of war and summoned fallen warriors to Valhalla. They are also the guides of the dead, escorting dead kings and heroes to the afterlife. In addition to their role as psychopomps, these divine women may also be associated with life after death. The Valkyries play an important role in the hall of the slain, as it is they who carry horns of mead to Odin's guests. This mead may be an elixir of immortality, as it was obtained from a goat that fed on the World Tree (often a symbol of longevity or immortality).[66]

One of the reasons mistletoe was considered sacred may be its liminal quality. In Celtic tradition (as well as in other cultures), things that are liminal, that exist in between two things or that are neither this nor that, are considered to have great potential for benefit or misfortune. They often have a supernatural quality to them and are thought to be powerful, dangerous, or significant. For example, the turning points of the year are liminal, being neither summer or winter, spring or autumn. They are points in time that exist between the worlds and, therefore, much closer to the Otherworld than the rest of time. During these times, beneficial or dangerous events may take place. Certain sacred sites or locations function in a similar fashion, as a portal between the worlds.

One of the best examples of liminality is the power attributed to May dew— dew collected at dawn on Beltaine. There are at least three liminal aspects to this substance: it is water that derives from neither rain or sea (nor river or well); it is collected at dawn (which is neither night or day) at Beltaine (which is neither winter or summer). There are many other examples of liminal objects, situations, places, time periods, events, and divine figures in Celtic myth and folk tradition. In the collection of medieval Welsh tales known as *The Mabinogi*, the divine figure Lleu responds to his wife's deceitful inquiry as to how he might be killed in the following manner:

> It is not easy to kill me with a cast. One would have to spend a year making the spear that was thrown at me, working on it only when people were at prayers on Sunday . . . I cannot be killed in a house, nor outside, neither on a horse nor on foot.[67]

This type of concept may be very old. In a Hindu tale concerning the great god Indra, the deity makes the following remarks:

> "It is now sunset, a dangerous time; it is neither night nor day.
> And Virtra must certainly be killed, for he is my enemy . . .

But he cannot be slain, even by the gods . . ."
Then he [Indra] saw a mass of foam like a mountain in an ocean.
"This is neither wet nor dry, nor is it a weapon.
I will throw this at Virtra and kill him in a moment.[68]

Like Indra's "mountain of foam," mistletoe is neither this nor that. Nor is it a weapon, although it was used as one. The plant's physical features and earthly manifestation exhibit a number of liminal qualities. It is produced by seed, but cannot be cultivated in the earth like other plants. It is neither a shrub nor a tree. It lives on something that has weakened vitality (its host tree), yet exhibits and maintains its life force during the depths of winter. It is a plant that grows in the air and seems to have no roots. In so many ways, mistletoe appears to exist between the worlds.

Because things that are liminal seem to defy classification, they are free from the limitations of things that can be classified or defined. For example, if a person encounters someone standing beneath a bunch of mistletoe, they are able to free themselves from the restrictions of convention and take certain liberties. Under the auspices and protection of this indefinable plant ("this tree which is not a tree"), one can therefore obtain a kiss from the person standing underneath the mistletoe, who is, of course, also in a very liminal position. Being outside the protection of normal societal conventions, he or she cannot refuse to give the other person a kiss. Moreover, the first person risks no penalty for obtaining that kiss.[69] It is interesting to note that the person standing under the mistletoe is placed in the liminal situation by being unaware that they are in the presence of the sacred plant. This brings to mind the ritual gathering of sacred plants that are most effective when the person is not looking for them. In any case, we can now understand the symbolism that lies behind the custom of hanging mistletoe at the Yuletide season, a turning point of the year, which is very liminal indeed.

In many areas of Britain, the strong pagan associations of mistletoe caused it to be banned from the greenery used to decorate churches during the Christmas season. In other areas, however, it was permitted and commonly used. It was, in some cases, customary to keep the Yuletide bunch of mistletoe throughout the year for good luck and replace it with a new one the following Christmas Eve. In a few instances, mistletoe was even placed on the church altar. It was left there during the entire Yule season, during which time "a general pardon and liberty" was proclaimed throughout the city. This further demonstrates the perceived liminal quality of the plant, as certain activities were tolerated and people pardoned for these actions.[70]

In many cultures, things not allowed during the rest of the year were permitted and overlooked during the New Year's celebrations. A similar state of affairs was customary at the Celtic New Year (Samain). Certain thefts and pranks and the custom of guising (which included men dressing as women, a very liminal situation) were tolerated during this important season. Eventually, some of these customs were transferred from the eve of the old pagan New Year (October 31) to that of the Gregorian New Year (December 31). The traditional use of mistletoe at the Yuletide season may be one of these "transferred" Samain customs.[71] Recall that the Scottish mistletoe ceremony traditionally took place at Samain.

We can perceive a number of liminal aspects in the story of Balder's death. In this tale, he is both helped and hindered by the gods. Part of his struggle for survival took place on Earth and part took place in the Otherworld. Even though he is impervious to weapons, he is slain by a weapon made of mistletoe. Neither a tree or a shrub, it was excluded from the oath the other plants were required to make. Due to its exemption from the pledge that protected Balder's life, it plays a role in his demise, which included the possibility of rebirth, although this was prevented by Loki.

We can see why mistletoe played such an important role in Celtic and Norse tradition. Its power is evident in its many healing applications and its dangerous aspects as well. It can survive on nothing all winter long, remaining evergreen while flourishing in a tree that seems to be dead. This plant, which grows neither in heaven or on Earth, exists in a charmed state between the two, prospering and thriving of its own accord. It appears to derive its power magically from this liminal state, tenaciously displaying the enchanted existence of its vital spark. It was considered very potent and powerful, and was at the same time beneficent and dangerous, terrible and holy.

The connection of mistletoe with a ritual associated with the Moon may attest to its perceived powers of life and death, and the birth that follows death. Its emergence "out of nowhere" and its ability to exhibit a life force of mysterious origin during the darkest time of the year suggest an association with symbolism of the new Moon, which appears from the darkness of the void. These important concepts, and the connection between the vital essence of plants and the phases of the Moon, may have found expression in ancient times in a Druidic ceremony associated with the gathering of this sacred elemental entity.

Witches, Hares, and Warrior Queens

The Moon may also be associated with a group of archetypal female figures from early Celtic tradition, which includes goddesses, witches, and warrior queens. The same Classical accounts that describe the Druids' lunar-based rituals and the gathering of sacred plants also describe a number of Celtic women remarkable for their bravery, tenacity, character, and skill. The notable courage of Celtic women, as well as the belligerence of the average Gaulish female, is mentioned by several writers. Both Classical writings and early Irish texts preserve tales and accounts of mortal and legendary women who served as leaders and rulers, Druids, seers, warrior queens, bards, satirists, and doctors. They even mention several respected women who taught the arts of war to men.[72]

The writers who recorded the details of these paragons of female strength and individuality were struck by the contrast between the attitudes and roles of Celtic women and the repressed situation (and consequently repressed attitudes) of many Greek women. Even though Roman women enjoyed relatively high familial and social status, Roman writers also went to some lengths to note the vigor and independence of women in the Celtic tribes they encountered.[73] While Celtic society (like all ancient societies about which we possess more than scant archaeological knowledge) was patriarchal in nature, these accounts seem to suggest a somewhat more equitable arrangement regarding the roles, functions, and status of men and women in Celtic society. Although women did not have equal rights with men, within the system, some women optimized their position and potential through the use of their will, character, intellect, and abilities (with no small amount of perseverance, determination, defiance, and spirit). Indeed, much the same thing could be said for women in modern society!

One of these notable women was Kamma, a priestess of Artemis who lived in Galatia. The worship of Artemis was probably introduced by the Romans who often adopted the veneration of foreign deities, bringing these cults with them as they occupied new territories. Kamma's husband was killed by a kinsman who was in love with her. When she was forced to marry her husband's murderer, she tricked him by persuading him to drink poison from a cup from which she had also drunk. She declared to Artemis before dying that her action was an act of sacrifice, and that she had outlived her husband only for this day of revenge, remaining faithful to his memory even after his death.[74]

Another memorable Celtic heroine is the British warrior queen Boudicca. She was the wife of Prasutagus, King of the Iceni (a Celtic tribe in southeastern Britain), renowned for his prosperity during the Romano-British period. To ensure the safety of his kingdom and people after his death, Prasutagus named Caesar his heir, along with his two daughters. After his death, however, Prasutagus' kingdom was plundered by Roman soldiers. The nobles of the Iceni were stripped of their hereditary estates and the king's relatives treated like slaves. His wife was flogged and his two daughters raped.

As a response to this outrage, Boudicca roused her people to take up arms. She inspired other tribes to join her expedition, which was successful in a number of military campaigns. Her army, consisting of over 120,000 troops, sacked and destroyed several Roman towns, including what would later become London. Confident in the wake of success, many warriors brought their wives with them, setting them up in carts around the edge of the battlefield to witness their victories. Boudicca herself was said to ride across the field of battle in a chariot with her daughters before her. Roman forces otherwise occupied in the west of Britain were forced to return to deal with the rebellion. Boudicca's army was eventually trapped and defeated. Rather than become a captive of Rome, the great queen took her own life by drinking poison.[75]

The effects of the uprising and its stunning early victories over imperial troops and territories were quite a blow to Roman resources and egos. Dio Cassius mentions that, in addition to the sacking of cities, the rebels killed 80,000 Romans. He writes: "All this . . . the Romans sustained at the hands of a woman, something that in fact caused them the greatest of shame."[76] Dio Cassius, in words that reflect his incredulity and respect, describes this remarkable figure as follows:

> . . . the one person who most roused them to anger and persuaded them to go to war against the Romans, the one person thought worthy of leading them and who directed the course of the whole war, was Boudicca, a woman of the British royal family who possessed more spirit than is usual among women.[77]

In addition to noting her strength, heroism, and skillful abilities as a leader and warrior, various accounts refer to Boudicca's physical appearance. She was evidently "very tall, and grim in appearance, with a piercing gaze and a harsh voice." She had long, fair hair that grew down to her hips and always dressed in the same fashion: a great gold torque around her neck and a multicolored tunic folded around her, over which was a thick cloak fastened with a brooch, sometimes carrying a spear.[78]

One of the most fascinating details of Boudicca's story concerns a ceremony she is said to have performed in a sacred grove. In the ritual, she invoked the aid of the goddess Andraste (probably a goddess of battle and victory). The ceremony evidently included a rite of divination involving the use of a hare. After inspiring her people with a speech and invoking her goddess, Boudicca released a hare from the fold of her tunic. It ran on "what was for them the lucky side," causing the people to shout for joy. It is presumed that the direction in which the hare ran served as a prognostication of the positive outcome of the battle. Dio Cassius records that the British Celts performed these activities ". . . to the accompaniment of sacrifices, feasting and orgies in their various sacred places, but especially in the grove of Andraste. This is the name they give to [the goddess] Victory, and they regard her with particular reverence."[79]

Dio Cassius also records the contents of what he maintains are speeches given by Boudicca, which are very interesting and quite inspiring. They are, however, likely to have been written by Dio Cassius himself (for the most part) to achieve a dramatic effect in his written accounts. It is possible, however, that the speeches may preserve the essence of some of what Boudicca is reported to have said to her people. After releasing the hare, she is said to having spoken the following words to her goddess:

> I thank you, Andraste, and I call upon you woman to woman . . . as one who rules over [the] Britons . . . experts in the art of war. Through this the

women too possess the same valour as the men. As queen, then, of such
men and women I pray to you and ask for victory, safety and freedom . . .
For us . . . may you alone, Lady, for ever be our leader.[80]

The use of a hare in this remarkable ritual of divination is highly intriguing. In general, the hare does not seem to have played a prominent role in early Celtic animal
lore or symbolism. Hares are depicted on a ceramic flagon from 4th-century B.C.E.
Germany, along with images of geese, boar, deer, and a dog, attesting to the animal's connection with the hunt. It may have been considered a propitious offering,
as hare fur was found in two offering pits from Britain. There is a stone statue of a
Gaulish hunter god who carries a large hare in his arms. The deity is naked except
for a torque and cloak, and, as there is a phallic emphasis similar to other images
of hunter deities, it may be that these figures represent fertility and abundance as
important integral aspects of the hunt. The hare was probably also associated with
fertility due to its ability to multiply rapidly and prodigiously.

Archaeological evidence shows that hares (as well as deer and fish) were
widely hunted in many Celtic areas. In light of this, it is interesting to note that
Caesar writes that the Britons considered the hare taboo as a food source.[81] This
may suggest that, for these tribes, the hare was a particularly sacred animal. While
we do not know the exact reasons for its veneration, its symbolic status may have
to do with its inclusion in Boudicca's quasi-religious ceremony and rite of divination. Later traditions concerning the hare may shed some light on how it was perceived by the British Celts.

In British folklore, the hare was associated with luck (both good and bad), as
well as with witchcraft. In many areas of Britain, it was considered unlucky to
encounter a hare, and to dream of a hare signified that death or misfortune might
befall someone in the family. However, in other regions, meeting a hare was considered lucky; a wish could be made as soon as the hare had passed. A hare's right
foot carried in the pocket was used to ward off rheumatism, and hare's feet were
considered good-luck charms. In some cases, only a white hare was unlucky, and
to see a black one was a sign of good fortune.[82]

A more beneficent presentation of the hare is preserved in this excerpt from a
Scottish Highland poem that reflects the voice of the hare, bemoaning the fact
that it has been caught.[83]

Whoever reads my testimonial, I was unquestionably virtuous,
Without gloom or servility in my nature.
I would not eat rank grass, what was food for my kind
Was the fine herbs of the moorlands . . .
Tis a sad tale to tell that I am tonight laid low . . .
Not thus was I at the Martinmas season,
Frisking and sporting mid the rough hills . . .

I was at home on the heaths where my father and ancestors
Were sportive, merry and spirited.

It is almost tempting to see some vestige of Boudicca's divinatory rite in the polarity of traditions concerning the variable propitious nature of the hare in British
folklore.

Numerous folk traditions record the belief that witches were able to turn
themselves into hares. Giraldus Cambrensis, writing in the 12th century, mentions
this belief as already quite old at that date. Witches in the shape of hares were supposed to steal the milk of cows and sheep lying out in the fields. These witches-in-
hare-form were often hunted, but usually escaped. They could only be shot with
a silver bullet. If a hare was wounded in the chase, a similar injury could later be
found on the body of a local witch.[84]

As late as 1662, Isobel Gowdie, a woman from Auldearne in Scotland who was
accused of witchcraft, "confessed" that she and other members of her coven transformed themselves into hares by repeating the following verse three times:

I shall go intill a hare,
With sorrow and sych and meikle care;
And I shall go in the Devil's name
Ay while I come home again.

To return to human form, the women were reported to say:

Hare, hare, God send thee care,
I am in a hare's likeness now,
But I shall be in a woman's likeness even now.[85]

What led to the association of hares with witches and nocturnal or supernatural
escapades? Many of the habits and activities of the hare are nocturnal in nature,
and this may underlie their association with night and, hence, with magic. Hares
feed at night, often lying under cover during the daytime. They are known to be
busy and active under the light of the Moon, but return to their homes as the Sun
rises. Their abode may be little more than a slight depression in the ground in
which they sit at daybreak, seeming almost to vanish, their fur blending in so well
with its surroundings.[86] The fields where the hares live (and where they can be
seen to disappear as if by magic) were nearby (or identical with) the fields in
which the family or community's herds grazed.

In addition, in the springtime of the year, the common brown hare becomes
the "mad March hare," moving about at all times of day rather than being active
at night, often galloping around the fields and engaging in strange ritualistic combats.[87] Anything that threatened the health or fertility of the herds posed a serious
threat to the continuation of life and the community. Fear for the safety of the
herds and their produce was a reasonable reaction to an animal whose behavior

may have seemed mysterious or unpredictable, and whose primary activities took place in the darkness of night, a period of time associated with the supernatural.

We can perceive a progression of ideas, from mysterious nocturnal animal to dangerous supernatural woman, both associated with nightime. An elusive animal that roams the pastures at night and disappears before one's eyes with the light of day—surely a sign of supernatural and possibly malevolent beings—whose behavior may be unpredictable or enigmatic and, hence, perhaps dangerous, is transformed into a magical figure intent on destroying the safety and security of the community's resources and livelihood.

Similarly, certain female figures in the community came under suspicion for a variety of reasons, including age, lifestyle, personality or character, or knowledge of herb lore or other traditions that had come to be misunderstood over time and considered potentially harmful or demonic in nature. These women came under the watchful gaze of both the clergy and the community. In some cases, suspicions or misgivings gave way to associations with nocturnal activities, sorcery, transformation and magical flight, and, ultimately, with threatening the health and welfare of society. The hare's nocturnal activities, and its unusual habits and abilities, led to its association with night, the Moon, and eventually, with witches. Its connection with the Moon and forces of potential darkness (beneficent or destructive) helped the hare make the leap from nocturnal animal to witch's familiar or witch's alter ego. This nocturnal or lunar association is widespread, as the hare is considered to be a lunar animal in many cultures worldwide.[88]

How are folklore traditions pertaining to witches connected with an early warrior queen of the British Celts and her use of a hare in a rite of divination? The answer may lie in the symbolism associated with certain divine female figures or deities and the evolution of that symbolism over time.

As we have seen, the number three was extremely significant in Celtic tradition. Various deities were conceived of in both single and triple form. An inscription to The Lugs was found in Celtiberia, and the Irish tribal deity known as The Dagda had three primary names. Various trios of female figures also existed. There were three manifestations of the goddess Macha, and Bridget is described as having two sisters, both also named Bridget. A carved relief of three water nymphs or healing goddesses decorated Coventina's well in Britain, and a set of three mother goddesses (probably influenced by Roman iconography and religious traditions) was venerated in Roman Britain.

In addition, groups of three (or nine, three times three) divine or supernatural women are common in Celtic myth and legend. There is an early inscription to The Three Lamia (the three witches) in Britain, and legends of a few centuries later record the existence of three divine women who accompanied King Arthur to the Otherworld. Pomponius Mela wrote about nine priestesses who inhabited a holy island located between Britain and Gaul. They were said to be able to predict the future, cure disease, and control the elements. Nine witches are mentioned in the medieval Welsh tale of *Peredur*, and, in the early Welsh mythic poem *Preiddau Annwfn* (The Spoils of Annwn), the poet Taliesin states that his poetry was "uttered" from a cauldron of inspiration, which was kindled by the breath of nine maidens.

It is interesting to note that the sacred vessel mentioned by Taliesin is described as "the cauldron of the chief of the *Un*world" (referring to the Otherworld or Underworld), and that it had a "ridge of pearls around its brim."[89] From this vessel or place of darkness, the flame of inspiration or wisdom was created. We have already examined the analogy between the darkness that precedes creation and symbolic images such as the womb, cauldron, or cosmic ocean. Pearls, of course, are jewels associated with the ocean, which is itself often associated with the Moon. While we may be reading too much into Taliesin's description, some of these ideas may come into play.

Perhaps the best-known Celtic trio of divine women is the three sisters from early Irish tradition: The Morrígan, Macha, and Nemain. The Morrígan is often perceived solely as a goddess of battle and death, but (as I have demonstrated in a recent academic paper) she is also associated with sexuality and fertility, abundance and the land.[90] Macha is associated with battle and sovereignty, the land and its fertility, female power, prophecy, and horses. Nemain, said to be the wife of Nét (an early Irish god of war), appears primarily as a symbol or harbinger of death, hovering over bodies that lay strewn on the battlefield. All three women are referred to at various times by the epithet *Badb*, "scald-crow or raven," a bird associated with darkness, death, and prophecy.

In numerous traditions (including Celtic, Hindu, and other European cultures), deities who exhibit a pronounced martial or destructive aspect are often also associated with life and abundance. The two aspects were perceived as necessary and complementary parts of the whole, rather than opposing or conflicting aspects. This natural cyclical duality was transformed by Christian ideology into a battle between light and dark, good and evil. Thus, this early trio of powerful female figures who were, in part, associated with death, magic, and destruction came to be viewed with great trepidation and suspicion, much like the hare and the witch. The dark aspect of their character was emphasized, and over time, they came to be feared, perceived as malignant harpies or hags. A reflection of these divine figures is found in modern Scottish and Irish folktales, which feature a group of three witches or hags.

Like Boudicca, the Morrígan, Macha, and Nemain may be described as warrior queens. All of these women (whether mortal or divine) had an unusual degree of authority and power, which they could use to control or influence the forces of life and death. This female power may have been viewed as unnatural or threatening.[91] In addition, these women had connections with magic, prophecy, and transformation. The awe-inspiring (but also unsettling) feminine power associated with warrior queens and other noteable female figures, as well as their connection with death and magic (and hence, also with night), may have eventually led to their characterization as witches or witch figures.

While the exact details of this transformation cannot be outlined with certainty (and while these associations are far from conclusive), it may be that there is some connection between early goddesses or queens of battle and death with the later figure of the witch. Originally associated with magic and power, life and abundance, protection and destruction, their darker aspects and magical abilities as well as their female power and autonomy were misunderstood and eventually feared. Once venerated and shown great deference and respect, they were later shunned and persecuted. Where once their strength protected the people through magic or warfare, both of which served to preserve society and its life forces, this aspect, perhaps considered inappropriate for women in later times, was perceived only as threatening or destructive. The early symbolism of darkness as an integral part of a whole that also contained light or life came to represent only that which was evil or malicious (and also nocturnal). The transformation from powerful, protective battle queen to malevolent witch was complete.

Witches and other supernatural women were directly associated with night, reputedly holding meetings or performing solitary rites under the light of the Moon. The Moon, as we have seen, excels at displaying a great capacity for self-transformation and can cause changes in others as well. It exerts a tremendous influence on certain elements of the natural world, affecting the tides and the behavior of man and beast. Witches were also said to be able to harness and control the elements of nature and affect the shape or behavior of people and other creatures. The independence of the witch and her ability to transform herself or others into various shapes was viewed as particularly threatening. This capriciousness, this instability of form, made the shape-shifting female dangerous, powerful, and frightening in the extreme. What was clear by the light of day was obscured, indistinct, and highly changeable by the light of the Moon.

What did the hare signify to the Celts of Britain and to the warrior queen Boudicca? Why was it used in an important rite of divination? While the answer to this may never be known, it may be that the hare's escapades under the moon-lit sky, and its subsequent association with night and the supernatural formed part of its early religious symbolism.

Divination was considered to be most effective when performed at liminal points in time (whether of the year, the month, or the day), as these were considered to be closer to the Otherworld, the source of wisdom in Celtic tradition. For this reason, many divinatory rites were practiced at Samain, the most liminal time of all. Night was also a very liminal time, and, as many tales demonstrate, it too was closely associated with the Otherworld. As Samain was the start of the new yearly cycle, so night was the start of the new daily cycle. Both symbolize the cosmic darkness from which life emerges. The nocturnal hare, which may have been considered a lunar animal in Celtic ideology, was reasonably associated with the darkness and potential of night. Its use as a sacred divinatory agent makes a great deal of sense in this context.

We can now also understand the evolution of strong, sacred female figures from queens or goddesses to witches or hags. Multi-aspected, highly respected, and widely venerated goddesses (some of whom were warrior queens), mortal warrior queens (whose strength and power exceeded that of the traditional female role), female magicians, herbalists, midwives or diviners, and a variety of women who did not fit in (and who thus fell under the suspicious eye of the church or a community under stress) all share a number of common attributes. Their character or skills marked them as unusual or out of the ordinary, particularly in the new Christian schema. They exhibited power, strength, independence, and initiative, characteristics perhaps once accepted or respected, but eventually less so. Their association with darkness and, in some cases, with the Moon may have contrasted too sharply with the solar aspect of the Christian male deity.

Even the gentle hare, because of its association with night and the Moon, became a target for suspicion. At one time, its connection with the darkness may have symbolized its link with the fertile liminality of the darkness from which the Celtic day emerged, a source of creation and origin whence knowledge might be gained if the Otherworld powers were properly respected or propitiated. The night, presided over by the Moon, was a holy time and place associated with transformation and knowledge of the divine.

Boudicca's skillful use of a creature associated with the Moon, the night, and the power of the Otherworld suggests her possible role as a priestess of Andraste and demonstrates her desire to utilize the divine forces around her to transform her difficult and perilous situation into one of victory and empowerment. Just as the Moon undergoes a powerful series of remarkable transformations throughout its course, Boudicca's role as battle queen and prophetess required a transformation from royal consort to leader, guide, and avenging mortal goddess. In her protective and destructive guise, she uses a sacred hare, a magical lunar animal, in a rite of divination associated with battle and death, but, ultimately, intended to promote the continuity of life.

$$\text{☽ ☽ ☽}$$

Meditations and Exercises

The following exercises can help you connect with the power of the Moon associated with liminal times and places.

1) The Celts demonstrated their covenant with the natural world by swearing by the elements—including land, sea, and sky, and the Sun and Moon—to do or not do various things. Create a personal oath or pledge to the elements utilizing

the number three, seven, or nine as its structural basis, that includes whichever features of the land or elements of the cosmos are most sacred to you. Making a solemn pledge to powerful entities can be a potent and empowering step toward undertaking an important task or setting out on a path of transformation. Remember that swearing by the elements is binding and not something to be taken lightly.

2) Think about the three classes of sacred persons that existed in Celtic society (Druid, bard, and seer). Do you feel an affinity—intellectually, creatively, or spiritually—with one of these paths or functions? Druids and poets (and perhaps by inference, seers) trained with distinguished and respected elders and professionals for many years to become masterful at their vocation or craft. What methods of training might you pursue to achieve a similar level of mastery? Consider private and group instruction, college and university resources, holistic practitioners, libraries and lecture series, personal reading, exploration, and meditation. Keep in mind issues of dedication, professionalism, experience, intuition, and respect for the ancestors.

3) What are your beliefs concerning immortality and the rebirth of the soul? How do these beliefs affect your daily life and the decisions you make? Take some time to reflect upon these important concepts and explore how they relate to the lunar cycle. Read about how other cultures perceive and interpret these spiritual ideas, or arrange a discussion group with like-minded people to explore how you can use the inherent power of these beliefs and cycles to live your lives most fully.

4) An important part of Druidic training was the memorization of traditional wisdom associated with various aspects of culture and society, including poetry, history, law, genealogy, and religious beliefs and practices. You may have an interest in traditional lore associated with myths, deities, herbs, astrology, poetry, folklore, or charms, as well as the genealogy of ancestors (or respected or inspirational historical or divine figures). How might memorization of the information associated with your area of interest or expertise affect your experience of it? Create mnemonic devices or rhymes to help you remember. Explore how working mentally and orally with traditional lore deepens your comprehension and experience of it.

5) The Celts offered beautiful works of gold, silver, bronze, and other materials to their gods, including jewelry, weapons, miniature objects, and symbols. It is reasonable to assume that they offered the fruits of the earth and the flocks as well, as these were things of great value to them. What can you offer the gods and the ancestors? This may be something you create yourself (art, poetry, music), an herb or plant you grow or gather, seasonal cakes or ale cre-

ated from local ingredients, the undertaking of a pledge or activity, or principles such as loyalty, respect, dedication, industry, inspiration, creativity, or gratitude. We often ask for blessings or assistance without completing the circle by making a pledge or offering ourselves. Reflect upon the cyclical nature of life as expressed by the Moon's phases and the seasons, and on the importance of reciprocity in your dealings with the Otherworld. At the new Moon, ask the gods or spirits to show you how best to express your admiration and respect.

6) Learn about herbs and plants considered sacred in the cultural or spiritual tradition that most interests you. These may be healing herbs, magical plants, sacred trees or shrubs, or plants that sustained the lives of the people. In Celtic culture, this would have included spelt, barley, oats, wheat, hazelnuts, berries, crab apples, and various wild plants and roots. These plants that "give life" are extremely sacred and can serve as powerful ritual elements. Read about the history and culture of the society in question and see which plants were eaten, utilized, and revered. Explore their varied practical and medicinal applications, as well as their use in various magical rites.

7) There are many Celtic deities who are only known to us through a single Classical reference or inscription. Even so, learning their names and associated symbolism are an important first step toward understanding their nature, power, and attributes. We can show our reverence and move toward knowing these deities by taking the time to understand the culture in which they were worshipped, and by comparing them with other Celtic gods.[92] Then, equipped with this practical knowledge, we can turn to the world of the divine to help us connect with and learn more about these gods and goddesses. Create a ritual to contact and honor one of these lesser-known Celtic deities. Include a chant that incorporates their name, titles or epithets, and attributes (if known). Indicate your desire to be respectful, and your wish to know more about them. Create a small altar for daily use and with the chanted invocation light a sacred flame and present offerings to show your good intent.

8) Create a ceremony you can use to gather sacred plants or herbs from the wild using symbolic elements from the Druidic or folklore rituals described above. Include the observation of the phase of the Moon, the importance of the way in which the plant is discovered or encountered, what sort of implement is used, whether the left or right hand is significant in gathering, a charm or incantation spoken or intoned before culling the plant, and the use of a cloth of some symbolic color or fabric in which the plant will be gathered. What will be the plant's purpose or uses? How will it be stored or ritually consecrated? Set some aside for making tinctures or herbal incenses, scattering in vessels of water, or strewing on the ground for protection or purification.

9) How has our exploration of liminality (things that are neither this nor that, or are in between) informed, changed, or deepened your understanding of folk customs, including the sacred divisions of time and space? How can we mark and utilize the temporal turning points (year, month, and day) in our spiritual practice? Reflect also upon the sacred divisions of the land, which can be reflected in our organization and use of sacred space. What other things can you now perceive as liminal? Keep in mind issues of respect, propitiation, and protection as you work with liminal concepts, as they have potential for danger as well as blessings and change.

10) Reflect upon the conceptual evolution in which goddesses of life and death (and warrior queens who embody some of their attributes) may have been transformed into the negative image of the witch. Many of the witch's activities were shadowy or nocturnal, some taking place under the light of the Moon. We can see that darkness is neither evil nor malicious, but the natural and necessary balance of light. How can you honor and promote the power of both light and dark in your own life, without giving in to societal preconceptions or fear? How are these ideas associated with autonomy and your ability to grow or to transform yourself? What aspects of darkness and of female power are still considered threatening in our society? Meditate on the image of the witch and her animal familiars. Do some journal or poetry writing, or record your dreams or meditations, to help you connect with these ideas. Reflect on your ability to use the image of darkness (which balances and creates light) to effect positive change in your life and in society.

11) Create a ritual or ceremony to connect with the god of the Underworld. You may want to include symbols of life, death, and transformation, cauldrons or vessels of water, and lunar symbols, stones, or animals (swans, cranes, ravens, bulls, cows) or Moon-related plants (club moss, water pimpernel, mistletoe). Taliesin describes the cauldron of the god of the Unworld as a source of inspiration, decorated with pearls around its rim. This may suggest its identity as a vessel of creation as well as its association with the primal ocean. Meditate on the image of the cauldron of inspiration, whose fire was kindled by the breath of nine sacred women. Work toward deepening your understanding of the primal darkness that precedes the creation of light or life, its parallels with lunar symbolism, and the interconnection between powers of light and dark, and life and death.

12) Women have traditionally been the guardians of certain kinds of power and are often associated with liminal points of time, transitions, and passages (birth, marriage, initiation, and death). Explore the lives of ancient women and how they were viewed in other periods of history. While there is almost no evidence for matriarchal society in either history or prehistory, women have enormously shaped the events, culture, and history of the world. Read about

powerful women who transcended cultural and sexual limitations to improve and cocreate their world. Make of list of their restrictions or limitations, as well as examples of how they lived within (and outside of) these restrictions. Note what rights women did have in society, and how they used these rights wisely and effectively. In what roles could women perform and excel? How can these stories serve as a guide for women in this modern age?[93]

13) Create a ritual to honor the Moon and its phases using elements from the Classical accounts concerning the spiritual beliefs and practices of the Celts. You may wish to model your ritual after the one below.

Celtic Lunar Ritual

Perform the ritual at the new Moon, either alone or in a group of three, seven, or nine people. Decorate the altar with oak and mistletoe, images of sacred animals (hare, swan, raven, crane), symbols of the Moon, and symbols of transformation (perhaps what you would like to see transformed in your life). Place a cauldron or vessel of water into which you have strewn herbs associated with the Moon in the center. Include symbols of the Underworld god (antlers, cauldrons, etc.), as well as those of other deities you wish to honor.

Begin by making an offering of ritual cakes you create yourself from traditional grains or other ingredients. These may include safe and edible symbolic or magical herbs. The cakes may be sprinkled with dew during preparation or during the ritual if you are able to gather some. Make an offering of a ritual beverage as well, perhaps ale or mead (as in the selago rite).

Symbolically "cull" a sacred plant (oak, mistletoe, or other herb) and present it in a clean, white cloth, offering it to the gods, the ancestors, and the spirits of the land.

Next, have each person recite a piece of poetry or lore (either traditional or created specifically for the ritual) pertaining to the Moon, lunar cosmology or symbolism, lunar plants, animals, stones, or charms, the power and sacredness of women, or themes of transformation and renewal. If possible, memorize in advance what you are going to offer and present. This will make the experience much more meaningful and powerful.

Sitting on the floor or in a circle, meditate on the image of the cauldron of the Unworld. This vessel may symbolize all three types of cauldrons found in Celtic tradition: the cauldron of renewal or transformation, the cauldron of abundance, and the cauldron of inspiration. Reflect deeply upon the concept or image of the primal darkness from which life emerges, as well as on the sacred balance between powers of life and death. Visualize the flame kindled from the breath of nine sacred women.

After the meditation, come forward individually to make a pledge or offering to the gods. This may consist of stones, flowers, herbs, artwork, poetry, or something else you have created. Then, using an oath you have created yourself that honors the Moon and other elements, make a pledge to begin, change, or transform some aspect of your life.

Thank the gods, the ancestors, and spirits of the land for their blessings and guidance, and ask for their continued support in your quest for renewal and transformation. This may be personal, or for the benefit of family, loved ones, or society in general. When the ceremony is concluded, pour the herb-strewn water around the base of an oak or other sacred tree, and place a portion of the cakes and ale outside under the moonlight for the gods.

ATENUX
(THE RETURNING NIGHT)

SACRED NUMBERS
AND LUNAR RECKONING

Why is a night moonlit, and another (so dark)
That thou seest not thy shield out of doors?
Why is a stone so heavy? Why is a thorn so sharp?
Skilled minstrel, why dost thou not tell me?
Does thou know where night awaits day?

—TALIESIN, *Y CYMMRODOR*

In early hunter-gatherer societies, keeping track of the seasons was important for the survival and continuity of the tribe. Since seasonal changes are generally visible to the naked eye, a complicated system of time measurement may not have been necessary in earliest times. People could remember from year to year the changes in weather, landscape, flora, and fauna that heralded the movement of animals or the appearance of certain kinds of plants and wild foods.

With the advent of agriculture, however (which took place in Europe around 3500 to 2500 B.C.E.), decisions pertaining to planting and harvesting required a more refined sense of timing. A mistake in either direction could spell disaster, and so the measurement of time was considered vitally important. Because of this, the creation and maintenance of calendar systems was often the responsibility of the priesthood or sacred class, whose members were able to devote sufficient time to their study and application. In addition to maintaining the calendar, these priests would also have supervised rites to propitiate the gods in order to regulate seasonal deviations and bring about good weather.

In earliest times, the most obvious unit of short-term time measurement was the day, which is governed by the Sun. However, as people needed to keep track of longer periods of time, the Moon, which governs the month and its internal periods of time, was used for more long-term reckoning. Unlike the weather, the Moon was reliable and could be counted on to provide essential temporal information. It is not surprising, then, that the lunar month came to have a great deal of religious significance. The new Moon, which was generally used to herald the start of each lunar cycle, became the object of veneration and festivals, and the subject of praise, gratitude, and priestly proclamations.[1] The veneration of the new Moon has continued into modern times, and in folklore traditions, as we shall see, it is the new Moon that is considered most significant.

Mystical number symbolism associated with the lunar cycle was often expressed by or incorporated into religious and mythological traditions. The Moon completes one revolution in its orbit around the Earth every 27.32 days; the period from one new Moon to the next is 29.5 days. The average of these cycles is equivalent to approximately twenty-eight days, a figure often used as a general indicator of the length of the lunar month. Both twenty-seven and twenty-eight figure in the numerical symbolism, however.

In addition to its association with the length of the lunar month, twenty-eight may have been significant due to its component factors, four and seven. In Celtic tradition, the year and the land were divided into four equal parts (which will be discussed later on). Four therefore symbolized "the whole" or entirety of something. The lunar cycle may be divided into four sections: new Moon to first quarter, first quarter to full Moon, full Moon to third quarter, and third quarter to new Moon.

Seven was also an extremely significant number. Peoples' lives were sometimes divided into periods of seven years, and certain adventures or experiences took place during or after seven years. When the chief Druid of the people of Nemed lit the first fire at Uisneach (the sacred center of Ireland), it blazed for seven years, and from that fire was kindled "every chief fire and every chief hearth" in Ireland. The festival of Samain is reported to have lasted for seven days, with the day of Samain itself in the middle and three days on either side.[2] In many cases, seven seems to have been associated with the Otherworld, the fairies, and various sacred persons or events. Therefore, twenty-eight may represent the internal periods of sacred time (seven) that exist within the whole (four).

There are also a number of interesting associations related to the number twenty-seven. The lunar zodiac, which is believed to have originated in Babylonia and spread to lands as far ranging as China and medieval Europe, has twenty-eight "mansions." However, other traditions maintain that there are twenty-seven constellations in the lunar zodiac. In Hindu mythology, the Moon, which is some-times called King Soma, has twenty-seven star wives with whom he spends one night each month.[3] In Celtic tradition, the number twenty-seven was quite significant. We have seen that three was a very sacred number to the Celts, and therefore nine (3 x 3) and twenty-seven (3 x 9) were also very important. Twenty-seven is almost as common in legend as nine, in fact. Interestingly, it is often expressed in terms of a group of twenty-seven, with the addition of a leader or other member, making twenty-eight in all. Finn's warriors were sometimes grouped into three companies of nine (plus a leader), and Cathbad and his twenty-seven men were reported to have killed the foster brothers of Conchobor's mother, Ness.[4]

Prior to the adoption of the seven-day week from Romano-Christian tradition, the Irish Celts appear to have had an earlier nine-day "week" or period of time measurement called a *nómad*. This consisted of either nine days and nights, or nine periods of eight hours (which equals three days). In Old Irish, the word "nómad" was also used to refer to a "ninth part" of something. Time reckoning by the nómad breaks the lunar cycle up into three sections of nine, plus the void Moon.[5] Here we can see the familiar representation of twenty-seven with an additional part. The word was also sometimes used to indicate the ninth day of the Moon, and in the Welsh laws, the ninth day of the month often marked the end or the beginning of a period of time.[6]

As we have seen, nine was an extremely sacred number. It was widely used in folk tradition, and associated with spells, divination, and folk cures. In Scotland, the "need fire" was kindled by nine men using nine kinds of sacred wood. Nine hazels of wisdom were said to grow at the well of Otherworld wisdom. In the mythological account of the early settlers of Ireland, the sons of Mil retreated "over nine waves" to elude the magical powers of the Tuatha Dé Danann. The Welsh poet Taliesin maintained that he was not made from a mother and father, but created from nine sacred things, including fruits, flowers, and earth, and water from the ninth wave.[7]

The word nómad could also refer to nine periods of eight hours, or three days and nights. This time period is often mentioned in Celtic contexts, and figures prominently in shamanic cultures as well. Significant illnesses or ordeals often last for three days and nights, during which time the person exists in a liminal state between the worlds. Those who enter Otherworld dwellings often have adventures lasting for three days and nights as well. Here we might remember that three days and nights is the length of the period of the void Moon, a liminal time when the Moon is "neither old nor new." We can see that the numbers three, nine, and twenty-seven (as well as four and seven) all played a significant role in Celtic mythological tradition, and that these very numbers also form an important part of any lunar system of time measurement.

The Gaulish Lunar Calendar

One of the most interesting archaeological discoveries connected with Celtic culture and religion occurred in the year 1897 in central France. A fragmentary Gaulish bronze tablet was uncovered that dated from the 1st century B.C.E. The tablet appears to be a timetable of religious festivals and other significant events. Known as the Coligny Calendar, it is the oldest extensive document surviving from ancient Gaul. It originally consisted of a large bronze plate, five feet by three-and-a-half feet, engraved with a sophisticated calendar system. It even had holes punched along the left-hand side into which movable pegs could be inserted to mark the days.[8] Before being deposited into the earth, the calendar seems to have been deliberately broken, which may signify that it was intended as an offering or used as some part of a religious ceremony.[9]

The calendar was comprised of sixty-two consecutive lunar months and two additional (intercalary) months, one inserted at the beginning of the cycle and another in the middle.[10] It is interesting to note that the calendar spans a period of five years; Classical author Diodorus Siculus mentioned that the Continental Celts held sacrifices (large religious assemblies) every five years.[11] The Coligny Calendar is especially interesting in that it reckons time by nights. Its markings indicate that time was divided into months and half-months.[12] The word *atenux* (which probably means "returning night") marks the division of the month into a "bright half" and a "dark half." The year itself was also divided into two similar halves.[13]

The first half of the year begins with a month called *Samon*, and the second half with a month called *Giamon*. These words are related to the words for summer and winter in the modern Celtic languages (compare them with *sàmradh*, "summer," and *geamhraich*, "winter" in Scottish Gaelic).[14] In early Irish tradition, Samain, which heralded the start of the New Year, also served as the beginning of the dark half of the year. Strangely, Gaulish *Samon* (like Old Irish *Samain*) incorporates the root-word *sam* which means "summer."[15] While this may seem confusing at first, the words in question may actually mean "summer's end," referring to the season just passed.[16] Likewise, the name *Giamon*, which includes the root *gam*, meaning "winter," may mean "winter's end." Samon (summer's end) began the dark half of the year, and Giamon (winter's end, which corresponds with the Irish festival of Beltaine) was the start of the bright half of the year.[17]

Many of the words marked on the Coligny Calendar are believed to indicate the names and dates of festivals. Most of these are concentrated in the first half of the year (sam, the dark half). A similar concentration of wintertime religious activity occurs in other European ritual calendars.[18] The Coligny Calendar is the best evidence we have to support the theory that holidays similar to the great Irish seasonal festivals of Samain, Beltaine, Imbolc, and Lugnasad may also have been celebrated in other parts of the Celtic world.[19] In addition to Samonios (which is cognate with Old Irish Samain), the calendar also indicates that a festival was held on August first,[20] the date of the Irish holiday called Lugnasad.

The months that make up the Coligny Calendar are of two types. In each twelve-month period, there are six months that are thirty days long and six months that are twenty-nine days long. The thirty-day months are described as *mat,* meaning "good" (compare with Old Irish *maith*), while the shorter months are described as *anm* (probably an abbreviation of *an mat-*, "not good").[21] These terms were probably used to designate the months as propitious or nonpropitious, either for particular activities or in a more general sense. In a number of Irish tales, Druids were consulted in order to ascertain which days were propitious for battle or other undertakings. Their knowledge and authority was such that they could even delay actions taken by kings and queens. In one story, the warrior queen Medb wants to engage in battle with the Ulstermen on a particular day, but is prevented from doing so by her Druids for a period of two weeks (half a lunar cycle).

Lunar Calendars of the Ancient World

Lunar-based calendars were also used by other ancient peoples, including the Greeks, the Babylonians, the Hebrews, and others.[22] An exploration of how these calendars were constructed and utilized may help us better understand the Gaulish calendar.

Like the Coligny Calendar, the Muslim calendar is comprised of six months of thirty days and six months of twenty-nine days. These appear in a regular alternating pattern, which actually creates a bit of a problem in terms of lunar reckoning. A true lunar year should always start on the day of the new Moon. However, if the calendar begins on a new Moon and then proceeds to simply alternate between twenty-nine- and thirty-day months, the calendar will become out of sync with the Moon. In this case, the third year will start the day before the new Moon; the sixth year will start two days before the new Moon; and so on. In thirty years, the calendar will be exactly eleven days out of sync with the solar year, and so the Muslims added in the eleven days, scattering them throughout the thirty-year period. This prevented any year from starting a full day ahead of or behind the new Moon. The cycle consists of nineteen "lunar" years of 354 days and eleven of 355 days, and would seem to solve the problem. But does it?

The difficulty is that the lunar year (whether 354 or 355 days in length) does not exactly align with the solar year and the cycle of the seasons.[23] The lunar year is about eleven days shorter than the 365-day solar year. However, if you just add eleven days at the end of the lunar year, the next year will not start with a new Moon. What to do? One solution is just to wait twenty years. If you start the solar year with the new Moon, it will get more and more out of sync, but every twentieth solar year will start on the new Moon again of its own accord. In this system, a twenty-year cycle is made up of nineteen lunar years of twelve lunar months each, with seven lunar months left over.[24]

The Babylonians, however, were not willing to let their calendar fall seven months out of sync with the seasons. They distributed the seven leftover lunar months throughout the nineteen-year cycle, inserting them one month at a time, and as evenly as possible. The intercalary months were added into the third, sixth, eighth, eleventh, fourteenth, seventeenth, and nineteenth years of the larger cycle. Their lunar year was thus never more than about twenty days out of sync with the Sun. This gave the Bablyonians a nineteen-year cycle comprised of twelve years made up of twelve lunar months and seven years made up of thirteen lunar months. This type of lunar-solar calendar was very popular in ancient times because it adjusted for the seasons and preserved the sanctity of the Moon and its cycles. The Hebrews and the Greeks adopted this calendar from the Babylonians, and it was even used for a few centuries by the early Christians.[25]

How did the Gaulish Celts solve their lunar-solar calendar dilemna? They appear to have inserted thirty-day intercalary months at alternating two-and-a-half- and three-and-a-half-year intervals. While Pliny wrote that the Gauls utilized a thirty-year cycle of some kind ("it is the moon that marks out for them the beginning of months and years and cycles of thirty years"), the Coligny Calendar seems to have more in common with the nineteen-year system used by Greek and Babylonian mathematicians.[26] The Gauls certainly had contact with the Greeks, but it is also reasonable to assume that Druidic knowledge was sophisticated enough to come up with a practical and smooth-running system on its own.[27] The learned classes of the Celts (like those of other peoples) would likely have been able to devise an accurate system of time measurement, even if this was influenced by the traditions of neighboring cultures.[28]

Classical reports mention that the Druids studied "the size of the universe and the earth," as well as "the stars and their motion." Lucan refers to the Druids' claim to understand astrology as well as the secrets of the divine, and Cicero mentions that the Druid Divitiacus had knowledge of natural phenomena. As students of the natural universe, the Druids would have had an interest in meteorological phenomena and the movement of both Sun and Moon.[29] And, as we have seen, both Caesar and Pliny speak of the Druidical reckoning of time by the Moon.[30]

One feature of the Coligny Calendar that may help support the idea of native innovation or adaptation is the pattern of alternation of *mat* and *anm* (good and not good) months. In other lunar calendars, these thirty- and twenty-nine-day months follow a regular pattern of alternation. If this were maintained throughout the Coligny Calendar, both Samon and Giamon (the months that included the sacred festivals that began the dark and bright halves of the year) would be mat months of thirty days each. This would seem a reasonable way to arrange the sacred calendar.

However, there seems to have been a deliberate adjustment in the Coligny Calendar so that the first half of the year (the ritually more important half) both begins and ends with a mat (good) month. Likewise, the second half of the year begins and ends with an anm (not good) month. Perhaps the Gauls felt it was important to surround the dark, or more significant, half of the year with good months, either to mark the importance of this sacral time or to help them make it through the long months of winter.

Another aspect of the calendar that aligns with other native religious concepts is the focus on a sacred division into two distinct parts. The calendar reflects a three-fold parallel division of time into two halves (light and dark), which may illustrate the importance and antiquity of such a division. In this system, the month, the year, and the larger cycle were all divided into light and dark halves. This primal division into two contrasting yet complementary parts also took place in connection with the land, and may have formed part of the division of sacred space as well as sacred time.[31]

An Ancient Division of Space and Time

In *Celtic Heritage*, Alwyn and Brinley Rees write extensively about the two-fold division of space and time.[32] Some of the earliest traditions pertaining to the division of the land of Ireland show it as conceptually divided into two halves, north and south. While both halves were significant, the north generally took precedence, which may be a parallel with the deference shown to the dark half of the year. The north was symbolically associated with kingship, dignity, and learning, and the south with music, food production, and "those who serve." These are conceptual rather than political associations or divisions, and both halves contain important and complementary attributes.

Later, a secondary development took place, and the land was divided in two once again, making a total of four provinces, with the addition of a sacred central point or province.[33] At this stage, new sets of attributes became associated with the four provinces, as well as with the center. In the Irish tale *The Settling of the Manor of Tara*, a list of about twenty attributes are mentioned as being associated with the various provinces. The primary attributes of each province or direction, however, are as follows: battle in the north, music in the south, prosperity in the east, learning in the west, and sovereignty in the center.

In addition, the medieval Irish text *Saltair na Rann* records that certain "winds" existed that were connected with each of the directions and associated with various colors. There were four winds in each of the main cardinal directions, with two winds between each of these.[34] The colors associated with the four primary winds were: north (black or dark), south (white or shining), east (purple; in other contexts, red or a reddish-purple), and west (dun, a light yellowish brown, yellow in other traditions). The use of these four colors (black, white, red, and yellow) is ancient in origin and found in primal and indigenous artwork worldwide. In addition, these are the first four colors that receive a name in many languages (black and white are named first, followed by red, and then yellow or green).[35]

A similar evolution seems to have taken place in connection with the division of sacred time. Samain and Beltaine, the two most prominent Celtic feast days, may have been the earliest sacred days in the original two-fold division of the year. Imbolc and Lugnasad may have been introduced to the tradition later. Evidence for the early observance of Imbolc is scarce, and stories associated with the god Lug and the festival of Lugnasad suggest that this holiday may have been added later, perhaps to complement the addition of Imbolc.[36]

The early two-fold division of time was expressed on three different levels in the Coligny Calendar in relation to the month, year, and five-year cycles. The division of the lunar month into two halves (mat and anm) presents some interesting challenges.

Each lunar month was made up of two parts, the first half consisting of fifteen days, and the second half of either fourteen or fifteen days (depending on the type of month).[37]

The word *atenux* was inscribed between the two halves of the lunar month. This word has been interpreted as meaning "renewal" or the "returning night," and would seem to be a reference to the return or renewal of the lunar crescent at the time of the new Moon.

However, the word *atenux* occurs at the middle of the lunar month. If the month started with the new Moon, to what does atenux refer? Perhaps it signifies the height of lunar light and power at the time of the full Moon. In light of what we know about lunar calendars, however, this would be quite unusual.

In many ancient systems of time reckoning, cyclical time (whether of the day, month, or year) begins at a sacred starting point (midnight, the new moon, the new year) and proceeds to an apex or turning point (noon, the full moon, the halfway point of the year). It then continues around this point and begins a return back to the place from whence it came.[38] This is precisely what we see in the Coligny Calendar where the term *atenux* ("returning night") is found in the middle of the month and corresponds with the time of the full Moon. The beginning of the cycle is the pivot of the system, the dark time of death and of creation (the void Moon/new Moon and Samain).

The Unbearable Complexity of Light and Dark

We have seen that the ancient Gauls characterized the winter/Samon half of the year as mat (good) and the summer/Giamon half as anm (not good). These characterizations may be connected with concepts associated with the availability of food and, hence, the continuation of life. At Samain, it was hoped that the harvest had reached its successful conclusion, although of course, this was not always the case. If it were successful, however, food stores would be at a yearly high: the crops would be in; the herds would be culled; the wild-boar hunt would have taken place; and wild foods would have been gathered. At this season of plenty, feasting would have occurred, as well as rites of propitiation, acts of divination, and religious ceremonies to offer reverence and thanksgiving.

While the initial part of the winter season was a period of relative plenty, as winter progressed, food stores would have become depleted. This may be why more religious rituals took place in the dark half of the year, in order to protect the stores of food and the people. The dark half of the year was "surrounded" or "capped" by mat months in a purposeful fashion, and these protective months may have served to preserve or improve the quality of this dark and potentially difficult time, much like a magical charm or formula.

Similarly, beneficent titles were sometimes used to safeguard against danger and invoke beneficial properties. By referring to things as good, the people sought to propitiate potential destructive forces and draw forth positive benefits or energies. For example, the fairies were often referred to as The Good People or The Good Neighbors. These designations not only showed respect, but were used to deter mischievous or malicious activities by the inhabitants of the sid-mounds. These epithets were utilized in the hopes that "what the fairies were called, they would be."

A similar situation may have existed in earlier times in connection with the Continental deity Sucellos, The Good Striker. He is often pictured with a wheel (perhaps symbolic of the sky or the Sun) and a great club. He may be similar to the Irish deity known as The Dagda, who owned a club that wielded life from one end and death from the other. By referring to Sucellos as The Good Striker, the people may have sought to ensure that his powers were used for blessings rather than misfortune. Surrounding the dark half of the year with mat (good) months and characterizing it as mat may have served to encourage and ritually call into being the characteristics the people hoped it might have.

Why would the bright half of the year be characterized as anm? While the weather was generally good during this half of the year, food was often far from plentiful. There would have been access to milk and cheese, foods gathered from the wild, and some animal foods (the result of hunting). However, it was not yet known if the harvest would be successful. Grains could not be harvested until August or September, and the grain supply from the previous harvest would be depleted. In fact, in Scottish Gaelic tradition, July was sometimes referred to as the "lean" or "hungry" month. But why purposefully characterize the bright half as anm? The reasoning behind this may have to do with the very concepts of duality we have been discussing, as well as the symbolism associated with creation.

Samain was the turning point immediately preceding the dark half of the seasonal cycle, when the creation or rebirth of the New Year took place.[40] Darkness did not symbolize evil, of course, but rather the cosmic darkness preceding birth or rebirth, the place where life was created. In a similar fashion, the ancient Gauls maintained that they were descended from Dis Pater, a god of the Underworld. He was not a dark or sinister figure either, but a powerful and multi-aspected deity associated with abundance, sexuality, fertility, wild creatures, and plenty—all things connected with life and life energies. If the darkness of the Underworld and its potentially beneficent deity were associated with the place of origin—a womb or cauldron where life, plenty, and fertility were created and distributed—we can see why darkness (and the dark half of the year) would be considered mat. Perhaps this perception and characterization, and the placement of mat months on either side of it, described what the dark half in fact was considered to be, as well as what it was hoped it could be.

The light half of the year, while not necessarily anm in all ways, could be a time of more scarcity (in some ways) than the dark half. In fact, great rituals of propitiation and protection took place at Beltaine. It was not simply a fun, frolicsome holiday concerned with greenery, flowers, and casual sex. While folkloric accounts describe ceremonies that included fires, dancing, and feasting, the holiday also had a very serious aspect. Drought, hail, and disease could do harm to crops, animals, and people, and survival was not yet guaranteed. For this reason, somber rites of propitiation and protection took place at Beltaine. These occurred even in the last century in some areas. The lighting of fires was probably *not* associated with Sun worship, as is commonly supposed, but utilized the long-revered element of fire to invoke the powers of protection, purification, and fertility.

What about the different patterns of light and dark represented in the monthly and yearly cycles of the Coligny Calendar? While Samain began (and was included in) the dark half of the year, it may be incorrect to associate this time of year with waning or diminishing properties.[41] It was the beginning of the New Year and, as such, would reasonably be associated with waxing characteristics. From the dark point of creation, life energies began to increase and grow. Beltaine, although outwardly embodying sunshine and joy, was actually the beginning of the waning period, when seasonal activities and energies progressed toward the end of the year. As Samain starts the new yearly cycle, so the new Moon starts the new monthly cycle. The important concept here is the significance of the turning point, and the driving force behind it has to do with creation, movement, and becoming, as seen in Table 4.

The patterns and symbolism associated with the reliable and life-affirming cycles of the Moon demonstrate the concept of life or light arising from a point of darkness, which is the place of creation. This idea can be expressed ritually, observed, and commemorated in various man-made systems of time measurement, which, of course, have really been cocreated with nature. As we can see in the Coligny Calendar, the new Moon was of great significance in Celtic time reckoning. We can envision a system of correspondence similar to that expressed in Table 5 and 6 as having formed part of some native Celtic systems of belief and perception.

However they were conceived of or expressed in various parts of the Celtic world, great significance was attached to these liminal points in time and space. The turning points were "neither this nor that," and therefore contained great power and potential for blessings or misfortune. They may have been considered independent points in time and, as such, believed to contain the whole of existence within themselves.[41] This may well have formed part of the religious ideology and symbolism associated with the rituals that took place at these times. As these points in space and time were closer to the Otherworld, communication and

Table 4. The Seasonal Turning Points, Their Symbolism, and the Phases of the Moon

TURNING POINTS	SYMBOLISM	MOON PHASE
Samain	Death and turning point but also the point of creation of light/life, followed by waxing/increasing energies	New Moon
Beltaine	Fullness of light, but also the start of a waning period of light/life and returning movement toward the darkness	Full Moon

Table 5. Lunar Calendar Associations

FESTIVAL	SEASON	DAY	MOON
Imbolc	Spring	Morning	Waxing
Beltaine	Summer	Afternoon	Full
Lugnasad	Autumn	Evening	Waning
Samain	Winter	Night	Dark/New Moon

Table 6. Lunar Directions, Attributes, and Colors

FESTIVAL	DIRECTION & ATTRIBUTE	COLOR	SEASON	LUNAR PHASE
Samain	North— Battle	Black	Night/ Winter	Void/New Moon
Imbolc	East— Prosperity	Purple (red)	Morning/ Spring	Waxing Moon
Beltaine	South— Music	White	Afternoon/ Summer	Full Moon
Lugnasad	West— Learning	Dun (yellow)	Evening/ Autumn	Waning Moon

interactions between the worlds were possible, and special events and rituals took place. Divination was performed, offerings were made, and blessings were sought, and from that point on, a new cycle could begin.[42]

The Daughter of the Twelve Moons

In a number of early European cultures, the Moon was used to ascertain when certain religious holidays were held. In many cases, the new Moon closest to the time of the holiday or feast day determined when its rites and celebrations took place. Bede mentions that, in early English tradition, the new Moon nearest the Winter Solstice was known as *Módranicht*, Mother's Night. This holiday was called *Dísablot* in Old Norse tradition, Offering to the Goddesses. Two weeks later, *Géol* or *Jól* (modern Yule) was held, a high feast day held at the first full Moon after the Winter Solstice. Many traditions became associated with the twelve nights between this new Moon and full Moon.[43]

Did the new Moon play any role in determining when Celtic assemblies were held? Gustav Lehmacher makes some interesting observations that may indicate that a similar system was used in Celtic society. He points out that the modern Irish names for the days of the week all derive from Latin, except one: *An Luan* (Monday). Despite its appearance, the word does not come from the Latin word for Moon *luna*, (as in Latin, *dies lunae*, or French *lundi*), but from Old Irish *lón*, a word derived from Old Celtic *louknos*, meaning "light, brightness, or glow." [44]

In early Irish sources, there are several references that seem to connect Monday with the Feast of Beltaine. The people of Partholón (early mythical invaders of Ireland) land on a Tuesday, which is said to be the "fourteenth of the month" (perhaps the full Moon).[45] They later perish due to a plague on "the calends of May," which "came upon them on a Monday."[46] Indeed, the Irish sometimes refer to May first as *Luan Lae Bealtaine*, "the Luan of Mayday." What is the significance of this phrase?

A hint may be found in a Scottish Gaelic folktale, recorded from the storytelling of Coinneach MacLeoid, in which the Moon is mentioned in association with swans:

> Once there were two "swan princesses," both of whom were so beautiful that it was impossible to say which was the lovelier, even when they were side by side. Eventually, one of the princesses laid a spell upon the other, so that she would be forever going "from height to height in the shape of a bird, graceful over the sea but awkward over the land, sweet-voiced under the moon, but dumb and silent under the sun." To this day, it is said, the swan is still thus enchanted.[47]

This story may have served to explain natural characteristics of the swan, but it also seems to suggest an association between the swan and the night sky. The old people evidently explained that during the dark period of the Moon, the swan was "dusky hued," which may allude to a connection between the swan and the actual light of the Moon. Significantly, elsewhere in the tale the swan is referred to as the Daughter of the Twelve Moons, which suggests that there were twelve "moons" (or lunar months) in all. Lehmacher proposes that this is the significance of the word *luan*. It may not have referred to the Moon *per se*, but to the lunar month or cycle (or more specifically, to its beginning).

If this is the case, it may be that each lunar month was referred to as, and started with, a luan, which referred to the brightness of the returning new Moon. Hence, the Luan of Beltaine was the new Moon that began the month in which Beltaine took place, or which occurred closest to the time at which Beltaine festivities should be held. If this is the case, Samain would have been held on or near a new Moon as well. The four Celtic holidays are currently held on the first of the month (November, February, May, and August), but it may be that they originally took place on the old "first of the month," which, in lunar terms, would have been the new Moon.

This supposition is borne out in a number of medieval and more recent folkloric accounts, which mention the early pagan feast days. In the *Dindshenchas* we find the phrase *día lúain Loga* ("the day of the lúan of Lug"). This refers to the festival of Lugnasad and means "the first day of the lunar month dedicated to Lug."[48] In Old Irish, the word *lúan* means "radiance" or "light" as well as "moon." Many centuries later, in areas of Ireland and Scotland, the ritual period of Lugnasad was associated with the period of a fortnight (two weeks), which suggests the lunar reckoning originally used to celebrate Lugnasad (its ritual period calculated in conjunction with a phase of the Moon).[49] In Cornwall, the Fair of Morvah, a very interesting Lugnasad survival, was held on the Sunday closest to August 1 and was believed to celebrate a wedding, which had taken place in ancient times "on the first day of the harvest Moon." The new Moon is a much more likely candidate than the full Moon for this event, as the sap of plants was believed to be on the increase during the waxing of the Moon (and hence gathering or harvesting should be done before the full Moon). Irish popular belief held that the Moon's waxing period was more propitious than its waning period.[50] In addition, in Scottish folk tradition it was customary for marriages to take place at the new Moon.[51]

The luan of Mayday was the new Moon of Beltaine and, because of the word *lon*'s association with the Moon (the object itself, and the light of the new Moon), it formed the basis for the native Irish word for Monday (a day that, in Latin and Anglo-Saxon traditions, was the day of the Moon).

What of the Moon and the symbolism associated with the swan? In Irish myth and legend, various people (mortal or divine) are transformed into swan form. In many cases, there are two swans, symbolizing two lovers, a tradition that may have its origin in the fact that swans mate for life. In addition, there is a symbolic connection between these nocturnal "flights" and meetings of lovers that take place under the light of the Moon. Other waterbirds (including swans) appear in various tales as women who have been changed into bird form.[53] In many cases, these transformations take place around the time of Samain. We can perceive a series of related images linking swans and waterbirds with women, water, and the lunar cycle, as well as with transformations that occur during liminal periods of time, such as Samain, Beltaine, and the new Moon.

☾   ☾   ☾

Meditations and Exercises

Try these interesting techniques for putting yourself in touch with the symbolic power of numbers and the Moon.

1) Create a lunar calendar based on your observations of nature. Even if you live in the city, you can record which birds stay year round and which migrate, note which plants bloom along the streets, highways, or in urban parks, and watch the stars pass through the heavens. In making your calendar, divide the year into lunar months and name these based on natural events or other symbolic or spiritual associations (Frost Moon, Bud Moon, Samain Moon, etc.). Observe weather patterns, plants, trees, flowers, animals, stars, planets, and winds. Devise a method to keep the lunar year aligned with the solar year, adding the appropriate number of days to the calendar each year (at the end, the middle, or interspersed as sacred intercalary days).

2) Meditate on the significance of numbers as they occur in your daily life, and their more esoteric symbolism. Do you have any preconceptions or intuitive feelings about the significance of certain numbers? Spend some time thinking about the quality, symbolism, and inherent power of various numbers, and see if you can come up with ways to incorporate them into your mundane or magical activities. Don't be overly rigid or superstitious in the use or application of numbers, but see which patterns arise and flow naturally. Work with numbers associated with the Moon and keep a record of your ideas and revelations.

3) Observe the cycles of the stars as they appear in your area. In the past, people from many cultures observed and named the shapes and symbols they perceived in the patterns of the stars. Modern constellations derive from Greek, Roman, and even Middle Eastern perceptions, but there are other options to choose from. You can create your own "zodiac" by exploring the shapes created by the stars of the night sky. Take into account the cycles of nature, birds and animals, and sacred or mythological figures or symbols, and see what shapes you can perceive in the stars. Note their relationship to each other and to the Moon.

4) Create your own ritual calendar, using the patterns and cycles of the natural world as a guide. This can be divided into two, three, four, or more sections, and may be lunar and/or solar. Will there be propitious or unpropitious days, cycles, or seasons? Feast days, sacred seasons or periods of time, lunar months, and smaller internal units may all figure in your system. Give appropriate names to these periods of time based on elements of nature, deities, or seasonal or other sacred symbolism. Include the ancient seasonal customs of your spiritual or biological ancestors, or devise modern ways to celebrate and express these ancient ideas. Meditate on the significance and flow of the seasons, and remember to show respect for the historical origins of things and for the ancestors.

5) Take some time to learn about swans and other waterbirds and see what significance they may hold for you. Do you feel that their connection with the sky and water suggests a connection with the Moon? There are a number of interesting Celtic myths involving swans, as well as legends in which women are transformed into cranes. Read some of these tales and then go out into nature and spend time in the presence of these wonderful birds. Swans and waterbirds often gather and feed in ponds and lakes (even in urban settings). See what these sacred creatures have to teach you. Paint or draw images of the birds or write poetry inspired by their symbolism and your experiences with them.

6) The tables in this chapter suggest a correlation between the turning points of the year, the four directions and their attributes, times of the day, and phases of the Moon. How do you feel about this set of correspondences? Does it resonate well for you or does it seem forced or artificial? Using your intuition and experience, take some time to reflect on these cycles to ascertain the flow of energies that formed these patterns and associations. This work will deepen your awareness of the meaning of each of the individual turning points. If you do find a naturalness or integrity in this system, it can serve as an excellent basis for seasonal or monthly rituals or other magical workings.

HORNED GODS AND ENCHANTED BIRDS

LUNAR SYMBOLISM IN CELTIC ART

*The crane of Inis Geidh has been alone
from the beginning of the world,
without any other crane with her.*

—NENNIUS

Art and myth are often described as reflections of the inner beliefs and concerns of a culture. We have seen that the Moon played an important role in the Celtic perception and measurement of time, in legends and beliefs concerned with creation, and in the observance of sacred festivals and holy days. What role does it play in the artwork of the Celts? Crescent Moon shapes or other forms that may represent the Moon are rare in Celtic art. However, among the striking and highly stylized portrayals of human and animal forms and wonderful interweaving curvilinear designs, some examples do exist.

A gold coin commemorating the reign of Tasciovanus, king of the British tribe known as the Catuvellauni, features a horse on one side and a number of abstract designs on the other, including several crescent Moon shapes.[1] A coin of the Carnutes (the Celtic tribe in whose territory the Gaulish Druids held their annual gathering) depicts a human head with long wavy hair, possibly female. A series of dots or circular shapes seems to ornament the hair, as does a small crescent shape near the left side of the coin.[2] A pair of bronze horse bits from 1st-century B.C.E. Britain are decorated with disks and circles, as well as a crescent Moon.[3] A gold-colored repoussé bowl from Switzerland portrays a ring of hornless deer above whom appears an alternating pattern of circular and crescent shapes, perhaps representing the Sun and the Moon.[4] In addition, a sandstone pillar from Germany, dated to between the 4th and 3rd centuries B.C.E., is decorated with beautiful curvilinear patterns, including a number of crescent-Moon shapes.[5]

More abstract crescent shapes appear on a number of other artifacts. The ornamentation on a 2nd-century B.C.E. bronze Irish scabbard plate from Lisnacrogher (County Antrim) includes a fabulous curvilinear pattern that seems to outline a series of elaborate crescent designs.[6] A black graphite polished pottery dish from Bavaria features a central figure that may be a Sun symbol surrounded by seven half circles, which could represent the Moon.[7] Decorative motifs found on a Hungarian pot and an Austrian bronze flask (both dating to the 4th century B.C.E.) incorporate a number of interesting and abstract designs that appear to include a variety of crescent shapes.[8]

Clearer evidence of lunar symbolism appears during the Romano-Celtic era, probably due to the influence of Classical art forms and lunar symbolism associated with the goddess Diana. A silver gilt lunar-shaped pendant from the sacred spring at Aquae Sulis (modern Bath) is thought to have formed part of a scepter or other liturgical regalia worn or used by a priest (although it could also have been an offering).[9] The bronze head of a British celestial deity was decorated with rays of light that seem to emanate from it, above which is an upturned crescent.[10] A Romano-Celtic clay horse from Belgium adorned with a Moon-shaped pendant and a number of gold and silver solar pendants from Wales and Scotland found in connection with lunar amulets also date from this period.[11]

Perhaps the most unique representation of the Moon comes from the artwork of the Picts. These Celtic peoples inhabited Scotland between 300 C.E. (or earlier) and 900 C.E. They are known for their distinctive art style, which portrayed animals, birds, and fish as well as more abstract designs. Pictish art was used to decorate a variety of objects, including silver jewelry, and was also engraved on standing stones. One abstract design, known as the crescent and V-rod, is comprised of a crescent-Moon shape, sometimes ornamented with curvilinear patterns, augmented by a V-shaped double arrow symbol.[12]

While it is not entirely certain what meaning or message lies behind the Pictish artforms, it is possible that animal symbols were associated with particular tribes and the other designs with important members or classes of society, or other significant concepts associated with Pictish culture or religion. In any case, the crescent and V-rod is often considered one of the most representative and fascinating examples of Pictish expressions.

Celtic Deities of Sun, Moon, and Sky

The Moon appears to play some role in the artwork of the Celts. While images of the Moon are not frequently encountered (except among the Picts), they are not necessarily less common than representations of the Sun, the stars, or other celestial phenomena. In terms of religious iconography, the early veneration of the sky and the Sun among the Celts is well-attested. Evidence pertaining to the worship of the Moon is much more difficult to identify. There are a number of Celtic deities who display celestial aspects or attributes, which makes it all the more surprising that so little material pertaining to lunar deities has survived. Indeed, the existence of well-represented solar and celestial cults suggests that it is possible that deities associated with the Moon were also venerated. The best-known celestial gods of the British and Continental Celts include:

1) Taranis: A Gaulish deity (possibly also venerated in the British Isles) whose name means The Thunderer. He is sometimes shown with a weapon or lightning symbol, a spoked wheel, and an oak (symbols frequently associated with sky gods).[13]

2) Loucetius: A British deity whose name means Brightness or Lightning, invoked at Bath along with Nemetona (Goddess of the Sacred Grove). This divine couple is also known in Gaul, where they were probably invoked for healing purposes.[14]

3) Nodons/Nodens: A British god whose name means either He Who Bestows Wealth or Cloud-Maker. His well-attested cult was primarily focused on his temple located on the banks of the Severn (Lydney Park). He was invoked as a god of healing, as images of dogs, the Sun, and water abound at the site. His name is cognate with that of Nuadu Argatlám, an early king of the Tuatha Dé Danann. Nuadu was a champion and seer also regarded as an ancestral figure of the Irish (much as Dis Pater was by the Gaulish Celts). He received a silver arm after losing his in battle, and his magical sword was one of the treasures of the gods of Ireland.[15] Some see a conceptual continuity between the sword of Nuadu and the Sword of Light found in much later Scottish and Irish folktales.

4) Belenus: A widely worshipped deity whose name means Shining or Bright or Brilliant One. Inscriptions on altars dedicated to Belenus have been found in northern Italy, Gaul, and the British Isles. There is a well-documented association in Celtic tradition that links the Sun with healing properties. Images of Sun wheels are frequently found at Celtic healing springs. Belenus himself was often invoked at healing wells, and this (along with the meaning of his name) suggests that he was a deity who may have had solar attributes.[16]

5) Lug/Lugus/Lleu: A widely worshipped deity or god-type, known in Ireland as Lug, in Britain and Gaul as Lugus, and in later Welsh tradition as Lleu. Lugus' name is commemorated in Lugdunum (modern Lyon) and Luguvalium (Carlisle in Britain). The Irish deity Lug was called Samildánach (Many-Skilled) and is portrayed as a multitalented young warrior, magician, and poet. In the *Mabinogi*, Lleu Llaw Gyffes (Bright One of the Skillful Hand) is transformed into an eagle, residing for a period of time in the top of an oak tree. The eagle and the oak are symbols of a solar or celestial deity.[17]

Certain female deities also display solar or celestial aspects. The British goddess Sulis was invoked and commemorated at the healing springs at Aquae Sulis. Her name is associated with a Celtic word for the Sun, and molds for making amulets (some of which resemble a solar wheel) were found at her sanctuary.[18] Many women seem to have patronized the Romano-Celtic temple, perhaps seeking help with childbearing disorders (votive images of breasts were found at the site). A likeness of the Roman Moon goddess Luna (a figure associated with women and fertility) was also found at the shrine.[19]

In Roman Britain, as well as on the Continent, there are numerous images of divine females known as the *Matronae* (Divine Mothers). These may appear in single, double, or triple form, and seem to have been primarily concerned with fertility and abundance. Clay figures of the single goddess are frequently shown nursing babies, and some of these wear lunar amulets around their necks (probably influenced by imagery associated with the goddess Diana, who assisted women in childbirth).[20]

The archetypal Celtic goddess of sovereignty, associated with horses, the land, abundance, and prophecy, may also be connected with solar imagery. There are a number of well-known manifestations of this figure: the Welsh Rhiannon (Divine Queen), the widely invoked Gaulish, British, and Continental goddess Epona (Divine Horse Goddess), and the Irish horse goddess Macha (whose nickname was Grían, Sun).[21] In Irish sources, the goddess of sovereignty presents a golden cup or goblet of wine or red ale to the intended king, which some have interpreted as a symbol of the Sun.[22] It is interesting to note that, while two of the Old Irish words for the Moon are neuter (*ésca*, later masculine, and *ré*, later both masculine and feminine), the commonly used word *gelach* is feminine. In addition, *grían*, the Old Irish word for Sun, is also feminine.[23]

With all the extant evidence pertaining to celestial and solar deities, it seems strange that there is such scant testimony concerning the existence of lunar-related gods or goddesses. Archaeological evidence has shown that sacred space in Ireland, Britain, and Gaul was focused on a sacred central point, often incorporating a pit or shaft into which objects were placed as offerings to the Underworld deities. Offerings were also made in pools, lakes, springs, and peat bogs, which may support a focus on the Underworld and the deities associated with it.[24] As we have seen, Underworld gods may be connected with darkness or night. Caesar's comparison of a Gaulish ancestral god with the Roman Dis Pater (the counterpart of the Greek god Pluto) is interesting as Dis occupied only a minor place in the Roman pantheon. This suggests that the attributes of the Gaulish deity were quite well defined. In his book on Gaulish religion, Jean Louis Brunaux even goes as far as to say that the Gaulish deity was in fact a god of night.[25]

There is also a female figure associated with the night sky. This is the goddess Sirona, a widely worshipped deity venerated at thermal healing sanctuaries in eastern Gaul, Brittany, Hungary, and the Rhineland. She seems to have been a goddess of healing, as she was sometimes paired with native Celtic versions of Apollo (who displays solar and healing aspects), as well as with Grannus, Belenus, and other potentially solar-aspected Celtic gods. Clay figurines found at Sirona's shrines sometimes portray the seated goddess accompanied by a lap dog (thought to be a symbol of healing). At other locations, imagery associated with the goddess includes grain, fruit, and snakes, probably symbolizing abundance and regeneration.[26] Sirona was sometimes worshipped on her own without a consort, suggesting that she was originally an independent deity worshipped in her own right prior to the Roman era. The name of this powerful, versatile, and widely worshipped goddess, a divine figure who was venerated throughout Celtic Europe, is particularly enlightening; it is related to a word meaning "star" and may therefore be translated as Divine Star Goddess.

If the Celts venerated gods and goddesses associated with the sky, the Sun, thunder and lightning, the clouds, and the stars, they must also have recognized deities associated with the Moon.[27] As the divine was considered manifest in all aspects of the natural world, it is reasonable to assume that the numinous was perceived in and expressed by the image of the Moon (as well as better-documented elements of the natural world). In light of these facts, I suggest that it is possible that the Moon was perceived as a female divinity, much as the Sun and the stars were venerated through the medium, symbol, and divine character of goddesses such as Sulis, Macha, and Sirona.[28]

The Moon in Irish Myths and Legends

What of the other spiritual and cultural mirror of society, the myths and legends associated with a particular era or people? The Moon does make an appearance in the body of myths, tales, and pseudo-historical texts attributed to the early Irish period. One of the most intriguing early Irish texts is *Lebor Gabála Érenn* (literally, The Book of the Taking of Ireland, more commonly referred to as The Book of Invasions). Some regard the text as a vast repository of pagan lore, while others maintain that it is primarily influenced by and derived from Christian sources. A more balanced and widely accepted view is that this medieval pseudo-historical document draws on elements of pagan Irish as well as Christian belief, with a hearty helping of classically influenced sources and other aspects of medieval European learned traditions.

One section of the text provides genealogical information pertaining to the Tuatha Dé Danann (The People of the Goddess Danu), the old gods and goddesses of Ireland. It mentions three grandsons of the Dagda who were best known as the consorts and husbands of Ériu, Banba, and Fotla, the eponymous goddesses of the land of Ireland. These were Mac Greine (Son of Sun), Mac Cuill (Son of Hazel), and Mac Cecht (Son of Plough). One passage describes the three gods as follows:

> The three sons of Cermat, son of the Dagda were Mac Cuill, Mac Cecht,
>   Mac Greine.
> Setheor was the name of Mac Cuill, and the sea was his god;
> Tetheor was the name of Mac Cecht, and the air was his god,
> with its luminaries, the moon and the sun;
> Cetheor was the name of Mac Grene [sic], and the earth was his god.[29]

Each of the three figures is associated with an aspect of the native Irish perception of a triune cosmos, which was comprised of three worlds or realms associated with Earth, Sky, and Sea/Underworld. Here Mac Greine (Son of Sun) is not directly associated with his namesake, which seems to form part of the sky realm of his brother Mac Cecht, along with its other important luminary, the Moon.

A text sometimes associated with *Lebor Gabála* is *The Roll of the Kings,* an annal compiled to record various events (battles, plagues, births, etc.) that were supposed to have taken place during the reign of various early Irish kings. These include a number of eclectic and fantastical happenings, such as those associated with *Fiachu Finscothach* ("There were flowers of wine in his reign, which they used to press in glass vats") or *Fiachu Findoiches* ("All the cattle of Ireland had white heads in his reign"). A number of celestial events are recorded in these annals. In the time of Flann mac Máel-Sechlainn, "two suns were seen to run together in one day," while during the reign of Conglach mac Máeil-Mithig, "two fiery columns appeared, a week before Samain, which illuminated the whole world." The Moon is mentioned twice, once during the reign of Finnachta Fledach, when "the moon was turned to blood as a portent," and once during that of Aed Oirdnide, when it was "coloured like blood" (*esca ar dath no fola*).[30] Classical accounts mention the reaction of a Gaulish army to an eclipse of the Moon, and it may be that the Moon's coloring was regarded as a significant omen or portent.

The Moon is also mentioned in the Middle Irish text *Accalam na Senórach* (Tales of the Elders of Ireland). In this text, St. Patrick asks Cailte about the myths or origin legends associated with various people, places, and things. When asked about the origin of two famous waves (Tonn Cliodna and Tonn Téite), Cailte provides the appropriate legend, during which he describes Cíabán, a warrior of Finn's retinue:

> Such was that warrior that, as the moon in her great fifteenth surpasses
>   the stars of heaven,
> That warrior, in his form and shape, surpassed the sons of the king and
>   chieftains of this world.[31]

King Conchobor is described in a similar fashion in *The Intoxication of the Ulstermen:*

A broad-eyed, royal, gigantic warrior . . . in the middle.
Comparable to a moon in its great fifteenth was his countenance,
his visage and his face.[32]

At one point in the *Accalam*, it is Cailte who poses a question to Patrick: "What year is there in which there is a month without a moon, a moon without a month, and a month that contains three moons?" Patrick replies:

The quartile year that occurs between two millenia, one preceding and one following.

The first month of that year is the one without a moon, but the following month has a moon, (but it is not a month in this instance because of the moon supporting it).

The third month contains three moons:

the first-moon of the first month that we counted in dealing with the question before us,

and the first-moon of the quarter before us of the same month that passed,

and the third moon is the moon of the Kalends of the actual era of that month.[33]

Rather than engaging in a lengthy discussion of this complicated passage, suffice it to say that it is evident the medieval Irish displayed a healthy interest in and knowledge of lunar reckoning and observation. Cailte goes on to ask Patrick, "When is the quartile year that you spoke to me of?" "Last night was its first night," said Patrick. "And when does the month come that contains the three moons?" "It begins tomorrow evening," said Patrick, "and the day following."[34] This last statement alludes to the previously mentioned belief that the day began with the night that preceded it.

References to lunar phenomena are also found in the early Irish tale *Cath Maige Tuired* (The Battle of Moytura). In one scene, the god Lug has arrived at the court of Tara and seeks permission to enter the hall. He mentions in turn his many skills (builder, smith, champion, harper, warrior, poet, sorcerer, physician, cupbearer, and metalworker), but the gods already possess people skilled in these areas. When Lug points out that he is the master of *all* of these skills (hence, his epithet *Samildánach*, Many-Skilled), he is permitted to enter. Perceiving Lug's many powers, King Núadu wonders if the newcomer might help the Tuatha Dé Danann free themselves from the oppression of the Fomoire.[35]

A council is held and, as a result, Núadu exchanges seats with Lug. The text states, "So *Samildánach* [Lug] went to the king's seat, and the king arose before him until thirteen days had passed." On the next day, Lug, the Dagda, and Ogma, along with the smith god Goibhniu and the divine physician Dian Cecht, began a secret conference on Grellach Dollaid. The secret conference lasted for a year, "so that Grellach Dollaid is called the *Amrún* (Great Secret or Plan) of the Men of the Goddess [Danu].”[36]

Núadu, whose name may mean Cloud-Maker (suggesting a celestial association) "arose before" Lug (who also may have a solar or celestial aspect) for thirteen days. On the fourteenth day, a great gathering took place that lasted for a year. One has to wonder if the thirteen days that preceded the start of the conference had some connection with lunar time reckoning, perhaps indicating a sacred or auspicious period of time (half a lunar cycle) that preceded the start of the next yearly cycle. In the Coligny Calendar, time is reckoned by half-months. Prior to the start of each half-year (or "year" of twelve half-months, at Samonios and Giamonios), an intercalary month was inserted.[37]

Lug, a newcomer to the court of Núadu, occupies the seat of precedence for thirteen days. Perhaps his arrival signified the appearance of the new Moon, whose waxing powers continued unabated until the full Moon on the fourteenth day, when the sacred conference began. Conversely, this radiant god may be associated with the light of the full Moon, whose power lasted for thirteen more days. At the end of that time, the void Moon occurred, heralding the start of the next yearly cycle as mentionend in the tale, as well as making way for the new Moon. This is all highly conjectural, of course, and the thirteen or fourteen days may simply have referred to a hallowed or auspicious period of time associated with status, divinity, or another socially relevant concept.[38]

Finally, one of the most interesting mythological settings in which lunar symbolism occurs is a tale that concerns a sacred object belonging to Manannán mac Lir (a god associated with the sea). Two women, Aoife and Iuchra, were in love with the same man. Iuchra became jealous and placed an enchantment upon Aoife so that she appeared in the form of a crane, so to remain for 200 years, "in the noble house of Manannán." As she placed her spell upon Aoife, Iuchra says to her:

> You shall always be in that house with everyone mocking you,
> a crane that does not visit every land; you shall not reach any land.[39]

The curse may signify that Aoife was fated to fly through the air without reaching any land for rest (similar to the curse landed upon Étain, who was buffeted about in the shape of a scarlet fly, unable to reach land or rest for many years). It may also be that she is meant to dwell in the house of the sea god for 200 years, unable to fly about (or land), not able to properly exist as a crane. Whatever the exact meaning, Aoife endures her fate. Upon her death, Manannán made a bag of the bird's skin, which was known thereafter as the "crane bag." It was described as a "treasure of power with many virtues," a vessel into which Manannán put "every precious thing he had" (including his shirt and knife, a belt belonging to Goibhniu, and several other rare and valuable objects).[40]

One fascinating detail pertaining to the crane bag is found in this description of the bag and its association with the tides and the sea:

When the sea was full, its treasures were visible in its middle;
When the fierce sea was in ebb, the crane-bag in turn was empty.[41]

What is the significance of this passage? The crane bag is clearly connected with the sea as it is a possession of the sea god. In addition (and on a more mundane level), cranes are waterbirds. The crane bag itself is associated with the sea in the above description, in particular with the tide. The tide, of course, is controlled by the Moon. Thus, in effect, it is the Moon that controls the visibility of the contents of the crane bag. Perhaps the crane bag represents some aspect of the sea itself, or supernatural elements that existed beneath the waves? A woman transformed into the shape of a bird who lives in the house of the sea god and flies through the skies without reaching land could certainly be interpreted as symbolizing the movement of the Moon. But what does the crane represent? How was this creature perceived by the Celts, and why was it associated with transformed or shape-shifting women?

Transforming Women and Enchanted Birds

The crane has a number of interesting attributes. Early artifacts show that, in some cases, it was associated with war or hostility. This connection is corroborated in later legendary sources. The Irish god Midir owned three hostile cranes that discouraged travelers from stopping at his dwelling and were able to deprive warriors of their courage and their will to fight. The crane also displays other attributes. Along with a variety of aquatic birds, it was associated with healing springs and therapeutic thermal waters. Many birds also served as symbols of divinity or as servants and messengers of the gods.[42]

In later Scottish and Irish folktales and legends, the crane is almost always associated with shape-shifting and transformation, most frequently with transformed women. A version of the story of Aoife mentioned above was preserved in a ballad in which Oisín encounters a woman called Miadhach who is in crane form and asks to hear her story. Miadhach (whose name means Honorable, Dignified, Noble) tells Oisín that she and her foster sister were in love with the same man. As a result of her unwillingness to give him up, she was transformed into the shape of a crane for 295 years.[43]

Cranes and supernatural women appear in several stories associated with Finn mac Cumaill. When he was a child, Finn was saved from falling over a cliff by his grandmother, who was transformed into a crane. In the tale of *The Hag of the Temple,* Finn also encounters enchanted cranes. Here, an old woman (Cailleach an Teampuill) had four warrior sons who were transformed into the shape of cranes.

They could only be returned to human form if they received a drop of blood from the skull of the legendary Connra Bull, which was owned by the Cailleach Bhéara.

A form of Irish magic existed called *corrguineacht* that seems to have had some connection with crane symbolism (*corr* means "crane" in Old Irish). The poet or magician performing the rite stood on one leg (much like a crane), using one hand and closing one eye to perform a type of poetic curse or satire known as *glam dicinn*.[44] In *The Battle of Moytura*, several *corrgunechai* (sorcerers) assisted the Tuatha Dé Danann in battle. They refer to the power of their craft, which will deprive the opposing warriors of two-thirds of their strength (reminiscent of the powers attributed to Midir's cranes).[45] As with the sons of the Cailleach an Teampuill, this story also demonstrates a connection between war (or warriors) and cranes.

In early times, the crane was venerated for its association with healing, therapeutic springs and waters, shape-shifting and transformation, and power in battle. As time went on, it seems to have developed an air of mystery, even inspiring a certain amount of fear or dislike. Its flesh was taboo in early Ireland. Modern folk tradition holds that it had the power to bring death to anyone who ate it. In the eastern part of Scotland, it was believed that certain people could be done away with instantly by shaking a bridle at them and saying, "Raven's flesh and crane's flesh come out thy way." In addition, a rite existed in the Highlands that could be used to bring about the death of someone who had lived too long or was in some other way unwanted. Those who wanted to perform the ceremony yelled through the keyhole of the room in which the person lay, saying: "Will you come or will you go? Or will you eat the flesh of cranes?"[46]

Eventually, cranes also seem to become associated with women who were considered mean or unpleasant. St. Columba evidently transformed two women who refused to show him reverence or respect into cranes. Verses collected from Scottish oral tradition mention that the armor of Columba protected against fairy arrows as well as the screeching or gnawing of cranes. A disagreeable Scottish woman, the daughter of MacDougall of Lorne, was given three nicknames associated with cranes: The Black-Bottomed Crane; Parsimony, the Evil Black Crane; and The MacDougall Crane. As late as 1955, a child on the Isle of Skye was warned against going into a certain room, being threatened with the possibility that the *corra-ghritheach* was there.[47]

In addition, there are a number of references in Scottish tradition to "three crooked cranes" and "three gnawing cranes." Perhaps these refer to concepts similar to those embodied in descriptions of the three hostile cranes of Midir. A trio of cranes is also found on a Gaulish stone carving whose inscription reads *Tarvos Trigaranus*, The Bull with the Three Cranes. It depicts a bull standing beneath a willow tree (often associated with water) along with three cranes. Similar imagery is found on another Gaulish relief, which portrays the head of a bull, three large aquatic birds, and (on another side of the monument) the figure of a woman. Two additional reliefs depict a great crane speaking into the ears of a female head. The association with women is emphasized in a bronze figurine of a triple-horned bull with the busts of three female figures on its back.[48]

Perhaps these images are meant to express elements of an early tradition concerning three goddesses associated with cranes, not unlike the three *Mórrigna* (Mórrigan, Macha, and Nemain), who were associated with ravens. Both the crane and the raven were connected with magic, shape-shifting, transformation, battle, and death. In addition, the flesh of both creatures is mentioned in the Scottish folk rite mentioned above. Ravens play a prominent role in Norse mythology, where they are also associated with war and the slain.[49] Odin had two ravens that flew about the world from dawn to daybreak. At that time, they returned to perch on the god's shoulders to speak into his ears, passing on information concerning all they had seen.[50] Perhaps a similar idea is expressed in the image of the crane that speaks into the ears of the female figure. If so, there may be an additional connection with wisdom or prophecy (an attribute shared by the raven in Celtic contexts).

Indeed, the whole scenario is reminiscent of that described in a previous chapter concerning the degradation of the raven goddesses. The original respect shown to this trio of divine crane women, who were symbolically or ideologically connected with healing, transformation, and magic, as well as warfare, shape-shifting, and death, may have degenerated into a superstitious dislike and fear of the crane, and its subsequent association with mean or unpleasant women.[51]

The early veneration and supplication of these goddesses at healing springs (perhaps the source of the willow-tree iconography), the prayers and offerings that may have been made for assistance in battle (where life is supported through strength and victory), and the taboo on eating the flesh of the crane (the sacred animal of these goddesses) all attest to the original status of these figures, as well as to the sanctity afforded the creature that served as their symbol or helper. The imitation of the crane's stance in a form of magic that could be used for either beneficent or malign purposes would have placed it in a liminal and somewhat shaky position. Over time, its primal connection with gods and divinities shifted to a more shadowy association with supernatural characters, and ultimately with disliked or mistrusted people. From healing goddess to harpy; from war goddess to witch. There is one element, however, that has not yet been explored. What of the bull depicted with the three cranes or three divine women?

The Mountain of the Horned One

The bull has been venerated in Celtic tradition since earliest times. It symbolized wealth, fertility, and power. The strength, ferocity, and virility of the bull were greatly admired, and bulls were sometimes offered as great sacrifices. In the early

Irish ceremony known as the *tarbh-fheis* ("bull feast"), bulls were used to help decide the election of the next king. Bulls were also associated with healing shrines and celestial deities—perhaps one thread of the overall pattern in which cranes and bulls were connected.[52] Numerous figures of three-horned bulls exist, as well as images of bull-horned gods. We also have evidence of various related divine titles, such as Deiotaurus (Divine Bull) and Donnotaurus (Lordly Bull), a name resembling that of the great bull known as the Donn from the great Irish epic *Táin Bó Cuailgne*.[53]

There were also several female deities associated with cattle. The name of the goddess Boand, the eponymous spirit or personification of the River Boyne, may derive from *bó* ("cow") and *find* ("bright, white, or blessed"), giving She of the White Cattle or perhaps White or Blessed Cow [Goddess]. On the Continent, the goddess Damona (Great or Divine Cow) was venerated at a number of healing springs, often surrounded by imagery associated with fertility (ears of grain) and regeneration (serpents).[54] Later, fairy cattle are featured in both Irish and Scottish folk contexts. Scottish tradition mentions supernatural water bulls that emerge from bodies of water to mate with and bestow blessings upon the human herds. Interestingly, all three of these examples demonstrate a connection between cattle and water or fertility.

The horns of bulls make an appearance in the iconography of the horned or antlered god, a deity associated with fertility, abundance, hunting, animals, and the Underworld. In some cases, the horned god is portrayed as a warrior, symbolizing the protection of the people, which ensured the preservation and continuation of life. There is great emphasis on animal horns in many Celtic contexts (whether bull, stag, or ram), manifesting in images of composite supernatural animals, such as birds with horns or birds combined with horned beasts.[55] These may reflect aspects of the religious concepts embodied in artwork in which bulls are depicted in association with birds.

How and why are these creatures connected? One possibility is that both the crane and the bull exhibit a relationship with the sky. Birds are well connected with the celestial realms, and it has been suggested that the horns of the bull symbolized the horns of the crescent Moon.[56] The Moon is certainly associated with bulls in other religious traditions. We have already seen that certain Indo-European sky gods drove chariots across the sky pulled by either horses or oxen. Examples from Greek mythology attest to "solar" horses and "lunar" mares or oxen, as with the chariot driven by the Moon goddess Selene, which was pulled by either horses or oxen. The Hindu god Shiva was said to ride a milk-white bull called Nandi through the skies. Originally a malevolent storm god, he was called *shiva* ("auspicious") in order to propitiate him. Later, he appears as a wrathful avenger and a herdsman of souls, a deity associated with yoga and asceticism with a pronounced erotic aspect. Interestingly, one of Shiva's symbolic attributes is the crescent Moon.[57]

Bulls play a prominent role in *Tain Bó Cuailgne*, a saga that tells of the conflict between Ulster and Connaught over the possession of a huge, supernatural bull known as the Donn (Brown, Dark) of Cooley. His rival is another huge bull called the Findbennach (the White-Horned). These bulls are the result of a series of metamorphoses undertaken by a pair of herdsmen. These men were "practiced in the pagan arts," able to change themselves into any shape. They pass through various forms (ravens, stags, champions, water beasts, etc.) and eventually enter two springs of water, emerging as the two great bulls.[58] Here again, we see the association of bulls with water. In addition, the bulls only manifest after a number of transformations, suggestive of the potent transformations of the Moon.

At the end of the tale, the bulls engage in a great battle. The Findbennach is killed, but the Donn dies as a result of his efforts. The details of the combat are quite interesting, and there is some speculation that it represents a contest between two early Irish bull deities or symbolizes a struggle between the dark Moon (the period of the void Moon) and the crescent Moon.[59]

The description of the battle of the two bulls is potentially significant. The dark one and the white-horned one meet on the top of a hill. The dark bull places his foot on the white bull's horn, preventing it from moving, thereby keeping it in position "all day until nightfall." The dark bull finally releases his hoof, sending the horn of the white bull flying to a nearby mountain known as Sliab nAdarca (The Mountain of the Horn).[60] The two bulls fight until nightfall, during which time they are apparently not visible (the men of Ireland can only hear the "uproar and fury" of the bulls in the darkness). When morning comes, the dark bull, weakened and exhausted, is seen moving westward with the remains of the Findbennach hanging from his horns. The white-horned bull remains hanging on the horns of the Donn all day. At nightfall, the dark bull enters the lake near Cruachan (in the west of Ireland). Later, he emerges with the vanquished white bull still on his horns. As he stops to drink at various locations, parts of the white bull fall to the ground, and certain places are said to be named for them (The White One's Shoulderblade, The Bull's Brow, etc.).[61] At the end of his wandering, the Donn falls dead at a location known as Druim Tairb (The Ridge of the Bull).

If this scenario does, in fact, represent a lunar combat of some kind, the constituent elements may perhaps be interpreted as follows. The dark Moon and the crescent Moon meet on the top of a hill. The dark Moon keeps the last remnant of the old lunar crescent in the sky all day until nightfall, when he releases it and sends it flying to the top of a nearby mountain (i.e., "into the sky"?). This is the last night of the old lunar cycle and the final appearance of the waning crescent Moon. The two bulls continue to fight until the next nightfall, during which time neither is visible. This is the first night of the void Moon.

The next morning, the dark bull emerges with the "dead" white bull hanging from his horns. The void Moon is victorious, and the old horned Moon is dead. The remains of the old Moon remain on the dark bull's horns all day. At night, the dark bull enters a lake in the west (i.e., he "sets" or "descends"). This is the second night of the void Moon.

The dark one then emerges from the water one last time, and the remnants of the old Moon are scattered over the Earth. Exhausted after his victory, the dark bull falls dead at the end of his wanderings. This is the third and final night of the void Moon.

Why would the void Moon have been mythologized? The dark bull must vanquish the white-horned one (the old Moon of the previous lunar cycle) in order for the new Moon to appear. This exemplifies the well-attested motif of creation rising from darkness: the new day, month, or yearly cycle all begin in darkness, from which time and creation emerge. Perhaps it is no coincidence that the dark bull is associated with the east of Ireland (from where he "rises" to ascendancy in this battle) and the white bull with the west (where the old moon "sets" or is vanquished).

There are several details that support this theory. The *Tain* mentions that one of the magical virtues of the Donn was the "magical lowing" or "roar" he made every evening as he returned to his home.[62] It has been suggested that the roar made by the bull every night is somehow associated with the tide. Poseidon, the Greek god of the sea, was known to be represented by a bull. In addition, Teach Duinn, the home of the Irish deity Donn, was also known as An Tarbh (The Bull). One of his epithets was *Donn na Binne*, Donn of the Peak or Donn of the Horn (animal horn). A sacred hill associated with this figure was Knockfirinne, where it was said that the fairy hares on the hill were Donn's pets.[63] The hare, of course, is a lunar animal.

Mystical Traditions and the Celestial Realms

We have explored many centuries of British, Gaulish, and Irish artistic, religious, and mythological traditions having to do with the Moon, sacred animals, and lunar and celestial deities. Is there any evidence of the Moon or the night sky playing a role in the mystical traditions of the Celts? In the medieval Welsh tale of Taliesin, the inspired young poet is credited with uttering a number of fascinating poems. In one of these, he mentions the stars and the night sky:

> *I know the stars' names from the North to the South . . .*
> *I was in the Court of Dôn before the birth of Gwydion . . .* [64]

The Court of Dôn (*Llys Dôn*) is a Welsh term for the constellation we call Cassiopeia. As we saw in a previous chapter, Taliesin refers to the stars and other cosmogonic elements in Cad Goddeu ("The Battle of the Trees") where he describes his previous incarnations: "I was rain-drops in the air, I was stars' beam."[65] This poem has marked affinities with Amairgen's incantation of creation or manifestation which includes the phrases: "I am a wind in the sea/I am a tear-drop of the sun." Near the end of the poem, the Druid and poet asks "Who invokes the ages of the moon?"[66]

The archetypal Celtic poet and seer is a figure who demonstrates a profound connection with the Otherworld, as well as with the world of nature. He is able to "see" into the other realms and poetically or mantically communicate the nature of these worlds to other members of his society. Here, the phases or ages of the Moon are one element used to illustrate the depth of the poet's wisdom and abilities. These cycles are mentioned by Mircea Eliade, who writes:

> The phases of the moon—appearance, increase, wane, disappearance, followed by reappearance after three nights of darkness—have played an immense part in the elaboration of cyclical concepts.[67]

He points out that these concepts find expression in many creation scenarios, in which various floods or catastrophes do away with humanity, only to result in a new "regenerated" culture, race, or society. In many cases, the new population group emerges from a mythical ancestor who escaped the catastrophe, or from a lunar animal. These cyclical myths and beliefs show that, from a lunar perspective, the death of the individual and the periodic death of humanity are necessary so that purification, revitalization, and regeneration may occur. As with the three days of darkness prior to the new Moon, all life force must return to the primordial chaos, waters, or darkness from which it came in order to be reborn or transformed.[68]

This scenario plays out in numerous cultures around the world, and may also be found in an Irish text. *Lebor Gabála Érenn* describes five mythological "invasions" or peoples who inhabited Ireland prior to the arrival of the Gaels (the Celts). Each group is associated with various primal happenings, including the formation of the land and bodies of water, and later, the development of the first skills and elements associated with society. Each population group exists for some time, but each is eventually wiped out by flood, war, or disease. Each new "invasion," however, results in an additional level of growth and transformation.

There is a structural as well as an ideological correspondence between these modes of passage: from darkness to light, from the preexistence of a people to its manifestation (often from a mythical ancestor), and from life to death to rebirth.[69] The Moon is clearly the preeminent symbol of all of these cycles and transformations. In Celtic tradition, cyclical creation scenarios were reenacted and commemorated during the sacred ceremonies associated with Samain, the start of the New Year. Mythical ancestors, divine figures that survived the ages in animal form, and lunar animals all make an appearance in the mythology and symbolism of the Celts. The Gauls maintained their descent from a mystical ancestor associated with the darkness and life-giving potential of the Underworld, the realm into which the Moon sank in the morning and whence it emerged at night (the beginning of the

Celtic day). Artwork depicting sacred animals connected with lunar symbolism, tales that allude to the transformative powers of these creatures and their associated gods and goddesses, and the plentiful evidence of celestial gods whose ranks included a divine star goddess all allude to the elusive, yet strangely ubiquitous, presence of the Moon in Celtic myth and legend.

☽   ☽   ☽

Meditations and Exercises

Consider these activities as ways to better understand the symbolic relationship of the Moon, the celestial realms, and your own inner life.

1) Design a piece of artwork that utilizes traditional Celtic styles or motifs and incorporates designs or symbols representing the Moon. This can be a sacred item to be used in ritual, such as a vessel, bowl, or cauldron, and may also feature symbolism associated with gods or goddesses of the Sky Realm. This object will benefit from being created and consecrated during a particular phase of the Moon.

2) Create a poem or chant to venerate and invoke the gods of the upper world, such as Taranis (The Thunderer), Nodons (Cloud-Maker), Belenus (Bright One), and Lugus, as well as Sulis (Eye/Sun), Macha/Grían (Sun), or Sirona (Divine Star). Include attributes associated with these deities (light, warmth, fertility, abundance, protection, healing, skill, women's concerns, and sovereignty). Decide if this piece of liturgy will be used for daily veneration or chanted or recited at special times of the day, month, or year.

3) Meditate on the figure of the goddess Sirona, the Divine Star. Imagine yourself approaching one of her shrines, located near a holy spring or well. Do you envision the goddess alone or with a consort? What symbolism is apparent at the site (grain, fruit, snakes, etc)? Once you have entered a meditative state, explore Sirona's connection with the crystal-clear water that wells up from under the ground, as well as the nature of her sacred dwelling or celestial abode. How does the goddess appear to you, and what are her powers? See if she has a gift of healing, abundance, or regeneration for you. Remember to make an offering of gratitude, perhaps a stone or crystal that resembles the luminaries of which she is the sovereign goddess. Ask this night goddess about any Celtic goddesses of the Moon, whose names may include roots like *gel*, "bright," or *ésca* or *ré*, "Moon" (pertaining to the Moon's connection with the measurement of time), along with the feminine divine ending, *ona* (as in Sirona, Epona, etc.).

4) Using a drum, rattle, or shamanic journeying tape, see if you can travel to and view the location and interconnection between the three worlds (Earth, sea/Underworld, and sky). Ask the gods of both the Upper and Lower Worlds to help you understand how these worlds are connected, and what their powers and attributes are. Bring your power animal or spirit helpers with you, and journey to the gods of the night sky (clouds, stars, sky, Moon, water, etc.) to see what they have to teach you. Remember to thank the spirits when you are done.

5) What do you make of the tale of Lug's arrival at Núadu's court, and the fact that Lug is given precedence over Núadu (who rises before him for thirteen days). Do you think there is some cosmogonic or lunar significance to this, or to the subsequent commencement of a great gathering that lasts for a year (the Amrún of the goddess Danu)? Or do you view the story as a representation of Lug's preeminent wisdom and skill, which would have been associated with a leader's fitness to rule? Whichever interpretation you favor, create a short retelling of the tale that emphasizes those aspects of the story (and the characters) you find most significant.

6) The crane bag of the sea god Manannán mac Lir contained many treasures and could only be seen when the "sea was full." How do you perceive the connection between the crane, the waters, and the Moon? In exploring these concepts, create your own facsimile of a crane bag (perhaps from the skin of an animal or bird you consider sacred, or containing objects or relics associated with such a creature). Whether you hunt the animal yourself in a sacred manner (asking permission to do so, using the animal wisely, and giving thanks afterward), or use an animal already dead from natural causes, remember to perform a ceremony to create a sacred bond between yourself and the spirits of the natural world, and show your gratitude and respect. Once this has been accomplished, decide what sacred objects you will carry in the bag. Are there symbols of the Moon or the sea inside? It would be auspicious to create and consecrate the bag during a significant or propitious period of the Moon (or the tide), and use it in a ritual of meditation.

7) Why do you think the image of the crane degenerated over time (as well as that of women associated with cranes)? Does it have to do with the bird's connection with water (and perhaps also with the Moon), or its association with magic and shape-shifting, which might have been misunderstood or mistrusted by the incoming religion? Write your own myth pertaining to cranes, women, magic, the sea, the Moon (or other associated elements) that expresses your understanding and perception of these sacred concepts.

8) Do you think the horns of a sacred white cow or bull represented the crescent Moon in the religious iconography of various early cultures? Does a battle

between bulls representing the old Moon and the void Moon make sense in light of the recurring images and elements we have encountered in our journey? Take some time to look back at earlier chapters, making note of things that might support either of these possibilities. If you do not agree with one or both of the statements, then use the information we have explored to come up with alternate suggestions (or even alternate myths) to explain the battle of the bulls in the *Táin*.

9) The mystical poetry attributed to Amairgen and Taliesin makes use of repetitive and ritualized language in which the poet expresses what he is or has been (I was . . . I am . . .). Do you think there is a shamanic element to these poetic expressions or experiences? After entering into a deep meditative state, write or spontaneously create your own poem of transformation using your unfolding spiritual vision or experience as its basis. Try this exercise at each new Moon or New Year's rite to see how your experience grows and transforms over time. Eventually, you may come up with a somewhat set version, which can serve as an intense incantory vehicle that you can use to create a powerful Samain or new Moon ceremony or experience.

QUEEN OF THE NIGHT

THE CELTIC GODDESS OF THE MOON

And near him stood the Lady of the Lake, who knows a subtler magic than his own—
Clothed in white samite, mystic, wonderful . . . a mist of incense curl'd about her,
and her face well nigh was hidden in the minster gloom.

—ALFRED, LORD TENNYSON, "THE COMING OF ARTHUR"

We have been searching for evidence of veneration of the Moon in Celtic tradition, including information pertaining to a deity associated with the Moon. We will now turn our attention to a series of medieval Welsh tales preserved in manuscripts dated to the 14th and 15th centuries, but clearly reflecting stories much older than that. They are the Four Branches of the *Mabinogi*, whose name is thought to refer to an earlier collection of related tales concerned (to varying degrees) with a group of divine and semidivine characters associated with the figure of Mabon (Divine Son, similar to the British god Maponos). While these tales reflect a number of medieval and Christian elements, they are also the medieval expression of what may be considered native British mythological themes.[1]

The Fourth Branch of the *Mabinogi* relates the story of the family of Dôn, an early British ancestress or mother goddess. Her name is often said to be the Welsh equivalent of that of the Irish goddess Danu. Celticist John Koch asserts that the origin of their names cannot be the same. The underlying root of Danu's name is probably an Indo-European word meaning "river," found in the names of rivers located throughout the vast territories once inhabited by the Celts, including the Danue, the Dniepr, and various rivers named "Don" in Britain and on the Continent. Dôn's name (as it is spelled in the medieval manuscripts) must instead come from a root word meaning "earth."[2] However, some of the earliest texts that contain the Irish goddess's name show it spelled with an "o" (Donu/Donann). Certainly both goddesses function as divine ancestresses or mothers of the gods, and Danu herself is explicitly described as the Mother of the Gods in early Irish tradition.[3]

The story of the Welsh ancestress Dôn's divine family is set in Gwynedd in the north of Wales, and features her brother, Math (who reigns as king of Gwynedd), and two of her children, Gwydion and Arianrhod (also spelled Aranrhod). Both

Gwydion and Math are powerful magicians, and the story is replete with elements of myth and magic.[4] What follows is a synopsis of the tale of Arianrhod, which appears in the Fourth Branch of the *Mabinogi*.

Math, son of Mathonwy, was lord of Gwynedd in the north and could only live while his feet were in the lap of a maiden, except in time of war. One of Math's nephews, Gilfaethwy, falls in love with Math's "footholder," Goewin, and he and his brother, Gwydion, devise a ruse to send the king away from the court on war-related business. They tell Math about some remarkable animals in the south of the land known as "pigs," that were given to Pryderi, son of Pwyll, by Arawn, king of Annwfn (the Welsh Otherworld). Posing as poets, the two men travel to Pryderi's court to try and obtain the animals for Math. Their scheme is not successful, so Gwydion conjures magical dogs and horses out of mushrooms, trading these for Pryderi's pigs. The magical illusion does not last, however, causing Pryderi and his army to move toward Math's realm in retaliation. Math sets out for battle and, while he is away, Gilfaethwy sleeps with Goewin against her will.

During the battle, Pryderi is slain. Math returns home to discover that Goewin is no longer a virgin and, therefore, cannot serve as his footholder. He proposes reparations for the loss of her honor, offering to marry her and put possession of the realm into her hand. (This episode probably concerns the Celtic goddess of sovereignty). He punishes Gilfaethwy and Gwydion by transforming them into stag and deer, wild boar and sow, and male and female wolves, condemning them to mate with each other (their genders alternating with each transformation) as a fitting punishment. When their shame and humiliation are ended, both men are bathed, dressed, and returned to the king's confidence.

Math then asks their advice concerning the replacement of his footholder. Gwydion suggests Math's niece, Arianrhod. She is summoned before the king, who asks her if she is a maiden. She replies, "I do not know other than that I am." Math extends his magician's rod (certainly a euphemism) and holds it down low, asking her to walk over it. "Step across this, and if you are a maiden, I will know it." She steps over the rod and spontaneously gives birth to a fine, yellow-haired boy, as well as a second entity described only as "some little thing." The first child is named Dylan, and, as soon as he is named, he makes for the sea. Gwydion furtively wraps the other "little thing" in a coverlet and hides it in a small chest at the end of his bed.

One day, Math hears a cry from the chest and opens it to discover a fine little boy. He raises the boy, who develops at a prodigious rate—a common motif in Celtic tales associated with the childhood of divine or semidivine figures or heroes. One day, Gwydion takes the lad to Caer Arianrhod (the Fortress of Arianrhod) and presents him to his mother. She is angry that Gwydion has come in an apparent effort to disgrace her and curses the boy, refusing him a name, arms, or a bride. Due to the scheming and magical machinations of Gwydion, however, she is tricked into presenting the boy with a name (Lleu) as well as arms.

Later, a bride is conjured for him out of flowers by Math and Gwydion and named Blodeuwedd (Flower Face).

Blodeuwedd and Lleu wed, but she soon falls in love with another man, Gronw. The lovers plan to kill Lleu, and Blodeuwedd, feigning concern over his safety, asks her husband in what manner his death may be accomplished. A number of taboos surround his demise, but the lovers perform the necessary tasks. Gronw casts a poisoned spear at Lleu, who utters a horrible scream and flies off in the form of an eagle. Math and Gwydion are downcast at Lleu's disappearance, and Gwydion wanders far and wide in search of his nephew. He finds Lleu in a sorry state, sitting in the top of an oak tree in the shape of an eagle, weakened and ill. Gwydion sings three magical *englynion*, each of which causes the eagle to come closer to him. Eventually, the eagle lands on Gwydion's knee, and the magician is able to transform Lleu into his own shape. The best doctors are summoned, and Lleu is healed. He kills Gronw and transforms Blodeuwedd into an owl, condemning her to a state of disgrace and exile. He regains possession of his kingdom and, thereafter, reigns happily and successfully.[5]

The Moon Gives Birth to the Sea and the Sun

The Fourth Branch is full of mythological symbols. Indeed, we could devote an entire chapter to deciphering and illuminating these themes. We will, however, restrict our exploration to elements that pertain directly to our quest. One of the most important clues to the possible identity of our long-sought Moon goddess is the name of Lleu's mother, Arianrhod, which means "Silver Wheel," which could well be an epithet for the Moon. Her two children also appear to be associated with cosmogonic elements, as one of her sons is associated with the ocean, and the other (as we shall see) with the Sun. John Koch feels that her name might once have designated "a goddess of the heavens, perhaps specifically of the moon." He points out the relevance of her son Lleu's name (which means "light") and reminds us that a compound of this word (*lleuad*) is still one of the modern Welsh words for "moon."[6]

When Arianrhod is asked to step over Math's magic rod, it is apparent that she is not a maiden or virgin. This may be a medieval interpolation or interpretation to some degree, as virginity was highly valued in Christian tradition. Various sources attest to a differing set of social standards in earlier Celtic society. In addition, in mythological terms, sexuality is often indicative of a divine figure's association with fertility and abundance, a trait that would have been venerated and respected.

Arianrhod's first child is Dylan Eil Ton, whose name may be interpreted along the lines of Sea, Son of Wave. As soon as he receives his name, he sets off for the water, where he immediately takes on the nature of the sea, swimming as well as the best fish in the ocean. Sadly, he is later killed by his uncle, Gofannon, the divine smith, which event is known as one of the Three Unfortunate Blows of the Island of Britain.[7]

The name of Arianrhod's other son, Lleu, is cognate with that of the Irish deity Lugh. Lugh, as we have seen, is a many-skilled deity who may possess a solar aspect. In the Fourth Branch, when Gwydion seeks to trick Arianrhod into providing her son with a name, he and the lad pose as shoemakers, producing marvelous shoes on a ship moored outside the entrance to Caer Arianrhod. They purposely send incorrectly sized shoes to her, persuading her to come in person so they can measure her foot properly. After she arrives on the ship, she watches the young boy make a very skillful cast, killing a wren perched on the deck of the ship. Smiling, she remarks, "It's with a skillful hand (*llaw gyffes*) that the fair-haired one (*lleu*) has hit him!" Gwydion points out that she has named her son (much to her chagrin). The boy's new name, Lleu Llaw Gyffes, The Fair One of the Skillful Hand, is clearly similar to that of Lugh Samildánach (also called Lugh Lamfáda), The Many-Skilled Bright One (of the Long Arm).[8]

Later, when Lleu's wife asks him in what manner he may be killed, he replies that it is not an easy task (attesting to his divinity). He explains that he cannot be killed in a house or outside, neither on a horse or on foot, and only with a spear that was worked on when people were "at prayers on Sunday" (i.e., during a sacred period of time). We have seen this sort of liminal symbolism before in association with mistletoe and other elements of Celtic lore. The spear is another link between Lug and Lleu, as the Irish deity also owned a magical spear, one of the four sacred talismans of the Tuatha Dé Danann.[9] Having been pierced with the poisoned spear, Lleu flies off in the form of an eagle into the top of an oak tree. Both the eagle and the oak are commonly associated with solar or celestial deities in Indo-European tradition. Maximus of Tyre stated that the Celts represented their Zeus (i.e., celestial father or tribal deity) by means of a high oak tree.[10] A silver cup from Lyon in France (originally Lugdunum, The Fortress of Lugus) depicts a tree (perhaps oak?) with mistletoe, an eagle, and a deity (probably Lugus).[11]

The magical poems Gwydion sings refer to Lleu's tree as an oak growing on a high plain "between two lakes," and mentions that "rain wets it not, nor does it melt." This sounds like a description of a sacred tree situated on a hill or a plain (which were used as ritual sites), liminally existing between two lakes (bodies of water are also common divine elements).[12] It is not destroyed by either fire or water, both considered powerful primal cosmogonic elements. In the third poem, Gwydion even refers to Lleu in the tree as a "stately prince in his temple," surely an indicator of his status as a divinity.[13]

After Lleu has been transformed back to his original form, he punishes his unfaithful wife by changing her into an owl. She is never again to show her face in the light of day and will ever after experience the enmity and fear of the other birds. Lleu, a solar-aspected divinity, transforms his unfaithful mate into a creature associated with night. The two will, hence, never cross paths, and she will remain apart from him in a state of exile. Although she was made from the flowers of the oak (a tree associated with Lleu), the meadowsweet (in Scottish Gaelic, *Crios Chuchulainn*, the Belt of Cú Chulainn, the mortal son of the Irish god Lugh), and the broom (whose sunny, yellow color is mentioned in numerous Irish and Welsh texts), Blodeuwedd is clearly not destined or worthy to be the consort of this bright, skillful god.[14]

Perhaps an older prototype of Arianrhod's story told of a Moon goddess (Silver Wheel) who gave birth to two sons, one associated with the ocean (Sea, Son of Wave) and the other with the Sun (Bright One of the Skillful Hand). Her inexplicable actions and her apparently unreasonable anger may be easier to understand in terms of this earlier tale, in which the birth of her children created great difficulties for her. We have seen that she did not seem to know she was pregnant, which may suggest that she was visited unaware by a mysterious or divine lover of some kind, a scenario we will explore in the next section. If this is the case, her answer to Math and her surprise and shame at giving birth makes perfect sense.

One of the children leaves and enters the realm of the sea, where he apparently does not cause any more problems for her. This is made certain by the death of the sea child, brought about by her brother, the divine smith. Arianrhod may have thought that the second child disappeared or did not survive. When, with no warning, she is faced with the lad's presence, she reacts in what is really an understandable fashion. She had been unaware of her own conception and did not choose the situation for herself. She had also experienced shame and humiliation in her uncle's court. Perhaps she sought solitude and restoration in her divine fortress, a peace that was shattered by Gwydion's arrival with the child.

Arianrhod's refusal to grant her son a name, arms, and a wife (three things necessary for a young man's entrance into adulthood) has given rise to a great deal of speculation and commentary. In doing these things, she denies him access to an important rite of passage and prevents his transformation into a mature and fully empowered being. Perhaps she was intuitively or prophetically cognizant of the "bright" nature of the lad or aware of his potential destiny (a theme common to many Celtic myths).

I suggest that an earlier version of the story may have existed that featured a goddess of the Moon, a respected deity of the celestial realms, whose potential power and importance are supported by that of divine figures like Sulis and Sirona. Unwittingly, she gave birth to a solar-aspected son, whose rise to power threatened her own dominion over the skies. In order to maintain her position, she tries to prevent his ascension to power in any way she can. Her attempts at self-preservation are thwarted by the magic of her brother and her uncle. The lad is almost destroyed by his unfaithful wife, but once again is saved by his uncle. The flower bride is transformed into a bird associated with the night, the world of the boy's mother (a figure who also tries to oppose him). Despite the efforts of both women, the young god is successful and takes control of his kingdom. While I do not suggest that the religious practice of the Celts was predominantly focused on Sun worship, myths pertaining to the dominance of the Sun over the Moon are found in a number of other cultures. If at least some of these interpretations are accurate, the actions of this fallen and euhemerized divinity take on a new meaning as we examine all the available information in an attempt to restore her to some semblance of what may once have been her original and venerable form.

The Lover of the Moon Goddess

One often-discussed element of the story is the absence or unknown identity of the father of Arianrhod's sons. Some have suggested that her uncle Math is their father, for, after she steps over his magic rod, she gives birth to two children. Others feel that her brother Gwydion may be Lleu's father, due to the care and diligence he exhibits in raising him. Sacred incest is common in many mythological traditions, often producing children of a divine nature. One frequently occurring motif in Celtic myth is the "sister's son," an important familial relationship in both the mortal and divine realms. (Lleu, of course, is Gwydion's sister's son.) Both paternal options are worth considering, yet there is another possibility.

In Irish and Scottish tradition, legends are told of women who unwittingly becoming pregnant due to the visitation (often unknown to them) of a trickster or supernatural figure associated with the sea—sometimes a member of the mer-folk or seal people. For example, in the Irish tale King Cormac and King Conn, a magical otter lord lies by the daughter of King Cormac as she is swimming and fathers the child Conn upon her. The event does not appear to be fully understood or realized by those involved. Conn is raised as Cormac's heir, but he is pitted against a child of Cormac's second wife (with Gaibhne Gow, the blacksmith). Conn later tricks Finn mac Cumhaill into helping him take the kingdom from his grandfather, but Cormac's true son defeats Conn and causes his death by the same otter lord who sired him.[15]

As in the tale of Arianrhod, in this story, a king's daughter is mysteriously pregnant with a child whose nature derives (in part) from a being associated with water. The child has a sort of half-brother, and one of the children has dealings with a smith. In some Irish sources, the god Lugh is said to have been fostered by Goibhniu, the divine smith; in others, by Manannán mac Lir, a god of the sea, illustrating the diverse and disparate branches of the tradition. In both tales, however, the sea child is eventually killed.

When Math asks Arianrhod if she is a maiden, she says she knows not but that she is (i.e., "as far as I know, I am"). When she gives birth, there is both surprise and disgrace (as well as a lack of clarity as to who the father is). These elements also appear in the well-known Scottish ballad "The Great Selchie of Sule Skerrie." A woman singing to her child says, "Little ken I my bairn's father, Far less the land

that he staps in." A great selkie then appears at the end of the bed and announces
that he is the child's father. The woman is not pleased by this revelation, saying it
was "na weel" that he came and "gave a bairn" to her. He gives a bag of gold to the
woman and asks her to give him the child to raise:

> An' it sall pass on a simmer's day,
> When the sin shines het on evera stone,
> That I will tak my little young son,
> An' teach him for to swim his lane [alone].[16]

Once again, a woman is mysteriously made pregnant by an unknown figure that
appears to be associated with the sea. She is not happy about her situation, which
came upon her unawares. The sea father offers to raise the child; in the *Mabinogi*,
neither child is raised by its mother. He also says he will teach it to swim, reminiscent of Dylan's marine nature.[17]

Folklorists working in the eastern part of Scotland reported a conversation
pertaining to a woman called Brita who scorned men, but was said to have taken
a seal lover at the time of the Lammas stream or summer high tide. She evidently
bore children whose fingers and toes were webbed.[18] This piece of lore is quite
remarkable. The woman had not had any interaction with mortal men (like
Artemis and also, perhaps, Arianrhod), and yet has children who partake of the
nature of the sea (the domain of the seal people). The supernatural union takes
place at the high tide of Lammas or Lugnasad, the feast day associated with Lugh,
the Irish counterpart of Lleu. There is also a reference to a "hot summer's day" in
the Selkie ballad, although this may simply pertain to good swimming weather.
However, it is interesting to note that it is in August, the month associated with
Lugnasad, that the Welsh seal colonies give birth to their young.[19]

Many folk traditions comment on the humanlike appearance or semblance of
the seal, and numerous stories tell of marriages between humans and seal folk
(unions that are often ill-fated). There appears to be some connection between
Lleu/Lugh and Lugnasad, unions between women and supernatural lovers associated with the sea, and the birth of offspring who are associated with the ocean
(offspring who are, in some cases, killed or drowned in the water, sometimes in
seal form).[20] Whatever the original myth may have been, it has a parallels in Irish
and Scottish folk legends, as well as in earlier medieval tales and lore.

One final story serves as an illuminating parallel to the tales already described.
It is found in a group of Irish tales known as *Balor on Tory Island*. Here, Lugh is
sired by a trickster on the daughter of a king (perhaps a reflex of Gwydion or a
crafty sea person as the father of Lleu, uniting with Arianrhod, the daughter of the
kingly figure Beli Mawr). The trickster also sires other children at the same time
who are at least half-siblings to Lugh. One version of the story states that Lugh had
two brothers who were born at the same time as he, which brings to mind the

inscription to the "triple Lugs" from Galicia. In both versions, Lugh's siblings are said to have fallen into the sea or escaped in seal form into a body of water, much like the oceanic wanderings of Dylan.[21]

Other details of the story also help fill out the original matrix of the tale. Evidently, it was foretold to Balor that, if his daughter gave birth to a son, the child would kill its grandfather. Therefore, he kept the girl locked away so that no man had access to her.[22] A young man called Cian, who is the father of Lugh in earlier Irish sources as well, managed to sleep with the girl and was killed as a result. The enraged Balor ordered her and the child to be set adrift in a boat. They survived thanks to the help of a smith called Goibhleann, who also made a spear for the child when he was growing to manhood. Later, Balor is angered when Goibhleann tries to retrieve his magical cow and threatens to destroy all of Ireland. Lugh makes a skillful cast, blinding Balor and killing him with his spear.[23]

There are a number of obvious parallels between this tale and that of Arianrhod. She is the daughter of a king who seems to have had no interaction with men, but who is mysteriously pregnant. The father may have been a trickster like Gwydion or a sea lover, which explains how she could have been unaware of her situation. The birth of her son Lugh/Lleu and another son associated with the sea (into which he escapes or perishes) is the cause of much trouble and consternation. A smith figure helps the child (much as Goibhniu is said to have fostered Lugh) and even kills the other sibling in the Welsh version. The smith makes a spear for the young man in this story, while in *The Battle of Moytura*, Lugh engages the help of Goibhniu and his two brothers in making magical weapons to help the Tuatha Dé Danann in battle. It may be Goibhniu who created Lugh's spear as well. Lugh and Lleu are famed for their skillful casts, and both are associated with magical spears. Interestingly, according to Dindshenchas tradition, one of Lugh's wives is an unnamed bride who was unfaithful to him with Cermait, son of the Dagda (reminiscent of Blodeuwedd).

In one version of the tale, the children are described as having been born, not to the mother or central figure, but to twelve women who guard the princess from men. We have seen that there is no mention of Arianrhod having relations with men.[24] Numerous Celtic tales refer to groups of thirteen people, comprised of twelve auxiliary members who assist, follow, or focus on a single sacred or esteemed figure or leader. This is interesting in light of the story variant above. In addition, a Breton folk ceremony that will be discussed in the next chapter took place on a hill surrounded by twelve stones. After descending the hill, the participants walked around a large stone that symbolized the Moon.[25] Here, the twelve surround the one, which is representative of the Moon. These stories can perhaps help us understand the elements and symbolism associated with the myth of Arianrhod, and bring her character and divinity into clearer focus.

The Death of the King of Winter

Birds play a significant role in the stories and iconography of Lugh/Lleu/Lugus. The archaeological record shows that, in several Continental contexts, the god Lugus was associated with ravens, although this may not have been true in all Celtic areas. An early stone altar portrays a youthful deity with one hand raised in some sort of oratorical gesture (perhaps similar to the *corrguineacht* posture assumed by Lugh in *The Battle of Moytura*). Two ravens are depicted speaking into the ear of the deity, who in turn seems to be providing them with information or instructions. There is an obvious parallel with the two ravens of Odin, a deity who shares other attributes with the god Lugh.[26] It also brings to mind the Gaulish monument that depicted two cranes speaking into the ear of a divine female.

The Lugh/Lleu/Lugus archetype is also associated with the eagle. This bird is regarded as the king of birds in many cultures and is often associated with celestial gods. It is specifically connected with solar cults over a wide area.[27] Another bird associated with Lleu is the wren, the small bird he killed with his skillful cast. This act earned him his name, much as Lugh obtained his epithet Lamfada (Of the Long Arm) from his skillful cast against his grandfather, Balor. What does the wren represent in the tale of Lleu and Arianrhod? Perhaps a discussion of Celtic traditions associated with the wren may shed some light on the underlying symbolism of the story.

Wrens play an important role in an unusual ceremony that takes place near the end of the calendar year. In Ireland, St. Stephen's day (December 26) is associated with a rite and procession known as the "hunting of the wren." On that day, small boys go out and kill a number of wrens, which are then carried about on a holly bush or decorated wooden tray. During the procession, the youths sometimes wear straw masks or animal horns or skins. They shout and laugh boisterously, singing traditional songs and beating on homemade skin tambourines as they go from door to door demanding money or drinks.[28] The first group of boys that brings a wren to the house is believed to bring luck for the coming year. If no welcome is given, however, the wren may be buried near the hall door of the house, an act thought to prevent luck from entering the house.[29]

The wren-boy processions customarily take place at night. At noon of the following day, the wren bushes were thrown away, and the wrens buried in the ground with a penny (reminiscent of coins or metal objects offered to the Underworld powers in earlier times). An excerpt from one version of the wren boys' song goes as follows:

The wren, the wren, the king of all birds,
On St. Stephen's day was caught in the furze,
Although he is little his family is great
Put your hand in your pocket and give us a treat.

Sing holly, sing ivy, sing ivy, sing holly,
A drop just to drink it would drown melancholy . . .[30]

The wren hunt takes place in Wales on Twelfth Night, the last night of the Christmas festivities. The wrens are carried in a wren house decorated with ribbons on top of a long pole, or on a small bier covered with a sheet. The wren seems to have some connection with love or fertility in the Welsh ceremony (rather than with luck, as in the Irish procession). In the 1600s, wrens were carried by young men to their sweethearts and carols were sung. In houses where there were no sweethearts, beer drinking took place instead. In the 1800s, young men carried the wrens about at night, visiting the houses of couples that had been married in the previous year. In some areas, the newlyweds invited the wren boys into their homes, where they received money instead of drink. Sometimes the procession arrived early in the morning before the couple had arisen, and water was sprinkled over them as they lay in bed (suggesting a connection with fertility).[31] Regional songs were sung that referred to the wren as the ruler of all birds:

Joy, health, love and peace . . . By your leave
Here we sing concerning our King [the wren] . . .
Now Christmas is past, Twelfth Day is the last,
To the old year adieu, *great joy to the new,*
Please turn the King in.[32]

Why was the wren called the king of all birds? Why was it associated with luck or fertility, treated with honor and respect, and yet hunted and killed near the turning of the year? An exploration of traditions and lore associated with the wren in earlier Celtic contexts may help us answer some of these questions.

A number of early Irish texts refer to the wren as an instrument of prognostication. Wrens, ravens, and scald crows were all described as having associations with prophecy. Many omens and portents were connected with the flight and activities of the wren (many of which had to do with its appearance in certain directions). It was known by several names, including *dreoluccán*, *drean*, and *druí*. In a famous quote in which he rejects the methods of divination used by the Celts (as well as other heathen activities and earthly pleasures), Colum Cille is reported to have said, "I adore not the voices of birds, nor sneezing nor lots in this world, nor a boy nor omens nor women. My druid is Christ the son of God (*Is é mo draí Críost mac Dé*)." The cleric may have been making a pun on the word *draí/druí*, knowing that it was also used to refer to the wren, a bird associated with prophecy. In Welsh, the word for wren is *dryw*, which (like Old Irish *druí*) is also a word for Druid.[33] In addition to its connection with words pertaining to Druids, in some contexts, the wren was referred to as a prophet (*fáth*), seer (*fithidh*), poet (*file*), or man of art (*fear dána*), probably due to its associations with wisdom and prophecy.[34]

Later, the wren makes an appearance in a story relating to another cleric, Saint Moling. In his solitude, the saint (who was said to be a prophet) kept three animals as pets: a fox, a fly, and a wren. In one tale, the wren kills the fly. The angry cleric curses the bird, saying "Let his dwelling be forever in empty houses, with a wet drip therein continually. And may children and young persons be destroying him." Here, he refers to the bird's habitat, its association with wet weather, and the hunting and destruction of the wren by young people (perhaps indicating that the wren hunt was practiced in medieval times).

Information about the wren's status as the king of all birds (as well as the first specific reference to the hunting wrens) is found in an 18th-century Irish poem. The wren is described as falling into the hands of its enemies and being brought "from kingship to death." The wren himself speaks of his former status, and mentions that "hosts of eagles" once submitted to his power.[35] The supremacy of the wren over the eagle is also mentioned in a 19th-century Irish manuscript that tells the story of an assembly of birds convened for the purpose of deciding who among them should have the leadership. It was decided to give the privilege to the bird that could fly the highest, an honor awarded to the wren, who flew safely under the eagle's wings.[36]

This motif is explained more clearly in versions of the tale collected from Scottish Gaelic folk tradition. The eagle and the wren were engaged in a contest to see who could soar the highest. After making a great ascent, the eagle could not see the wren, and so called out to it. The wren replied, *Tha mis' an seo, os do chionn* (I am here, above you); it was perched on the eagle's back.[37] In Irish folk tradition, the eagle revenges itself on the wren by putting a spell on it so that it could not fly higher than the gable of a small house. In another tale, however, the wren manages its own revenge, putting a spell on the eagle so that it can never have more than two young each year. The wren, on the other hand, is capable of producing many offspring (hence, the song reference to its small size, but great or numerous family).[38] The well-attested cleverness of the wren is mentioned in a number of folktales, where it is also described as outwitting the fox. Its association with wisdom or prophecy is said to account for the common saying, "A little bird told me."[39]

The wren also seems to have a connection with themes of betrayal. In medieval and early modern stories, wrens are described as giving warnings to the enemy in battle situations. Modern Irish anecdotes exist in which Jesus himself is betrayed by a wren. The many types of calls emitted by the wren include sounds that seem to indicate alarm or warning (including the bird's familiar scolding chatter).[40] Perhaps this is the source of the bird's association with warnings, messages, or betrayal. This association is particularly interesting in light of the theme of betrayal that runs through the tales of Lleu.

There are several possible ways of interpreting the lore associated with the wren. Originally, it seems to have been connected with prophecy and divination, as well as with Druids, seers, and other men and women of wisdom. This may have led to its portrayal in folktales as a bird clever enough to outwit the eagle (and later, the fox). Its association with native methods of divination, Druidic wisdom and lore, and other pagan themes may account for its unpopularity with early churchmen. This, in combination with its characteristic call, may have led to its connection with warnings or betrayals. Hence the bird's lamentation of its fall "from kingship to death," which may have been acted out in a ritual slaying around the time of Jesus' birth.

What about the veneration paid to the bird during the wren boys' procession? We have seen that the eagle was frequently associated with the Sun. One wonders if these year-end customs reflect traditions originally associated with the Winter Solstice rather than Christmas, due to Anglo-Saxon or Norse influence in Ireland and Wales. Perhaps the wren symbolized the spirit of winter, which was killed at the time of the Winter Solstice in order for the Sun/solar bird to regain power. Interestingly, as wrens feed mainly on insects and spiders, they often have difficulty making it through the winter. During the dark half of the year, many of the small creatures perish.[41] While the "winter bird" was clever enough to "outwit the sun" for some time (and was therefore afforded great respect), it eventually had to die in order for the light of the Sun to return and increase in strength. Perhaps this is why the wren boys' processions took place in the darkness and why the wren bushes were destroyed at noon, when the Sun's power was at its height.

It is also possible that this custom, like many others associated with the New Year, were transferred from Samain, the old Celtic New Year. This may be the source of the wren's association with luck and fertility, things commonly sought and solicited by many cultures at the time of the New Year's celebration. The wren's association with the word for Druid may derive from the Druid's role as priest and prognosticator, presiding over the Samain rituals and ceremonies. With the adoption of the Gregorian calendar, the symbolism behind the older New Year's customs may have become less clear, and the old ways, diminishing in power and prestige, less of a focus. The early veneration of a "Druid bird," associated with prophecy, Druidic wisdom, and Samain rites and divination, may account for its unpopularity among early church figures, even to the point of naming it as a betrayer of Christ in later sources. Perhaps this led to the symbolic hunting and slaying of the wren at the end of the old year and the start of the new.

While we may never know exactly how these traditions originated, or which one of the interpretations is most nearly correct (if any), we can perceive a number of related or causative themes and elements that are (or have been) connected with the wren. Lleu, who is associated with the eagle, kills a wren, an act that earns him his name and starts him on the road to adulthood, power, and kingship. Perhaps this act prefigures or reflects themes present in the early modern or medieval wren hunt. The triumph of the Sun/solar bird over the Druid bird may represent the perceived triumph of Christianity over paganism and the growing authority of Christian clerics over the traditions of the Druids.

It is also possible that the story of Lleu represents a struggle between the wren (the bird of winter or the dark half of the year, which began at Samain) and the eagle (the bird of the Sun and perhaps also of summer, the bright half of the year). The primal meaning of the contest between these creatures may lie in a mythic story whose origins are lost to us.

The tradition that the wren was king of the birds, along with related traditions linking the wren with the eagle, was explored by E. A. Armstrong in *The Folklore of Birds*, where he attempts to trace the connection back to ancient times and suggests that its basis is mythological.[42] The power and status of Lleu's mother, Arianrhod, whose original and venerable association with darkness and night may have degenerated over the course of time, is usurped by her son, whose solar aspect may have been more acceptable in the early Christian and medieval periods. Like his Irish counterpart, Lugh (whose appearance at the court of Tara creates quite a stir), Lleu's arrival at the fortress of Arianrhod results in a chain of events, and causes many changes to take place in the realms of the gods.

The Primal Divinity of the Silver Wheel

A number of clues that may help us understand the divine nature of Arianrhod are found in the names and attributes of her family members. These barely euhemerized figures mentioned in the *Mabinogi* and other Welsh sources appear to reflect attributes of early British deities. Arianrhod is the daughter of Dôn, a mother goddess or ancestress who seems to be the progenitor of what may be called the Welsh pantheon. Dôn's name may be cognate with that of Danu, a powerful goddess who seems to head the deities of Ireland, and who is referred to in the title *Tuatha Dé Danann*, The People of the Goddess Danu. Dôn is the sister of Math, son of Mathonwy.

In the *Triads of Britain*, Dôn's husband or consort is a figure called Beli Mawr (Beli the Great). He is an ancestor deity credited with establishing several royal lines in Wales. He is specifically said to be the father of Arianrhod, as well as of Caswallan, Lludd, and Llefelys, figures known from other Welsh tales. Some have postulated that Beli's name may be related to that of Belenus, a solar-aspected deity associated with healing waters, although this is not certain. Dôn is credited with a number of divine offspring including Gwydion, a powerful magician; Gofannon, whose name means Divine Smith; Amaethon, a Divine Ploughman (Welsh *amaeth*, "agriculture, labor"); Arianrhod (Silver Wheel); and Gilfaethwy, whose rape of Goewin leads to the testing and trials of his sister.[43]

Gwydion and Gofannon are associated with magic and smithcraft, skills revered in Celtic society. Amaethon's skill may reflect the third function of Indo-

European society, as outlined by Georges Dumézil (kingship/priesthood, warriors, farmers). A similar distinction existed among the Tuatha Dé Danann, who held that their "people of skill" (*aes dána*) were gods and their farmers and herders (*aes trebtha*) "non-gods."

Arianrhod's name and character may reflect an earlier strata of divine figures, similar to the primal nature of her parents. In addition to being a sacred ancestress, Dôn seems to be associated with cosmogonic elements to some degree. Her divine dwelling, Llys Dôn (The Court of Dôn) is the constellation Cassiopeia. Arianrhod also has a dwelling associated with the celestial realms. Caer Arianrhod (The Fortress of Arianrhod) is a popular Welsh name for the Corona Borealis. In addition, according to Welsh folk tradition, there is a reef off the coast of Gwynedd also known as Caer Arianrhod. The reef is reputed to be the remains of the island castle where Arianrhod was tricked into giving arms to her son, Lleu.[44] It is apparently only visible during low tide, suggestive of the Moon's connection with the ocean and the tides, and bringing to mind the tidal appearance of the crane bag of Manannán mac Lir.

In the *Mabinogi*, Gwydion and Lleu journey along the seashore between Caer Dathl and Abermenai, at which point Gwydion fashions a magical ship out of seaweed. The pair then proceed to the port of Caer Arianrhod. Abermenai (the mouth of the Menai, or the Menai strait) lies between Anglesey and the rest of Wales. On its southern edge is Caernarvon, near which the reef or fortress of Arianrhod may be seen. Later in the tale, Lleu and Gwydion proceed along a particular route that leads by the sea toward Bryn Arien (Silver Hill, perhaps associated with Arianrhod in some way). At the top of Cefn Cludno, they mount horses and proceed toward Caer Arianrhod.[45] In addition to an earthly fortress associated with the sea and the tides, Arianrhod lives somewhere in or near the Corona Borealis. Both her worldly and Otherwordly dwellings seem to support an association with the Moon.[46]

The author(s) of the medieval Welsh tales of the *Mabinogi* drew from a wide variety of sources, including popular tales and lore, triads, proverbs, genealogies, legal texts, motifs from Irish (and international) tales, as well as traditional British mythological material. Proinsias Mac Cana feels that the majority of the main incidents in the Four Branches derive from this mythological layer and cites a number of parallel figures in support of this:

1) The focus on the family of Dôn, who may correspond in name (as well as elements of form and attribute) to the divine people of Ireland known as the Tuatha Dé Danann

2) Manawydan ap Llyr, the British equivalent of the Irish sea god Manannán mac Lir

3) Gofannon, the Divine Smith, parallel with the Irish smith god, Goibhniu

4) The importance of figures like Rhiannon (Rígantona, Divine Queen), Teyrnon (Tigernos, Divine Lord), and Mabon (Maponos, Divine Son)[47]

Mac Cana discusses other mythological themes present in the Four Branches, stating that most of the narrative revolves around familiar mythical themes of sovereignty, the Otherworld, and the birth of the hero. He writes that some less obvious elements "may continue archaic and all but forgotten religious forms: for instance, Georges Dumézil has discussed the curious condition by which the magician-king Math is always obliged, except in time of war, to keep his feet in the lap of a virgin girl and has related it to an ancient Indo-European myth and ritual of kingship."[48]

Mac Cana also points out the strong character of most of the female figures in the *Mabinogi,* quite unusual in light of the era in which it was written. In the medieval period, when courtly traditions prevailed, most women were beautiful, unobtainable, and passive figures dominated by their fathers or husbands. While Branwen and Cigfa are, for the most part, passive characters affected by events beyond their control, Rhiannon and Arianrhod are powerful and assertive female characters that Mac Cana describes as "literary reflexes of the Celtic goddess in some of her many aspects."[49]

An Early British Cosmogonic Tale?

Having explored information pertaining to Arianrhod's divine family, their attributes, and sacred dwellings, we can avail ourselves of this knowledge and indulge ourselves in postulating a prototype of what may originally have constituted an early British myth.[50]

Before men came to the island of Britain, the land was inhabited by the gods of Annwfn. First were Dôn and Beli Mawr, the divine ancestress and ancestor of the gods. Dôn, the mother goddess, lived in her celestial court, Llys Dôn, and bestowed many gifts upon the land. From her flowed streams of wisdom and rivers of abundance. She had a brother called Math, the son of Mathonwy. Math was a great king and magician. He was responsible for the fertility of the land and ruled over it with diligence and justice.

Dôn's consort, Beli Mawr, was a great warrior who provided healing and protection to those in need. He had three sons, Lludd, Llefelys, and Caswallan, and, with Dôn, he created the goddess Arianrhod. Dôn had four other children, all sons: Gofannon, Amaethon, Gwydion, and Gilfaethwy. Gofannon was the Divine Smith, master over the elements. Amaethon was the Divine Ploughman, as well as a magician. He taught the art of magic to his brother, Gwydion, who became a powerful conjurer and shape-shifter. Once, Amaethon stole a stag, causing a war between one of the Chiefs of Annwfn and Gwydion (which led to Cad Goddeu,

"The Battle of the Trees"). Dôn's fourth son, Gilfaethwy, fell in love with Goewin, Math's virgin footholder, and slept with her against her will. This led to more war and caused strife and difficulty for his sister, Arianrhod.

Arianrhod, the Silver Wheel, was a powerful goddess of the celestial realms. Her parents presented her with Caer Arianrhod, a divine fortress in which she traveled through the skies. After the rape of Goewin (who guarded the sovereignty of the land), she was no longer fit to be Math's footholder. On the advice of Gwydion and Gilfaethwy, Arianrhod was summoned to her uncle's court. Although her sovereign realm was that of the sky (rather than the Earth or the lower world, which were ruled by other gods), she agreed to come to see if she could be of assistance.

When she reached the court, Math tested her, asking her to step over his magic rod. As she did so, she gave birth to two sons, quite unexpectedly. One son had the nature of the sea, and so was called Dylan Eil Ton, Sea, Son of Wave. As soon as he was named, he made for the sea, where he could swim as well as any fish. He would not have been happy living with his mother in the starry skies, and so it was fitting that he should live in the sea, as her power also extended to the realm of the ocean.

The second son caused her great concern. She knew in her heart that this child, though small and poorly formed, might one day become a threat to her power. Therefore, she shunned the boy, who was carried off and raised by his uncle, Gwydion, Arianrhod's brother. The nature of her sons caused quite a commotion among the gods of Annwfn, and the fact that neither was raised by its mother was the subject of some concern, as well as a source of shame to her. Arianrhod retired to her celestial fortress where she processed through the skies with grandeur and nobility as she had always done, causing the waves to ebb and flow, and wondering to herself what was to come.

She often caught sight of her son, Dylan, swimming over the tops of the waves, and this brought lightness to her heavy heart. One day, however, word came to her that Dylan had been killed by another uncle, Gofannon. Some said it was an accident, others that he sought retribution for the shaming of his sister. Arianrhod grieved for her child. She locked herself inside her fortress, refusing to see anyone.

Time passed, and her second son grew to be a bright and able child. Eventually, when it was perceived that the omens were auspicious, Gwydion brought the boy to meet his mother. Arianrhod reacted with surprise and anger. Her grief for Dylan was still keen, and the disgrace she had experienced in her uncle's court was fresh in her mind. As she looked upon the boy, she could sense his potential. She knew that, in order to maintain her own power, she must refuse to help him, as hard as it was to do. Gwydion was angry at her reaction, and spoke harshly to her.

Arianrhod understood that her brother's actions were well intentioned, but out of self-preservation she was forced to make a difficult choice. She was revered among the gods as a good and noble ruler of the Sky Realm, where she made her circuit every twenty-eight days, turning her face toward all parts of her kingdom as she went. She knew every star intimately and moved in harmony with the sea.

It gave her pleasure to see her mother's dwelling as she passed by, remembering the honor shown to her by her parents (as well as many of the other gods) in entrusting her with this realm. Honor and power were important, and she meant to hold onto them. Although it pained her heart to do so, she told Gwydion that she would not give the lad a name, nor award him weapons.

Gwydion stormed off, determined to help the boy he had lovingly raised. He devised a scheme and, using his magic, created a ship out of seaweed. He and the lad posed as shoemakers, luring Arianrhod onto their ship, which was moored outside her castle. Once on board, she watched the boy kill a wren with a single cast and commented that it was with a skillful hand (*llaw gyffes*) that the fair-haired one (*lleu*) had killed the small bird. In doing this, she had inadvertently given her son a name, a step toward empowerment. When she realized this, Arianrhod became very angry. Although she knew her reaction was likely to be perceived as cold and heartless, because of the importance of her divine role she felt compelled to follow her path.

After some time had passed, Gwydion and young Lleu engaged in another ruse. Posing as bards, they entered Arianrhod's castle. With the aid of Gwydion's magic, they convinced Arianrhod that a great army was poised outside her fortress. She provided arms to all the men and gave permission for the lad to carry arms as well. The illusion was dropped, and, much to her dismay, she discovered that she had given arms to Lleu. Her rage was great, as was her fear. Her son had taken another step forward in his ascension to power. In desperation, she then denied him a wife from any race then on Earth.

In retaliation, Gwydion and Math created a woman for Lleu from the flowers of the fields and called her Blodeuwedd (Flower Face). This woman was not of their divine race and so did not possess their noble characteristics. She soon fell in love with another man, and together they plotted her husband's demise. Blodeuwedd's lover cast a magical poisoned spear at Lleu, who uttered a great scream and flew off in the form of an eagle. Gwydion searched high and low for his fosterling, finally locating the ailing youth in the top of an oak tree. Gwydion sang three magical *englynion* to him, coaxing him down from the tree. After he restored Lleu to his original form, he summoned healers, and the young man's health was restored. Lleu transformed his disloyal bride into an owl, a bird of night, exiling her to the darkness. He killed her lover and retook control of his kingdom.

This is the story of Arianrhod and her son, Lleu, which tells how one of the sons of Dôn created strife that led to the downfall of his sister, a wise and noble goddess of the Moon. She gave birth to two sons, the first associated with the realm of the sea and the other with that of the Sun. After her second son acquired his power, his light eclipsed that of his mother. She was then considered a lesser ruler of the sky, even though her power had been bestowed by Dôn and Beli Mawr. In spite of her trials, she maintained her noble bearing and performed her duties in a regal manner as she had always done. She turned her face toward every part of her realm as she traveled through the skies, urging on the sea and the tides, smiling upon the stars, and shining her light upon all those who remembered the greatness of her power.[51]

Crystal Charms and Silver Branches

One of the most intriguing details pertaining to Arianrhod is her name—Silver Wheel. The images evoked by this epithet are striking, and lead us to wonder what attributes were assigned to silver in Celtic tradition. The earliest phases of metal-working in Celtic regions focused on the mining of copper, tin, and gold. From these metals, alloys were produced to create a great diversity of bronze jewelry, weapons, and artifacts. Later, iron came onto the scene.[52] Native silver was mined in Britain, Ireland, and continental Europe, but does not seem to have been very common until the Roman era and again in the Viking Age, when the Norsemen introduced the use of silver on a large scale to most of Europe.[53] Some silver items were produced prior to the Roman and Viking eras, however, including silver disks, plaques, ornaments, brooches, and finger rings.[54] In the first few centuries of this era, the Picts were also renowned for their wonderful silver work, producing beautiful chains, plaques, rings, brooches, bowls, and sword fittings.

There are also several massive silver torcs from the Continent, but these may exhibit an Eastern influence, similar to the famous Gundestrup Cauldron, believed to have been commissioned by Celts, but produced by Thracian silversmiths. Overall, the most common use for silver seems to have been in the production of coins. If silver was mined, but not commonly used prior to the medieval period (except in the case of the Romans and the Picts), it may be that the circumstances that led to this situation also led to the perception of silver as a rare and valuable substance, perhaps even more valuable than gold, a scenario that exists in other cultures.

Silver has a number of interesting associations in Scottish folk tradition, particularly in connection with protective amulets and healing charms and stones. Healing stones had been used in Scotland since ancient times. Adamnan tells how Broichan, the chief Druid of the Pictish court at Inverness, was cured of his illness by drinking water in which a white pebble from Loch Ness had been dipped.[55] Some of the most potent healing stones in Scottish tradition consist of round, oval, or egg-shaped pieces of rock crystal wrapped in silver settings. These stones were held by certain Highland families and were widely reputed to possess healing properties. Often, the silver-wrapped stones were suspended on silver chains and dipped in water to impart their healing essence to the liquid. This was then given to those in need of healing, reminiscent of the Pictish healing stone. Some of the stones were also used to grant wishes, bestow victory, or provide protection against the evil eye.[56] While quartz pebbles and crystals have had magical associations since the earliest times in Scotland, other charm stones connected with healing or protection are also known. One of these is the Lee Penny, a piece of car-nelian set in a piece of a silver coin. The common element in many of these charms is the use of silver in the setting, the chain, or both.

Silver had a number of protective qualities, and silver coins often served as amulets.[57] New calves were given "silvered water" to drink for health and protec-tion, as were children believed to be in danger of the evil eye. To prevent witches from stealing milk, the first three draughts obtained from the cow were milked through a gold ring or over a silver coin.[58] Silver had other associations with witches and transformation. If a witch was encountered in animal form, arrows barbed with silver or muskets loaded with silver coins could be used to force him or her to regain human form.[59]

In other folk contexts, silver was associated with luck and abundance. On St. Columba's Day, the woman of the house would bake a bannock of oats or rye, placing a small silver coin into the cake. The head of the household then cut the cake into as many pieces as there were children in the family, and whoever got the coin was given part or all of the crop of lambs for the year. The baking of sacred cakes into which objects associated with luck or abundance were placed (includ-ing silver coins) also took place on other holidays, including those that were orig-inally pagan feast days.[60]

Objects of a particularly magical or sacred nature (especially those associated with the Otherworld) are often described as being silver. The MacCrimmons, hereditary pipers to Clan MacLeod, were given a silver chanter by a fairy woman who married one of the early MacLeod kings.[61] Magical branches, which served as a token of passage between the worlds (associated with healing, magic, music, and gifts from the Otherworld) were sometimes silver in color. In *Cormac's Adventures in the Land of Promise*, a magical silver branch is given to King Cormac by Manannán mac Lir. The branch is described as follows: "Delight and amuse-ment enough it was to listen to the music made by the branch, for men sore-wounded, or women in child-bed, or folk in sickness would fall asleep at the melody which was made when that branch was shaken."[62]

Both silver and crystal feature in *The Voyage of Bran*. One day, while wander-ing off alone, Bran heard magical music that caused him to fall asleep. When he awoke, he saw "a branch of silver with white blossoms," which he took with him back to his royal house. A fairy woman appeared to the host and sang fifty quatrains to Bran, which began:

> A branch of the apple-tree from Emain I bring, like those one knows;
> Twigs of white-silver are on it, crystal brows with blossoms.[63]

Silver seems to be associated with healing, water, magic, abundance, protection, transformation, and gifts from the Otherworld. As such, it is a fitting element to appear in connection with a goddess of the Moon.

Argante, Arianrhod, and Morgan le Fay

The element in Arianrhod's name that means "silver" derives from an Indo-European root word *arg*, which means "to shine," "white," "the shining or white metal," "silver." From this root came words in numerous languages having to do with silver and, eventually, with money, as with the French word *argent*.[64] These words also appear in Celtic languages: Old Irish *argat/airged*, Breton *arc'hant*, and Welsh *arian* (as in Arianrhod).[65] The Old Celtic form of the word (*arganto-*) is commonly found in place names, as well as in the Gaulish personal name Arganto-marus.[66]

There is another divine figure from British legendary tradition whose name includes a word meaning silver. This is Argante, an Otherworldly figure referred to only once in the Arthurian sources. She is mentioned in the *Brut* of Layamon, written around the turn of the 12th century. This is the first English vernacular version of the Arthurian legend and the second major poetic adaptation of Geoffrey of Monmouth's *History of the Kings of Britain*. While Layamon's work took as its immediate model the *Roman de Brut* of Wace and the *Ecclesiastical History* of Bede, some new material in the work is thought to have been added by the author.[67]

Layamon was a parish priest who lived near the upper reaches of the Severn River. His audience was comprised of common people rather than courtiers.[68] He preferred the archaic style and ancient virtues of earlier epics, where heroism and the supernatural mingled freely, avoiding popular references to courtly love and chivalry.[69] The atmosphere of Layamon's writing is closer to the Welsh tradition that informed some of Geoffrey of Monmouth's work, and many native characters seem to retain their original qualities. Layamon's work also appears to include elements of Celtic mythology familiar to us from other sources, and it may be that, living near the Welsh border, he had access to British folklore and local legends that a French author like Wace did not have.[70]

The death and disappearance of King Arthur are given a particularly mystical setting in the *Brut*, where Arthur is said to have traveled to Avalon to see someone called Argante.[71] Arthur's final scene is described as follows, as Arthur speaks his final words to his kinsman Constantine, son of Cador, duke of Cornwall:

> *I shall go forth to Avalon to the fairest of maidens*
> *To* Argante *the queen, the comeliest of fays*
> *And she shall heal my wounds and make me healthy and sound,*
> *By preparing for me health-giving potions.*
> *And then I shall come again into my own kingdom,*
> *And I shall abide with my Britons in joyous bliss.*[72]

Layamon goes on to describe two magnificently clad women who carry Arthur by boat over to Avalon, where he dwelt with "the fairest of spirit-folk" and whence he was fully expected by the Britons to return. This is the only specific reference we have to Argante. How are the women associated with Arthur's Otherworld voyage described in other Arthurian sources?

Neither Argante nor Morgan le Fay appear in Geoffrey of Monmouth's first work, *The History of the Kings of Britain,* completed around 1138. This narrative simply states that the mortally wounded Arthur was carried off to the Isle of Avalon so that his wounds could be treated. Geoffrey tells us that he handed his crown over to his cousin, Constantine, in the year 542.[73] Next is Wace's *Roman de Brut,* the first full account of the Arthurian story in French, written in the latter half of the 12th century. This text states that the mortally wounded Arthur had himself carried to Avalon to heal his wounds, and that he is still there, his return eagerly awaited by the Britons. While the author does refer to a number of characters that also appear in Welsh legendary sources, no mention is made of Morgan or Argante in this narrative either.[74]

It is in another work by Geoffrey of Monmouth that Morgan le Fay first appears. This is the *Vita Merlini* (The Life of Merlin), completed in 1148. There is much in this, Geoffrey's third work, that may be the creative interpolation of the author (including stories pertaining to Arthur and Merlin), yet certain elements clearly derive from early Welsh poems, as well as Scottish legends associated with Lailoken.[75] In the text, we are told that Morgan lives with eight of her sisters on the Isle of Avalon. Nine Otherworldly maidens also appear in Welsh tradition, where their breath is said to kindle a great cauldron located in Annwfn, the Welsh Otherworld. In the *Vita Merlini,* Morgan is noted for her learning, her healing powers, and her ability to shape-shift. She is also credited with receiving Arthur into the Otherworld and taking on the task of his healing:

> The island of apples, which men call "the Fortunate Isles," gets its name
> . . . because it produces all things of itself . . . There nine sisters rule by a
> pleasing set of laws those who come to them from our country. She who
> is first of them is more skilled in the healing art, and excels her sisters in
> the beauty of her person. Morgen is her name, and she has learned what
> useful properties all the herbs contain, so that she can cure sick bodies.
> She also knows an art by which to change her shape . . . After the battle
> of Camlan . . . Morgan received us with honour . . .[76]

She appears next in the works of Chrétien de Troyes, believed to date from between 1170 and 1190 (although some argue that his first work may have been composed as late as the mid 1180s). An educated and well-trained writer, Chrétien's highly innovative work drew on well-established themes and traditions connected with scholarly rhetoric and formal literary conventions and were, therefore, focused on themes of courtly love. These stories are primarily concerned with the knights of Arthur's court rather than the king himself, from whom the focus seems to have strayed. Chrétien does incorporate motifs drawn, to some degree, from Celtic folklore, particularly those relating to adventures and enchantments. Morgan is mentioned in his earliest surviving piece, *Erec and Enide*, where she is described as the friend of Lord Guingamar, Lord of the Isle of Avalon. The tale describes how she made an ointment to heal the wounds of her brother, Arthur, a task she also performs in *Yvain (Le Chevalier au Lion)* where she is described as Morgan the Wise.[77]

The *Brut* of Layamon, which refers to Argante as the supernatural queen who ferries Arthur to the Otherworld to heal him, is thought to date from between 1189 and 1199. It may, therefore, appear next in the chronology, although it is possible that this position is held by Giraldus Cambrensis, whose *On the Instruction of Princes* was composed sometime in the 1190s. Arthur's Otherworldly grave and the authority and healing power of Morgan are mentioned by Giraldus as follows:

> "The burial place is now known as Glastonbury, and in ancient times it was called the Isle of Avalon. It is indeed almost an island, being surrounded by marshes." And so in the British language it was called Inis Avallon, or Apple Island, since apples grow there in abundance. Then too Morgan, the noble matron and lady ruler of those parts, who was closely related by blood to King Arthur, transported Arthur after the Battle of Kemelen (Camlan) to this island, now called Glaston, to heal his wounds.[78]

The *Prose Merlin* of Robert de Boron, in which Merlin is somewhat reinvented from his original appearance in Geoffrey of Monmouth, was probably written in the beginning of the 13th century. Morgan appears in this text as one of three daughters of Ygerne:

> The peace was thus ratified on both sides, and Uther Pendragon took Ygerne as his wife, and gave her daughter [Morgawse] to King Lot of Orkney ... The daughter who became the wife of King Lot later gave birth to Mordred, to my lord Gawain, to Agravain and Gareth and Gaheris. Another daughter, a bastard, was married to King Neutre of Sorhaut. Finally, on the recommendation of the whole family, the king sent the daughter named Morgan to school at a convent. She was so gifted that she learned the seven arts and quite early acquired remarkable knowledge of an art called astronomy ... She also studied nature and medicine, and it was through that study that she came to be called Morgan the Fay.[79]

The *Vulgate Cycle*, a series of stories created by an unknown writer or writers, became the most popular account of the Arthurian legends in the latter part of the Middle Ages. Many new elements appear in these tales, including the love of Lancelot and Guinevere as an important element in Arthur's tragic undoing (shifting the focus from his heroic deeds to his personal life), the intertwining of the Round Table and the Grail legend, and Merlin's enchantment and imprisonment by his beloved Nimue.[80] In one of the stories that comprise this cycle of tales (the *Estoire de Merlin*), Morgan is described as cheerful, beautiful, well-proportioned, a good singer, and "the warmest and most sensual woman in Britain." She is reported to have learned astronomy and other subjects from Merlin: "she became an excellent scholar and was later called Morgan La Fée because of the marvels she wrought." While she is generally described as calm and agreeable, the story also mentions that, when her anger was aroused, she was very difficult to appease, sounding like a goddess figure who demanded respect.

Morgan le Fay is the presiding genius (and chief troublemaker) in *Sir Gawain and the Green Knight,* a tale that has survived in a single manuscript dated to the 14th century. Here, Morgan devises a scheme with which to test Arthur's court, as well as to try and shock Guinevere, presumably because the queen exposed Morgan's love affair with the knight Guimar. As in other accounts, Morgan's power derives from that of Merlin, and the origin of both figures seems to lie in the world of Celtic myth.[81] In one part of the tale, a beautiful young woman is accompanied by an elderly woman who turns out to be Morgan, "an ancient one . . . highly honoured by all those high-born around her." This "venerable and ancient woman" is described as wrinkled and old, her throat and chin draped in concealing veils, with a squat, thick body. Gawain is said to have saluted the older woman first, "scraping very low," prior to taking the young woman in his arms.[82] Later in the story, the Green Knight reveals to Gawain the identity of the old woman:

> *The mighty Morgan the Fay, who lives on my manor,*
> *Whose mastery of magic is manipulated with craft,*
> *Learned to a large degree from the lore of great Merlin—*
> *For indeed she had a long and a lasting love with that crafty wizard,*
> *Who is known to your country's knights as one of fame.*
> *Therefore Morgan the Goddess rightly is her name.*[83]

The Green Knight goes on to describe how Morgan sent him in disguise to Arthur's halls to see if everything was as splendid as its reputation made it out to be. He mentions that Morgan, "the aged lady," is the daughter of Ygerne, or Igraine, the Duchess of Tintagel, as well as Arthur's half-sister and Gawain's aunt. He invites Gawain to come back to his manor to visit with his aunt, Morgan, and be merry in his house.

In Malory's *Le Morte d'Arthur,* published in 1485, we encounter Morgan and a number of other divine female figures. In the tale, Arthur is led away in a ship "wherein were three queens: one was King Arthur's sister, Queen Morgan le Fay, the other was the Queen of Northgalis, and the third was the Queen of the Wastelands. Also there was Ninive, the chief lady of the lake, . . . and this lady had done much for Arthur . . ."[84]

While a full examination of the legend of Morgan le Fay is beyond the scope of this chapter, we can examine the primary elements and attributes associated with Morgan, as well as the chronological order of references to Morgan and Argante. Keeping in mind that the dating of certain Arthurian texts is unclear or debated, a general timeline pertaining to Argante, Morgan le Fay, and other Avalonian women may be as shown in Table 7, opposite.

It is interesting to note the variation in the number of women who ferry Arthur over to Avalon or who attend him to heal his wounds. Nine sisters are mentioned in the *Vita Merlini*, two woman in Layamon (one of whom is Argante), and three or four women in Malory's text (Morgan and two queens, as well as the Chief Lady of the Lake, Ninive), not to mention Morgan's various solitary appearances.[85] It is unclear if Argante and Morgan are the same figure, or if Argante is one of the other queens of Avalon (perhaps one of Morgan's eight sisters). The traditions are fascinating in any case, and in the texts, we can perceive an early and continuing representation of an Otherworld queen and ruler associated with a passage across the water to the Otherworld realms—a wise, learned, and respected figure skilled in many arts and noted for her powers of healing, as well as magic and shape-shifting in later texts.

There are a number of similarities of theme and function between Arianrhod and Argante, especially if the latter is the same as, or similar to, the figure of Morgan le Fay. Both are powerful, supernatural women known for their Otherworld connection and habitation, and associated with Earthly and supernatural bodies of water, some of which are known for their healing properties. Both women possess the ability to grant or withhold weapons from male figures—in Arianrhod's case, her son, Lleu, a hero and king, and in Arthurian sources, a number of kings and heroes.[86] Morgan's reputation as a magician seems to grow and degenerate over time as she is transformed from a beneficent, healing goddess to a manipulative and deceitful sorceress, passing through intermediate stages as a beautiful, skilled magician and a wily, yet generally honorable, trickster. While I would hesitate to make a direct connection between the figures of Argante and Arianrhod, it is interesting to note their association with specific Otherworld locations, their profound connection with magic, feminine power, and bodies of water, and their ability to give or withhold arms from male figures, as well as the appearance of words denoting silver in their divine epithets.

The Shining One

We have followed the veneration of the Moon through its various manifestations in a number of ancient, shamanic, and historically attested cultures, from the pantheons of Indo-European cultures to the rise of the great Neolithic monuments, from Druidic rituals to early modern folk practices. We have also watched the

Table 7. Chronology of Arthurian Sources

WORK AND DATE	
Geoffrey of Monmouth, 1138	No mention of Argante or Morgan le Fay
Geoffrey of Monmouth, *Vita Merlini,* 1148	First mention of Morgan. She is learned, skilled in many arts, capable of shape-shifting. Heals Arthur's wounds. She is said to have eight sisters.
Wace, second half of 1100s	No mention of Argante or Morgan.
Chrétien de Troyes, 1170–90	Morgan mentioned, associated with healing.
Brut of Layamon, circa 1189–99	Argante, a beautiful, Otherworld queen appears. She and another woman ferry Arthur to Avalon.
Giraldus Cambrensis, 1190s	Morgan, "matron and lady-ruler" of Otherworld. Takes Arthur to Avalon to heal him.
Robert de Boron, *Prose Merlin*, early 1200s	Morgan le Fay, learned, gifted, and skilled. Plots against Arthur, steals his sword.
Vulgate Cycle, Anon., later Middle Ages	Morgan is learned, gifted; also lovely, sensual. When roused to anger, she is difficult to appease.
Sir Gawain and the Green Knight, 1300s	Morgan the Goddess, ancient, wise, and revered; Magician, shape-shifter, and schemer
Thomas Malory's *Morte d'Arthur*, 1485	Morgan le Fay, along with two other queens (and the Lady of the Lake), takes Arthur to Avalon for healing

Moon's enigmatic but persistent appearances in the realms of Celtic art, myth, and legend. Yet the Queen of the Night is elusive, her symbols and portents veiled behind the mists of time and hidden under a fog of obscure language and mythology. Her face peers out at us from behind a cloudbank of half-forgotten legends as she rises out of waters whose ebb tide reveals a little of the ancient story lines, medieval chronicles, and well-worn folk charms that chart her course.

As we will see in the next chapter, the Moon was considered a beloved and respected friend in Celtic folk tradition, a divine measurer of time whose phases guided the lives of mortals. She was adored and venerated in Scottish folklife, hailed as "a glorious jewel," a "divine guidant of the clouds and stars," "a celestial lamp" whose light shines on the world below, and a "queen-maiden who steers the tides."[87] In this guise, she is the Silver Wheel, a bountiful queen of the celestial realms who illuminates the world during its time of darkness, and whose power is great enough to move the mighty ocean.

In early Britain, she may have gone by the name Silver Wheel, but in other regions and eras, she is likely to have had other descriptive titles. While many words for the Moon in Indo-European languages are related to the month (or time measurement in general), other lunar terminology is connected with words pertaining to the concept of "brightness." For example, an Old Irish word for the Moon, *gelach*, contains a color term, *gel*, which means "fair, white, bright, or shining."[88] Perhaps other early Celtic terms or titles associated with the Moon and its divinity contained this or a similar root word. We know that the names of various Scottish lakes, streams, fords, river mouths, and meadows contain the word *gel*. A number of Scottish river names derive from related Pictish terms (*gelidios* or *gelidia*), which denote "the white or pure one," and may reflect the well-attested association of rivers or bodies of water with female deities.[89]

This concept of brightness also appears in connection with several Welsh words for the Moon (*lleuad* and *lloer*). These derive from an Indo-European root (*leuksna-*), which produced words denoting brightness or light, as well as words referring to the Moon. This root is found in Old Irish *luan*, "light, brightness, Moon, perhaps specifically the new Moon," Old Prussian *lauxnos*, "stars," and Latin *luna*, the goddess of the Moon.[90] Just as the roots *gel-* and *leuksna-* (meaning "bright" or "shining") produced words that referred to the Moon (as well as a female Moon deity), perhaps the word *arg* ("to shine"), found in words denoting shining and silver, eventually found its way into the names of at least two British female divine figures, one of whom may be associated with the Moon.

Whatever her title and whatever her name, it is the radiance of the Moon's resplendent and most sacred light that has fascinated and guided us throughout the ages. A divine, luminous being that is ever changing, yet always the same, she is the ruler of the night skies, and a lamp that lights our way. As it was said in a traditional Scottish folk prayer: "Sacred be each thing which she illumines."[91]

☽   ☽   ☽

Meditations and Exercises

Explore these inspiring activities to gain a better understanding of the nature and power of the Queen of the Night.

1) We have seen that the names of the divine ancestresses Danu and Dôn may be related and that both serve as mother of the gods. Their names may derive from words meaning "earth" or "river," and may be connected with the concept of divine gifts or skills. In Celtic tradition, the seat of wisdom lies in the Otherworld and is often described as a well from which the sacred streams of knowledge flow. Do you think there is a connection between these divine women and the concepts mentioned above? You may want to undertake a journey or meditation to connect with these ancient goddesses and see what imagery or information is presented to you.

2) If you have not read the *Mabinogi*, I highly recommend Patrick Ford's translation. It is thoroughly readable and enjoyable, with an excellent introductory chapter. Explore these stories in some detail to help you understand the characters and themes associated with Arianrhod. *The Mabinogi* by Proinsias Mac Cana is an excellent follow-up once you are familiar with the stories. It can help you understand the many strands of tradition from which these tales were woven, as well as the symbols and elements embedded within them.

3) Do you think Arianrhod's name and the nature of her two children support our interpretation of her story as an early myth concerned with cosmology and the like? Who do you think her sons' father was (Math, Gwydion, or an Otherworld lover), and how does his identity and nature affect the children's attributes, character, and destiny? In addition, what is the significance of the twelve women who guard the king's daughter in *Balor on Tory Island*? Meditation can serve as a useful tool to discover additional layers of significance in this mythological scenario.

4) The wren has a number of interesting associations and plays an important role in the wren-boy processions of Ireland and Wales. The legends and attributes of the wren lend themselves to a number of possible interpretations. Which of the theories previously presented resonates with you in terms of authenticity and viability? How else might the symbolism of the wren be interpreted?

5) Create a chart that maps out the genealogy of the family of Dôn. Include the names of these divine characters, the meaning of their names or epithets, and their primary attributes. Can you perceive any themes or relationships beyond the ones presented in this chapter? Take some time to reflect upon the primal

nature of these sacred figures and see if you can discern any other pertinent mythological motifs or patterns.

6) At an auspicious time of the lunar cycle, light thirteen small candles in a crescent in front of you. Take a spiritual journey that focuses on an ascent to the Sky Realm, and see if you can envision the celestial dwellings of Dôn and her daughter (Llys Dôn and Caer Arianrhod). What sorts of images pertaining to these goddesses and the various elements of the Sky Realm come to you? Set down your experiences in a journal or create a piece of poetry or liturgy based on the images you experience and the entities you encounter.

7) Try your hand at a re-creation of the original version of Arianrhod's story. After reading through her story in its entirety, take some time to look back through this chapter carefully, making note of the important themes and elements. Let the story and its symbolism ruminate in your unconscious for three days and nights prior to writing. See what connections, images, and ideas your inner mind brings to light.

8) After examining the various uses and attributes of silver, can you think of any other possible interpretations of the name Silver Wheel? We have seen that decorative silver disks existed that may have had a ritual or symbolic purpose. Chariot wheels are another possibility, perhaps connected with the lunar chariot. We know that gold disks symbolized the Sun in a variety of early contexts, as did Sun crosses and spoked wheels, strengthening the possibility that a silver wheel was associated with the Moon. Meditate on the various motifs pertaining to silver, including its association with healing, protection, and Otherworld gifts and connections. How might these be associated with the Moon? Write a piece of poetry that expresses these concepts and your personal exploration of them.

9) Do think there is any connection between Argante, Morgan le Fay, and Arianrhod? In addition, do you feel their attributes form a pattern of correspondence or follow any perceptible line of symbolic development? What do you make of the various lunar-related words associated with the concept of brightness? How might the light of the Moon, shining against the darkness of the sky and illuminating the unknown, have formed part of their sacred origins or legendary evolution?

THE PATH OF THE WHITE MARE

CELTIC LORE AND
LUNAR FOLK TRADITIONS

Though I am old with wandering,
Through hollow lands and hilly lands
I will find out where she has gone,
And kiss her lips and take her hands;
And walk among long dappled grass,
And pluck till time and times are done
The silver apples of the moon,
The golden apples of the sun.

—WILLIAM BUTLER YEATS, "THE SONG OF WANDERING AENGUS"

The age-old patterns of lunar observation and time reckoning, and the deeply imbedded traditions associated with the worship and veneration of the Moon, also find expression in the folklore of Celtic countries. These customs were widely practiced, and many were alive and resonant well into the 20th century. Beyond the context of medieval myth and legend, the Moon played a role in early charms and incantations that bridged the gap between paganism and Christianity, incorporating elements of both traditions. In the 8th-century poem *Saint Patrick's Breastplate*, the reciter invokes the strength of the Trinity and the power of various elemental forces:

Today I go forth with
The strength of the Skies
The brightness of the Sun
The splendor of the Moon
The brilliance of Fire
The swiftness of Lightning
The speed of the Wind
The depths of the Ocean
The steadfastness of Earth
And the steadiness of Rock.[1]

The Moon plays an integral role in a Latin love charm found in an early manuscript from the British Isles. Known as the *Leiden Lorica,* the poem invokes various apostles and archangels, yet also includes elemental forces sacred to other magical traditions. The last line appears to be an echo of the early triune cosmos of Sky, Earth, and Sea/Underworld.

> *I adjure you, heaven and earth and sun and moon and all stars,*
> *Lightning and clouds and winds and rain and fire and heat,*
> *To purify the heart of (beloved one's name) for the sake of my love.*
>
> *I adjure you, nights and days, darkness and light,*
> *to purify the heart of (name) for the sake of my love.*
>
> *I adjure you, all trees and stones and hours and minutes,*
> *to purify the heart of (name) . . .*
>
> *I adjure you, birds of the sky and all beasts of the field,*
> *beasts of burden and . . . fish of the sea . . .*
>
> *I adjure you . . . all wonders and powers that*
> *are above the sky and the earth,*
> *under the sky and the earth, and under the sea . . .*

Some time later, the 12th-century writer Giraldus Cambrensis (Gerald of Wales), in his *History and Topography of Ireland,* comments upon the Moon at some length. His discourse reveals the pervasive influence of Classical and medieval sources on early Irish and British learning and written lore. Giraldus relates how, when the Moon was "at her meridian," the ocean recalled its waters to its "hidden lairs," leaving the coasts of Britain dry, yet filling the Irish coasts near Dublin. He mentions that, when the Moon was "recovering her light" and beginning to grow beyond "her half size," the western seas became rough and tempestuous, swelling more and more until the time of the full Moon, when "the moon has attained the full perfection of her roundness." Then as her "fires decrease and she turns her face away," the swelling of the waves evidently also decreased.[2]

Giraldus describes a number of concepts related to the perceived connection of the Moon with bodies of water and its effect on the liquid essence inherent in all living creatures. This is a belief we will encounter in much later Celtic folklore as well.

> Indeed Phoebe is to such an extent a source and influence on all liquids,
> that according to her waxing and waning she directs and controls not only
> the waves of the sea, but also the bone-marrow and brains in all living

things as well as the sap of trees and plants. When she is deprived of her full light you will notice that all things lose their fullness. But when she has attained her complete roundness, you will find that bones are full of marrow, heads of brains, and other things of sap.[3]

Several centuries before the publication of this learned exposition, a deep appreciation of the Moon and the beauty it brings to the natural world and to our lives appears in a poem attributed to the Irish hermit Suibne Geilt. Written in the 8th century, Suibne's poem describes his humble but beloved shelter in the wilderness:

> My little room in Túaim Inbir:
> No dwelling could be more sturdy
> With its attendant bright stars
> With its sun, with its moon.
> It is Gobbán who made it . . .
> It is as bright as being in a garden.[4]

Celtic Lunar Folk Traditions

Folklore relating to the Moon has been recorded in every region associated with Celtic language and culture. While there is insufficient time and space to present all the pertinent folklore, examples are presented from many of the Celtic countries.

Ireland

In Ireland, the new Moon was considered the most important of the Moon's phases. Its appearance was greeted in most parts of the country with a ceremony, which, if not carried out, was believed to result in misfortune. On Clear Island (off the coast of Cork), when women saw the new Moon, they blessed themselves and offered a short prayer, *Slán beo go bhfága sí sinn,* "May she leave us in good health." It is still a fairly widespread practice in certain parts of Ireland for people to bless themselves when they first see the new Moon.[5]

Marriage divination rites were also associated with the Moon. Young women looked at the reflection of the "young May Moon" in their mirror, hoping also to see their future husbands looking over their shoulder.[6] When people viewed the new Moon for the first time, they bent down and picked up three lumps of clay and put them around their necks to make their future partners appear in a dream that very night. In County Mayo, when they saw the first new Moon of the new year, they put a bit of clay under their right side and recited the following rune:

> New moon, true moon, New Moon trick,
> Bring to me my true love quick.
> The colour of (his/her) hair, the clothes (s)he'll wear,

And may (s/he) appear to me this night in my dream,
And the day (s)he'll be married to me.[7]

Others believed that, when they saw the new Moon for the first time, if one of their garments were turned inside out, they would receive a present. Turning money in the pocket upon seeing the new Moon resulted in having twice as much the next time the new Moon appeared. It was considered unlucky to see the new Moon through glass or through a window, and misfortune might occur if it was seen over the left shoulder.[8]

The Moon had a significant effect on many facets of life. People born under certain phases of the Moon were said to be influenced by it in various ways. It was believed that the insane were far worse during the full Moon, and that sleeping under the moonlight could in itself cause insanity. Signs and portents associated with the weather, the appearance of the sky, and the May Moon were carefully noted on Beltaine. These were considered indicative of the weather to be expected in the upcoming summer season.[9] A halo around the Moon was thought to portend a storm or rain.[10] The appearance of the Moon on the eve of Samain was also used as a guide to the weather during the winter season. If the Moon was clear, it meant fine weather. If clouded over, the degree of this foretold a similar proportion of rain. Clouds racing over the Moon were a warning of coming storms.[11]

The phase of the Moon could also affect the efficacy of healing charms. Folk cures for many ailments were often carried out in such a way so that the disease disappeared as the Moon was on the wane. One folk cure for corns was started during the waxing Moon and just before the full Moon, so that, when the cure was completed in twenty-one days, the Moon was once again waxing.[12] Some cures were said to be more effective if carried out under the light of the Moon. Herbs were sometimes gathered in the moonlight in the belief that the medicine made from them would be more effective.[13]

There are a number of Irish folk stories pertaining to the Man in the Moon, a figure known variously as Domhnall na Gealaí (Donald of the Moon), Seán na Scuab (Sean of the Brooms), or Tadhg na Scuab (Tadhg of the Brooms). In some of these tales, a lazy only child, spoiled by his mother, refuses to perform a simple task and is cursed by her with the phrase: "May the Moon take you with her!" The next day (which was Sunday), the boy was collecting sticks in the woods. The Moon came down to him and said she was going to take him away with her. Although the boy pleads with her, his efforts are in vain, and there the boy lives to this day. When the Moon is full, he is said to look down upon young children to warn them of what will happen if they don't do what their mothers say. In another version of the story, the Man in the Moon is an ordinary fellow carrying a bundle of broom on his back (on a Sunday as well). On returning from the woods, he encounters a "wee man" who grants him three wishes, one of which is, "I wish I were the man in the moon!"[14] It is interesting to note that, while the markings on the Moon represent a transplanted male figure, the Moon itself is female.

Scotland

In Scotland (as in many other countries), the phases of the Moon were observed before certain types of activities were performed. Journeys or undertakings were rushed or delayed in order to have them occur under the correct influence of the Moon. People often stood outdoors at night "to see what the night was doing." The Moon, the stars, and the constellations were observed, and a prayer was offered to the bright Moon, popularly referred to as "the glorious lamp of the poor."[15] Folklore collected as late as the 17th century noted that the Highlanders "reckoned time not by months of thirty or thirty-one days but by four weeks, computing by the Moon, which they observe in almost all matters."[16]

The new Moon was believed to encourage growth in substances, and the appearance of the new crescent (which led to the waxing phase) was considered the proper time for sowing and planting. An exception to this was made in the case of onions and kale, which tended to go to seed if they were sown during the increase of the Moon.[17] It was believed that if a cow and bull mated during the first quarter of the Moon, a bull calf would be born, but if they united during the waning Moon, a cow calf would result.[18] It was lucky to cut one's hair during the waxing Moon, and some mothers took little snips of their children's hair for luck during that time. The new Moon was considered propitious for setting out on a journey and for all new undertakings. Until recent times, marriages in the Orkneys always took place during the waxing Moon phase.[19]

The waning Moon was a good time for ploughing, reaping, and cutting peat. Only during this phase would the moisture leave the peat so it would dry properly.[20] During the waning Moon, the essence of things were also thought to wane or decrease. For this reason, hazel and willow for making baskets (and pine wood for making boats) were not cut during this phase, as it was believed the sap of the plant went down into the root. This made the wood brittle and crumbly, "without pith, and without good." Similarly, animals were not killed for food during the waning Moon, for the meat would be neither plump or fatty, "tasteless and without sap."[21] Eggs laid during the waning Moon were used in hatching, rather than those laid during the increase of the Moon (as the latter were thought to be difficult to rear). The waning Moon was also the proper time to geld animals.[22]

In early times, many people in Scotland, both young and old, kept a coin in their pockets known as the *peighinn pisich*, "the lucky penny." They turned the coin in their pockets three times at the first glimpse of the new Moon. In the modern era, some people still turn a coin (preferably a silver one!) in their pockets for luck at the new Moon. In some areas, when you saw the new Moon, it was propitious to put your right hand around your left foot and then make a cross on your palm with spit, reciting a short Christian prayer.[23] All over the Highlands, in addition to the widespread custom of turning money at the first sight of the new Moon, it was also customary to bow to the new Moon when it was first observed.[24]

In the 1600s, when people in the Highlands saw the new Moon, they turned around three times and cast a handful of grass at the Moon to thank the Creator for its presence. They sometimes also cut a cross in ground and said "I have wounded you, Earth, before I am wounded." They believed that by doing this they would not be harmed or wounded during the course of that lunar month.[25]

On the first Monday of each quarter, the house was blessed with water obtained from a wise woman. In earlier times, the day associated with the Moon (luan) was understood to be the new Moon. The new Moon, which began each quarter of the year (corresponding to the pagan holidays), was a good day for averting the evil eye or drawing lovers to each other. It was also the correct day to part from a lover. The new Moon was believed to be the favorite day for men and women "of the evil eye" to practice their *dubh-cheilg* ("black art"). Additionally, it was the day on which men and women who had the skill of the *frith* ("augury") practiced their visions.[26]

Healing charms also made use of the phases of the Moon. Large stones known as "child-getting stones" were visited by women during the waxing Moon in the hope they would conceive. In Moray, branches of woodbine were cut during the waxing period of the March Moon, twisted into wreaths, and kept until the following March. Children suffering from fever or consumption were passed three times through them to effect a cure.[27]

The Moon is mentioned in a folk charm for making a love philter using a highly prized plant known as the *mòthan* (perhaps the bog violet). In this charm, a woman goes down on her left knee and plucks nine roots of the plant. She knots these together into a ring and places it into the mouth of the girl for whom it was made. While doing so, the woman invokes the King of the Sun, the Moon, and the stars, as well as the Sacred Three. Later, if the intended man kisses the girl while she has the ring in her mouth, he will fall in love with her and be bound to her everlastingly "in cords infinitely finer than the gossamer net of the spider and infinitely stronger than the adamant chain of the giant."[28]

We have seen how, in ancient times, the Moon played an important role in the timing of seasonal rites. This was also the case with the early Celtic feast days, as well as later folk customs and festivals. Dr. Michael Newton, a specialist in Scottish Gaelic traditions, describes the timing of these seasonal customs most eloquently:

> The Gaels celebrated the round of the year with seasonal festivals inherited from their pre-Christian past. The most important . . . were the "Quarter Days," organized generally according to the solar year, but adjusted to the lunar calendar by holding celebrations on the new moon.

The dark always preceded the light, and therefore the new day starts with dusk, just as the new year begins with the start of winter.[29]

Oral tradition played a huge role in the culture of traditional societies. Songs, poems, advice, and practical information all formed part of a remarkable system of knowledge and lore. Thousands of proverbs were preserved in the memory of everyday people. Even in modern times, bards and storytellers commit hundreds of lengthy tales to memory and can often remember from whom they were learned.

Traditions, information, and lore pertaining to the Moon formed part of the oral record, as this knowledge was considered practical, and perhaps also spiritual, in nature. This was but one branch of the vast body of traditional wisdom associated with the natural world preserved in the memories of traditional bearers and elders. It was recorded that, prior to the year 1800:

> . . . There was many a one of the Highlanders who could tell the names of his ancestors for many generations back. Also, although they could neither read nor write, they took note of the time, and he who did not always learn the day of the month and the age [that is, phase] of the moon, was considered a man void of intelligence. The people who were of old would tell when the new moon would come, when it would be full or in the quarter, as well as though they had an almanac.[30]

As an elderly gentleman in the Isle of Eigg was quoted as saying, "The men of old were observant of the facts of nature, as the young folk of today are not."[31]

Wales

In Welsh tradition, the circumstances surrounding the birth of a child were thought to influence its life in a number of ways. Those born at night were said to be able to see visions, ghosts, and phantom funerals. Children born during the new Moon would be eloquent; those born during the last quarter had excellent powers of reasoning.[32]

Cornwall

In Cornwall, it was considered unlucky to see the new Moon through glass, but if viewed outdoors, money turned in the pocket would enable one to make a wish. It was believed that, to ensure good luck, you should spit on the palm of one hand and cut or strike it across with the palm of the other upon seeing the new Moon. If a child was born during the waning Moon, the next child would be of the opposite sex. If born during the waxing Moon, however, the next child would be of the same sex. An early death was predicted if a child was born during the void Moon. It was also believed that, on the first day of the month (which, in earlier times, coincided with the new Moon), the word "rabbits" should be the first word spoken, perhaps demonstrating some connection with the widespread tradition that the rabbit or hare is a lunar animal.[33]

Cornish tradition stated that, if you picked up sticks on a Sunday, you would be taken up into the Moon, as in the Irish tale of the Man in the Moon. It was also believed that, if a piece of tin was placed in a bank of *muryans* (ants) during a certain phase of the Moon, they would turn it into silver. The muryans were believed by Cornish miners to be the "little people" in a state of decay of the earth. It is interesting to note the connection here between the Moon, silver, and the inhabitants of the Otherworld.

An interesting piece of lore has been recorded concerning club moss, considered good for treating eye diseases in Cornish folk tradition, as it was in early Irish tradition. On the third day of the Moon (the void Moon), when the new crescent is seen for the first time, the knife that will be used to gather the club moss is presented to the Moon, saying: "As Christ healed the issue of blood, do thou cut what thou cuttest for good." At sunset, the person washes his or her hands and, kneeling, cuts the moss, which is then wrapped in a white cloth and boiled in fresh water from the spring nearest to where the plant was growing.[34] This ritual includes familiar elements from early Irish and more recent Scottish rituals associated with the gathering of sacred plants. These include the use of a special knife, kneeling while gathering the plant, and wrapping the plant in a white cloth.

Brittany

In Brittany, a sacred ritual of circuiting survived at Locronan that was held every seven years. In this rite, the participants walked around a sacred hill on a pathway twelve kilometers long and containing twelve stations marked by sacred stones. The procession began in the west, rather than the east, as in other ceremonies (a feature found in Scottish folk rites associated with the Moon, as we shall see in the next section). The participants proceeded in a sunwise circle, rising northward, descending eastward, and then proceeding toward the south. After completing a circuit of the hill, they climbed it, descending in the west. During their descent, they walked three times around a huge stone that represented the Moon. This stone stood near a wood called Nevet (Sacred Place, similar to the words *nemed* and *nemeton*, which mean "sacred" or "sacred place" in the older Celtic languages).

Apart from the remarkable existence of a huge stone that represented the Moon, the appearance of twelve station stones is interesting in light of other traditions we have encountered (twelve maidens who guarded a thirteenth, etc.) Twelve stones surrounding a larger, central stone also appear in an account of an early pagan ritual from Ireland. Written by a somewhat biased Christian writer, the account refers to the worship of a figure called Crom Cróich, the "king-idol" of the pagan Irish, god of all the people who lived in Ireland prior to the coming of Patrick. First fruits were offered to this deity at Samain, when the people gathered to worship him. Evidently, twelve subsidiary stones existed at the site around the central stone that represented the idol.[35] While the Irish Celts were not likely to have been monotheists, it is possible that they gathered at Samain to offer the fruits of field and flock to their gods. The existence of a primary central stone surrounded by twelve others is interesting in light of the Breton ritual.

Traditional Proverbs, Rhymes, and Riddles

Many proverbs, rhymes, riddles, and weather omens have been collected over the last century or more, a few examples of which are presented here (arranged by country):

Cornwall

See the new Moon through glass, you'll have trouble while it lasts.
A Saturday Moon if it comes once in seven years it comes too soon.
Two full Moons in May, neither good for corn nor hay.
Sunday's Moon is a sailor's dread.

Ireland

What exists since the time of Adam and has not yet reached five weeks of age?
   (The Moon.)
What is it that is a fortnight in growing and a fortnight in dying?
   (The Moon.)
It exists from the beginning of the world and yet it is not a month old.
   (The Moon.)
A little white sheet on the side of the house,
and no one could go to weave it.
   (Moonshine.)
I see it sitting and standing, I see it on the blossom of the gorse
Neither fog nor dew causes it to fall, and it never stops walking.
   (The Moon.)
A white mare in the lake,
And she does not wet her foot.
   (The Moon shining in the water.)[36]

In relation to this last riddle, it is interesting to note the place name Aichearra an Ghearráin Bháin (Short-cut of the White Gelding) mentioned in *Fairy Legends from Donegal*. The term *gearrán bán* occurs in a number of place names and is said to mean "the Moon." One wonders if there is some connection with early representations of the lunar chariot drawn by horses (often, but not always, by mares).

Scotland

It is in Scottish tradition that we are fortunate enough to have a record of the wonderful folk prayers offered to the new Moon when first perceiving her each month. Alexander Carmichael describes how men and women went up onto the highest hill or knoll in the region in order to look for the new Moon. They began looking in the west (as in the Breton ritual), turning slowly in a sunwise direction on the right heel until they saw the Moon. When the Moon appeared, they called out, "See! See! See!" and there was much competition as to who saw it first. Heartfelt prayers of praise were then offered to the Moon, a "jewel of guidance in the night" and a "queen-maiden of good fortune"[37]:

> *Welcome to you, New Moon*
> *Jewel of Guidance, of Affection.*
> *I am bending my knee to you*
> *I am offering my love to you . . .*
> *I am lifting my eye to you*
> *New Moon of the Seasons.*
> *Welcome to you, New Moon . . .*
> *Queen of my Love.*[38]

. . .

> *When I see the New Moon,*
> *It is fitting for me to lift my eye*
> *It is fitting for me to bend my knee*
> *It is fitting for me to bow my head.*
>
> *I praise you, Moon of Guidance*
> *Now that I have seen you again*
> *Now that I have seen the new moon*
> *Beautiful Guide on the Pathway.*[39]

The Moon plays a role in other Scottish folk prayers utilized for a variety of purposes. In a popular charm for plucking yarrow, the incantation includes these words:

> *May I be an island in the sea*
> *May I be a hill upon the shore*
> *May I be a star in the waning moon*
> *May I be a staff for the weak.*[40]

A lengthy poem in praise of Brigit (which includes the "The Descent of Brigit") was recited to invoke protection, so that neither "sun, fire, beam nor moon" would burn the person, nor "river, brine, flood nor water" drown them (reflecting the earlier, perhaps Druidic, perception of the destructive powers of fire and water).[41] In The Invocation of the Graces (a charm whose power is attributed to Brigit), the following gifts are invoked:

> Power of the love of the skies be yours
> Power of the love of the stars be yours
> Power of the love of the moon be yours
> Power of the love of the sun be yours.[42]

The beauty and abundance of these prayers attest to the veneration of the Moon in Celtic popular tradition, probably over a period of many centuries. As it is unlikely that charms and prayers invoking and worshipping the Moon were produced during the Christian era, it is reasonable to assume that they derive their majesty, resonance, and power from the early widespread worship of the Moon, the beloved and awe-inspiring Queen of the Night who has been worshipped, hailed, and welcomed since time and times began.

The Horned Women

In his *Irish Fairy Book*, Alfred Graves mentions a story collected by Lady Wilde known as The Horned Women. The tale is interesting in and of itself and may contain lunar-related themes and motifs. In the story, a rich woman is sitting up late one night carding and preparing wool when there is a knock at the door. She asks who it is, and a voice replies, "I am the Witch of the One Horn." Thinking her neighbor is playing a prank, the woman opens the door. A woman with a horn on her head and carrying wool carders in her hand enters. She begins to card wool furiously, saying every so often "Where are the others? They delay too long!"

A second knock follows, and the woman feels compelled to open the door. A second witch, with two horns on her forehead, enters with a spinning wheel. "Give me place," she says, "I am the Witch of the Two Horns." She sits down and begins to spin vigorously. The knocks continue until twelve witches have entered the woman's dwelling. They sit busily spinning, carding, and weaving, singing an ancient rhyme. They speak no word to the frightened woman, who can neither move nor speak as their spell is upon her.

Finally, one of the witches calls out to the woman in Irish, demanding that she rise up and bake them a cake. The woman is not able to find a vessel to bring water from the well for the baking, so the witches tell her to use a sieve (an item often associated with witches in folk tradition). The sieve does not work, of course, and the woman sits down by the well and weeps. She hears a voice telling her to "take yellow clay and moss, and bind them together" (a mixture that enables the sieve to hold water). It then tells her to return to her home and, once outside, cry aloud three times that "the mountain of the Fenian woman and the sky over it is all on fire."

She does this, causing the witches to rush out of her house in alarm. They utter wild lamentations and fly off to Slievenamon, their chief abode. The voice (which is the Spirit of the Well) tells the woman to prepare her house against the enchantment of the witches should they return. In order to break their spells, she sprinkles "feet-water" (the water used to wash one's feet at night) outside on the threshold. While she was out, the witches had prepared a cake using the blood of her family. She breaks the cake into bits and places them in the mouths of each sleeping family member to restore them. She also takes the cloth the witches had woven and places it half inside and half outside of a chest with a padlock on it, and locks the door.

The witches are not long in returning, and they cry out angrily for vengeance. They order the vessel of feet-water to open the door for them, but it replies it cannot, as it is scattered on the ground. The door likewise cannot open as it is securely fastened. They demand obeisance of the cake they had made, but it replies that it is "bruised and broken." The witches rush back through the air to Slievenamon, "uttering strange curses on the Spirit of the Well who had wished their ruin." The woman and her house are left in peace, and it is said that a mantle dropped by one of the witches was hung up by the woman as a reminder of the night's remarkable events. Evidently, this mantle has been in the possession of the same family from generation to generation, for five hundred years.

There are a number of elements in the tale possibly associated with lunar symbolism. Thirteen women figure in the story, a primary character and twelve witches. They have horns on their heads and are associated with spinning and weaving. They appear late at night and fly away and return several times. The woman receives the help of a water spirit, who tells her to bind a sieve with clay and moss (clay is used in lunar-related love spells, and club moss has been mentioned previously). There are also a number of liminal elements—water poured on a threshold and a mantle locked halfway in and halfway out of a chest. The presence of twelve horned women who arrive one by one late at night and enter the dwelling of the main female character, spinning and weaving and chanting, may suggest a connection with themes related to the Moon.

The Folk Who Go Widdershins

We have previously discussed the various ways in which night, darkness, and the Moon became associated with magic and the supernatural. In earlier eras (and even in modern times), many felt that night was "closer" to the Otherworld or the supernatural than the day. Fairies and other spirits became more active after sundown, and people born during the night were said to be able to see ghosts and spirits invisible to "the children of the day."[43] Irish folk tradition maintains that night belongs to the fairies or spirits, and that it is therefore fitting for humans to withdraw to the security of their homes and hearths at night. Until fairly recent times, country people in Ireland said that it was not appropriate to be outside at all hours of the night, as one might disturb the fairies.[44]

Staying up late was also considered inappropriate, as it was commonly believed that the dead silently approached the house every hour between 10 p.m. and midnight, hoping to find all quiet inside. For this reason, ashes or water should not be thrown outside at night. To show respect, one should retire early and leave seats arranged for the ancestors around a well-made fire after having swept the hearth area.[45] It was also considered unwise to whistle outside or call children by their name at night, as this drew attention to oneself and one's children (in whom the fairies might take more than a passing interest). With the coming of the dawn, the darkness is dispelled, and the approach of the light of the Sun sends spirits to their own abodes. It is almost as if our night is their day, and our day their night.[46] Indeed, many descriptions of the Otherworld seem to indicate that this sacred realm is a mirror of our own world in a number of ways.

The names of the four directions and their traditional associations and attributes suggest that this was the case. In Celtic and other Indo-European traditions, ritual activity generally began in the east and proceeded in a sunwise (or clockwise) fashion. The Old Irish word for south is *dess*, from which we get the term *deosil*, which means "in a sunwise fashion" (i.e., from the east, moving toward the right or the south). If movement is made in the opposite direction (to the left), one then approaches the north. In Old Irish, the word for north is *túath*, used in compounds to denote northern or left/on the left. The word later came to mean "wicked" or "evil" because of its connection with anti-sunwise movement. In fact, the fairies were sometimes referred to as "the people who go widdershins" (the opposite of deosil, referring to counterclockwise movement toward the left or the north). The word túath was also used to describe certain magical figures or activities: a witch was a *ban-túathach*, the fairies were called *tuath-geinte*, "people of (or who go toward) the north or left side," and Druidism was sometimes referred to as *túathcherd* (northern or left-hand craft).[47]

East is the direction of the rising Sun, and ritual activity followed the natural movement the Sun, whose light moves toward the south as the day progresses. Movement in the opposite direction is therefore movement toward the darkness. Sunwise movement makes sense in our world, yet it may be that movement toward darkness or night was the natural pattern of movement for inhabitants of the Otherworld. The sacred quality of primal darkness and night (which preceded the Celtic day) made it a natural part of the sacred order of things for the gods and spirits of Celtic tradition. In this hallowed state of existence, their primary luminary (like the Sun in our world), may have been the Moon.

The Dew of the Goddess

We have already encountered a variety of words and phrases associated with the Moon in various Celtic languages. Some of these refer to lunar time reckoning and some to the brightness of the Moon. Other lunar terminology may also be of interest, as language can tell us a great deal about how a culture views the world around it.

In Old Irish, the new Moon was referred to as *gealach núa* or *núadha*. The word *ré*, which can mean "moon," also means "a space or interval of time," as in the phrase *a reib coisicartha*, "at hallowed seasons." The term *tríchtach* referred to a "moon" of thirty days, probably alluding to the difference between "moons" (or lunar months) of twenty-nine or thirty days. The term *gel* was used to describe the color of one of the winds associated with the four directions. Precious objects made of "'white silver" (*gel-argad*) are often mentioned in the myths, and one of the sacred Otherworld plains was known as Mag Argat-nél, The Plain of Silver Clouds. Another fascinating phrase is *druchta dea*, "dew of a goddess." This was a kenning for corn and milk, and may have had an additional sense pertaining to some facet of a poet's training (i.e., inspiration coming to the poet from the darkness of the Otherworld, much as dew appears on the morning grass during the night). This phrase is particularly interesting, as it was believed that the Moon caused the morning dew.[48]

Many of these phrases produced similar terms in Scottish Gaelic and modern Irish. In Scottish Gaelic, the new Moon is referred to as *gealach úr, ré nuadh*, or *an solus úr*, the third phrase meaning "the new [bright] light." The Moon's path is *triall na gealaich*. The *tarbh-boidhre* was a monster or demon, or a god capable of changing himself into many forms, which may have had some connection with the Moon's transformations and the lunar symbolism of bull's horns. In addition, we find several interesting plant names: *lus-na-h-oidhche* (literally, "plant of night"), the deadly nightshade, and *lus-nam-mios,* "moonwort" (plant of the lunar month).

In modern Irish, the new Moon is *geal úr*, the crescent Moon *corrán gealaí*, the first phase of the Moon *tús gealaí*, and the full Moon *geal lán or lán na ré*. *Oíche ghealaí* is "a moonlit night," and *an ré ghealaí* refers to "the visible Moon." The word *geal* ("white," "bright," etc.) is often used to indicate brightness, "as of the Moon, moonlight." It is also associated with words pertaining to clarity, gladness, and goodness, as in *lus na gealaí* or *sailchuach na gealaí,* "honesty," the name of a plant better known as the violet.[49]

In modern Welsh, the Moon is either *lleuad* or *lloer*. The last quarter of the Moon is *cil y lleuad* (literally "recess" or waning of the Moon), and a honeymoon is *mis mêl* ("a month of honey"). Clearly, there exists in the Celtic languages a rich and vibrant vocabulary pertaining to the Moon and her brilliance. As in earlier times, when roots like *gel, leuksna,* and *arg* (used to refer to things brilliant) produced words for the Moon (and for silver), the modern language of the Moon and the night sky can tell us much about how these sacred elements were perceived, and perhaps also worshipped.

$$\quad\mathbb{D}\quad\quad\mathbb{D}\quad\quad\mathbb{D}$$

Meditations and Exercises

Use the power of words and the gifts of the natural world to help put you in touch with the Moon and its sacred symbolism.

1) Create your own protective charm to be used upon rising each morning, in which you invoke the power of the Moon and other elemental forces sacred to you. This invocation may include three, nine, or thirteen elements in total, in keeping with other examples of traditional folk charms used for protection.

2) Take a trip to the library or used book store to read about how traditional cultures utilized the phases of the Moon in their daily lives (including growing and gathering plants for food, medicine, or magical purposes). See if you can utilize this ancient wisdom in your own daily life or seasonal activities. The phases of the Moon can be utilized in the magical use of plants and herbs, whether you have access to a garden, public wilderness area, or fields and forest. Be careful when culling wild plants for ingestion that they are gathered well away from roads or industrial areas. Also, make sure your activities do not disturb the ecological balance of the area.

3) At an appropriate phase of the Moon, try some of the rituals associated with love or marriage divination as described in this chapter. Gather the necessary plants and ingredients from the wild whenever possible. Notice if these rites are more potent when performed during a particular Moon phase (or on the quarter days).

4) Create a monthly ritual to be used when first viewing, greeting, and blessing the new Moon. Utilize some of the traditional folk elements presented above, or use these as a basis for your own creation. Compose and recite a short prayer to the Moon that can be easily memorized for use at the beginning of each lunar month.

5) Design a silver amulet of some sort to carry in your pocket. This can be turned three times for luck or a wish upon seeing the new Moon and can also be carried in your pocket as a general protective talisman. You may wish to use a circular shape (evoking silver coins/wheels) and include lunar stones, herbs, or symbols.

6) Make a list of activities that were traditionally performed (or not performed) during the various phases of the Moon. Follow these customs for a period of at least three months to see how they resonate with you. Are you able to perceive a connection between the Moon and the liquid "sap" or essence of living things?

7) Read the folklore and customs associated with club moss or the bog violet, and try gathering them according to the time-honored rites. Write a poem or journal entry about how it feels to be following in the footsteps of the ancestors as you work with the elemental gifts of the natural world.

8) What do you make of the Breton ritual that featured twelve outlying stones and a central stone that symbolized the Moon (and its similarities to the Irish ceremony)? Discuss various possible interpretations for the common motif of one primary element or figure with twelve additional figures (making a total of thirteen).

9) Find out if your family has preserved any lunar proverbs or lore. Ask your parents, grandparents, aunts, and uncles if they remember any sayings or customs from their childhood days. You may also want to create your own sayings or rituals based upon your experience of the Moon and its influence and attributes.

10) What do you make of the tale of The Horned Women? There are a number of possible lunar elements in the story, including the motif of twelve-plus-one, horned female figures, and nocturnal spinning and weaving. Do you think the story has a particular message to impart? This powerful tale may serve as inspiration for a painting or drawing.

11) The inhabitants of the Otherworld may be associated with night and counterclockwise movement. In early Irish tales, this was associated with cursing and bad omens. It may also have been used for decreasing magic (banishing sickness, reducing negative influence, etc.) What do you think about the directions and the fairies' connection with night, widdershins movement, and magic?

12) In Celtic tradition, the fairies are not tiny winged creatures that live in teacups, but appear as full-sized men and women. They are often striking in manner or appearance, and very skilled and powerful. They are fond of beauty, good manners, optimism, generosity, skill, true love, music, dancing, and merriment, as well as hunting, processions, ball games, and the occasional battle (disliking the opposite aspect of these attributes). It is important to show your respect for them and make offerings to them. Bread or cakes, butter, honey, milk, cream, and ale have all traditionally been utilized. Create an altar or special corner in which to leave offerings and show your love and respect, using seasonal flowers and greens, and symbols of things of which the síd-dwellers are fond. Use

these on the feast days or quarter days (the turning points of the year), during appropriate phases of the lunar cycle, and at the turning points of the day (dawn, noon, dusk, and midnight).[50]

13) Look back through the words we have explored that are associated with names for the Moon (including word-elements meaning bright, white, pure, sacred, etc.). Meditate on these words and sounds, and see if you can intuitively ascertain a divine name for the Moon goddess. This may include root words like *gel*, *leuksna* (as in *luna*, etc.) or *arg* (as in Argante or Arianrhod). The feminine divine suffix *-ona* (as in Epona and Sirona) may be useful, as well as the endings *-a*, *-ana*, etc. Let the Otherworld guide you in your exploration. Chant some of these names to see if one or more of them rings true for you. This name can be used in your daily observances as well as in yearly or monthly rituals and invocations.

A GODDESS TRANSFORMED

THE INEXPRESSIBLE
MYSTERY OF THE MOON

*The "numinous" is the deepest and most fundamental element
in all strong and sincerely felt religious emotion.*

—RUDOLPH OTTO, "THE IDEA OF THE HOLY"

The worship of the Moon in Ireland and the British Isles has taken many forms over the years. It is still honored in a sort of half-remembered way whenever someone turns a silver coin in their pocket or finds themself standing in the doorway, gazing upon the face of the Moon in a state of reverie for longer than they'd realized. From the embroidered symbols on a shaman's cloak and the carefully planned alignments of long-forgotten stone circles, to the gold and white spheres that hung from the maypole in certain parts of Ireland to represent the Sun and the Moon, humankind can but try to symbolically express its wonderment at and connection with the Moon.[1] These ritualized attempts at remembrance are described eloquently by Nicolai Tolstoy:

> . . . Religion is a product of the unconscious, and reveals itself almost exclusively through revelatory symbols, liturgical language and rituals reenacting a Mystery which is essentially inexpressible.[2]

We are fortunate to know at least some details of the rituals once used to worship the Moon, to mark and commemorate its phases, and to express gratitude for its luminous light. In these and other religious rites, a connection with the past lends intensity to the experience of ritually expressing a connection with the numinous and the divine. This is true for each successive generation. The past (whether perceived or actual) is imbued with properties of mystery and arcane knowledge from the accumulated wisdom and experience of the ancestors, which are passed on to the elders of the next cycle. It is our fascination with and apparent need for mystery as well as a physical or spiritual experience that fuels the search for a connection with the Other. Fadel Gad speaks about these perceptions of the past and their connection with the mysteries of existence (using the widespread attraction to ancient Egypt as a metaphor):

> [People are drawn to Egypt] because it is a mystery, and everyone wants to solve a mystery. It draws you in because you are engaged in trying to answer the why and the how. But I believe the why is more important than the how. Egypt speaks to the "one within" and that one within is a mystery by itself.[3]

The same can be said about ancient Celtic religion (as well as that of many other ancient cultures). Our fascination with the past, particularly its sacred rites and the search for divine wisdom, is the most recent manifestation of an impulse that has been part of the human experience for a very long time. Most cultures look to the past for strength, guidance, and inspiration. The deities, ancestors, and sages of any given culture breathe life into the spirits and experiences of those who now live on the Earth. In this way, the cycles of past, present, and future are intertwined, and the existence of each is assured, all three an integral and sacred part of the web of life and the spiral of time.

The Wisdom of the Ages

The cyclical nature of time was expressed in the sacred writings of the Greeks and the Hindus. They felt that time was comprised of various successive eras, each one inferior to the last. In both traditions, the current era was considered the most degraded or corrupt. People, therefore, looked back to an earlier time when humanity existed in a theoretical Golden Age. They also looked forward to the point in time that heralded the end of the cycle. The concept of a degraded age that leads to death and decay may be a frightening prospect to the modern Western mind, and an idea that does not appear to serve us emotionally or spiritually. However, by now we should be able to see that darkness and death are symbols of the healing, purifying, and welcoming void that precedes the creation and rebirth of all life. Gad discusses the sacred nature of darkness:

> Egyptian mythology provides us with a valuable perspective on our "dark" moods. Today we associate darkness with negativity. We're afraid of it because it represents the color of death. . . . But in ancient Egypt, the highest god, Nun, is represented by the darkness from which the light, On, was created.[4]

This concept finds expression in the mythological tradition of many cultures and, as we have seen, was an extremely important theme in early Celtic religion and mythology. Gad goes on to describe the cosmic void as follows:

> It is the ocean of darkness. . . . We came from darkness. It is who we are. . . . Throw your desires into this place. You will be amazed to at how they come into form.

It can be possible to solve the mystery of the one within by exploring . . .
[these] mysteries.[5]

The Moon is one of the most potent symbolic expressions of these concepts, which may be why lunar worship has played such an important role in the religious ideologies we have been exploring. The concept of renewal, which results from a journey to the void (or to the past), forms an integral part of many religious systems. The wisdom of the ancestors is thus brought forward into the present time, demonstrating that time and existence partake of a spiral or cyclical nature, and that the worlds are connected.

In *The Concept of the Goddess*, Juliette Wood discusses this need for connection with the past, claiming that, "When the present attempts to link itself to the past," the past becomes "an image of what one was or has left behind, and of what once was and could be again."[6] In this way, the past becomes "a template for possible renewal in the future." The legend of King Arthur fits this template nicely. He is the good king during whose rule the land and the people prosper. Society flourishes under the influence of energies or entities both wise and enlightened. For over a thousand years, it was popularly believed that Arthur was not dead, but simply resting and healing in the Otherworld realms, one day to return to lead the Britons to their former glory. Other divine or legendary figures have exerted a similar effect on the hearts and minds of the people (Merlin, the ancient Egyptians, the Druids, etc.).[7] Common to all these legends is a sincere and heartfelt yearning for wisdom, wholeness, and a connection with the divine and the self. Inherent in this desire is the bridging of past, present, and future. The religious symbolism of the Moon, her patterns of transformation and eternal promise of renewal, draws upon and nourishes these same ideas and impulses.

The Rebirth of the Moon Goddess

During the second half of the 1700s and into the 1800s, German and English poets of the Romantic era expressed a joyous, liberating, and life-affirming sensibility that celebrated kinship with nature, the connection between this world and the supernatural, and the concept of ancient wisdom. Reacting against the Christian ethos (Puritanism in particular) and the triune demon of science, industry, and technology, their language gained intensity as these movements progressed, blossoming forth during the dawning of the 1900s. Love, sex, and the body were resanctified, and a New Age was proclaimed in certain circles. This age focused on and drew inspiration from what were called the old religions—the perceived and somewhat factual beliefs and practices of Greco-Roman paganism in particular.[8] Poets such as Keats, Shelley, Swinbourne, and Yeats brought these images to life with such power and relevance that their words continue to evoke a sense of reawakening and a yearning for the glorified past in modern-day readers.

The need to emotionally, spiritually, and even physically express these ideas became so strong that seekers, spiritualists, and occultists began meeting to discuss (and in some cases, ritually enact) the ideas about which they had formerly only been reading or speaking. One of these groups, The Golden Dawn, was particularly influential, drawing its ideology from ritual magic texts of the Middle Ages, which had generally been utilized only by upper-class males, elements of Greco-Roman and in some cases Celtic mythology (such as it was understood at the time), aspects of folklore and folk custom, and (in terms of the rituals) the practices of the Masonic Temples.[9]

A parallel movement arose over time primarily concerned with witchcraft and magic (both ceremonial and folk-based), resulting in the modern religion known as Wicca.[10] It, too, draws on Masonic ritual elements and ceremonial magical practices, as well as Celtic and other European folk customs and a wide range of other sources, both ancient and modern, creating a remarkably fluid, potent, and spiritually relevant tradition. Often touted as The Old Religion of Europe—preserved and practiced through the centuries by European witches—the diverse origins of Wicca resulted in the creation of a new spiritual tradition whose numbers increase exponentially each year. Despite variations in practice and belief, in general, Wicca may be described as a beneficent Earth-honoring and nature-worshipping religion that focuses on the use of positive magic and ritual (group or solitary) to bring healing to the self and others, honor the gods and spirits, attain wisdom, accomplish certain goals (none of which may result in the harm of another), and honor and empower the sacred that exists within every person.[11]

Although popular books on the subject present various derivations for the name of the religion, the word "wicca" actually derives from the Indo-European root *weg*, meaning "to be strong or lively." From this root come other words, including "waken," "watch," and "wait," as well as "vigor," "velocity," "surveillance," and "vigil." Associated Old English words include *wacan*, "to wake up, arise" and *wacian*, "to be awake" (from the Germanic word *waken*). Also related are "Wicca," "witch," "bewitch," and "wicked," which derive from Old English *wicca*. *Wicca* referred specifically to a male sorcerer or wizard, the feminine form being *wicce* ("witch"). Both are from Germanic *wikkjaz*, meaning a "necromancer" or "one who wakes the dead."[12] Here, we can see the connection with words like "waken" and so forth (having to do with strength or life energy). An Anglo-Saxon word is not likely to have served as the name of a great pan-European movement, yet the word does invoke a number of positive images: a group of people who have awakened, who watch and learn, who strive to awaken the traditions or energies of those who have gone before, and whose spiritual beliefs and energies are vigorous and strong.

One of the most noteable innovations of the movement is its focus on, and concern with, the veneration and resanctification of the feminine divine principle. This varies among Wiccan or neopagan groups or practioners: some focus almost exclusively on a modern goddess figure, others see the divine as manifest in a god and goddess (The Lord and The Lady). Others are polytheistic in belief and practice, and yet others are eclectic in their beliefs, drawing on a number of historical traditions, including animism and shamanism.[13] In many instances, however, one of the primary attributes or manifestations of the female divine is a pronounced association with the Moon. While seasonal rites take place on the quarter days, solstices, and equinoxes, full and new Moon rituals are also held, often considered as important as the Sabbaths.

In an attempt to redress the imbalance of earlier religious systems and as a response to changes in modern society, these traditions never allow the feminine to take a backseat. If a religion is no longer relevant, it tends to die out or radically transform itself. Modern paganism or Earth religion is a healthy, respectful, and necessary reaction to the inadequacies and imbalances inherent in modern cultural and spiritual paradigms and organizations. It is a natural response to a lack of reverence for nature and the current emphasis on money, materialism, and technology. It also draws attention to the lack of meaningful and effective social and spiritual institutions, and positive, elder-supported outlets for the expression of the emotional and spiritual. Many religious forms arise in response to the conditions of the world surrounding them, demonstrating the ability (and necessity) of spiritual systems to adapt, grow, and transform. It would have been surprising, in this light, if the modern Earth religions had not come into existence.

The Wisdom of the Ancestors

The neopagan movement is often criticized for a lack of historical accuracy in terms of its claims of ancient heritage and continuity of belief and practice, as well as inaccuracies pertaining to ancient beliefs, history, or tradition. The movement could benefit from the support and expertise of academics, and should turn to improved and updated sources, training programs, and research methods if it is to be taken seriously and afforded the respect it deserves. In this way, respect for the gods and the ancestors (part of the neopagan creed) can become a physical and literal part of the spiritual practice as well as the ideology of this growing religion.

In a spiritual sense, improved research methods show the greatest respect toward those who dwell in the Otherworld realms. Learning about who the ancestors were and what they really believed is crucial in forming and maintaining a link with the experiences and wisdom of the past. As with any new religion, a well-defined and accredited system of education will come with time, along with the hope that it not fall prey to the pitfalls, dogma, and corruption of many other organized systems. Until that time, neopagans must learn from whatever resources are available to them, taking that knowledge out into the world (as well as into the ritual circle and the wilderness) as a foundation for spiritual learning and experience. Reliable information, well-supported training, and respectful research are vitally important. But without physical manifestation, the past (in some measure) cannot be brought forward to exist and flourish in the here and now:

> What we know of ancient spiritual practices doesn't need to remain purely academic. Most people perceive the Egyptians' rituals as primitive and esoteric, but perhaps there is a better way to use what they believed to better our understanding of the world today.[14]

The rituals of some ancient cultures are remarkably effective for those in the modern era. The rapidly increasing numbers of modern students and adherents of shamanism, for example, attest to the power of these primitive and esoteric methods, which in reality are more sophisticated and effective than most people realize. Other rituals, however, may be time-, place-, or culture-specific, requiring thoughtful and respectful adaptation in order to be practical or relevant in the modern age. One desire or impulse behind many religious acts is that the worldly, physical, or human manifestations of the inexpressible attempt (to the best of their ability) to honor and form an effective link between the worlds. This impulse was part of Celtic Iron Age pagan religion and exists in Earth-honoring spiritual movements of today. And, in this response to these natural, innate, and universal needs, the Moon shines forth as a sacred guide to those below, lighting our way and welcoming us back to the void. The Moon shows us that life is re-created from darkness, that the worlds are connected, and that past, present, and future are woven from the same spiraling and luminescent thread of existence.

> *High Priest: Hear ye the words of the Star Goddess.*
> *She in the dust of whose feet are the hosts of heaven,*
> *and whose body encircles the Universe.*
>
> *High Priestess: I who am the beauty of the green Earth,*
> *and the white Moon among the stars, and the mystery of the Waters,*
> *and the desire of the heart of man, call unto thy soul.*
> *Arise, and come unto me.*
>
> *For I am the soul of nature, who gives life to the universe.*
> *From me all things proceed, and unto me all things must return.*[15]

☽   ☽   ☽

Meditations and Exercises

To mark the culmination of your journey (which is also a beginning), use your personal knowledge and experience of the material presented in this book to create a ritual and celebration honoring the Moon (and youself!). Here are a few recipes and suggestions you may enjoy.

A number of herbs and plants are associated with the Moon in various traditions (older and more recent). These can be used to make herbal incense, to decorate yourself or your surroundings, in cooking, or for seasonal crafts.[16] A lunar herbal incense can be prepared from moonwort with a combination of either jasmine, rose and violet, or clary sage, orris root, and star anise (depending on your preference). Other herbs associated with the Moon are adder's tongue, cleavers, coolwort, duckweed, sea holly, water lily, and stonecrop. Experiment with your own herbal blends for use as incense or potpourri (either fragrant or symbolic). Irises or lilies may be used to decorate the room or the altar, and necklaces of dried rowan berries, rosebuds, or star anise can be worn during the ceremony. A number of plants associated with the Moon are frequently used in cooking. You may want to hold a dinner or potluck supper after the ritual, using dishes prepared from these plants.

Selene's Salad: Wash and prepare lettuce, chickweed, purslane, watercress, and cucumbers. Serve with a dressing made from tahini, sea salt, and coriander.

Celestial Slaw: Toast sesame seeds in an iron skillet. Place some butter in the pan and add large, round, thinly sliced pieces of red cabbage. Fry evenly on both sides, adding soy sauce and tahini, until well cooked. Sprinkle with sesame seeds prior to serving.

Phoebe's Pumpkin Surprise: Cut up small, sweet organic pumpkins (suitable for eating) into halves or quarters. Cook in a hot oven until tender. Ten minutes prior to serving (while still in the oven), drizzle with maple syrup (to which you may add some orange zest and ground ginger). Cook a little longer and then serve. You may want to serve natural herbal teas (ginger, citrus, anise) along with some gingerbread after the meal. Wintergreen, anise, and ginger teas are good digestives.

Sacred Cakes: In Scotland, sacred cakes or "bannocks" were made at each of the quarter days (Imbolc, Beltaine, Lugnasad, and Samain). These were, in most cases, oatcakes made from oat flour (called oat "meal" in Britain), butter and salt (although Beltaine bannocks were sometimes washed with a coating of whipped eggs, milk, and cream).[17] To prepare, mix together one cup of oat flour, a pinch of baking soda, and ¼ teaspoon salt. Add one teaspoon melted butter and a bit of hot water sufficient for mixing. Roll the dough on a board well coated with oat flour. Cut into shapes and bake in the oven at 375 degrees until nicely cooked (dry). Orange or lemon zest, or a bit of powdered ginger or finely chopped candied ginger can be added for variation.

Rowan Jelly: Wash and drain almost-ripe rowan berries. Simmer in a pot of water for about forty minutes, or until the water is red and the berries are soft. Strain the juice from the berries carefully, and discard the berries. Measure the juice and return to the pot. Add sugar (regular sugar, or birch or date sugar), one pound for each pint of juice that you have. Boil rapidly for half an hour, or until the jelly sets quickly when a sample is placed on a cold plate. Skim well, put into small jars, and cover tightly. Rowan jelly is traditionally served with wild game (such as grouse or venison) or with mutton, although it is also good on fresh baked bread or oatcakes.

Fairy Butter: Wash a quarter pound of fresh butter in orange-flower water. Beat together with the pounded yolks of five or six hard-boiled eggs. Blanch two ounces of sweet almonds and pound to a paste with a little orange-flower water. Add a little grated lemon peel and a little sifted sugar (of whatever type). Mix together and work through a colander with a wooden spoon. Soak vanilla cookies or biscuits in white wine, and pile these on top of the fairy butter. (Conversely, the fairy butter can be put on top of cookies, shortbread, or sweet oatcakes).[18]

Sacred Beverages: Serve ginger beer or anise liquor during or after the ritual. If you brew, ale made from coriander, sweet flag (wild iris), wintergreen, or clary sage is also appropriate.[19] In 1703, Martin Martin reported that, in Scotland, "violet whey" was used as a cool and refreshing drink, especially for those with fevers. A drink made from whey in which violets had been boiled can be an interesting celebratory beverage, especially in the summertime.

Bendachtan éisci fort!
The Blessings of the Moon upon you!

JOURNEY TO THE GODDESS

A MOON MEDITATION

A question, my elder, where did you come from?

That is not difficult: along the columns of age . . .
Along the magic hill of the wife of Nechtan . . .
Along the land of the sun,
Along the dwelling place of the moon . . .

—*IMMACALLAM IN DÁ THUARAD* (COLLOQUOY OF THE TWO SAGES),
EARLY IRISH WISDOM TEXT

To read something is to learn it, to be shown it is to know it, to experience it is to understand it. It is only in the last few millennia that we have become separated from the experience of the divine. In an age when technology, science, and consumerism have become the new gods, that which can neither be seen nor measured has been pushed to the extreme fringe. What if the same held true for invisible abstracts such as love, truth, or honor? For more than 99 percent of the time humans have inhabited Earth, the invisible presence—and reality—of the divine realms and their inhabitants have been part of daily existence. Far from superstitious belief or wishful thinking, this connection with the source or origin of all life, blessings, and wisdom is a profound and sophisticated experience. This experiential chapter has been provided for those who actively seek and welcome the journey, as well as for those who are new to the adventure.

Moon Meditation

Sit quietly for a few minutes with your eyes closed. Imagine the stress and worries of the day melting downward, from your head to your toes, becoming grounded in the earth and then transmuted into healing energy. Focus on your breathing and let your mind become still.

Envision yourself standing on the shore of the ocean or a large body of water. In your mind's eye, look down at your feet and feel the waves lapping against your toes. Notice that you are now wearing some unusual garments, including a hooded cloak. See if you can feel the sand beneath your feet, as well as the grass, stones, or shells that may also be there. Listen to the sound of the water until you are completely in touch with the moment and place in which you find yourself.

You look out over the water and notice something approaching. As it comes nearer, you see that it is a boat with silver fittings whose prow is carved with elaborate ornamentation. A lone figure steers the boat with a long silver oar. As the boat approaches, see if the person is young or old, male or female. Make note of his or her garb, as well as the symbolic pendant or amulet hanging around his or her neck. The figure may speak to you or silently motion for you to enter the boat. Check your intuition to see if this is the right thing to do.

When you are ready, step into the boat. Connect with the tangible feeling of the wooden planks under your feet and the wickerwork seat you have been ushered toward. Hold onto the sides of the boat and feel the silver fittings and ornate carvings with your fingers. The figure in the boat may speak to you, telling you who he or she is or giving you information or instructions. Spend some time connecting with this person and his or her energy. Feel yourself merge with the smooth floating motion of the boat, the wind or air around you, and the feel of the journey itself. Notice if it is night or day, and whether the face of the Moon is visible.

After some time, you realize that the boat has pulled up onto a narrow beach on an island you have not seen before. Before leaving the boat, thank your guide and see if he or she has any instructions for you. Step onto the shore, noticing everything around you. Take time to connect with the land, the trees, and the fragrant air, as well as with any birds or animals you may encounter. Walk around the shore for a while, and then climb the small hill in front of you. Explore this world fully with all of your senses.

After awhile, you come upon a small stone doorway covered with moss. In front of it lies a patch of violets, white and purple. Blue and gold irises arise from the moist soil nearby. Sit down in front of the doorway, connecting with the earth and the plants around you. Reaching into your pocket, you pull out a stone of some kind. Set the stone on top of the doorway as an offering. When you are ready, pull your hood over your head, and let yourself journey into the darkness of the stone doorway.

Feel yourself travel down into the Underworld. You may enter a dark passageway, walk down steps, or fly or float down a long tunnel. Do not force the experience, but keep yourself open and aware, letting yourself feel the journey with all of your senses.

Eventually, you see a lighted area and emerge to find yourself in a stone cavern. A small river runs through the cavern; the water is dark but clear. Three torches project from the cavern walls to light your way. On a large stone ledge or platform, you see an altar. On top of the altar stands a large silver cauldron. Black pearls line the rim of the cauldron, and its surface is decorated with images of deities and magical symbols. Approach the cauldron with humility and respect. Peer inside, and see what is there.

After some time, you become aware of a presence in front of you, just beyond your gaze in the shadows of the cavern. You hear the tinkling of small bells, a sound that reminds you of the summer stars. You hear the rustling of her gown before you can see her. It is the Goddess of the Moon. She is arrayed in a woven tunic made of purple and silver fabric and a sparkling cape of darkest blue fastened with a silver brooch in the shape of a hare. She wears a silver torc and bracelet, and small silver bells adorn her feet.

You have entered the sacred Underworld dwelling where the Moon goddess rests during the day. Make a sign of respect toward her, and wait for her to speak. She holds out her clasped hand, which is closed around an object. Turning her hand palm-side up, she opens it to reveal what is inside. Look at the object in her hand, and hear what she has to say. Her words may be difficult for you to interpret. In the Otherworld, things are sometimes the same as in our world, yet they may also be different, as in a mirror image. You may be able to understand her speech intuitively, even if it is not the same as your own. What does her voice sound like? Does it remind you of water, or of stars?

Interact with her as seems fitting, remembering to show her great respect. Her presence may be overwhelming, but it is also beneficent. See what it is she wishes to impart to you, and use your intuition to ascertain whether you should speak to her or even offer her something. If appropriate, you may ask her for healing, transformation, or guidance.

When you sense that your time with her has come to an end, make a final gesture of respect toward her, and thank her either mentally or verbally. She turns and walks away from you toward an inner chamber where she sleeps in a bed covered with furs, in a room lit by a multitude of small candles that look like stars. After leaving her presence, you look toward the river and see the boat waiting for you. This time, it is empty. Step carefully down a set of stone steps and enter the boat. It will proceed of its own accord, moving down the river that flows out of the cave to the left.

After some time has passed, you emerge from the Underworld, out into the light of day. The sunlight may seem too bright at first, but your eyes adjust to it. The trees here are covered with leaves, and small birds sing from their branches. The river has transformed into a country stream that gurgles merrily through the fields and meadows. It is late afternoon, and soon you will be able to see the faint outline of the crescent Moon far up in the sky. For now, let yourself enjoy the ride. Spend time floating through this landscape, enjoying the water, or perhaps walking about on the land.

At last, you can clearly perceive the rising of the Moon. Take this moment to greet and thank the Goddess of the Moon. If you have not previously made an offering to her, do so now. When you feel yourself ready to return, turn and notice the small, thatched cottage on your left. Step out of the boat and walk onto the grass. You notice that the doorway of the cottage is framed with wild roses. A small silver vessel of water sits on a ledge by the window frame. Take a sip from the vessel and offer your thanks. Open the wooden door of the house. As you enter the welcoming darkness of the cottage, you awaken to find yourself back at home.

CONCLUSION

THE VOICE OF THE GODDESS

Thou art the pure love of the clouds
Thou art the pure love of the skies
Thou art the pure love of the stars
Thou art the pure love of the moon.

—EXCERPT FROM TRADITIONAL SCOTTISH FOLK PRAYER

Throughout our journey to discover and understand the worship of the Moon in Celtic tradition, we have uncovered a number of recurring themes. These have appeared in almost every source we have encountered, which underscores their importance to the Celts and other cultures as well. Some of the most significant elements related to lunar veneration and the archetypal characteristics of Moon goddess include:

• Fertility (water/ocean, plants/forests)

• Cycles of life and death

• Creation

• Gateways and portals

• Important transitions in women's lives (childbirth, coming of age, marriage)

• The potency and sanctioned expression of women's sexual energies

• The creative or intuitive mind

• Transformation, healing, and rebirth.

While neither Sun worship nor Moon worship alone can be said to have formed the basis for Celtic (or other early European) religious traditions, the widespread occurrence and persistence of such important themes certainly attest to the deep awareness and veneration of these elements of nature in the tradition. The respect and religious feelings the Celts expressed toward other facets of the natural world have long been recognized and documented, particularly those associated with sacred groves, hills or fairy mounds, and bodies of water. The Moon can now be seen as an integral and very prominent part of Celtic spiritual beliefs.

Who is the Celtic Moon Goddess? She is the silver-clad mistress of the place of origin, the keeper of the Underworld cauldron of wisdom, healing, and transformation. The mother of the Sun and the ocean waves, her celestial chariot is drawn by a team of sacred white oxen or deer whose horns may be seen at the beginning and end of her monthly journey. She wears a cloak of darkest blue speckled with stars and hemmed with the morning dew; her head is adorned with a ring of mistletoe and other sacred plants. She has been welcomed on Earth by majestic stone circles, shamanic and druidic rituals, and prayers of the common people. She is the mysterious light in the night sky that guides and illuminates our path. Whether envisioned as a white mare in Ireland, a silver wheel in Wales, or a beloved friend in Scotland, whether goddess, witch, or enchantress, she is the Queen of the Night.

GUIDE TO PRONUNCIATION

This appendix is included at the behest of an interested reader and friend who suggested that people might like to know how to pronounce the foreign names and words mentioned in the text.

Uttering the sacred names of deities or spiritual beings is considered a powerful method of contacting the divine in many traditions, and, all spiritual considerations aside, it is nice to know how to say the words we read. Instead of using the International Phonetic Alphabet (which may be unfamiliar to many readers), I have provided a pronunciation guide based on English phonetics and common usage. The stressed syllable is in capital letters, and the name of the language for which a pronunciation is being provided is listed first in parentheses.

The "ch" in Celtic languages is pronounced like the "ch" in Bach or loch (not as in the word "choose") and the Welsh double-"l" sound is made by placing the tongue as if you were going to say "l," but then (keeping the tongue in place) saying or "hissing" a "th" sound on either side of the tongue. I hope this will be helpful and informative in your further study and exploration!

Accalam na Senórach (Old Irish) AH—guh—luv nah Shen—ORE—ach

Amaethon (Middle Welsh) ah—MAY—thon

Amairgen (Old Irish) AH—ver—gin

Amrún (Old Irish) AHM—roon

Andraste (Old British) ahn—DRAHS—tay

Annwfn (Middle Welsh) ah—NOO—vin

Annwn (Middle Welsh) AH—noon

Aoife/Aife (Old Irish) EE—fuh

Argante (Old British) ahr—GAHN—tay

Arianrhod (Middle Welsh) Ar—ee—AHN—hrode

Atenux (Gaulish) ah—TEN—oox

Awenyddion (Middle Welsh) ah—wen—UH—thee—on ("th" as in bathe)

Banba (Old Irish) BAN—vuh

Belenus (Gaulish) BEH—leh—noos (or perhaps Beh—LEH—noos)

Beli Mawr (Middle Welsh) BEH—lee Mow—err (rhymes with hour)

Beltaine (Old Irish) BEL—tih—nuh (modern BEL—tayne)

Blodeuwedd (Middle Welsh) Bloh—DAY—weth ("th" as in bathe)

Boudicca (Old British) Boo—DEE—kuh

Bríg (Old Irish) BREEGH

Brug na Boinne (Old Irish) BROOG nah BO—ih—nuh

Cad Goddeu (Middle Welsh) CAD GO—thay ("th" as in bathe)

Caer (Middle Welsh) KIRE (rhymes with fire)

Cailleach Bhéara (Modern Irish) CALL—ach VARE—uh

Cath Maige Tuired (Old Irish) CATH MIE—guh TOO—reth (final "th" as in bathe)

Cernunnos (Gaulish) CAYR—nu—noss or Cayr—NOO—noss

Cerridwen (Middle Welsh) CAYR—ihd—wen or perhaps Cayr—IHD—wen

Coligny (French) COLE—in—yee

Cormac (Old Irish) CORE—mac

Cruithni (Old Irish) CROOTH—ni

Cú Chulainn (Old Irish) COO CHULL—in

Dagda (Old Irish) DAGH—da

Damona (Continental Celtic) Dah—MOE—nah

Deosil (Scottish Gaelic) JESH—ull

Dindshenchas (Old Irish) Dinn—HEN—uh—chuss

Dôn (Middle Welsh) DONN

Emer (Old Irish) EH—ver

Englynion (Middle Welsh) en—GLUNN—ee—un

Epona (Gaulish) Eh—POE—nuh

Ériu (Old Irish) AYR—ee—yoo

Fili (Old Irish) FIH—lih

Findbennach (Old Irish) Find—BEN—ach

Fotla (Old Irish) FOT—luh

Gelach (Old Irish) GEL—ach

Gilfaethwy (Middle Welsh) Gil—VITHE—wee ("th" as in bathe)

Goibhniu (Old Irish) GOV—nee—yoo

Goidelic Goe—ih—DELL—ick

Grían (Old Irish) GREE—uhn

Gwion Bach (Middle Welsh) GWEE—uhn BACH

Gwydion (Middle Welsh) GWUD—yuhn

Gwynedd (Welsh) GWIN—eth ("th" as in bathe)

Imbolc (Old Irish) IHM—olk

Iuchra (Old Irish) YOOCH—ra

Lebor Gabála Érenn (Old Irish) LEH—verr Gah—VAHL—uh AYR—inn

Lleu Llaw Gyffes (Middle Welsh) LLAY LLOW (rhymes with how) GUH—fiss

Luan (Old Irish) LOO—un

Lug (Old Irish) LOOGH

Lugnasad (Old Irish) Loog—NAH—sath ("th" as in bathe, modern LOO—
   nuh—sah)

Lugus (Gaulish) LOOG—uss

Mabinogi (Middle Welsh) Mah—bih—NOE—gee

Mabon (Middle Welsh) MAH—bon

Macha (Old Irish) MAH—chuh

Manannán mac Lir (Old Irish) Mah—nah—NAN mac LEER

Manawydan (Middle Welsh) Mah—nah—WIH—dan

Maponus (Gaulish) Mah—POE—noos

Mari Lwyd (Modern Welsh) MAH—ree LOO—wid

Mathonwy (Middle Welsh) Mah—THON—wee

Miadhach (Old Irish) MEE—ah—thach ("th" as in bathe)

Morrígan (Old Irish) MORE—ih—gun or More—REE—gun

Morrígna (Old Irish) More—REEG—nuh

Mug Roith (Old Irish) MUGH ROYTH

Nemain (Old Irish) NEH—vin

Nómad (Old Irish) NOE—vath ("th" as in bathe)

Núadu (Old Irish) NOO—uh—thoo ("th" as in bathe)

Ogam (Old Irish) AH—guhm (modern Scottish Gaelic OE—wuhm)

Ogma (Old Irish) OGE—muh

Oisín (Old Irish) Ah—SHEEN

Peredur (Middle Welsh) Peh—REH—deer

Pryderi (Middle Welsh) Prih—DAYR—ee

Pwyll (Middle Welsh) POO—will ("ll" as above, or, use "th" as in think, rather than "l")

Rhiannon (Middle Welsh) Hree—AH—nun

Samain (Old Irish) SAH—vin (modern SOW—in, first syllable rhymes with how)

Samildánach (Old Irish) Sah—vil—DAH—nuch

Síd (Old Irish) SHEETHE (same as English sheathe, modern SHEE)

Sirona (Gaulish) Sih—ROE—nah

Sucellos (Gaulish) Soo—KELL—oss

Suibne Geilt (Old Irish) SOOV—nuh GELT

Sulis (Old British) SOO—liss

Táin Bó Cuailgne (Old Irish) TOYN BOE COOL—in—yuh

Taliesin (Middle Welsh) Tahl—YEH—sin

Taranis (Gaulish) Tah—RAHN—iss

Tarbh-fheis (Old Irish) TARV FESH

Tarvos Trigaranus (Gaulish) TAR—wose Tree—gah—RAHN—oos

Toutatis (Gaulish) Too—TAH—tiss

Tuatha Dé Danann (Old Irish) TOO—uh—thuh DAY DAH—nin

Tuige (Old Irish) TOO—guh

NOTES

Foreword

1 Alexander Carmichael, *Carmina Gadelica: Hymns and Incantations* (Edinburgh: Lindisfarne Press, 1992), 285.

First Lunation

1 Patrick Moore, *The Moon* (New York: Rand McNally/Royal Astronomical Society, 1981), pp. 8-9.
2 Moore, *The Moon*; Kopal Zdenek, *The Solar System* (Oxford: Oxford University Press, 1973), pp. 70-71.
3 Zdenek, *The Solar System*.
4 Moore, *The Moon*, pp. 10-11; Zdenek, p. 71.
5 Moore, *The Moon*, p. 11.
6 Moore, *The Moon*, p. 10.
7 http://es.rice.edu/ES/humsoc/Galileo/Things/moon.html
8 http://es.rice.edu/ES/humsoc/Galileo/Things/moon.html
9 http://es.rice.edu/ES/humsoc/Galileo/Things/moon.html
10 http://es.rice.edu/ES/humsoc/Galileo/Things/moon.html; Moore, *The Moon*, pp. 12-13.
11 Zdenek, *The Solar System*, pp. 74-84.
12 Moore, *The Moon*, pp. 18-19.
13 Moore, *The Moon*, pp. 18-19.
14 Moore, *The Moon*, pp. 22-23; Zdenek, *The Solar System*, pp. 86, 91.
15 Moore, *The Moon*, pp. 6-7, 24-25; Zdenek, *The Solar System*, pp. 91-92,
16 Calvert Watkins, *Dictionary of Indo-European Roots* (New York: Houghton Mifflin Co., 2000), p. 51.
17 Carl D. Buck, *A Dictionary of Selected Synonyms in the Principal Indo-European Languages* (Chicago: University of Chicago Press, 1949), pp. 1006-09.
18 www.seds.orga/billa/psc/fullmoons.html. Other cultures, of course, have their own Moon terminology and lore. This is, for the most part, outside the scope of this book (although words for the Moon and its phases in Celtic languages and its associations in Celtic folklore will be examined in a later chapter).
19 http://nssdc.gsfc.nasa.gov/lunar/blue_moon.html
20 John Lust, *The Herb Book* (New York: Bantam, 1987), p. 572; Paul Beyerl, *The Master Book of Herbalism* (Custer, WA: Phoenix Publishing, 1984), pp. 351-52.

Second Lunation

1 Mircea Eliade, *The Sacred and the Profane* (New York: Harcourt Brace, 1987), pp. 156-57.
2 Many popular works emphasize the significance of the full Moon (rather than the new Moon). In many historically attested religious traditions, however, the new Moon is the most significant phase of the lunar cycle, and its reappearance is an extremely important event. Folklore associated with the full Moon does exist in many cultures, although not necessarily in greater quantity than that associated with the new Moon (or the waxing and waning phases of the Moon). This special reverence for the new Moon is found in numerous traditions (including Celtic, as we shall see). That being said, I do not mean to imply that the full Moon was not considered powerful or significant. Its power and beauty still inspire awe to this day. As an example, after a recent snowfall, I was out walking in the woods one night without the aid of a flashlight or the benefit of any modern light source. As I walked along, I realized I could see the landscape around me quite clearly. The Moon was full that evening, and its light, reflected off the snowy ground, was nothing short of marvelous. The scene was beautiful and surreal, and I marveled at the power of the full Moon's brilliant light. Its radiant face seemed close and personal, like a

friend who was there to guide my way, and at the same time it was awe-inspiring, almost incomprehensible. I felt blessed to experience this brief interlude during the writing of this book and to explore one of the many reasons the full Moon has acquired its lore and status.

3   The Moon's phases also provided a basis with which to compare the attributes of the Sun, which we will discuss further on.

4   Eliade, *The Sacred and the Profane*, pp. 156-57.

5   Mircea Eliade, *Rites and Symbols of Initiation* (Woodstock, NY: Spring Publications, 1995), pp. 9, 36.

6   This concept exists (in various forms) in Judeo-Christian tradition, Hinduism, Buddhism, Shamanism, and other indigenous religious systems (as well as modern Earth religions).

7   These concepts are discussed at some length by Eliade in *The Sacred and the Profane*, as well as in *Rites and Symbols of Initiation* and *The Myth of the Eternal Return* (Princeton, NJ: Princeton University Press, 1971).

8   We should not confuse this concept with the frequent association of light with goodness and darkness with evil that is found in certain (but not all) religious systems. It should be clear by now that darkness is necessary and beneficial. If a seed cannot go into the dark soil, it cannot be born and have life. If we do not sleep, we cannot survive. If the Sun or Moon do not set, they cannot rise again. Wholeness and balance cannot exist without both light and dark, winter and summer, male and female energies. These dualities are complementary, not antagonistic, and form an intrinsic part of creation, existence, and the sustenance of life. A spiritual path that focuses too heavily on either half of these ideas (male, light, summer; or female, dark, winter) does not embrace or show reverence for the whole of existence.

9   Eliade, *The Sacred and the Profane*, pp. 148, 184-88.

10 Eliade, *The Sacred and the Profane*, p. 180.

11 C. Kerényi, *The Gods of the Greeks* (London: Thames and Hudson, 1951), p. 32. In other sources, including Homer, only one Moira is spoken of, a single spinning goddess described as "strong . . . hard to endure . . . destroying." Robert Graves, *The Greek Myths* (London: Penguin Books, 1960), p. 48 states that, at Delphi, only two Fates were worshipped (those of birth and death). This may be due to a myth variant that stated that, in some cases, Zeus might intervene in the decision-making process pertaining to the length of a person's life, thereby making the role of Lachesis the Apportioner obsolete.

12 Kerényi, *The Gods of the Greeks*, p. 32; Graves, *The Greek Myths*, pp. 48-49. This description may be an analogy for the dark recesses of the ocean or the night sky being illuminated by moonlight.

13 Graves, *The Greek Myths*.

14 Eliade, *Rites and Symbols of Initiation*, pp. 42-46.

15 Eliade, *Rites and Symbols of Initiation*, p. 46.

16 Eliade, *The Sacred and the Profane*, pp. 156-57.

17 Eliade, *The Sacred and the Profane*, pp. 156-57.

18 In previous centuries, scholars and aristocrats theorized that ancient and/or "uncivilized" peoples (a.k.a. "primitives and savages," those who were not Christian, white, and middle-to-upper class, as well as the recipient of a classical or ecclesiastical education) engaged in simple-minded superstition, rather than any sort of "real" religion. They existed in "less enlightened times" and "barbarous places," and lived in a state of darkness and ignorance. In their pitiful state, many of these apparently heterogeneous and misguided souls evidently worshipped the Sun. This way of thinking is, of course, outmoded, inaccurate, patronizing, and ethnocentric in the extreme (although it still exerts a considerable impact in our day and age). Religious concepts pertaining to the sacrality of nature (including the Sun and the Moon) formed part of many belief systems and varied widely over time and in different regions. Based on what we know of ancient cultures (as well as modern primal cultures), there is no reason to assume that their beliefs were any less sincere, well thought-out, or sophisticated than the large religious systems of today.

19 Eliade, *The Sacred and the Profane*, pp. 156-57.

20 Whether or not it is historically accurate, in the minds of some the Sun has become associated with patriarchal, monotheistic religions, which are considered the antithesis of Earth-honoring spiritual systems that embrace the divine feminine as well as the divine masculine. At least some ancient solar-focused religions (whether they existed in patriarchal societies or more egalitarian settings) are likely to have been Earth-honoring. Many of these were probably polytheistic, embracing powerful male and female deities. It is next to impossible to ascertain what ancient peoples believed (regarding the Sun or other spiritual concepts) based solely on archaeology, which is the only source we have for most ancient or prehistoric cultures. Without written records or other hard evidence (as well as sufficient expertise and objectivity), it is difficult (as well as dangerous, in terms of accuracy and issues of respect) to overgeneralize or hypothesize about ancient religious beliefs. Even where we do have written records, the variations of belief are myriad (and sometimes surprising). For example, Hinduism is a polytheistic "pagan" (non-Christian) religion, in which male deities associated with the Sky Realm and/or creation are worshipped. There are also many powerful Hindu goddesses whose worship is widespread. Hindu society is profoundly hierarchical and patriarchal, and women have little power. Norse religion was also pagan, polytheistic, and presum-

ably Earth-honoring, and while early Norse society (like most early societies) was patriarchal, the status of women appears to have been higher than that of Hindu society. In this mythological setting, the Moon was masculine and the Sun feminine.

21 Eliade, *The Sacred and the Profane*, pp. 156-57.

22 Eliade, *The Sacred and the Profane*, p. 158.

23 Eliade, *The Sacred and the Profane*, p. 158. Some religious systems that maintained a strong solar focus also preserved the concept of darkness as the source of creation (often equated with the primordial ocean).

24 Eliade, *The Sacred and the Profane*, pp. 157-58.

25 Eliade, *The Sacred and the Profane*, p. 158. Eliade cites relevant examples from the end of antiquity, such as Emperor Julius' treatise *On the Sun King*, and Proclus' *Hymn to the Sun*.

26 Eliade, *The Sacred and the Profane*, p. 158.

27 Eliade, *The Sacred and the Profane*, p. 158. While Christianity caused religious, political, and cultural changes in areas where earlier religions had long flourished, it did not always reject the sacred character of the natural world. Irish monastics in particular were famous for beautiful poetic and spiritual observations about the land in which they lived. Nature could be considered holy in that Yahweh was said to have created it. In addition, Jesus told his followers that, if they sought him, they had only to look underneath a stone (meaning that he, and the sacred, were present everywhere). This is, however, somewhat different than the belief that nature is sacred in and of itself, no matter how it came into existence. Owing to variations in Biblical interpretation and a growing concern for the environment, an increasing number of Christians seek to deepen their connection with the natural world. The ability of New Age spiritualities to accommodate these impulses is noteworthy.

28 In Celtic tradition, sovereignty is personified as a female figure, a powerful goddess who, in some cases, appears to have had solar attributes. In addition, the word for the Sun in many Celtic languages is feminine.

29 Eliade, *Rites and Symbols of Initiation*, p. 42.

30 Eliade, *Rites and Symbols of Initiation*, p. 42.

31 Eliade, *Rites and Symbols of Initiation*, p. 42.

32 Eliade, *Rites and Symbols of Initiation*, p. 46.

33 It is believed that the solar year was adopted as a unit of time measurement during the later Egyptian era (at least in terms of recorded history). Most other historical cultures (including those of the earlier Egyptian eras) had a lunar year that fit into the solar year (the solar year consisting of twelve months of thirty days each, plus five added intercalary days). Before historical sources begin, other systems may have been utilized that were lunar-based (perhaps exclusively so). A lunar year, which consists of thirteen lunar cycles (of twenty-nine and one-half days each), would be eighteen and one-half days longer than a solar year. Alternately, a lunar year consisting of twelve lunar cycles would need to add eleven days to complete a solar year.

34 Mircea Eliade, *The Myth of the Eternal Return* (Princeton, NJ: Princeton University Press, 1971), pp. 51-52, 60-61.

35 Alwyn and Brinley Rees, *Celtic Heritage* (New York: Thames and Hudson, 1989), pp. 89-93, 98-99, 104-6. This custom is evident from the details of many well-documented cultures and their New Year's folklore. In Celtic tradition, this was most certainly the case. Samain, the end of the Celtic year and beginning of the next, was considered a "point outside of time." It was a very liminal period, when the Otherworld was more accessible and interactions between the worlds most probable (whether dangerous or beneficial). Certain types of ceremonies and texts recited or enacted by the Druids or religious personnel of the tribe would likely have cited historical, societal, and religious precedents.

36 Rees and Rees, *Celtic Heritage*, p. 114; John Carey, "Lebor Gabála Érenn," in John Koch and John Carey, *The Celtic Heroic Age* (Oakville, CT: Celtic Studies Publications, 2000), pp. 226-71. The medieval Irish pseudo-historical text *Lebor Gabála Érenn* (popularly referred to as The Book of Invasions) describes the various incoming waves of inhabitants (both mortal and divine) to the land of Ireland. Between the various "invasions" (which are not to be taken literally, as they function on a variety of semihistorical, literary, spiritual, and symbolic levels), a catastrophe often occurs, such as a flood or plague. This event often wipes out all or almost all of the current inhabitants. After a period of time, new people arrive and the pattern repeats itself.

37 In an upcoming chapter, we will explore the calendar systems of the Celts, as well as the possibility that the New Year and other sacred days were connected with the appearance of the new Moon.

38 Eliade, *The Myth of the Eternal Return*, pp. 58-59, 63-64.

39 This saying has been attributed to a number of Native American tribes.

40 Eliade, *The Myth of the Eternal Return*, pp. 63-64.

41 Nerys Patterson, *Cattle Lords and Clansmen: The Social Structure of Early Ireland* (Notre Dame, IN: University of Notre Dame Press, 1994), pp. 121-29.

42 Eliade, *The Myth of the Eternal Return*, pp. 56, 66-67; Rees and Rees, *Celtic Heritage*, pp. 89-94.

43 Lecture notes, Celtic Paganism Course at Harvard University taught by Patrick K. Ford (Spring, 2000). In native Celtic tradition, time was cyclical, as opposed to the Biblical concept of time as a linear event.

Third Lunation

1   Many traditional healers utilize spiritual healing techniques, but the shaman utilizes a method unique to shamanism. Magical techniques are also found in most cultures, but once again, the shaman is associated with very specific areas of magical expertise. The techniques involved with religious ecstasy are specific to the shaman, and not all techniques, nor all ecstatics, can be called shamanic.

2   Mircea Eliade, *Shamanism: Archaic Techniques of Ecstacy* (Princeton, NJ: Princeton University Press, 1964), pp. 3-4. We will use the word "shaman" to refer to practitioners of shamanic techniques in all parts of the world (keeping in mind that indigenous terms for this belief system and its practitioners exist in many languages).

3   Eliade, *Shamanism: Archaic Techniques of Ecstacy*, pp. 259-61. During initiations, candidates often experience a spiritual ascent to the Sky Realm that involves symbolism associated with the World Tree.

4   Eliade, *Shamanism: Archaic Techniques of Ecstacy*, pp. 4-8.

5   Eliade, *Shamanism: Archaic Techniques of Ecstacy*. While other forms of magic and religion are frequently found in societies in which shamanism is practiced, shamanism often (but not always) constitutes the oldest layer of spiritual belief or tradition in the community. Sometimes, other religious elements are present that may be earlier than (or parallel with) those of the shamanic tradition. In certain areas, these myths, ideas, and rites result from the general religious experience of the group, rather than those of a specific class of practitioner. And, apart from the areas of expertise just described, other aspects of religious life may not involve the shaman at all.

6   Eliade, *Shamanism: Archaic Techniques of Ecstacy*, pp. 5-7.

7   Eliade, *Shamanism: Archaic Techniques of Ecstacy*, p. 13. When a candidate is chosen by the clan, this is often determined by the quality of the candidate's ecstatic experiences.

8   Eliade, *Shamanism: Archaic Techniques of Ecstacy*, p. 13. The deliberate quest for magical or religious powers of a shamanic nature (or the granting of such powers by the gods and the spirits) involves the radical transformation of the person into a specialized technician. When shamanic powers are obtained through methods other than hereditary transmission, there is quite a bit of variation as to whether the candidate obtains these powers for the benefit of the tribe or for his or her own benefit. This type of work may not be strictly shamanic, as it does not imply a distinction in religious or social terms. A number of people in modern Western culture have become involved in the study of shamanism and its techniques. Many are able to learn the techniques of shamanic journeying for the benefit of themselves and others. Often, these journeys are used for healing, restoring soul parts or spiritual power, purification, protection, and gaining knowledge of the spiritual realms (as well as of one's own inner life and spiritual path). Quite a number of people have become masterful in these techniques, even where a social distinction is not always possible. Whether these people should be called shamans or masters of shamanic techniques is somewhat a matter of semantics, but also a matter of respect for the cultures from whom the techniques were obtained (and to whom a debt of gratitude is owed).

9   Eliade, *Shamanism: Archaic Techniques of Ecstacy*, pp. 13-14.

10   These spirits are different from tutelary spirits (spirits of place) and may or may not be different from the spirits the shaman summons for assistance during religious ceremonies.

11   Eliade, *Shamanism: Archaic Techniques of Ecstacy*, pp. 21-23, 33-38, 64-66, 81-85, 96-99, 106-7.

12   Eliade, *Shamanism: Archaic Techniques of Ecstacy*, pp. 84-85. In some cases, the shaman may control a limited number of spirits.

13   Eliade, *Shamanism: Archaic Techniques of Ecstacy*.

14   Eliade, *Shamanism: Archaic Techniques of Ecstacy*, pp. 168-75; Michael Harner, *The Way of the Shaman* (San Francisco: HarperSanFrancisco, 1990), pp. 50-53. The use of a drum is intentional and practical, as well as symbolic. The sound that emanates from the head of the drum when struck includes a primary tone or "fundamental," as well as a number of softer tones that are somewhat more difficult to perceive at first (but definitely present). Some of these consist of tones higher than the fundamental, which often have a ringing or bell-like quality, while others are low tones, booming and quite powerful. Many primal cultures recognize the inherent power of overtones and their potential for assisting people to enter into trance states or altered states of consciousness. With a small amount of training, a person can focus on and hear these sounds very clearly. Focusing on the overtones frequently results in an altered state in which the person experiences the sensation of movement or "flying" (in terms of the physical and spiritual bodies). Overtones occur in nature, and ancient man would have perceived them in a variety of natural settings. Focusing on these sounds would have revealed to early humans their inherent powers. Waterfalls, rushing water, and the wind are all potent sources of overtones. Some people are even able to perceive the overtones that emanate from electric devices like electric fans or refrigerators. In addition to the drum, the sound produced by rattles (or drums with bells) operates in a similar way, and these are also used in shamanic rites and journeys. It should also be noted that the rhythm or tempo used by shamans when drumming, rattling, or chanting is deliberate and highly functional. A tempo of two beats per second has been shown to entrain a person's brainwaves physically, often resulting in an altered state of consciousness. Therefore, this tempo is sometimes referred to as "theta rhythm." This rhythm will be familiar from the chants, rattling, or drumming of certain Native American cultures (although this has often been imitated or portrayed in a culturally insensitive manner).

15 Eliade, *Shamanism: Archaic Techniques of Ecstacy*, pp. 168-76.

16 Eliade, *Shamanism: Archaic Techniques of Ecstacy*, pp. 169, 172, 176.

17 Liam Mac Mathúna, "Irish Perceptions of the Cosmos," in *Celtica* 23 (1999).

18 These included seasonal gatherings, tribal assemblies to dispense justice or enact tribal business (including the inauguration of kings), and Druidic ceremonies.

19 The texts known as the *Dindshenchas* (The Lore of Places") mentions a number of special trees considered sacred to the early Irish: the Ash of Tortu, Éo Rosa (a yew), Éo Mugna (also a yew), and the Tree of Dathí (an ash). The early Irish writing system known as the *ogam* alphabet preserved information pertaining to native lore associated with a number of plants and trees. A. T. Lucas, "The Sacred Trees of Ireland," in *The Journal of the Cork Historical and Archaeological Society*, vol. 63 (1963). For an in-depth discussion of the Celtic World Tree, see my paper entitled "The Descent of the Gods," in *The Proceedings of the Harvard Celtic Colloquium*, vol. 21 (2001).

20 Hilda Ellis Davidson, *Myths and Symbols in Pagan Europe—Early Scandinavian and Celtic Religions* (Syracuse, NY: Syracuse University Press, 1988), pp. 23-24, 170, 180.

21 Tom Cross and Clark Slover, *Ancient Irish Tales* (Totowa, NJ: Barnes and Noble, 1969), p. 505.

22 Cross and Slover, *Ancient Irish Tales*, p. 507.

23 Eliade, *Shamanism: Archaic Techniques of Ecstacy*, p. 186.

24 Katherine Briggs, *An Encyclopedia of Fairies* (New York: Pantheon Books, 1976), pp. 131, 135, 137, 152-55, 158, 167-68. See also W. Y. Evans-Wentz, *The Fairy Faith in Celtic Countries* (New York: Citadel Press, 1990), pp. 23-225.

25 Eliade, *Shamanism: Archaic Techniques of Ecstacy*, p. 189; JohnCarey, "The Location of the Otherworld in Irish Tradition," in *Éigse* 19 (1982); Jean Louis Brunaux, *The Celtic Gauls: Gods, Rites and Sanctuaries* (London: Seaby, 1987). Archaeology has shown that the central point of many Celtic sacred sites was considered most important for contacting and making gifts to the gods. Ritual shafts and pits located at the center of sacred sites or sanctuaries have been found to contain jewelry, cauldrons, swords, the bones of sacred animals, the charred wood of sacred trees, and other items. These appear to be offerings to the deities of the Lower World. It is also possible that gifts appropriate to the deities of the Upper Realms (the smoke from sacred fires, herbs, or other offerings, or oblations that do not leave a trace in the archaeological record) may have also been made.

26 Eliade, *Shamanism: Archaic Techniques of Ecstacy*, pp. 186-87.

27 Anne Ross, *Pagan Celtic Britain* (Chicago: Academy Publishers, 1996), pp. 99, 132, 252, 344, 347.

28 Alexander Carmichael, *Carmina Gadelica: Hymns and Incantations* (Edinburgh: Lindisfarne Press, 1992), pp. 281-82. For examples of these kinds of prayers, see the hymns and charms given on pages 43, 48, 73, 83-85, 96-100, 131, 136-38, 140, 151, 159, 176, 178, 217, 237-39, 267-70, and 283-92.

29 Ross, *Pagan Celtic Britain*, pp. 99, 132, 252, 344; Eliade, *Shamanism: Archaic Techniques of Ecstacy*, p. 106.

30 Stanley Ireland, *Roman Britain* (New York: Routledge, 1991), pp. 181-90. See also Stuart Piggot, *The Druids* (New York: Thames and Hudson, 1975); T. G. E. Powell *The Celts* (London: Thames and Hudson, 1980); George Calder, ed., *Auraceipt na n-Éces* (Dublin: Four Courts Press, 1995). Secret "Druidic" languages are alluded to in several instances (including those associated with the *ogam* alphabet).

31 See the stories in *Ancient Irish Tales* by Cross and Slover for examples of Druidic attributes.

32 Patrick K. Ford, *The Celtic Poets* (Belmont, MA: Ford and Bailie, 1999), pp. xv-xxvii.

33 Martin Martin and R. W. Munro, *A Description of the Western Islands of Scotland Circa 1695* (Edinburgh: Birlinn, 1999), p. 79.

34 Ford, *The Celtic Poets*, p. xxvi.

35 Lewis Thorpe, ed. and tr., *Gerald of Wales—The Journey Through Wales/The Description of Wales* (London: Penguin Books, 1988) pp. 246-247.

36 Martin and Munro, *A Description of the Western Islands of Scotland*, p. 77. Martin also recorded a divinatory method from 17th-century Scotland in which a person from the community was singled out and taken to a remote place. He was wrapped in a cow's hide and left alone all night until "invisible friends" provided the answer sought. An early Irish tale describes a Druidic divination ceremony in which a person engaged in magical sleep while wrapped in a cow hide.

37 Eliade, *Shamanism: Archaic Techniques of Ecstacy*, pp. 173, 407-8, 467. In ancient India, for example, the sacrificial horse (in the shape of a bird) was responsible for carrying the sacrificer in his or her journey to the Sky Realm. In some cultures, shamans performed the role of the sacrificing priest.

38 Eliade, *Shamanism: Archaic Techniques of Ecstacy*; Ross, *Pagan Celtic Britain*, pp. 115-17, 172-220. Magical branches (sometimes adorned with bells) are mentioned in a number of Celtic tales and seem to have been associated with poets and seers, magicians, and Otherworld figures. Iron is featured in stories and folklore accounts and is associated with protection, and hence with danger. Several myths and artifacts refer to divine beings or animals that possessed three horns, and artwork from Britain and Gaul depicts a widely worshipped horned or antlered deity.

39 Eliade, *Shamanism: Archaic Techniques of Ecstacy*, pp. 229-34.

40 Ross, *Pagan Celtic Britain*, pp. 404-17.

41 Ross, *Pagan Celtic Britain*, pp. 99-100, 286-88, 404-17; Miranda Green, *Celtic Goddesses* (New York: George Braziller, 1996), pp. 184-87.

42 Trefor M. Owen, *Welsh Folk Customs* (Llandysul, Dyfed: Gomer Press, 1987), pp. 49, 54-58.

43 Eliade, *Shamanism: Archaic Techniques of Ecstacy*, pp. 116-19, 182-83, 190-92.

44 John J. O'Meara, ed. and tr., *Gerald of Wales—The History and Topography of Ireland* (London: Penguin Books, 1982), pp. 109-10

45 Eliade, *Shamanism: Archaic Techniques of Ecstacy*, p. 188.

46 Cross and Slover, *Ancient Irish Tales*, p. 179.

47 In Celtic folklore, magical encounters and healing events take place near stone pillars or standing stones, which are frequently associated with fairies, witches, and other supernatural characters.

48 Other tales have been recorded in which a king, hero, or other special candidate must travel to the Otherworld to complete a task, journey, or adventure, which precipitates the candidate's return home.

49 In shamanic tales, fairy wives are often jealous of the shaman's mortal wife and may try to steal or kill her children. This is also a well-known motif in Celtic legends, where fairies (or witches, a later stand-in for the fairies in Celtic folklore) are accused of stealing, or attempting to harm or abduct, mortal children.

50 In *Serglige Con Chulainn*, Cú's Otherworld lover wants him to stay with her in her world, but he continues on his quest and eventually returns to his home.

51 Eliade, *Shamanism: Archaic Techniques of Ecstacy*, pp. 73-81, 133n, 344, 361.

52 Eliade, *Shamanism: Archaic Techniques of Ecstacy*. This theme is widely seen in Celtic tradition. Cú Chulainn himself is offered assistance by a divine female figure, the Morrígan. His rejection of her offer of help (and her affection) outrages her, and results in her attempts to thwart his progress. However, when he sets out for his final battle, she tries to warn him by preventing his departure. In later Celtic-inspired tales, King Arthur's plans are repeatedly hindered by the sorceress Morgan le Fay. Yet, at the end of his life, she is one of the three Otherworldly women who ferry him to the Isle of Avalon to receive healing. Other divine Celtic women are said to have had dealings with kings, heroes, and other figures. Sometimes, they entice or lure the men into situations (beneficial or treacherous). They may divert them from their goals or fight with them magically, but may also assist them in their physical and spiritual quests. These women sometimes provide the heroes with information that enables them to accomplish nearly impossible tasks or endure or complete initiatory ordeals or adventures. Sometimes the women lead the men toward (or directly provide them with) magical branches or apples, weapons, or other objects associated with magical power, transformation, or immortality.

53 Eliade, *Shamanism: Archaic Techniques of Ecstacy*, p. 77.

54 Otta F. Swire, *Skye: The Island and Its Legends* (London and Glasgow: Blackie and Son Ltd., 1961). In some versions of this tale (and related types), the husband must search for the fairy wife who has abducted the child. Sometimes she is caught visiting our world and singing to the infant son in his bed. Many of these fairy songs were recorded in Scotland within the last century, including a number of songs attributed to the early fairy queen of Clan MacLeod.

55 Eliade, *Shamanism: Archaic Techniques of Ecstacy*, p. 82.

56 Eliade, *Shamanism: Archaic Techniques of Ecstacy*, pp. 47, 50n, 52, 91, 125, 132, 135-37, 339, 350; Anne Ross, *The Folklore of the Scottish Highlands* (Batsford: Barnes and Noble, 1976), pp. 77-80, 92; F. Marian McNeill, *The Silver Bough: Scottish Folklore and Folk-Belief*, vol. 1 (Glasgow: William MacLellan, 1977), pp. 90-94. The motif of the crystal mountain or palace encountered by heroes in their mythical adventures may derive from shamanic tales in which a crystal (or magical stone) detaches from the sky and falls to Earth. The stone is said to dispense wisdom, clairvoyance, and the powers of divination and magical flight. Crystal dwellings, trees, and other objects (often located or originating in the Otherworld) are also found in Celtic sources.

57 Eliade, *Shamanism: Archaic Techniques of Ecstacy*, p. 126.

58 Eliade, *Shamanism: Archaic Techniques of Ecstacy*, pp. 126, 136-37, 169; Patrick K. Ford, *The Mabinogi* (Berkeley: University of California Press, 1977), pp. 89-109.

59 Author's translation from Old Irish.

60 Author's translation from Old Irish.

61 George Calder, *Auraceipt na n-Éces* (Dublin: Four Courts Press, 1995), p. 91; Eliade, *Shamanism: Archaic Techniques of Ecstacy*, pp. 194 and n., 270, 403. Sacred tree climbing is also found in Brahmanic texts, where climbing a tree is a symbol of spiritual ascent. Altaic shamans climb 7 or 9 notches cut in a ceremonial birch to reach the farthest heavens.

62 Author's translation from Old Irish.

63 For many years, I have been quite interested in the overtone-rich "throat-singing" style practiced by the Tuvans of Central Asia. One group of Tuvan musicians, Huun Huur Tu, has released a number of popular recordings. The grandfathers of two of the group's members were shamans and one of the musicians has, in the past, performed a shamanic dance during their concert performance. The group has often performed in Boston and, over the years (through my own musical endeavors that include the use of overtones), I became acquainted with the group's manager. One night, after taking them out for dinner, Huun Huur Tu visited my home. They appeared to enjoy their visit, trying out various Celtic instruments I have on hand and looking at ritual objects around the house. I ride, and am fond of, horses (in both the earthly and spiritual sense) and have a number of horse-related

images on the walls. Several of the group's members are horse-herders and they commented on the beauty of some of these images. In speaking with one of the musicians, I was asked about these horse images. I explained my interest and relationship with them and one member replied, "Oh, that's your 'spirit.'" The group was also very interested in the mythological images depicted in a panel from the Gundestrup Cauldron (a large silver cauldron found in Denmark, possibly of Gaulish or Thracian origin, whose artwork may depict a number of Celtic deities). The panel in question features the horned god known as Cernunnos. I was asked about this figure, and described the horned god's powers and attributes in Celtic tradition. My words were translated for the others, who nodded and gave some brief commentary. The fellow then turned to me and said, "Yes, we have one of those."

64 Whitley Stokes, ed. and tr., *Sanas Chormaic* (Cormac's Glossary) (Calcutta: Irish Archaeological and Celtic Society, 1868), p. 160.

65 Sean Ó Duinn, *Forbhais Droma Damhgháire* (Dublin: Mercier Press, 1992), p. 103.

66 Eliade, *Shamanism: Archaic Techniques of Ecstacy*, p. 83; Ford, *The Mabinogi*, pp. xviii-xxv.

67 Ford, *The Celtic Poets*, pp. 159-81.

68 Ford, *The Celtic Poets*, pp. 183-87.

69 Carey, *Lebor Gabála Érenn*, in Koch, and Carey *The Celtic Heroic Age*, p. 259.

70 For example, the Sun and Moon are used to decorate the sacred chest in which Buryat shamans keep their magical objects (including their drum, stick-horse, fur, and bells).

71 Eliade, *Shamanism: Archaic Techniques of Ecstacy*, pp. 186-87.

72 Harner, *The Way of the Shaman*, pp. 21-24.

73 Harner, *The Way of the Shaman*, p. 327.

74 Harner, *The Way of the Shaman*, p. 292.

75 Harner, *The Way of the Shaman*, pp. 60, 62. *Qaumaneq* can also be obtained by the candidate directly, but only with the help of the spirits of the dead, the bears, or the Mother of the Caribou (the mythical beings from whom candidates know they may receive this power if they are sufficiently prepared).

76 Harner, *The Way of the Shaman*, pp. 292-93.

77 Harner, *The Way of the Shaman,* pp. 190-96. The sixth heaven is the level traditionally associated with the Moon, while the seventh heaven is associated with the Sun.

78 Eliade, *Shamanism: Archaic Techniques of Ecstacy*, p. 195.

79 Harner, *The Way of the Shaman*, p. 196

80 Harner, *The Way of the Shaman,*, pp. 76-77.

81 The reader will notice that no specific meditations or exercises were provided with this chapter. It is suggested that those who are interested read *The Way of the Shaman* by Michael Harner. This book is written by an accomplished anthropologist and shamanic specialist and is intended for Westerners. It distills the universal elements of shamanic traditions around the world into a practical, coherent, and powerful system of meditative exercises that have been used successfully by modern learners in many countries. Eliade's book *Shamanism: Archaic Techniques of Ecstasy* would serve as a good in-depth source for the concepts and practices of shamanism. There is no really reliable book on Celtic shamanism available as of the writing of this book (something I hope to produce in the future). Those who are interested in the shamanic elements of Celtic myth and religion might first acquaint themselves with the religion of the pagan Celts by reading about it in reliable sources (University presses and the like). Celtic myths should also be read (in good translations, rather than retellings). After having read Harner and Eliade, the shamanic elements of Celtic myths and religion will be readily apparent.

82 Mircea Eliade, *The Sacred and the Profane* (New York: Harcourt Brace, 1987), p. 11. Another important shamanic/Celtic parallel should be noted here. In many shamanic cultures, great reverence is paid to smiths and their craft. Often, the craft of the smith will rank just below the shaman's in importance and status. Yakut proverbial wisdom states "Smiths and shamans are from the same nest" and "A shaman's wife is respectable; a smith's wife is venerable." Buryat legend tells of the nine sons of the celestial smith who came to Earth to teach the art of metallurgy to men. Their first students were the ancestors of the families of human smiths. The sons of the celestial smith married the daughters of the Earth and are therefore the ancestors of mortal smiths. No one can become a smith unless he is descended from one of these families. Smiths are often said to have the power to heal and prophesy and are often associated with a number of magical practices. The smith is highly revered in Celtic tradition, where he is also credited with magical powers or associations. One interesting comparative example pertains to the Yakut smith, who receives his craft from a fairly dark-natured god who is the chief smith of the Underworld. This deity is said to reside in an iron house. He is able to repair the broken or amputated limbs of heroes, and is involved with initiating shamans of the underworld, "tempering their souls as he tempers iron." Iron houses feature in a number of Celtic tales and are often associated with magic and/or danger. The physician-deity Dian Cecht made a silver arm for the god Núadu to replace one lost in battle.

83 Eliade, *Shamanism: Archaic Techniques of Ecstacy*, p. 193. Note the connection of the bird's left wing with the Moon and its right wing with the Sun (an example of the connection between Sun/Moon and right/left, which is further discussed in the next chapter).

Fourth Lunation

1   Information about the goddess Artemis was derived from the following sources: Mark Morford and Robert J. Lenardon, *Classical Mythology* (New York/London: Longman, 1991), pp. 173-84; Thelma Sargent, *The Homeric Hymns* (New York: W.W. Norton and Co., 1975), pp. 58, 76; and Robert Graves, *The Greek Myths* (London: Penguin Books, 1960), pp. 55-56, 83-84. Additional sources included: Edith Hamilton, *Mythology: Timeless Tales of Gods and Heroes* (New York: Penguin, 1969), pp. 116, 137-38, 156-58, 174, 184, 239, 249-50, 255-56, 294, 297; C. Kerényi, *The Gods of the Greeks* (New York: Thames and Hudson, 1994); H. J. Rose, *A Handbook of Greek Mythology* (New York: E. P. Dutton, 1959). Due to the general nature and availability of this information, this chapter will not be as highly footnoted as other chapters. The interested reader may refer to the sources above for additional information or confirmation.

2   These are called Nereids, the early name of the nymphs who were originally associated with the sea (even though these popular nymphs are associated with other elements).

3   Numerous versions of mythological tales exist (and persist) in the world's mythological and religious systems. These are sometimes contradictory, other times complementary. The variations may be local or may have evolved through the repetition and variation of stories in oral tradition over the centuries. Sometimes the variants confuse the plot line or the connection between characters, while other versions are more helpful (perhaps more faithful to the original).

4   This image, of a star emerging from the ocean when the Sun had not yet shone its light upon the land, may reflect the image of the Morning Star, or the stars of the predawn hours. It may also be that Hera's curse refers to the darkness of night specifically, when the Moon, rather than the Sun, shines upon the Earth.

5   Information about Selene was derived from the same sources as that about Artemis (see footnote above) as well as pp. 210-11 in Graves, *The Greek Myths*, and p. 81 in Sargent, *The Homeric Hymns*.

6   Selene's imagery may be influenced by earlier representations of a Moon goddess who was associated with or took the shape of a cow depicted alongside the bull or horse of the Sun.

7   Sargent, *The Homeric Hymns*, p. 81.

8   Information about Hecate is derived from the following highly recommended source: Robert Von Rudloff, *Hekate in Ancient Greek Religion* (Vancouver: Thesis published by Horned Owl Publishing, 1999).

9   This is clearly similar to the concept of the three shamanic worlds. A comparable cosmogonic triad exists in Celtic sources, which we will explore in another chapter.

10   There is also a possibility that she was involved with the great mysteries at Eleusis.

11   It has sometimes been suggested that Hecate may represent the dark, chthonic side of Artemis, or that the triple-faced statues of Hecate represent a lunar deity comprised of Selene (reigning in the heavens), Artemis (reigning on Earth), and Hecate (reigning in the lower realms).

12   Von Rudloff, *Hekate in Ancient Greek Religion*, p. 112.

13   We might compare this passage with descriptions of the deities of the lower world as they appear in certain forms of shamanism, as well as with the *síd*-dwellers or fairies of Celtic mythology.

14   Von Rudloff, *Hekate in Ancient Greek Religion*, p. 104.

15   Von Rudloff, *Hekate in Ancient Greek Religion*, pp. 21-31.

16   Another example of the pairing of the Sun (Helios) with a possible lunar goddess comes from an account in which he is said to have had a wife called Neaira, The New One (possibly a reference to the new Moon). The story of their marriage or union may commemorate the apparent encounter of the Sun and Moon at the time of the new Moon (the phase of the Moon most associated with Hecate). Kerényi mentions a tale (which he does not describe or reference) involving "daughters of Hecate and Hermes," whom he takes to be identical with the two- or three-fold Charites. These two female figures were referred to as either daughters of Heaven (Ouranos) or of the Sun (Helios) and Light (Aigle, The Luminous, perhaps referring to moonlight). Aigle was one of the Hesperides, daughters of Night, of Atlas, or of Phorkys and Keto. Their joint name is connected with Hesperos, the star of evening. They were associated by name with sunset, evening, and the approach of Night. In one source, they are Hespera (The Vespertinal), Aigle (The Luminous), Erytheia (The Crimson), and Arethousa (a goddess of springs). In another source, they are listed as Lipara (Of Soft Radiance), Chrysothemis (Golden Law and Order), Asterope (Star-Brilliant), and Hygeia (Health). In Laconia, two Charites were worshipped, one called Kleta (The Invoked), and the other Phaenna (The Brilliant). These may be names for goddesses who seemed to appear during certain phases of the moon, especially during the dark nights of the festivals of the new Moon when the Moon might be invoked and the brilliant one welcomed. In Athens, two Charites were known as well: Auxo (The Waxing) and Hegemone (The Precursor—referring to the second half of the month in which the Moon precedes the Sun). Hegemone also seems to have been an epithet for Artemis. (It should be kept in mind that Kerényi and other scholars may have been influenced by the "over-lunarization" of goddesses by Robert Graves).

17   Many good books exist on the subject of Hindu mythology, and any reader who wishes to delve further into the topic would be richly rewarded by his or her efforts. These include: Wendy Doniger O'Flaherty, *Hindu Myths* (London: Penguin Books, 1975) and *Women, Androgynes and Other Mythical Beasts* (Chicago: University of

Chicago Press, 1980); David R. Kinsley, *Hindu Goddesses* (Berkeley: University of California Press, 1988). These are the primary sources utilized in researching this chapter.

18 Myles Dillon, *The Archaism of Irish Tradition* (Chicago: University of Chicago, 1969), reprinted from *Proceedings of the British Academy*, vol. 33 (1947).

19 O'Flaherty, *Hindu Myths*, pp. 50, 356.

20 O'Flaherty, *Hindu Myths*, p. 185.

21 John Carey, tr., "Lebor Gabála Érenn," in John T. Koch, and John Carey, *The Celtic Heroic Age* (Oakville, CT: Celtic Studies Publications, 2000), p. 265.

22 O'Flaherty, *Hindu Myths*, p. 119.

23 Roy Willis, ed., *World Mythology* (New York: Henry Holt, 1993), p. 71, and O'Flaherty, *Hindu Myths*, pp. 274-80, 349.

24 Clarified butter, or *ghee*, is considered to be a very sacred and health-promoting substance in traditional Indian medicine. Butter is highly regarded in Irish and Scottish folk charms as well.

25 O'Flaherty, *Hindu Myths*, p. 315. In the tale, when Parvati leaves to practice asceticism, she leaves behind two young sons (the deities Ganesa and Skanda) in the care of the Ganges. The text emphasizes her abandonment of the children, contrasting this with the Ganges, The Good Mother. In a Welsh tale we will explore in some detail in an upcoming chapter, the divine figure of Arianrhod (who may be a Moon goddess) gives birth to two sons. but abandons them as well. This is a large focus of the story, where her refusal or inability to raise the boys is a source of shame and conflict. Later in the Hindu tale, Shiva says to Parvati, "Let there be an end to your anger, Goddess. You abandoned Skanda when he wished to suckle at your breast, and you went off to perform asceticism, and so you will be called the Goddess Whose Breasts Are Not Sucked." In the Welsh tale, the uncle of the children later brings one of the boys to see his mother and she reacts with anger.

26 O'Flaherty, *Hindu Myths*, pp. 303-6.

27 O'Flaherty, *Hindu Myths*, pp. 30, 340, 341. A similar connection between animals and animal terminology is found in Old Irish, where the word *dam* may refer to an ox or cow, or a stag or doe (hind).

28 Kinsley, *Hindu Goddesses*, p. 14.

29 Kinsley, *Hindu Goddesses*, p. 14.

30 Information on the Mahadevi is derived from Kinsley, *Hindu Goddesses*, especially pp. 132-33, 138-41, 143-44, 149.

31 Some of the better-known Hindu deities are Indra, the King and chief of all the deities; Brahma, the Creator; Agni, the god of fire; Vishnu, originally a solar god, then supreme deity; Krishna (the dark one), an avatar of Vishnu; and Shiva (auspicious), the god of ascetics, the *linga* (sacred phallic symbol) and of cosmic destruction. Popular goddesses include: Lakshmi (good fortune), wife of Vishnu; Parvati (daughter of the mountain), wife of Shiva; Sita (the furrow), wife of Rama (an incarnation of Vishnu); Sarasvati (flowing), a holy river and the goddess of speech and knowledge, also wife of Brahma; Durga (difficult of access), an epithet of the Mahadevi in her fierce aspect; and Kali (the black goddess), a terrifying deity associated with battle, liminality, and the death and destruction that feed on and create life.

32 This duality also exists in Celtic mythology. For example, the warrior and tribal father god known as the Dagda, associated with a cauldron of nourishment and the harvest, was said to own a club that wielded life from one end and death from the other. At Samain, he unites with another great deity, the Mórrígan (Great Queen). She is primarily described as a goddess associated with battle and death, yet other sources indicate that she was also associated with the fertility of the land.

33 Information on Candamari and Camunda found in Kinsley, *Hindu Goddesses*, pp. 146-47.

34 O'Flaherty, *Hindu Myths*,especially pp. 157, 252 and O'Flaherty, *Women, Androgynes and Other Mythical Beasts*, pp. 241, 255-57. In one Hindu myth, Shiva is depicted riding Nandi the ox while wearing the Moon in his hair. He is contrasted with Vishnu, the solar deity, appearing as Hayagriva (the horse-headed) or Kalki (the centaur). In addition, the Asvins, a pair of horse gods or divine horsemen, were said to be the twin sons of the sun and a mare.

35 O'Flaherty, *Women, Androgynes and Other Mythical Beasts*, pp. 255-57, and Bruce Lincoln, *Myth, Cosmos and Society* (Cambridge, MA: Harvard University Press, 1986), various. One exception is the *Maharastra*, where the Moon is feminine in the usual Indo-European manner. In the various stages of Indian religious tradition, there is wide variety in terms of male and female dominance and focus (and this not necessarily in a linear progression). In some cases, the dominant, powerful or erotic woman is considered dangerous or undesirable, while in other cases, the dominant consort is the female. Some of the goddesses are docile, helpful wives to the powerful male deities; others are independent, powerful, and multifaceted. While early male dominance is seen in the Rig Veda, both male- and female-dominated hierogamies occur in the epics, with some leanings toward female dominance in the Puranas. Hinduism is a complex spiritual system, and therefore, generalization is not always possible or wise. This is, of course, true of most religions, ancient and modern.

36 H. R. Ellis Davidson, *Gods and Myths of Northern Europe* (New York: Penguin, 1964), pp. 37, 277-78.

37 O'Flaherty, *Women, Androgynes and Other Mythical Beasts*, p. 340. We will examine the gender of the words for the Sun and Moon in various Celtic languages (as well as the gender of the deities or divine figures associated with them) in an upcoming chapter.

38 O'Flaherty, *Women, Androgynes and Other Mythical Beasts*, pp. 77-81. It is interesting to note that, in Celtic tradition, a similar powerful female figure existed in the person of the goddess of sovereignty. She, too, was associated with the mare and also chose a human consort (the king), on whom she conferred the right to rule justly and successfully.

39 O'Flaherty, *Women, Androgynes and Other Mythical Beasts*, pp. 79-81. In addition to these early goddesses associated with the Moon, mares, sovereignty, and female power, several other goddesses are mentioned in the Rig Veda. Few hymns were devoted to them for, at this point, they were statistically less important than the male deities who dominated the pantheon at the time. While some goddesses from the early Vedic tradition seem to have diminished in power or disappeared, others survived and were worshipped in later Hindu tradition (Bhudevi, the Earth, and Sarasvati, for example). Most of the earliest evidence shows female deities in a less important position than male deities, quite the opposite of what has often been theorized (a transition from female to male focus or dominance). In addition, a variety of goddesses appear in later Hindu tradition who were not seen earlier or who did not receive much focus in the early period (including Parvati, Durga, Radha, Sita, and Kali). The Mahadevi does not appear until the medieval period in Hinduism, and there, she is the product of a carefully articulated theology. However, it is fascinating to note that the Devi is one of the female figures who (rather than being usurped) appear to have grown in power and significance over time.

40 O'Flaherty, *Women, Androgynes and Other Mythical Beasts*, p. 235.

41 O'Flaherty, *Women, Androgynes and Other Mythical Beasts*, pp. 255-57.

42 Lincoln, *Myth, Cosmos and Society*, p. 197 n8.

43 O'Flaherty, *Women, Androgynes and Other Mythical Beasts*, pp. 255-57.

44 O'Flaherty, *Women, Androgynes and Other Mythical Beasts*.

45 In Hindu tradition, various fluids (bodily and ritualistic) may be transmuted alchemically into one another, since they can function in the same way. Butter and honey are frequent metaphors for soma (which is compared to semen). The seed, or its metaphorical substitutes, were ritually ingested in certain ancient ceremonies. Milk and soma are considered to be the two quintessential foods (the first human, the second divine). Interestingly, butter and milk are considered extraordinary food sources in Celtic tradition, and both are frequently used in folk charms and rituals.

46 In one tale, Brahma is transformed into Candramas (a term that refers to the Moon), a being incarnate as a god and a sage.

47 O'Flaherty, *Women, Androgynes and Other Mythical Beasts*, p. 27.

48 Information in this section taken from Lincoln, *Myth, Cosmos and Society*, pp. 1-35.

49 Lincoln, *Myth, Cosmos and Society*, pp. 31-32. The Moon is also associated with other creation scenarios. In the *Aitereya Upanisad*, the original lone entity, Atman, creates the levels of the universe (heaven, atmosphere, Earth, and Underworld), as well as the primordial man, Purusa. Atman works on Purusa through "heat," a process of transformation well known in yoga and in shamanism, where ascetic heat is a sign of self-transformation. During the transformation, it is said that the Moon came from the mind.

50 Lincoln, *Myth, Cosmos and Society*, p. 3.

51 Lincoln, *Myth, Cosmos and Society*, p. 55.

52 Lincoln, *Myth, Cosmos and Society*, p. 1.

53 Lincoln, *Myth, Cosmos and Society*, p. 10.

54 Lincoln, *Myth, Cosmos and Society*, p. 15.

55 Lincoln, *Myth, Cosmos and Society*, p. 4.

56 Lincoln, *Myth, Cosmos and Society*, p. 15.

57 Lincoln, *Myth, Cosmos and Society*, p. 26.

58 Kinsley, *Hindu Goddesses*, p. 179. The Hindu goddess Aparajita was described as having the stars for pearls in her hair, the heavenly rivers for a girdle or belt, Mount Meru for her body, and the Sun and Moon for eyes.

59 Lincoln, *Myth, Cosmos and Society*, p. 30.

Fifth Lunation

1 Not continuously; they would have emigrated and returned during the various Ice Ages. Timothy Darvill, *Prehistoric Britain* (London: Routledge, 1987), pp. 28-29.

2 Darvill, *Prehistoric Britain*, pp. 29-34.

3 Darvill, *Prehistoric Britain*, pp. 35-36.

4 Darvill, *Prehistoric Britain*, pp. 37-38. Mammoth, bison, wooly rhino, and lions became extinct in Britain around this time. Existing animals were hunted primarily with spears.

5 Dogs or domesticated wolves were used for hunting as well as companionship. There may have been well-organized seasonal camps that were utilized for hunting at various times during the year.

6 Darvill, *Prehistoric Britain*, pp. 39-42.

7 Darvill, *Prehistoric Britain*, pp. 38, 41, 43.

8 Darvill, *Prehistoric Britain*, pp. 38, 41, 43.

9 Darvill, *Prehistoric Britain*, pp. 43-44.

10 Darvill, *Prehistoric Britain*, pp. 44-46.

11 As the land connection between Ireland and Britain was severed by 7000 B.C.E., the early inhabitants may have come by boat. It is likely that a variety of groups landed around the coast from parts of the western coast of Britain (although they could have also come from other parts of Europe).

12 Michael Ryan, ed., *The Illustrated Archaeology of Ireland* (Dublin: Country House, 1991), pp. 31-33, 39-40. In spring and summer, salmon would have been plentiful, and in autumn there would have been an abundance of nuts, berries, and fruit (as well as eels running downstream). During the winter, stores of food and wild pig would have been the primary food sources.

13 Ryan, *The Illustrated Archaeology of Ireland*, pp. 31, 33-40.

14 Darvill, *Prehistoric Britain*, pp. 48-49. These new techniques would have been especially welcome in areas suffering from rapid population growth or food scarcities.

15 Oak, alder, elm, and hazel were prevalent in southern Britain, and birch and pine in northern and western areas. The very north of Scotland and the Western Isles were mostly treeless.

16 Darvill, *Prehistoric Britain*, pp. 49-51.

17 Darvill, *Prehistoric Britain*, pp. 49-51.

18 Darvill, *Prehistoric Britain*, pp. 52-53. In addition to the reduction of trees and scrub, the activities of grazing animals prevented the regrowth of the forest

19 Darvill, *Prehistoric Britain*, pp. 54-56. Tools were made of flint and other kinds of stone, as well as antler, bone, and wood. Pottery of quite good quality was produced to make cooking pots and storage containers for food and liquids. Wood was used for bowls, pins, figurines, paddles, bows and arrows, fur and leather for clothes, and reeds and plant materials for baskets, matting, and string.

20 Darvill, *Prehistoric Britain*, pp. 49-51. There is some evidence for settlements by around 3000 B.C.E., including some the size of small villages. These are usually in sheltered areas, on well-drained soil, on low hills, or in river valleys. Buildings made of timber (and in Scotland, of stone), some with more than one room, would have been surrounded by fields and grazing areas. An average of six to twelve people lived in these small settlements.

21 Darvill, *Prehistoric Britain*, pp. 57-62. In some areas, the enclosures are regularly spaced, which supports the theory of periodic sacral use, as does the deposition of skulls or skeletons. Some sites seem to have been used primarily for ritual purposes, but there may not have been such a marked contrast or line between ritual and domestic activities as we perceive in our own culture.

22 Ryan, *The Illustrated Archaeology of Ireland*, pp. 47-48. These groups brought cattle, sheep, goats, domesticated pigs, wheat, and barley, as well as stone axes for clearing woodlands (for grazing and cultivation), ploughs and spades, flint and stone tools for harvesting, and stone querns for grinding the grain.

23 Earth floors (some with simple paving) may have been covered with straw, reeds, or skins, and single smoke holes served for ventilation.

24 Ryan, *The Illustrated Archaeology of Ireland*, pp. 59-62. Habitations needed to be close to water, arable land, grazing land, fuel, and building materials. Sheltered sites, and those facing south (which had more access to more sunlight and warmth) were popular. There is evidence of indoor fireplaces, refuse pits, and outside pits for storing grain.

25 Ryan, *The Illustrated Archaeology of Ireland*, pp. 47-48, 63. Some have theorized that, prior to the arrival of the Indo-Europeans, society was peaceful and matriarchal in nature. We clearly do not possess sufficient evidence to determine such religious or cultural beliefs. Weapons existed and were used since earliest times (some certainly in skirmishes). The type of defenses built could only have been needed against one type of animal: man. In addition, we should note that all of this takes place several thousand years prior to the arrival or influence of Indo-Europeans.

26 Darvill, *Prehistoric Britain*, pp. 63-64.

27 Darvill, *Prehistoric Britain*, pp. 64-67.

28 Darvill, *Prehistoric Britain*, pp. 68, 70-74. In some areas, people were buried without large mounds or tombs. Others were sometimes buried in the shafts of flint mines or in the boundary ditches of the ritual enclosures described above. It is interesting to note the evidence of trade at this time, primarily in flint, finished stone tools, quernstones, pottery, and jadeite axes. A ritualized system of trade based on gift exchange was likely in place, where one community passed goods on to the next without necessarily expecting immediate repayment. In this system, repayment or reciprocity may not happen for months or years, and may consist of a different type of item. This helps groups form alliances by making them obligated to each other for a variety of human interactions, including assistance during times of crisis.

29 Darvill, *Prehistoric Britain*, p. 68.

30 Darvill, *Prehistoric Britain*, pp. 73-74.

31 Ryan, *The Illustrated Archaeology of Ireland*, pp. 49-50, 55-56. Wooden items are not likely to have survived, and there are no examples of amber or jet beads from this era in Ireland.

32   Ryan, *The Illustrated Archaeology of Ireland*, pp. 56-57.

33   Ryan, *The Illustrated Archaeology of Ireland*, pp. 57-58.

34   A great many theories have been put forth regarding the meaning of these symbols. The most reasonable explanation is that they are entoptic patterns, designed to facilitate and represent experiences connected with altered states of consciousness, such as those associated with the shamanic journey. Shamans in many cultures describe seeing arcs, spirals, concentric circles, or geometric shapes in early stages of the journey, and the art of these cultures sometimes depicts these designs. This is true of Asian and Siberian shamanic cultures, as well as a number of Native American societies.

35   Ryan, *The Illustrated Archaeology of Ireland*, p. 58. A great deal of speculation has taken place concerning the meaning of these symbols and elements. It is probably best to shy away from great overarching theories concerning matriarchal societies and goddess figures, for, as we can see, there is no evidence to support such a supposition. Suggested reading includes: *Pre-Christian Ireland* by Peter Harbison, (London: Thames and Hudson, 1988), *Newgrange* by Michael J. O'Kelly (London: Thames and Hudson, 1982), and *Knowth and the Passage-Tombs of Ireland* by George Eogan (London: Thames and Hudson, 1986). These contain reliable information and many wonderful illustrations.

36   Ryan, *The Illustrated Archaeology of Ireland*, pp. 58-59.

37   Darvill, *Prehistoric Britain*, pp. 75-77.

38   Darvill, *Prehistoric Britain*, p. 88. In northern Wales and Scotland, the use of communal tombs lasted much longer than in other parts of Britain, but eventually (after about 2000 B.C.E.) changes in ritual forms and societal organization also affected these outlying regions.

39   Darvill, *Prehistoric Britain*, pp. 79-84.

40   Darvill, *Prehistoric Britain*, p. 86.

41   Darvill, *Prehistoric Britain*, pp. 88-90.

42   Darvill, *Prehistoric Britain*, pp. 90-91.

43   Darvill, *Prehistoric Britain*, pp. 92-94.

44   Darvill, *Prehistoric Britain*, pp. 94-95, 106. Single standing stones were also set up, perhaps to mark the pathways leading to upland grazing sites or seasonal camps.

45   Darvill, *Prehistoric Britain*, pp. 96-97.

46   Darvill, *Prehistoric Britain*, pp. 98-100.

47   Darvill, *Prehistoric Britain*, pp. 100-102. In *Pagan Religions of the Ancient British Isles* (London: Blackwell, Oxford University Press, 1991), pp. 37-44, Ronald Hutton discusses the controversy surrounding the isolated figure from Norfolk. It has been widely and popularly described as evidence of worship of a goddess or a great goddess, but no other evidence exists in these regions. There is also reason to believe that it may be a forgery.

48   Darvill, *Prehistoric Britain*, pp. 108-19.

49   Darvill, *Prehistoric Britain*, pp. 120-26.

50   At this time, rye was introduced to supplement previously grown grains, as it can be grown in less favorable conditions.

51   Darvill, *Prehistoric Britain*, pp. 122-32.

52   Ryan, *The Illustrated Archaeology of Ireland*, pp. 65-66. Yew is useful for timber, spear shafts, wheels, bows, and knife handles, but cattle will readily eat its leaves, which are poisonous to them.

53   Early outcrops of bedrock would have included the dull green of malachite or the bright blue of azurite, both carbonates of copper, which showed early prospectors where the ore lay.

54   Ryan, *The Illustrated Archaeology of Ireland*, pp. 68-74, 83-84.

55   People were either cremated or buried, sometimes in a crouched position (although more often lying on their sides). Sometimes the body had been ritually exposed to the elements and birds of prey prior to interment, the bones alone forming the burial. The dead were often buried individually in pits or small stone boxes (cists), sometimes grouped together in or under mounds of earth or stone. Over time, however, simple cremation was the most common method.

56   Ryan, *The Illustrated Archaeology of Ireland*, pp. 68-70, 84-88, 89-92.

57   Ryan, *The Illustrated Archaeology of Ireland*, pp. 100-2.

58   Ryan, *The Illustrated Archaeology of Ireland*, pp. 96-99.

59   Ryan, *The Illustrated Archaeology of Ireland*, pp. 100, 103.

60   Hutton, *Pagan Religions of the Ancient British Isles*, pp. 37-52, 101-2, 302-40. See also Lotte Motze, *The Faces of the Goddess* (Oxford: Oxford University Press, 1997), especially pp. 179-85.

61   Hutton, *Pagan Religions of the Ancient British Isles*, pp. 3-6. Much has been written and theorized concerning female figurines from Europe and the Near East that date to the Neolithic period. It is not often acknowledged that representations of phalluses are also found at many of the same sites.

62   Michael Herity and George Eogan, *Ireland in Prehistory* (London: Routledge, 1989), pp. 73-75; Hutton, *Pagan Religions of the Ancient British Isles*, p. 102.

63 Hutton, *Pagan Religions of the Ancient British Isles*, pp. 3-4.

64 Peter Harbison, *Pre-Christian Ireland* (New York: Thames and Hudson, 1988), pp. 65, 118.

65 Herity and Eogan, *Ireland in Prehistory*, p. 111.

66 Darvill, *Prehistoric Britain*, pp. 75, 97.

67 Ryan, *The Illustrated Archaeology of Ireland*, p. 54.

68 Hutton, *Pagan Religions of the Ancient British Isles*, p. 60; Harbison, *Pre-Christian Ireland*, pp. 94-95.

69 BBC Online Network, Thursday, April 8, 1999.

70 Graham and Anna Ritchie, *Scotland—Archaeology and Early History* (Edinburgh: Edinburgh University Press, 1991), p. 47. In one of the earlier class-one henge monuments (at Balfarg), a timber ring and stone rings were erected with a portico on the southwest side.

71 Ken Osborne, ed., *Stonehenge and Neighbouring Monuments* (London: English Heritage, 1995), p. 8; Hutton, *Pagan Religions of the Ancient British Isles*, p. 94. The northeast is aligned with the midsummer sunrise, and this northeast/southwest axis is evident in a number of sites, perhaps demonstrating a focus on the brightest and darkest points of the year. (The midwinter sunrise is associated with the southeast and the midsummer sunset with the northwest.)

72 Osborne, *Stonehenge and Neighbouring Monuments*, pp. 8-12.

73 D. V. Clarke, T. G. Cowie, and A. Foxon, *Symbols of Power at the Time of Stonehenge* (Edinburgh: National Museum of the Antiquities of Scotland, 1985), p. 78.

74 Hutton, *Pagan Religions of the Ancient British Isles*, p. 115.

75 Hutton, *Pagan Religions of the Ancient British Isles*, p. 117.

76 This is true of the smallest circles, which contain only five stones, as well as the larger ones, which are comprised of up to seventeen stones.

77 Ryan, *The Illustrated Archaeology of Ireland*, pp. 90-91; Harbison, *Pre-Christian Ireland*, p. 94.

78 Hutton, *Pagan Religions of the Ancient British Isles*, pp. 94, 117. The author points out that a study of the stone rings of Cork and Kerry (based on one set of criteria) showed that eleven out of thirty-seven surviving rings might have been aligned on the sky: three on the southern lunar maximum, three on the Winter Solstice sunset, one on midsummer sunset, and one on the northern lunar maximum. This is just under one-third of the circles, but is based only on one study.

79 Ritchie, *Scotland—Archaeology and Early History*, p. 61.

80 Ritchie, *Scotland—Archaeology and Early History*, pp. 58-59.

81 Ritchie, *Scotland—Archaeology and Early History*, pp. 55-58.

82 Ritchie, *Scotland—Archaeology and Early History*, pp. 30-31.

83 Clarke, Cowie and Foxon, *Symbols of Power at the Time of Stonehenge*, p. 45.

84 Ritchie, *Scotland—Archaeology and Early History*, p. 52.

85 Hutton, *Pagan Religions of the Ancient British Isles*, p. 36. Other sites in his survey do not seem to be aligned with either the Sun or the Moon.

86 Darvill, *Prehistoric Britain*, p. 85.

87 Hutton, *Pagan Religions of the Ancient British Isles*, pp. 59, 94, 109. White quartz stones and pebbles were popular in Scottish folk tradition, and are even known from some Pictish sites.

88 Hutton, *Pagan Religions of the Ancient British Isles*, pp. 104-6.

89 Hutton, *Pagan Religions of the Ancient British Isles*, pp. 115-17.

90 Daithi O hOgain, *Myth, Legend and Romance—An Encylopedia of the Irish Folk Tradition* (New York: Prentice Hall, 1991), p. 165.

91 O hOgain, *Myth, Legend and Romance*, pp. 166-67.

92 O hOgain, *Myth, Legend and Romance*, pp. 67-68. An in-depth look at the figure of the Cailleach is beyond the scope of this chapter, but will be explored in an upcoming work.

93 Rees and Rees, *Celtic Heritage*, pp. 134-39.

94 BBC Online Network, Thursday, April 22, 1999; also, *The Irish Times* on the Web. I am greatly indebted to Regina D'Anca for bringing this news article to my attention.

95 The oldest (prior to this potential discovery) was that made by Leonardo da Vinci around 1505.

96 George Eogan, *Knowth and the Passage-Tombs of Ireland* (London: Thames and Hudson, 1986), pp. 50, 96-97. The lunar "map" is on Orthostat 47. Illustrations of Orthostats 47-50 are provided in the book,and are described by the author as seeming to "guard" the inner chamber of the tomb.

97 It bodes well for possible future interpretation of other Neolithic markings if this design, which was formerly labeled "abstract" or "meaningless," has been properly interpreted as something meaningful and useful, whether that meaning is sacred or mundane.

Sixth Lunation

1   Stanley Ireland, *Roman Britain* (London: Routledge, 1992), pp. 15-16.

2   Ireland, *Roman Britain*, pp. 15-16.

3   Cultural and historical inaccuracy or embellishment, as well as the effects of cultural bias, often affect reports of foreign peoples written by those outside the culture. This was the case with some of the Classical accounts, as well as with medieval authors writing about Ireland and Wales, and British noblemen reporting on Scotland in the 17th through 19th centuries. Undoubtedly, it is still a problem in certain contexts due to the imperfect nature of human perception.

4   Ireland, *Roman Britain*, pp. 19-20.

5   Ireland, *Roman Britain*, p. 20.

6   Ireland, *Roman Britain*, p. 22.

7   Ireland, *Roman Britain*, p. 24.

8   Ireland, *Roman Britain*, p. 23.

9   Ireland, *Roman Britain*, pp. 23-24.

10 There may have been other religious figures in Celtic society as well, male and female, who engaged in divination, prophecy, and other religious rites. Accounts exist of people living on holy islands off the shore of Britain and Gaul, including groups of religious women living together in isolation. Plutarch, in his 1st-2nd- century C.E. work entitled *On the Disuse of Oracles*, mentions the reports of one Demetrius telling of remote and desolate islands around Britain, some of which were evidently named after gods or heroes. He himself had sailed to the nearest of these islands, reporting that only a few holy men who were held inviolate by the Britons lived there.

11 Ireland, *Roman Britain*, p. 185.

12 Ireland, *Roman Britain*, p. 187.

13 Ireland, *Roman Britain*, p. 22.

14 Ireland, *Roman Britain*, p. 16. Here we must keep in mind that it was to the benefit of those attempting to conquer the Celts to portray them as barbaric and liable to benefit from the civilizing ways of Roman authority and culture. The Romans had, in fact, only recently abolished human sacrifice themselves and, at the time of the writings, still tolerated (if not enjoyed) the gladiatorial games. It is important to keep in mind that most members of Celtic society would not have had access to "disposable" human life (such as slaves or prisoners of war) and that animals, jewelry, weapons, and other offerings or pledges would have been most common.

15 Ireland, *Roman Britain*, p. 183.

16 Ireland, *Roman Britain*, p. 181-82.

17 Ireland, *Roman Britain*, p. 183. Archaeology does, of course, provide us with the actual names of many native Gaulish, Continental, and British deities. Some were worshipped in more than one area, while others were quite localized. See Anne Ross, *Pagan Celtic Britain* (Chicago: Academy Publishers, 1996) for useful commentary on these deities and their names. In Britain: Sulis, Maponus, Epona, Nodons, Cocidius, Belatucadrus, Brigantia, Antenociticus, Condatis, Coventina, Latis, Camulos, Corotiacus, Loucetius, Rigonemetis, Olloudious, Callirius, Verbeia, Vitiris. In Gaul: Cernunnos, Taranis, Ogmios, Atepomarus, Belenus, Grannus, Vindonnus, Borvo, Bricta, Damona, Sequana, Glanis, Sucellos, Ialona, Ianuaria, Icovellauna, Lenus, Brixianus, Albiorix, Caturix, Artaios, Cissonius, Nemausus, Ritona, Rudiobus, Segomo, Teutates. In Continental Europe: Abnoba, Arduinna, Artio, Sirona, Inciona, Ladicus, Poeninus, Uxellinus, Gebrinius, Nantosuelta, Nehalannia, Rosmerta, Ucuetis, Bergusia, Vagdavercustis, Vasio, Visucius.

18 Ireland, *Roman Britain*, pp. 182, 186. These areas of Druidic expertise are reiterated by Pomponius Mela in the 1st century C.E., when he calls the Druids "teachers of wisdom" and mentions the instruction they provided to students in "secret locations" such as caves or hidden glades.

19 David Rankin, *Celts and the Classical World* (New York: Routledge, 1996), p. 261.

20 Rankin, *Celts and the Classical World*, pp. 260-61.

21 Rankin, *Celts and the Classical World*, p. 263. Following this disclosure, Rankin remarks that there is no evidence for a distinctively Celtic Moon goddess in Spain. He states, however, that there was *Luna Augusta* (perhaps referring to Roman influence in or near the area, and/or to the veneration of the Moon itself). The meaning of his statement is not entirely clear. It may be that he is alluding to a possible connection between water and Underworld deities and lunar gods or concepts associated with the Moon, while pointing out that there is currently no surviving evidence pertaining to an Iberian Moon goddess.

22 Rankin, *Celts and the Classical World*, p. 260.

23 Rankin, *Celts and the Classical World*, pp. 260-61.

24 Liam Mac Mathúna, "Irish Perceptions of the Cosmos," in *Celtica* vol. 22 (1999) and "The Christianization of the Early Irish Cosmos? Muir mas, nem nglas, talam cé," in *Zeitschrift fur Celtische Philologie*, vols. 45-50 (1997).

25 Edward Gwynn, *The Metrical Dindsenchas* (Dublin: School of Celtic Studies, Dublin Institute for Advanced Studies, 1991), 3:11.

26 This does not mean that Pictish society was matriarchal, but that candidates to replace a king could be chosen

from among the relatives of the queen (sons, nephews, etc.) See *Celtic Britain* by Nora Chadwick (N. Hollywood, CA: Newcastle Publishing, 1989), pp. 81-82. There were several methods of succession in Celtic countries. In some cases, it was patrilinear, but did not necessarily follow the custom of primogeniture. In many cases, tribal kingship was open to every adult male member of the royal line whose great-grandfather (or nearer ascendant) had been king.

27   Rankin, *Celts and the Classical World*, pp. 251-52.

28   Ireland, *Roman Britain* p. 189.

29   Jean Gricourt, "L'Ovum Anguinum en Gaule et en Perse," *Ogam*, vol. 6 (1954), p. 1.

30   Alexander Carmichael, *Carmina Gadelica: Hymns and Incantaions* (Edinburgh: Lindisfarne Press, 1992), p. 381.

31   Rankin, *Celts and the Classical World*, pp. 251-52.

32   Rankin, *Celts and the Classical World*, p. 186.

33   Rankin, *Celts and the Classical World*, p. 186.

34   Celtic beliefs may or may not have resembled similar doctrines from Hindu tradition.

35   The Celtic Otherworld mirrored this world in some aspects. Its landscape was remarkably beautiful and its inhabitants extraordinarily fair, wise, skilled, and powerful. Sadness, illness, war, and death did exist in the Otherworld, but seem to have been quite rare. There is no evidence of a belief in sin or punishment.

36   Rankin, *Celts and the Classical World*, p. 185.

37   The equation of Caesar's Dis Pater with the Celtic deity Cernunnos has been mentioned by a number of scholars, including Anne Ross and David Rankin. Theories that attempt to equate Cernunnos with Dis Pater may find some support in the following presentation of ideas: in the iconography of the horned or antlered god, he is often represented as ruling over a variety of creatures (perhaps as "lord of the animals"). In an early Welsh tale, a figure described as a "dark man" is perceived sitting on a mound, brandishing a powerful club, and demonstrating his power over a wide variety of animals. Another deity known for his use of a club is the Irish deity the Dagda. In addition to a cauldron of unending nourishment (reminiscent of the symbolism of abundance common to representations of horned deities), he possesses a magical club that wields life from one end and death from the other. Both the horned god and the Dagda display evidence of fertility associations, and the Dagda (like the Welsh figure on the mound) is associated with a sacred hill or mound (Uisneach, the cosmological center of Ireland). The Dagda may be similar to the Continental deity Sucellos (The Good Striker) who is also represented with a club. In addition, the British chalk figure known as the Cerne Abbas Giant is pictured with a great club and is quite phallic in nature. There is reasonable evidence to suppose that at least some of these deities were widely venerated and may have been considered tribal or father deities (similar to the concept of Dis Pater). They may represent regional or temporal variations of an early archetypal father or tribal deity, associated with fertility, abundance, animals and crops, and the powers of life and death, who owned a powerful club or a cauldron of nourishment, who was venerated at (or inhabited) a sacred mound, and who was sometimes represented with horns or antlers.

38   H. J. Edwards, tr., *Caesar—The Gallic War* (Cambridge, MA: Harvard University Press, 1997), 6:18. The italics are my own, to emphasize the direct connection between the statement about the Gaulish descent from a god of the Underworld and the measurement of time by nights rather than days.

39   Isaac Asimov, *Asimov on Numbers* (New York: Simon and Shuster, 1977), p. 182. It is interesting to note that the Egyptians, who used a solar-based calendar, considered the day to begin at sunrise, while for the Hebrews, who utilized a more lunar-based system, the day started at sundown. For this reason, certain Jewish holidays begin the night before. Christianity, which began as an offshoot of Judaism, still maintains remnants of this lunar-derived tradition in regard to certain holidays, such as Christmas and New Year's, which begin the night before (Christmas Eve and New Year's Eve). It is because of this ancient use of lunar-based systems of time measurement (which are discussed further on) that Celtic holidays also begin on the "eve" or night before (and not because of any direct connection between these cultures).

40   This may be the line of reasoning that underlies David Rankin's presentation of information concerning Iberian Underworld deities and the subsequent mention of a Moon goddess.

41   Ireland, *Roman Britain*, p. 189.

42   Tess Darwin, *The Scots Herbal: The Plant Lore of Scotland* (Edinburgh: Mercat, 1996), pp. 56-57.

43   Alexander Carmichael, *Carmina Gadelica: Hymns and Incantations* (Edinburgh: Lindisfarne Press, 1992), p. 157.

44   Carmichael, *Carmina Gadelica*, p. 366.

45   Ireland, *Roman Britain*, p. 189.

46   Darwin, *The Scots Herbal: The Plant Lore of Scotland*, p. 143.

47   In *Carmina Gadelica*, one plant (which is unnamed in the charm) was to be gathered "as Brigit culled it, with her one hand." A folk charm called the "Spell of the Counteracting" (used to counteract a spell that cast the evil-eye or other misfortune on someone) called for the plucking of yarrow in the manner that Christ, evidently, had done: "with his one hand." Another folk charm associated with the gathering of "tree-entwining ivy" describes the plant as having been plucked by Mary "with her one hand" as well.

48   Carmichael, *Carmina Gadelica*, pp. 146, 148, 154, 365-67, 611-13.

49 Ireland, *Roman Britain*, p. 189.

50 Nicholas Culpeper, *Culpeper's Complete Herbal and English Physician* (Glenwood, IL: Meyerbooks, 1990), p. 119, states that one of the author's sources, *Clusius*, "gives order that it should not touch the ground after it is gathered" (although this may be influenced by the Classical account).

51 Miranda Green, *The World of the Druids* (London: Thames and Hudson, 1997), p. 19.

52 John Lust, *The Herb Book* (New York: Bantam Books, 1977), 278; M. A. Grieve, *A Modern Herbal* (New York: Dover, 1971), p. 547; Culpeper, *Culpeper's Complete Herbal and English Physician*, p. 119. The association of mistletoe with the apple tree may also account for some of its mystique or prestige, as the apple was considered a very sacred tree, connected with passages to and from the Otherworld. Describing a mistletoe preparation used to treat epilepsy, Culpeper remarks that the mistletoe found on the oak is best.

53 Roger Phillips and Nicky Foy, *Herbs* (New York: Randon House, 1990), pp. 184-85. In some cases, the berries may not ripen until December, closer to the time of the Winter Solstice.

54 John Ayto, *Dictionary of Word Origins* (New York: Little Brown and Co., 1990), p. 351.

55 Phillips and Foy, *Herbs*, 184-85.

56 Edward Dwelly, *Faclair Gaidhlig gu Beurla—Dwelly's Illustrated Gaelic to English Dictionary* (Glasgow: Gairm Publications, 1994); Niall Ó Dónaill, *Foclóir Gaeilge-Béarla* (Dublin: Rialtas na hÉireann, 1977).

57 Lust, *The Herb Book*, p. 278-79. Mistletoe is a diuretic, stimulant, and vasodilator (although it may also have a sedative effect on the nervous system) and has been used to treat arteriosclerosis, digestive problems, epilepsy, high blood pressure, migraine, and a number of other conditions. Mistletoe was known in ancient times to help treat "the spreading disease" (cancer), and it is currently being used once again to treat certain forms of cancer. As a tea, mistletoe has been used as a wash for chilblains and leg ulcers and made into a compress for varicose veins. It has also been used to treat dizziness, cramps, and difficult menstruation. Large doses of mistletoe may have a detrimental effect on the heart. Eating mistletoe berries can be dangerous, particularly for children. Mistletoe should be used with care, preferably under medical direction. Darwin, *The Scots Herbal: The Plant Lore of Scotland*, pp. 175-76: In Scottish folk medicine, mistletoe was used (either alone or in combination with other herbs) in preparations for abscesses, heart palpitations, epilepsy, and fevers. See also Phillips and Foy, *Herbs*, pp. 184-85, and Richard Mabey, *The New Age Herbalist* (New York: Collier Books, 1988), p. 85.

58 Darwin, *The Scots Herbal: The Plant Lore of Scotland*, pp. 175-76; Culpeper, *Culpeper's Complete Herbal and English Physician*, p. 119. Culpeper's herbal states that Clusius maintained that, if mistletoe is hung around the neck, "it remedies witchcraft" (serves as a protective charm).

59 Darwin, *The Scots Herbal: The Plant Lore of Scotland*, pp. 175-76; Grieve, *A Modern Herbal*, p. 547.

60 F. Marian McNeill, *The Silver Bough: Scottish Folklore and Folk-Belief* (Glasgow: William MacLellan, 1977), p. 77.

61 Dwelly, *Faclair Gaidhlig gu Beurla—Dwelly's Illustrated Gaelic to English Dictionary*.

62 H. R. Ellis Davidson, *Gods and Myths of Northern Europe* (London: Penguin, 1964), p. 35.

63 Davidson, *Gods and Myths of Northern Europe*, pp. 182-89.

64 Grieve, *A Modern Herbal*, p. 548. While most herbal preparations involving mistletoe are used for disorders of the nervous system, Grieve's herbal mentions that certain older writers recommended it to treat sterility. This is not mentioned in either Culpeper's or Gerard's herbal, and it is unclear to which older writers the author is referring (or if she is referring to Classical accounts).

65 Davidson, *Gods and Myths of Northern Europe*, pp. 182-89.

66 Davidson, *Gods and Myths of Northern Europe*, pp. 28, 61, 143.

67 Patrick K. Ford, *The Mabinogi* (Berkeley: University of California Press, 1977), p. 105.

68 Wendy Doniger O'Flaherty, *Hindu Myths* (London: Penguin Books, 1975), pp. 83-84.

69 Alwyn and Brinley Rees, *Celtic Heritage* (New York: Thames and Hudson, 1989), p. 345.

70 E. and M. A. Radford, *The Encyclopedia of Superstitions*, ed. Christina Hole (New York: Barnes and Noble, 1961), pp. 233-35.

71 An examination of the nature of Scottish and Irish New Year's customs will reveal that a great many of these customs are similar to, or were probably transferred from, their original position at Samain-tide.

72 Rankin, *Celts and the Classical World*, p. 253.

73 Rankin, *Celts and the Classical World*, p. 245.

74 Rankin, *Celts and the Classical World*, p. 248.

75 Ireland, *Roman Britain*, pp. 59-63.

76 Ireland, *Roman Britain*, p. 63.

77 Ireland, *Roman Britain*, p. 64.

78 Ireland, *Roman Britain*, p. 64.

79 Ireland, *Roman Britain*, p. 67.

80 Ireland, *Roman Britain*, p. 66.

81 Miranda Green, *Animals in Celtic Life and Myth* (London: Routledge, 1992), pp. 38, 44, 48, 50, 63.

82 Radford, *The Encyclopedia of Superstitions*, pp. 181-83.

83 Carmichael, *Carmina Gadelica*, pp. 568-69.

84 Radford, *The Encyclopedia of Superstitions*.

85 Radford, *The Encyclopedia of Superstitions*.

86 Green, *Animals in Celtic Life and Myth*, pp. 38, 44, 48, 50, 63.

87 Frances Pitt "Animal Life," in *Nature in Britain* (London: Batsford, 1936), pp. 28-29.

88 The Chinese even see a "hare in the Moon" in the familiar lunar markings we call the Man in the Moon. This image is clearly visible around the time of the full Moon: the hare is seated or crouched, but rests its feet and belly on the left side of the Moon, as opposed to the bottom of the Moon. See the various works of Mircea Eliade for discussion of the hare as a lunar animal.

89 "Preiddeu Annwvyn (The Spoils of the Unworld,)" in John T. Koch and John Cary, *The Celtic Heroic Age* (Oakville, CT: Celtic Studies Publications, 2000), pp. 295-96.

90 See Sharon Price MacLeod, "Mater Deorum Hibernensium" in *Proceedings of the Harvard Celtic Colloquium*, vol. 19 (1999).

91 Certainly, the figure of the Irish warrior queen Medb was portrayed in quite a disparaging fashion, her strengths portrayed as folly or even weaknesses.

92 *Pagan Celtic Britain* by Anne Ross and *Celtic Goddesses or The Gods of the Celts* by Miranda Green are valuable resources for learning the names, attributes, and symbolism associated with these deities.

93 You can learn more about the rights and roles of women in Celtic society in the following sources: Fergus Kelly, *Early Irish Law* (Dublin: Institute for Advanced Studies, 1988), Rankin, *Celts and the Classical World*; Ronald Hutton, *The Pagan Religions of the Ancient British Isles* (Cambridge and Oxford: Blackwell, 1991); Ross, *Pagan Celtic Britain*; and Green, *Celtic Goddesses*.

Seventh Lunation

1   Isaac Asimov, *Asimov on Numbers* (New York: Simon and Shuster, 1977), pp. 166-68.

2   Alwyn and Brinley Rees, *Celtic Heritage* (New York: Thames and Hudson, 1989), pp. 156, 195, 340.

3   Rees, *Celtic Heritage* , p. 195.

4   Rees, *Celtic Heritage* , 194, 216, 315-16.

5   DIL, Dictionary of the Irish Language, based mainly on Old and Middle Irish materials, Royal Irish Academy, 1913-1976.

6   Rees, *Celtic Heritage* , p. 194. In addition, in Wales, the period of bright moonlight during the Harvest Moon is called *y nawnos olau*, "the nine light nights."

7   Rees, *Celtic Heritage* , pp. 96, 192-93, 230, 311.

8   Stuart Piggott, *The Druids* (London: Thames and Hudson, 1975), p. 49, 116.

9   Miranda Green, *The World of the Druids* (London: Thames and Hudson, 1997), p. 37.

10 Rees, *Celtic Heritage* , p. 85.

11 Rees, *Celtic Heritage* , p. 85.

12 Piggott, *The Druids*, p. 116.

13 Piggott, *The Druids*, p. 49.

14 Malcom Maclennan, *Gaelic Dictionary* (Edinburgh: Mercat Press, 1979).

15 Rees, *Celtic Heritage* , p. 85.

16 DIL. In Old Irish, the word *samain* was sometimes spelled *samuin*, and said to derive from *samfuin*, a word described as meaning the "death of summer." The word *fuin* means "end," but can also be used in the sense of "setting or sinking" (*fuin gréne* refers to the sunset, and means the "setting of the Sun").

17 Carl D. Buck, *A Dictionary of Selected Synonyms in the Principal Indo-European Languages* (Chicago: University of Chicago Press, 1949), pp. 1010-11, 1013-14. While there is great diversity in calendar systems (even among closely related Indo-European languages or population groups or within the same country), month names are generally based upon religious festivals or some element connected with the weather, vegetation, or harvest. Overall, there is a great deal of agreement regarding the early division of the year into winter and non-winter. Terms denoting winter may derive from Indo-European *gheim*, which gives Latin *hiems* and its related adjective *hibernus*, Welsh *gaeaf* and Old Irish *gem-red* (*red* = *ráithe* "season"). Indo-European words for summer derive from terms meaning "hot" or "burn," or even "good season, fine weather" (like Old Norse *sumar* and Old English *sumor*.

18 Rees, *Celtic Heritage* , p. 85.

19 The terms *Samain*, *Beltaine*, *Imbolc*, and *Lugnasad* are Old Irish words for festivals that were likely held in pagan times in all or most of Ireland. We do not know for certain if these holidays were observed in other Celtic countries. Modern and medieval accounts of these holidays may suggest that they were somewhat pan-Celtic in nature (perhaps with different names and varying customs). However, these names were obviously not used in other European countries, as they are Irish terms for Irish feast days. Neopaganism has incorpo-

rated these Irish words into its modern blend of ancient concepts and folk traditions from many lands and eras, with medieval and early modern occult traditions generally practiced by educated upper-class males. Obviously, all ancient people did not celebrate these four ancient Irish holidays. Each culture would have had its sacred days and traditional beliefs, although cultural or linguistic affinities may have resulted in certain parallels or similarities. It is also important to note that we do not have any evidence that the Celts celebrated the equinoxes or the solstices. While their astronomers would certainly have been aware of these events, they do not seem to have formed any part of the Celtic seasonal calendar. Folk customs associated with the solstices and equinoxes exist in many European countries, and in Celtic regions, these became part of the seasonal ritual calendar due to the blending of Germanic, Norse, Roman, Slavic, and other cultures with Celtic peoples and customs.

20 As mentioned in Green, *The World of the Druids*, p. 37. In the Gaulish context, the August first holiday is notated by the term *Rivros*. Anne Ross writes that this may mean Great Festal Month, a period of time consisting of two weeks before and two weeks after the date of the sacred day.

21 Rees, *Celtic Heritage* , p. 86. Similarly, the Athenian calendar contained months of thirty days called "full months" and months of twenty-nine days known as "hollow months." In Southeast Asia, calendars contained these two kinds of months, alternating in a regular sequence, which were referred to as "complete" and "defective" months.

22 Piggott, *The Druids*, pp. 116-17. Tamil calendar makers in southern India calculated eclipses by arranging shells or pebbles on the ground in a certain pattern to remind them of the necessary process or mathematical formulae. In 1825, one man who knew no theories of Hindu mathematics was able to predict a lunar eclipse to within four minutes of its exact time.

23 For this reason, Muslim calendar festivals shift over time, occuring at various seasons during the year.

24 Asimov, *Asimov on Numbers*, pp. 170-71.

25 Asimov, *Asimov on Numbers*, pp. 172-79, 190. This is still the basis for the Jewish calendar, which is why certain Jewish holidays fall on different days of the civil calendar (yet on the same day each year in the Jewish calendar). The early Christians continued to use the Jewish calendar for about three hundred years. Our current calendar is inherited from the Egyptians who used a solar calendar and were not concerned with the new Moon. A modified version of the Egyptian calendar was adopted by the Romans around 45 B.C.E. In the Egyptian system, there is an extra quarter day each year. To take care of this, it was established that every fourth year would be 366 days long (which accounts for modern custom of the "leap year"). This Julian year (named for Julius Caesar) was adopted by the Christian church at the Council of Nicea in 325 C.E.

Christianized Romans were also concerned about the date of Easter, which, at the time, moved about quite a bit. Some method had to be found so that the correct date for Easter could be calculated in advance using the Roman calendar. At the Council of Nicea, it was decreed that Easter was to take place on the Sunday after the first full Moon following the Spring Equinox. The date still moved about, but could be calculated in advance.

26 Piggott, *The Druids*, p. 116.

27 Other ancient peoples in Europe certainly possessed skill in astronomy. For example, ancient Romanian circular calendrical monuments made of stone and wood have been discovered, dating to the 1st century B.C.E.

28 Piggott, *The Druids*, p. 117.

29 John Carey, "A Tract on the Creation," in *Éigse* XXI, 1986. In later Irish tradition, even the Druid who raised St. Bridget was said to have studied the stars. Early Irish monks or men of learning evidently needed to know five things each day: the day of the solar month, the phase of the Moon, the tide, the day of the week, and the saint's day.

30 Piggott, *The Druids*, pp. 116-17. It was recorded that around the 1st century B.C.E., there lived among the Getae a semilegendary figure known as Dicineus who expounded upon natural and moral philosophy and taught such things as "the courses of the twelve signs and of the planets passing through them," "the whole of astronomy," and "the names of the three hundred and sixty-five stars. He was a figure of great repute who trained particularly wise and noble initiates, teaching them theology and "bidding them worship certain divinities and holy places."

31 Piggott, *The Druids*, pp. 116-17. All around the world, the elements of society are frequently divided into two halves, upper and lower, associated with heaven and earth, male and female, summer and winter, right and left, etc. This can be expressed in the two-fold division of countries, provinces, cities, villages, temples, halls, and kindreds. In Celtic regions, the distinctions of upper and lower (often used in connection with some natural feature of the land) or even great and little, were used to differentiate between neighboring villages or parishes, and there was often a sort of congenial rivalry between the two.

32 Rees, *Celtic Heritage* , chapter 4.

33 Rees, *Celtic Heritage* , pp. 92, 100-03, 122-23.

34 Carey, "A Tract on the Creation," 1986.

35 Rees, *Celtic Heritage* , pp. 385-86. The authors point out that the Kalmucks of Siberia also associate a different color with each direction. I would like to thank Benjamin Bruch for information pertaining to early order and development of color terms as found in Berlin and Kay's research on the topic.

36 Lug is pictured as a newcomer to the Tuatha Dé Danann, and this holiday (one associated specifically with agriculture, rather than with herding, like the other three holidays) is also likely to be a later addition.

37 Rees, *Celtic Heritage*, p. 87. Months of thirty days (with fifteen days in each half) were *mat* or good, and the months of only twenty-nine days (with fifteen days in the first half and fourteen in the second half) were *anm* or not good.

38 Emily Lyle, *Archaic Cosmos* (Edinburgh: Edinburgh University Press, 1991), pp. 90-91, 100.

39 Asimov, *Asimov on Numbers*, pp. 185-186. In most cultures, New Year's celebrations take place in spring or autumn. While spring is the beginning of the planting season, autumn heralds the end of the work year at harvest time, and since the work cycle has ended, a new year can begin. Early Celtic society supported itself in large measure by herding, and the patterns and activities associated with herding and keeping animals formed the basis for most of their holidays. Animals were brought back from summer pasture by the time of Samain, hunting was concluded, and where agriculture was a focus, the crops were in. Work associated with the bright half of the year was concluded, and thus, a new cycle began.

40 Many modern works suppose that the religious ideas and rites of most ancient peoples revolved around the waxing or waning properties of the Sun and its light. This may be true in some cases, or in certain aspects of some religious ceremonies, but it is not universally true. Nor is there is any reason to suppose that the theology and philosophy of ancient peoples were any less sophisticated than our own. Early religions would have considered many aspects of life and nature with complex spiritual beliefs and knowledge of natural science.

41 Rees, *Celtic Heritage* , p. 93.

42 It may be appropriate here to point out that the Celtic Lunar Tree Calendar, which is often described as having formed part of ancient Celtic pagan religion, was, in fact, a poetic and theoretic construct by the 20th-century poet Robert Graves (a specialist in Greek mythology). There is no evidence of such a system in Celtic tradition (or indeed, prior to Graves' 1949 classic work *The White Goddess*). There was, of course, a sophisticated system of tree lore in Irish tradition, some of which was connected with the ogam alphabet and the training of poets. To read more about Graves and his tree calendar, see Ronald Hutton, *The Pagan Religions of the Ancient British Isles* (Cambridge and Oxford: Blackwell, 1991), p. 145, also pp. 325-27, 332-35. To learn about ogam and the tree alphabet, see Damian McManus, *A Guide to Ogam* (Naas: Maynooth Monograph Series, 1997) and George Calder, ed., *Auraceipt na n-Éces: The Scholar's Primer* (Dublin: Four Courts Press, 1995).

43 Gustav Lehmacher, "The Ancient Celtic Year," in *Journal of Celtic Studies*, vol. 1 (1949-50). Their new year began on the new Moon nearest the Winter Solstice, and each month thereafter began with the new Moon and had its own special name. Sometimes intercalary months were inserted into this lunar system to regulate it in terms of the solar year (as seen in the Coligny Calendar and other similar systems).

44 Lehmacher, "The Ancient Celtic Year." In early Irish sagas, a *lón láith* or "hero's brilliance" shone from the face or head of certain Ulster warriors. See also Carl D. Buck, *A Dictionary of Selected Synonyms in the Principal Indo-European Languges* (Chicago: University of Chicago Press, 1949), pp. 54-55.

45 John Carey, "Native Elements in Irish Pseudohistory," in *Medieval Studies—Cultural Identity and Cultural Integration: Ireland and Europe in the Middle Ages* (Dublin: Fourt Courts Press, 1995).

46 John Carey, "Lebor Gabála Érenn," in John Koch and John Carey, *The Celtic Heroic Age* (Malden, MA: Celtic Studies Publications, 1995), pp. 226-27, 244.

47 Lehmacher, "The Ancient Celtic Year."

48 Edward Gwynn, *The Metrical Dindsenchas* (Dublin: School of Celtic Studies, Dublin Institute for Advanced Studies, 1991), 4: 415.

49 Máire MacNeill, *The Festival of Lugnasa*, (Oxford: Oxford University Press, n.d.) p. 16. Ms. MacNeill points out that *lúan* as used in the expressions *Luain Loga Lugnasa* and *Luan Lae Beltaine* is more likely to mean "the new moon or "the first day of the month" rather than "Monday" as it has sometimes been translated.

50 MacNeill, *The Festival of Lugnasa*, pp. 16, 384-85, 419.

51 Michael Hunter, *The Occult Laboratory*, (n.p.: The Boydell Press, 2001), p. 73. This information comes from a manuscript entitled *A Collection of Highland Rites and Customs* compiled in the late 1600s about folk customs in the Scottish Highlands.

52 Miranda Green, *Animals in Celtic Life and Myth* (London: Routledge, 1992), pp. 55, 139-40, 174-76.

Eighth Lunation

1 Stanley Ireland, *Roman Britain* (London: Routledge, 1986), p. 40.

2 T. G. E. Powell, *The Celts* (London: Thames and Hudson, 1980), p. 117. A less certain identification comes from a 1st-century B.C.E. coin of the Coriosolites in northwest France. This shows a face in profile that resembles a stylized Man in the Moon. The head is crescent-shaped and has wavy hair that suggests the rays of the Sun or Moon. In addition, there are two possible crescent shapes near the left side of the coin.

3 Powell, *The Celts*, p. 128.
4 Ruth and Vincent Megaw, *Celtic Art* (New York: Thames and Hudson, 1989), p. 46.
5 Megaw, *Celtic Art*, p. 131.
6 Megaw, *Celtic Art*, p. 195.
7 Powell, *The Celts*, p. 116.
8 Megaw, *Celtic Art*, pp. 96-97.
9 Miranda Green, *The World of the Druids* (London: Thames and Hudson, 1997), p. 112.
10 Green, *The World of the Druids*, p. 132.
11 Miranda Green, *Dictionary of Celtic Myth and Legend* (London: Thames and Hudson, 1992), pp. 153-54.
12 Graham and Anna Ritchie, *Scotland—Archaeology and Early History* (Edinburgh: Edinburgh University Press, 1991), pp. 159-65.
13 Anne Ross, *Pagan Celtic Britain* (Chicago: Academy Publishers, 1996), pp. 181, 252, 344, 349, 475.
14 Ross, *Pagan Celtic Britain*, pp. 228-29. Loucetius is often associated with Mars, who was originally a god of healing.
15 Ross, *Pagan Celtic Britain*, pp. 230-33. Nodons may also have had an aspect as a hunter deity, as he was likened to the Roman god Silvanus.
16 Ross, *Pagan Celtic Britain*, p. 472.
17 Ross, *Pagan Celtic Britain*, pp. 289, 319, 321, 346, 349.
18 Miranda Green, *Celtic Goddesses* (New York: George Braziller, 1995), pp. 94-96.
19 Green, *Celtic Goddesses*, pp. 93-96. There are a number of Celtic goddesses who were invoked at healing springs (some of which had thermal properties). Sometimes they were invoked with a consort, and sometimes independently.
20 Green, *Celtic Goddesses*, pp. 106-10.
21 Ross, *Pagan Celtic Britain*, pp. 286-87. The association of horses with the Sun manifests in a variety of Indo-European traditions, where the Sun, often depicted as a golden wheel or disk, is carried in a chariot drawn by horses.
22 Green, *Celtic Goddesses*, pp. 40-41, 70-74.
23 In Norse myth, night and day (symbolized by a girl called Sun and a boy called Moon) were drawn in chariots pulled by horses. H. R. Davidson, *Gods and Myths of Northern Europe* (London: Penguin, 1964), pp. 27-28.
24 Jean Louis Brunaux, *The Celtic Gauls: Gods, Rites and Sanctuaries* (London: Seaby, 1987), pp. 7-11, 27-31, 41-43.
25 Brunaux, *The Celtic Gauls: Gods, Rites and Sanctuaries*, pp. 45-46, 70. The name of this deity (Dis) literally means "rich," probably referring to attributes pertaining to abundance. This supports the interpretation of the ancestor god of the Gaulish Celts as a figure similar to Cernunnos, who is often shown with bags of coins or images of grain.
26 Green, *Celtic Goddesses*, p. 102.
27 Scattered references to the Sky Realm often make mention of the Moon ("Sun, Moon, and stars," etc.).
28 Powell, *The Celts*, p. 146 discusses the association of Celtic goddesses with the land and points out the fact that they often display aspects of both fertility and destruction. He describes the possibility of the Celtic goddesses being ". . . symbolized in the sun and moon, no less than in zoomorphism and topography."
29 R. A. Stewart Macalister, *Lebor Gabála Érenn* (Dublin: Irish Texts Society, 1956), pp. 193-95.
30 Macalister, *Lebor Gabála Érenn*, pp. 231, 239, 383, 395, 399, 401.
31 Ann Dooley and Harry Roe, *Tales of the Elders of Ireland* (Oxford: Oxford University Press, 1999), p. 113.
32 Tom P. Cross, and Clark H. Slover, *Ancient Irish Tales* (New York: Barnes and Noble/Henry Holt, 1969), p. 226.
33 Dooley and Roe, *Tales of the Elders of Ireland*, pp. 176-77.
34 Dooley and Roe, *Tales of the Elders of Ireland*, p. 177.
35 Elizabeth Gray, *Cath Maige Tuired* (Dublin: Irish Texts Society, 1982), pp. 39-43.
36 Gray, *Cath Maige Tuired*, p. 43.
37 Eoin Mac Neill, "On the Notation and Chronography of the Calendar of Coligny," in *Ériu* 10, 1926-28.
38 It is interesting to note, however, that Lug was at one time the owner of the crane bag, a sacred object that may have had a lunar connection (described below). In addition, in *Cath Maige Tuired*, Lug performs a magical incantation while standing on one foot and with one eye closed (similar to the description of *corrguineacht*, also given further on), a rite that may have some association with cranes.
39 Eoin MacNeill, *Duanaire Finn*, as quoted in Ross, *Pagan Celtic Britain*, pp. 357-58.
40 Ross, *Pagan Celtic Britain*, pp. 357-58.
41 Ross, *Pagan Celtic Britain*, pp. 357-58.
42 Ross, *Pagan Celtic Britain*, pp. 111, 302-3, 337. The characteristics associated with the swan, the raven, and the crane are amazingly consistent throughout the eras.
43 Ross, *Pagan Celtic Britain*, pp. 358-59, 361.
44 Ross, *Pagan Celtic Britain*, 356, 360-61.
45 Gray, *Cath Maige Tuired*, pp. 52-53.
46 Ross, *Pagan Celtic Britain*, pp. 330, 355, 369. It is interesting to note that, while crane flesh was taboo (or could cause a person's death), a bag made from the skin (which excludes the flesh of the bird) was a sacred object.

47 Ross, *Pagan Celtic Britain*, pp. 359-60. On Vatersay, it was considered a bad omen to hear a crane or heron at night.

48 Ross, *Pagan Celtic Britain*, pp. 278, 351, 361, 363-64. There are also examples of fittings for ritual buckets and cauldrons that portray birds emerging from the top of bull's heads.

49 H. R. Davidson, *Myths and Symbols in Pagan Europe* (Syracuse, NY: Syracuse University Press, 1988), p. 58.

50 Jean I. Young, *The Prose Edda of Snorri Sturluson* (Berkeley and Los Angeles: University of California Press, 1964), pp. 65-66.

51 Ross, *Pagan Celtic Britain*, 363-64.

52 Ross, *Pagan Celtic Britain*, pp. 384, 387; Miranda Green, *Animals in Celtic Life and Myth* (London: Routledge, 1992), pp. 119-22, 220-24

53 Ross, *Pagan Celtic Britain*, pp. 174-75, 385. Words denoting "bull" in the various Celtic languages have remained remarkably similar and consistent: Gaulish *tarwos*, Welsh *tarw*, Cornish *tarow*, Breton *tarv*, Manx *tarroo*, Old Irish *tarb*, and modern Irish and Scottish Gaelic *tarbh*.

54 Green, *The World of the Druids*, pp. 82-83, 103-4.

55 Ross, *Pagan Celtic Britain*, pp. 184-86, 219, 389. Bronze mounts from a cauldron in Denmark (early 3rd century B.C.E.) depict an owl and a bull's head—both symbols of night?

56 Perhaps this association underlies imagery in an Irish folktale concerning a cow with silver horns.

57 Heinrich Zimmer, *Myths and Symbols in Indian Art and Civilization* (New York: Harper Torchbooks, 1962), p. 198; Roy Willis, ed., *World Mythology* (New York: Henry Holt and Co., 1993), pp. 80, 135. Zeus took on the form of a white bull in order to seduce Europa. She sat on his back and he plunged into the water and swam away with her, coming ashore on Crete where he turned into an eagle and united with her.

58 Ross, *Pagan Celtic Britain*, p. 387; Green, *Dictionary of Celtic Myth and Legend*, pp. 183-85; Thomas Kinsella, *The Tain* (Oxford: Oxford University Press, 1970), pp. 46-50.

59 This struggle may be paralleled in a Scottish tale in which a Scottish bull is victorious in combat with an English bull, the whole scenario associated with a stone known as *Clach nan Tarbh* near Loch Lomond.

60 The word *adarc* refers to the horn of an animal and appears in a medieval Irish astronomical tract in a metaphor of the new Moon: *dacitur adharcach iat ar cuma an re nua* ('They appear horned like the new Moon'). The phrase *adharca bruic* means "badger's horns," referring to something imaginary or nonexistent. In Scottish Gaelic folk tradition, one of the lunar months is connected with *gealach bhuidhe nam broc* ("the yellow Moon of the badgers"). This October Moon (during whose light the badger is said to dry grass for its nest) is sometimes associated with a change in the weather.

61 Kinsella, *The Tain*, pp. 251-52. The Donn, like the two original herdsmen and the Scottish water bulls, is described as emerging from a body of water. We have previously mentioned possible lunar associations with the Neolithic tombs at Carrowkeel, which may have been positioned so that light of Moon would enter the inner chamber at midwinter (the full Moon on either side of the Winter Solstice). The tomb evidently points toward a hill called Knocknarea (Hill of the Moon), the burial place of Queen Medb of the *Tain*.

62 Ross, *Pagan Celtic Britain*, p. 214; Kate Muller-Lisowski, "Contributions to a Study in Irish Folklore: Traditions about Donn," from 1945 publication *A Study in Irish Folklore*, p. 193.

63 Muller-Lisowski "Contributions to a Study in Irish Folklore: Traditions about Donn," pp. 144, 155, 160-61. The Scottish Gaelic folk term *tarbh-boidhre*, which refers to either a monster or demon or a god capable of changing himself into many forms—a man, a horse, a bull, etc., with supernatural powers.

64 Patrick K. Ford, *The Mabinogi* (Berkeley: University of California Press, 1977), p. 172.

65 Ford, *The Mabinogi*, p. 184.

66 Koch and Carey, *The Celtic Heroic Age*, p. 265.

67 Mircea Eliade, *The Myth of the Eternal Return* (Princeton, NJ: Princeton University Press, 1954), pp. 86-87.

68 Eliade, *The Myth of the Eternal Return*, pp. 88-89. In many cultures, the festival that takes place just before the New Year is often when the events associated with creation are reenacted in order for the new and regenerated cycle to begin.

69 Mircea Eliade, *The Sacred and the Profane* (New York: Harcourt Brace, 1957), p.180.

Ninth Lunation

1 Patrick K. Ford, *The Mabinogi* (Berkeley and Los Angeles: University of California Press, 1977), pp. ix-x, 1-13.

2 John Koch, "Some Suggestions and Etymologies Reflecting on the Mythology of the Four Branches," *Proceedings of the Harvard Celtic Colloquium*, vol. 9 (1989), pp. 4-5.

3 Ford, *The Mabinogi*, p. 89. See also my article "Mater Deorum Hibernensium" in *The Proceedings of the Harvard Celtic Colloquium*, vol. 19 (1999) for a more complete discussion of Danu and related river names.

4 Ford, *The Mabinogi*, pp. 89-91.

5   Ford's translation of the Fourth Branch served as my source for this summary, as well as for my discussion of specific words or elements in the rest of the chapter. For this reason, I will provide page numbers only for specific references that may be difficult to locate.

6   John Koch, "Some Suggestions and Etymologies Reflecting on the Mythology of the Four Branches," *Proceedings of the Harvard Celtic Colloquium*, vol. 9 (1989), pp. 5-6. While Modern Welsh uses the word *olwyn* for "wheel," the older word is still found in the proverb *rhod heno, glaw 'fory*, meaning "wheel tonight, rain tomorrow" (referring to the wheel or ring of silvery haze, which sometimes appears around the Moon). Similarly, in Scottish Gaelic the phrase *tha roth mu'n ghealaich* ("there is a wheel around the Moon") refers to a misty halo of light seen around the Moon's orb.

7   Ford, *The Mabinogi*, pp. 98-99.

8   Ford, *The Mabinogi*, pp. 100-101. Gwydion is henceforth known as one of the "three golden shoemakers" of Britain. The fact that Lleu is associated with shoemaking is suggestive of his connection with Lugh/Lugus. Over the doorway to a shoemaker's college in Iberia was an inscription to the Triple Lugs. I am indebted to Leslie Jones for providing me with her notes for her presentation at the Harvard Center for Literary and Cultural Studies, 17 April 1998, "Lugh: The Shod God?"

9   Elizabeth Gray, *Cath Maige Tuired* (Dublin: Irish Texts Society, 1982), pp. 24-25.

10 Anne Ross, *Pagan Celtic Britain* (Chicago: Academy Publishers, 1996), p. 349.

11 Ross, *Pagan Celtic Britain*. An eagle also lived in the top branches of the Norse World Tree.

12 Ford, *The Mabinogi*, pp. 106-7.

13 Ford, *The Mabinogi*, p. 101. Lleu's parallels with Lugh are also evident in the description of his fosterage under Gwydion, and his growth and development. He was said to be capable of every kind of horsemanship, and was raised until he was "perfected in form, growth and size." The feast day associated with Lugh has a pronounced association with horses, and Lugh is "near to perfection" in aspect and ability.

14 Richard and Alastair Fitter and Marjorie Blamey, *The Wild Flowers of Britain and Northern Europe* (London: Collins, 1974), pp. 32, 106, 120. The oak tree (Welsh *derwen, dâr*) flowers between April and June, frequently in May (the month associated with Beltaine, *Calan Mai* in Welsh). The beautiful yellow flowers of the broom (Welsh *banadl*) appear during the same period as those of the oak tree. The fragrant, delicate white flowers of the meadowsweet (Welsh *erwain* or *blodau'r mêl*) appear between June to September, growing in woodlands as well as in wet places. In Scottish Gaelic, meadowsweet is known as *lus-chneas-Chuchulainn*, the "skin, waist or bosom" of Cu Chulainn.

15 Sarah Larratt Keefer, "The Lost Tale of Dylan in the Fourth Branch of the Mabinogi," *Studia Celtica* vol. 24-25 (1989/90), pp. 30, 31-32.

16 Keefer, "The Lost Tale of Dylan in the Fourth Branch of the Mabinogi," p. 33.

17 Keefer, "The Lost Tale of Dylan in the Fourth Branch of the Mabinogi," p. 30. A reference is made to Dylan in a later Welsh folktale (*Y Fôr Forwyn*, "The Mermaid"), which relates the adventures of a mermaid who is said to be the niece of Gwydion.

18 Keefer, "The Lost Tale of Dylan in the Fourth Branch of the Mabinogi," p. 31.

19 Keefer, "The Lost Tale of Dylan in the Fourth Branch of the Mabinogi," p. 29.

20 The Irish goddess Macha, who was venerated at Lugnasad, was (in one text) said to have a father whose name meant "ocean."

21 Keefer, "The Lost Tale of Dylan in the Fourth Branch of the Mabinogi," p. 32.

22 This may also have formed some part of Arianrhod's legend, which may be why the conception was so mysterious and the father undisclosed (as well as why such disgrace was attached to the birth).

23 Daithi O hOgain, *Myth, Legend and Romance: An Encylopedia of the Irish Folk Tradition* (New York: Prentice Hall, 1991), p. 276.

24 This is a characteristic she shares with Artemis. In addition, the twelve women who guard a thirteenth may have some connection with lunar numerology.

25 Rees and Rees, *Celtic Heritage* (New York: Thames and Hudson, 1989), pp. 196-97.

26 Ross, *Pagan Celtic Britain*, p. 320.

27 Ross, *Pagan Celtic Britain*, p. 246.

28 E. Estyn Evans, *Irish Folk Ways* (London: Routledge and Kegan Paul, 1957), pp. 211-12. The author says that, at one time, the wren-boy ceremonies involved a great deal of fertility symbolism, and were attended by men dressed as women. He also feels that, in spite of the English origin of certain associated rhymes, the wren-boy processions are degenerations of more elaborate performances of Irish origin, perhaps showing affinities with the mummer's plays (and like them, moved from an earlier association with spring).

29 Kevin Danaher, *The Year in Ireland* (Cork:London: Mercier Press, 1972), pp. 243-47.

30 Danaher, *The Year in Ireland*, p. 244. The wren's family is great in that it is large, with many possible offspring.

31 Trefor M. Owen, *Welsh Folk Customs* (Llandysul, Dyfed: Gomer Press, 1987), pp. 59, 63, 65-68.

32 Owen, *Welsh Folk Customs*, p. 64.

33 Brian Ó Cuív, "Some Gaelic Traditions about the Wren," in *Éigse* 19 (1982), pp. 57-58. Various scholars have dis-

cussed earlier roots that may underlie both of these words, as well as the Welsh word *derwydd*, "Druid, prophet," and other Irish names for the wren.

34 Ó Cuív, "Some Gaelic Traditions about the Wren." The 9th-century text known as *Cormac's Glossary* explores the association of the wren with Druids and prophecy, somewhat fancifully explaining the derivation of two of its names: *dreann* (from **dre*, perhaps meaning "small" and *én*, "bird") and *druí-én* (from *druí*, "druid," and *én*, "bird").

35 Ó Cuív, "Some Gaelic Traditions about the Wren," pp. 47-48, 53-54.

36 Ó Cuív, "Some Gaelic Traditions about the Wren," pp. 54-55.

37 Alexander Nicolson, *Gaelic Proverbs* (Edinburgh: Birlinn, 1996), p. 82. Alexander Forbes, in his 1905 *Gaelic Names of Beasts, Birds, Fishes, Insects and Reptiles* (pp. 347-48) states that the wren is also referred to as "the king of birds" in *The Death of Bran*.

38 Ó Cuív, "Some Gaelic Traditions about the Wren," pp. 60-61, 63. A Scottish rhyme also refers to a similar contrast between the heron and the wren (the heron shares similar characteristics with the crane, and the two are sometimes interchangeable).

39 Alexander Robert Forbes, *Gaelic Names of Beasts, Birds, Fishes, Insects and Reptiles* (Edinburgh, 1905), pp. 357-359.

40 Ó Cuív, "Some Gaelic Traditions about the Wren," pp. 64-66.

41 Bruce Campbell, *The Oxford Book of Birds* (Oxford: Oxford University Press, 1972), pp. 134-35. Owen, *Welsh Folk Customs*, p. 67; The scarcity of the wren and its subsequent return in the spring is alluded to in this excerpt from a song associated with a Welsh wren-hunt procession: "A little wren is the fellow about whom there is commotion . . . The rogue who was proud last night is now caught . . . He was placed under a sheet on a white bier of many colours . . . Ribbons of all colours encircle the wren, Ribbons in three turns enclose him instead of a roof. Wrens are scarce, they flew away, but they will return along the old meadow's path."

42 Ó Cuív, "Some Gaelic Traditions about the Wren," pp. 59-60.

43 Rachel Bromwich, *Trioedd Ynys Prydein* (The Triads of Britain) (Cardiff, Wales: University of Wales Press, 1961), pp. 281-82; Peter Shrijver, "On Henbane and Early European Narcotics" in *Zeitschrift fur Celtische Philologie*, vol. 51 (1999), pp. 17-45.

44 Bromwich, *Trioedd Ynys Prydein* (The Triads of Britain), p. 278.

45 Ford, *The Mabinogi*, pp. 99-101. On top of Twt Hill (near Caernarvon) are the scattered remains of a Celtic settlement, and from the jutting peak one can see sweeping vistas of the land below (including Caernarvon castle).

46 Ford, *The Mabinogi*, pp. 175-76.

47 Proinsias Mac Cana, *The Mabinogi* (Cardiff: University of Wales Press, 1992), p. 51.

48 Mac Cana, *The Mabinogi*, p. 51.

49 Mac Cana, *The Mabinogi*, p. 55.

50 This is, of course, a highly speculative and creative attempt to weave the elements at our disposal into a smooth-running narrative. For those who wish to read more about the *Mabinogi* and its cast of characters, the following are recommended: *The Mabinogi* by Proinsias Mac Cana, *The Mabinogi and other Medieval Welsh Tales* by Patrick K. Ford, and sections of *Celtic Heritage* by Alwyn and Brinley Rees (including, but not limited to, pp. 41, 51-53, 144, 176). It is possible that the slaying of Dylan by his uncle, Gofannon, is cognate with the story of the death of Bridget's son, Ruadán, at the hands of his uncle, Goibhniu (the Irish divine smith). Both sons are the product of a "mixed marriage" in the sense that the mothers are members of the primary divine pantheon, but the fathers are of another race (Fomorian, etc.) In many Irish tales, the paternity of the child appears to determine its character or outcome. Those with Tuatha De Danann fathers and mothers from other supernatural races are preeminent or successful (like Lugh), while those with Tuatha mothers and fathers from other races are not (like Bres).

51 Mac Cana, *The Mabinogi* , pp. 30, 130. It is interesting to note that, in the later poetry of the *cywydd* period, there is a late-15th-century allusion to the Tale of Math. Here it is Arianrhod, not Goewin, who is the footholder. It has been suggested that the two poets involved in the compilation of the text may have been quoting an earlier and more authentic version of the story of Lleu's conception (although we cannot know for sure). If this is the case, the story of Arianrhod may have even more interesting ramifications. A number of interesting academic explorations of this branch of the *Mabinogi* have been made. John Carey (*History of Religions* 31, 1991) believes that the tale's primary significance is inherited rather than synchronic, and that it displays (in a somewhat altered form) a myth of origins describing the end of a paradisal state of being (and the emergence of new conditions associated with the restrictions of mortality). Roberta Valenta (*Bulletin of the Board of Celtic Studies*, vol. 35, 1988) explores the actions and interaction of Gwydion and Arianrhod in terms of their transgression of conventional gender roles assigned to them by society.

52 Michael Ryan, ed., *The Illustrated Archaeology of Ireland* (Dublin: Country House, 1991), pp. 74-75, 105. Copper ores used by Bronze Age miners in Ireland contained traces of silver, arsenic, and antimony.

53 Ryan, ed., *The Illustrated Archaeology of Ireland*, pp. 125, 153-55.

54 Barry Cunliffe, *The Ancient Celts* (Oxford: Oxford University Press, 1997), pp. 26-27. The somewhat late appearance of silver as a widespread medium led James Mallory to the conclusion that the constant references to silver

among prestigious items mentioned in the *Taín* must reflect Irish experience in the 6th to 9th centuries (although other elements of the saga do seem to reflect earlier elements of Irish society). Ruth and Vincent Megaw, *Celtic Art* (New York: Thames and Hudson, 1989), pp. 58, 85, 116-17, 161, 166-67, 174-76, 179, 182, 190, 230. For example, a gold plaque engraved with silver (late 5th century B.C.E. Czechoslovakia), a group of silver disks (some decorated with triskeles, such as the 1st-century B.C.E. northern Italian disk also ornamented with repoussé heads), silver ornaments from the late 1st century B.C.E. in Hungary, a silver brooch and ring (4th century B.C.E. Switzerland), a silvered bronze brooch (4th century B.C.E. Austria), and a silver gilt finger ring (2nd-century B.C.E. Switzerland). Graham and Anna Richie, in *Scotland—Archaeology and Early History* (Edinburgh: Edinburgh University Press, 1991), pp. 108, 172-74, mention that silver spiral finger rings have been found in Scotland dating to quite an early period.

55   F. Marian McNeill, *The Silver Bough: Scottish Folklore and Folk-Belief*, vol. 1(Glasgow: William MacLellan, 1977), p. 91.

56   McNeill, *The Silver Bough: Scottish Folklore and Folk-Belief*, pp. 75-76, 92-94.

57   McNeill, *The Silver Bough: Scottish Folklore and Folk-Belief.*

58   McNeill, *The Silver Bough: Scottish Folklore and Folk-Belief*, pp. 146, 153.

59   Anne Ross, *The Folklore of the Scottish Highlands* (New York: Barnes and Noble/Batsford, 1976), p. 70.

60   Ross, *The Folklore of the Scottish Highlands*, p. 132.

61   McNeill, *The Silver Bough: Scottish Folklore and Folk-Belief*, p. 110.

62   Tom P. Cross and Clark H. Slover, *Ancient Irish Tales* (New York: Barnes and Noble/HenryHold, 1969), p. 503.

63   These textual references to silver come from the medieval period (as do those in the *Taín*).

64   Calvert Watkins, *Dictionary of Indo-European Roots* (New York: Houghton Mifflin, 2000), p. 5.

65   Carl D. Buck, *A Dictionary of Selected Synonyms in the Principal Indo-European Languages* (Chicago: University of Chicago Press, 1949), pp. 610-11. Edward Dwelly, *Faclair Gaidhlig gu Beurla: In Scottish Gaelic, airgiod-luachra* is the name of the herb meadowsweet, also known as *crios Cuchulainn*.

66   A. L. F. Rivet and Colin Smith, *The Place-Names of Roman Britain* (London: Batsford/Cambridge University Press, 1979), p. 257; Buck, *A Dictionary of Selected Synonyms in the Principal Indo-European Languages*, p. 610.

67   James J. Wilhelm, Layamon's *Brut* in *The Romance of Arthur: An Anthology of Medieval Texts in Translation* (New York: Garland Publishing, 1994), pp. 109-10. Layamon tried to avoid French phrases or stylistic expressions as in Wace. His Arthur acts more like an early British chieftain than a Norman monarch, and the author is always on the side of the Celts (rather than the Saxons or French).

68   Wilhelm, *The Romance of Arthur: An Anthology of Medieval Texts in Translation*, pp. 109-10.

69   Richard Barber, *King Arthur: Hero and Legend* (Suffolk: Boydell, 1986), pp. 40-41.

70   Barber, *King Arthur: Hero and Legend.*

71   Barber, *King Arthur: Hero and Legend.*

72   Wilhelm, *The Romance of Arthur: An Anthology of Medieval Texts in Translation* , p. 119.

73   Lewis Thorpe, ed. and tr., *Geoffrey of Monmouth: The History of the Kings of Britain* (Middlesex, UK: Penguin, 1966), p. 261.

74   Wilhelm, *The Romance of Arthur: An Anthology of Medieval Texts in Translation*, pp. 95-96.

75   Barber, *King Arthur: Hero and Legend*, pp. 24-25, 37, 49.

76   Barber, *King Arthur: Hero and Legend*. See also Basil Clarke, ed., "Vita Merlini" (Cardiff, Wales: University of Wales Press, 1975).

77   Barber, *King Arthur: Hero and Legend*, pp. 56, 59.

78   Wilhelm, *The Romance of Arthur: An Anthology of Medieval Texts in Translation*, pp. 7-8.

79   Wilhelm, *The Romance of Arthur: An Anthology of Medieval Texts in Translation*, p. 343. See also *The Prose Merlin*, p. 355, where Morgan le Fay is mentioned in a dialogue between Merlin and the Lady of the Lake: "Ah! Lady of the Lake, if you only felt some affection for Arthur! If you only knew what is being plotted against him! His sister Morgan, who he trusts completely, has just stolen his good and trustworthy sword Excalibur, together with the scabbard, and she has replaced it with one that looks identical but is worthless. And tomorrow he is to meet a knight in single combat! That means his life is in danger, because his sword will fail him when he needs it." Morgan's machinations to destroy Arthur continue, but the Lady of the Lake (Niviane) rescues him and restores to him his sword Excalibur.

80   Barber, *King Arthur: Hero and Legend*, p. 118.

81   Wilhelm, *The Romance of Arthur: An Anthology of Medieval Texts in Translation*, p. 399.

82   Wilhelm, *The Romance of Arthur: An Anthology of Medieval Texts in Translation*, pp. 425-26.

83   Wilhelm, *The Romance of Arthur: An Anthology of Medieval Texts in Translation*, pp. 463-64.

84   Wilhelm, *The Romance of Arthur: An Anthology of Medieval Texts in Translation*, pp. 529-30, 569.

85   Ygerne/Igraine is said to have had three daughters. Apart from the Lady of the Lake, three Otherworld queens are mentioned in Malory's text, bringing to mind the sacredness of three in Celtic tradition and goddesses who are triple-aspected, like Bridget, the Morrígan and Macha.

86   Wilhelm, *The Romance of Arthur: An Anthology of Medieval Texts in Translation*, pp. 295-97. These include the

Prose Merlin of Robert de Boron, the anonymous *Suite du Merlin* written in the early to middle part of the 13th century, the late-14th-century Italian *Cantare on the Death of Tristan* (where she gives an enchanted lance to Tristan) and of course, Malory's *Le Morte d'Arthur*.

87   Alexander Carmichael, *Carmina Gadelica* (Edinburgh: Lindisfarne, 1991), pp. 283-92.

88   Buck, *A Dictionary of Selected Synonyms in the Principal Indo-European Languages*, pp. 54-55. Another word meaning "bright, shining, pure, sacred," commonly found in Old Irish tales, is the word *find/finn* (cognate with Welsh *gwynn*, fem. *Gwen*), found in the names of numerous divine figures and heroes.

89   W. F. H. Nicolaisen, *The Picts and Their Place-Names* (Rosemarkie, UK: Groam House Museum Trust, 1996), pp. 18-19; W. J. Watson, *The Celtic Placenames of Scotland* (Edinburgh: Birlinn, 1993), pp. 440, 478. These include Geallaidh in Nairnshire and Moray, two Geldies in Aberdeenshire, Abergeldie and Loch Gellie in Fife, Inbhir Gheallaidh in Glen Lednock, Gellie near Kinross, and other Gellie burns.

90   Buck, *A Dictionary of Selected Synonyms in the Principal Indo-European Languages*, pp. 54-55.

91   Carmichael, *Carmina Gadelica*, p. 288.

Tenth Lunation

1   Thomas Kinsella, ed. and tr., *The New Oxford Book of Irish Verse* (Oxford: Oxford University Press, 1986), p. 12-13. Parts of this prayer could be envisioned as forming part of an earlier Druidic invocation. Here the poet summons the elemental powers (and the Christian deity) to protect against "the chants of false prophets, dark laws of the pagans, false heretics' laws, entrapments of idols, and the enchantments of women, smiths and druids."

2   John O'Meara, tr., *Gerald of Wales: History and Topography of Ireland* (London: Penguin, 1982), p. 59.

3   O'Meara, tr., *Gerald of Wales: History and Topography of Ireland*, p. 59.

4   Gerard Murphy, *Early Irish Lyrics* (Oxford, UK: Clarendon Press, 1956), p. 113. Gobbán is a divine smith.

5   George McClafferty, "I See the Moon, and the Moon Sees Me," *Sinnsear* 5, p. 67.

6   Kevin Danaher, *The Year in Ireland: Irish Calendar Customs* (Dublin: Mercier Press, 1972), p. 125.

7   McClafferty, "I See the Moon, and the Moon Sees Me," p. 68.

8   McClafferty, "I See the Moon, and the Moon Sees Me,"pp. 68-69.

9   Kevin Danaher, *The Year in Ireland* (Cork/Dublin: Mercier Press,1972), p. 87. See also "Scots Folklore Scraps," in *Folklore*, vol. 43 (1932). As late as 1932, it was recorded in Scotland that the weather of the next month was believed to be rainy if the new Moon had occurred on a Saturday (both the Moon and Saturn were associated with rain).

10   McClafferty, "I See the Moon, and the Moon Sees Me," p. 70.

11   Danaher, *The Year in Ireland: Irish Calendar Customs*, pp. 203, 218.

12   Dermot MacManus, *The Middle Kingdom* (Gerrards Cross: Colin Smythe, 1973), pp. 188-89. The cure consisted of walking bare-footed and bare-legged in a soft bog in a left-hand-wise circle (useful for decreasing magic) for fifteen minutes daily for a three-week period.

13   MacManus, *The Middle Kingdom*, pp. 69-70.

14   McClafferty, "I See the Moon, and the Moon Sees Me," pp. 71-72.

15   Alexander Carmichael, *Carmina Gadelica* (Edinburgh: Lindisfarne Press, 1992), pp. 283-84.

16   Entries from a manuscript entitled *A Collection of Highland Rites and Customs* compiled in the late 1600s, as presented in Michael Hunter, *The Occult Laboratory* (n.p.: The Boydell Press, 2001), p. 54. My thanks to Dr. Michael Newton for bringing this to my attention.

17   F. Marian McNeill, *The Silver Bough* (Glasgow: William MacLellan, 1977), pp. 57-58.

18   McNeill, *The Silver Bough*, p. 58; I. F. Grant, *Highland Folk Ways* (London: Routledge, 1989), p. 355.

19   McNeill, *The Silver Bough*, p. 58; Grant, *Highland Folk Ways*, p. 355; M. Bennett, *Scottish Customs—From the Cradle to the Grave* (Edinburgh: Polygon, 1992), p. 123. A report dating from 1874 in the northeast of Scotland mentioned that marriages were held either on Tuesdays or Thursdays (and more rarely on Saturday) during the increase of the Moon. Marriages were held in any month but May, a month considered unlucky for marriage (hence the custom of the June Bride).

20   A type of lichen called *corcur* (used to dye wool various shades of red to purple) was reported by Martin Martin in 1695 to have been scraped from stones during the decrease of the Moon, preferably in August when it was most ripe. As quoted in Tess Darwin, *The Scots Herbal—Plant Lore of Scotland* (Edinburgh: Mercat Press, 1996), p. 46.

21   McNeill, *The Silver Bough*, pp. 57-58.

22   McNeill, *The Silver Bough*, p. 58; Grant, *Highland Folk Ways*, p. 355.

23   Carmichael, *Carmina Gadelica*, p. 283.

24   McNeill, *The Silver Bough*, p. 58, 91; Grant, *Highland Folk Ways*, p. 355. Grant mentions that an elderly relative took that occasion to kiss the woman nearest to him, reminiscent of the liminal associations of mistletoe at the time of the New Year (which originally would have coincided with the new Moon).

25 From *A Collection of Highland Rites and Customs*, in Hunter, *The Occult Laboratory*, pp. 72, 76.

26 Carmichael, *Carmina Gadelica*, p. 642.

27 McNeill, *The Silver Bough*, p. 58, 91; Grant, *Highland Folk Ways*, p. 355.

28 Carmichael, *Carmina Gadelica*, p. 612.

29 Michael Newton, *A Handbook of the Scottish Gaelic World* (Dublin: Four Courts Press, 2000), p. 177.

30 *The Dewar Manuscripts*, as quoted in Newton, *A Handbook of the Scottish Gaelic World*, p. 102.

31 McNeill, *The Silver Bough*, pp. 57-58.

32 Trefor M. Owen, *Welsh Folk Customs* (Llandysul, Dyfed: Gomer, 1987), p. 144.

33 Kathleen Hawke, *Cornish Sayings, Superstitions and Remedies* (Trewolsta, Trewirgie, Redruth: Dyllanson Truran Cornish Publications, 1973), pp. 10-20.

34 Hawke, *Cornish Sayings, Superstitions and Remedies*, pp. 18, 31.

35 Alwyn and Brinley Rees, *Celtic Heritage* (New York: Thames and Hudson, 1989), pp. 196-97.

36 Vernam Hull and Archer Taylor, *A Collection of Irish Riddles* (Berkeley and Los Angeles: University of California Press, 1955), pp. 4, 5, 13, 14, 48.

37 Author's translation from the Scottish Gaelic in Carmichael, *Carmina Gadelica*.

38 Author's translation from the Scottish Gaelic in Carmichael, *Carmina Gadelica*.

39 Author's translation from the Scottish Gaelic in Carmichael, *Carmina Gadelica*.

40 Author's translation from the Scottish Gaelic in Carmichael, *Carmina Gadelica*.

41 Author's translation from the Scottish Gaelic in Carmichael, *Carmina Gadelica*.

42 Author's translation from the Scottish Gaelic in Carmichael, *Carmina Gadelica*.

43 Folk traditions maintain that the fairies are most active at the turning points of the year (particularly Samain and Beltaine). They are also active at the turning points of the day: dawn, noon, dusk, and midnight. Some of these associations are seen in Breton folk tradition, where the points of the compass are also associated with the time of day. East is, of course, associated with the sunrise, and proceeding in a sunwise direction, noon is in the south, sunset in the west, and midnight in the north. I am most grateful to Benjamin Bruch of Harvard University for bringing these traditions to my attention.

44 Rees, *Celtic Heritage*, p. 83.

45 Rees, *Celtic Heritage*, p. 83.

46 Rees, *Celtic Heritage*, p. 83.

47 DIL, 2 túath.

48 In addition, the polar star was called *an rélta a túaidh*, "the star of the north," and a comet is *ré mongach*, "a maned or hairy star." *Roth*, "a wheel" (cognate with *rhod* as in Arianrhod), also applies to a brooch.

49 Here, we might recall the Scottish love charm that cited the Moon as one of its empowerers, and which may have used the bog-violet in its preparation.

50 Recommended books on Celtic fairy traditions include: *The Fairy Faith in Celtic Countries* by Evans-Wentz (New York: Citadel Press, 1990) (ignore outdated theories, especially pp. 234-48 and 329-26, but enjoy the accounts recorded in the Celtic countries, pp. 23-225); *Fairy and Folk Tales of Ireland* by W.B. Yeats (New York: Macmillan, 1983); and *The Encyclopedia of Fairies* (New York: Pantheon, 1976) or *The Fairies in Tradition and Literature* (London: Routledge and Kegan Paul, 1977) by Katherine Briggs. Trust books by university presses, folklore associations, or trained folklorists in which accounts of fairies and fairy traditions are taken from actual oral reports.

Eleventh Lunation

1 Estyn Evans, *Irish Folk Ways* (London: Routledge and Kegan Paul, 1957), p. 274.

2 Nicolai Tolstoy, *The Quest for Merlin* (Boston: Little Brown and Company, 1985), p. 227.

3 Fadel Gad, "Egypt: Land of the Golden Mummies," in *Ions Noetic Sciences Review*, Dec. 2000, p. 46.

4 Gad, "Egypt: Land of the Golden Mummies."

5 Gad, "Egypt: Land of the Golden Mummies."

6 Sandra Billington and Miranda Green, eds., *The Concept of the Goddess* (London: Routledge, 1996), p. 15. The same may be said of things foreign or exotic, as well as things on the periphery of society.

7 Billington and Green, eds., *The Concept of the Goddess*, pp. 8-25. Wood describes the growth of another legend whose origins may be found in the works of certain poets, archaeologists, and seekers. This is the relatively modern legend of the Goddess, which began in the late 1800s, growing in popularity as a result of the feminist movement in the latter half of the 1900s. The legend theorizes that ancient people worshipped a great Mother Goddess and lived in peaceful and predominantly matriarchal societies. In previous chapters, we have encountered information that brings to light the historical problems of this theory (which have been generally ignored by its supporters). For many of the social and spiritual reasons presented in this chapter, the Goddess movement continues to grow in popularity, bringing a sense of connectedness, hope, and empowerment to women around the world.

Wood explores in some detail the theories and impulses that led up to the creation of this modern myth, a process also explored by Ronald Hutton in *Pagan Religions of the Ancient British Isles* (Oxford: Blackwell, 1991) and *The Triumph of the Moon* (Oxford: Oxford University Press, 1999).

8   Hutton, *The Triumph of the Moon*, pp. 1-42.

9   This process is explained in great detail in Hutton's *Triumph of the Moon*.

10 See Hutton, *Pagan Religions of the Ancient British Isles* (chapter 8), and *Triumph of the Moon*.

11 Gerina Dunwich, *Wicca Craft* (Seacaucus, N.J.: Citadel Press, 1997), pp. 10-17.

12 Calvert Watkins, *Dictionary of Indo-European Roots* (Boston: Houghton Mifflin, 2000), p. 95.

13 For an explanation of the modern origins of the Goddess (circa 1850 onward) see Hutton, *The Triumph of the Moon*, pp. 32-42; Juliette Wood, "The Concept of the Goddess," in *The Concept of the Godddess*, ed. Sandra Billington, and Miranda Green (London: Routledge, 1996), pp. 8-25; Lotte Motz, *The Faces of the Goddess* (New York: Oxford University Press, 1997); Hutton, *Pagan Religions of the Ancient British Isles* (Chapter 8).

14 Gad, "Egypt: Land of the Golden Mummies."

15 Excerpt from a traditional Wiccan blessing and ritual.

16 Paul Beyerl, *The Master Book of Herbalism* (Custer, WA: Phoenix Publishing, 1984), pp. 341-52.

17 F. Marian McNeill, *The Scots Kitchen* (Edinburgh: Mercat Press, 1993), pp. 174-75.

18 McNeill, *The Scots Kitchen*, pp. 165, 210, 221.

19 Stephen H. Buhner, *Sacred and Herbal Healing Beers* (Boulder, CO: Siris Books, 1998), pp. 199-203, 288-90, 298, 318, 304-6.

BIBLIOGRAPHY

Asimov, Isaac. *Asimov on Numbers*. New York: Simon and Schuster, 1977.

Bennett, M. *Scottish Customs: From the Cradle to the Grave*. Edinburgh: Polygon, 1992.

Billington, Sandra and Miranda Green, eds. *The Concept of the Godddess*. London: Routledge, 1996.

Briggs, Katherine. *An Encyclopedia of Fairies*. New York: Pantheon Books, 1976.

Brunaux, Jean Louis. *The Celtic Gauls: Gods, Rites and Sanctuaries*. London: Seaby, 1987.

Brunaux, John Ayto. *Dictionary of Word Origins*. New York: Little Brown and Co., 1990.

Buck, Carl D. *A Dictionary of Selected Synonyms in the Principal Indo-European Languages*. Chicago: University of Chicago Press, 1949.

Buhner, Stephen H. *Sacred and Herbal Healing Beers*. Boulder, CO: Siris Books, 1998.

Calder, George, ed. *Auraceipt na n-Éces: The Scholar's Primer*. Dublin: Four Courts Press, 1995.

Campbell, Bruce. *The Oxford Book of Birds*. Oxford: Oxford University Press, 1972.

Carey, John, and John Koch. *The Celtic Heroic Age*. Malden, MA: Celtic Studies Publications, 1995.

Carmichael, Alexander. *Carmina Gadelica: Hymns and Incantaions*. Edinburgh: Lindisfarne Press, 1992.

Clarke, D. V., T. G. Cowie, and A. Foxon. *Symbols of Power at the Time of Stonehenge*. Edinburgh: National Museum of the Antiquities of Scotland, 1985.

Cross, Tom, and Clark Slover. *Ancient Irish Tales*. Totowa, NJ: Barnes and Noble, 1969.

Culpeper, Nicholas. *Culpeper's Complete Herbal and English Physician*. Glenwood, IL: Meyerbooks, 1990.

Cunliffe, Barry. *The Ancient Celts*. Oxford: Oxford University Press, 1997.

Danaher, Kevin. *The Year in Ireland*. Cork/Dublin: Mercier Press,1972.

Darvill, Timothy. *Prehistoric Britain*. London: Routledge, 1987.

Darwin, Tess. *The Scots Herbal: Plant Lore of Scotland*. Edinburgh: Mercat Press, 1996.

Davidson, H. R. *Gods and Myths of Northern Europe*. London: Penguin, 1964.

———. *Myths and Symbols in Pagan Europe*. Syracuse, NY: Syracuse University Press, 1988.

Dillon, Myles. *The Archaism of Irish Tradition*. Chicago: University of Chicago Press, 1969.

Dooley, Ann, and Harry Roe. *Tales of the Elders of Ireland*. Oxford: Oxford University Press, 1999.

Dunwich, Gerina. *Wicca Craft*. Secaucus, NJ: Citadel Press, 1997.

Dwelly, Edward. *Faclair Gaidhlig gu Beurla: Dwelly's Illustrated Gaelic to English Dictionary*. Glasgow: Gairm Publications, 1994.

Edwards, H. J., trans. *Caesar: The Gallic War*. Cambridge, MA: Harvard University Press, 1997.

Eliade, Mircea. *The Myth of the Eternal Return*. Princeton, NJ: Princeton University Press, 1971.

———. *Rites and Symbols of Initiation*. Woodstock, NY: Spring Publications, 1995.

———. *The Sacred and the Profane*. New York: Harcourt Brace, 1987.

———. *Shamanism: Archaic Techniques of Ecstacy*. Princeton, NJ: Princeton University Press, 1964.

Eogan, George. *Knowth and the Passage-Tombs of Ireland*. London: Thames and Hudson, 1986.

Evans, E. Estyn. *Irish Folk Ways*. London: Routledge and Kegan Paul, 1957.

Evans-Wentz, W. Y. *The Fairy Faith in Celtic Countries*. New York: Citadel Press, 1990.

Forbes, Alexander Robert. *Gaelic Names of Beasts, Birds, Fishes, Insects and Reptiles*. Edinburgh, 1905.

Ford, Patrick K. *The Celtic Poets*. Belmont, MA: Ford and Bailie, 1999.

———. *The Mabinogi*. Berkeley: University of California Press, 1977.

Grant, I. F. *Highland Folk Ways*. London: Routledge, 1989.

Graves, Robert. *The Greek Myths*. London: Penguin Books, 1960.

Gray, Elizabeth. *Cath Maige Tuired*. Dublin: Irish Texts Society, 1982.

Green, Miranda. *Animals in Celtic Life and Myth*. London: Routledge, 1992.

———. *Celtic Goddesses*. New York: George Braziller, 1995.

———. *Dictionary of Celtic Myth and Legend*. London: Thames and Hudson, 1992.

———. *The World of the Druids*. London: Thames and Hudson, 1997.

Grieve, M. A. *A Modern Herbal*. New York: Dover, 1971.

Gwynn, Edward. *The Metrical Dindsenchas*. Dublin: School of Celtic Studies, Dublin Institute for Advanced Studies, 1991.

Hamilton, Edith. *Mythology: Timeless Tales of Gods and Heroes*. New York: Penguin, 1969.

Harbison, Peter. *Pre-Christian Ireland*. New York: Thames and Hudson, 1988.

Harner, Michael. *The Way of the Shaman*. San Francisco: HarperSanFrancisco, 1990.

Herity, Michael, and George Eogan. *Ireland in Prehistory*. London: Routledge, 1989.

Hull, Vernam, and Aecher Taylor. *A Collection of Irish Riddles*. Berkeley: University of California Press, 1955.

Hutton, Ronald. *The Pagan Religions of the Ancient British Isles*. Cambridge and Oxford: Blackwell, 1991.

———. *The Triumph of the Moon*. Oxford: Oxford University Press, 1999.

Ireland, Stanley. *Roman Britain*. New York: Routledge, 1991.

Jackson, Kenneth. *Studies in Early Celtic Nature Poetry*. Lampeter, Dyfed: Llanerch, 1935.

Kathleen, Hawke. *Cornish Sayings, Superstitions and Remedies*. Trewolsta, Trewirgie, Redruth: Dyllanson Truran-Cornish Publications, 1973.

Kelly, Fergus. *Early Irish Law*. Dublin: Institute for Advanced Studies, 1988.

Kerényi, C. *The Gods of the Greeks*. New York: Thames and Hudson, 1994.

Kinsella, Thomas. *The New Oxford Book of Irish Verse*. Oxford: Oxford University Press, 1986.

———. *The Tain*. Oxford: Oxford University Press, 1970.

Kinsley, David R. *Hindu Goddesses*. Berkeley: University of California Press, 1988.

Lincoln, Bruce. *Myth, Cosmos and Society*. Cambridge, MA: Harvard University Press, 1986.

Lust, John. *The Herb Book*. New York: Bantam Books, 1977.

Mabey, Richard. *The New Age Herbalist*. New York: Collier Books, 1988.

Mac Cana, Proinsias. *The Mabinogi*. Cardiff: University of Wales Press, 1992.

Macalister, R. A. Stewart. *Lebor Gabála Érenn*. Dublin: Irish Texts Society, 1956.

MacKillop, James. *Dictionary of Celtic Mythology*. Oxford: Oxford University Press, 1998.

Maclennan, Malcom. *Gaelic Dictionary*. Edinburgh: Mercat Press, 1979.

MacManus, Dermot. *The Middle Kingdom*. Gerrards Cross: Colin Smythe, 1973.

Martin, Martin and R. W. Munro. *A Description of the Western Islands of Scotland Circa 1695*. Edinburgh: Birlinn, 1999.

McManus, Damian. *A Guide to Ogam*. Naas: Maynooth Monograph Series, 1997.

McNeill, F. Marian. *The Scots Kitchen*. Edinburgh: Mercat Press, 1993.

———. *The Silver Bough: Scottish Folklore and Folk-Belief*. Glasgow: William MacLellan, 1977.

Megaw, Ruth, and Vincent Megaw. *Celtic Art*. New York: Thames and Hudson, 1989.

Moore, Patrick. *The Moon*. New York: Rand McNally/Royal Astronomical Society, 1981.

Morford, Mark P.O., and Robert J. Lenardon. *Classical Mythology*. New York/London: Longman, ca. 1985.

Motz, Lotte. *The Faces of the Goddess*. New York: Oxford University Press, 1997.

Murphy, Gerard. *Early Irish Lyrics*. Oxford, UK: Clarendon Press, 1956.

Newton, Michael. *A Handbook of the Scottish Gaelic World*. Dublin: Four Courts Press, 2000.

Nicolaisen, W. F. H. *The Picts and Their Place-Names*. Rosemarkie, UK: Groam House Museum Trust, 1996.

Nicolson, Alexander. *Gaelic Proverbs*. Edinburgh: Birlinn, 1996.

Ó Dónaill, Niall. *Foclóir Gaeilge-Béarla*. Dublin: Rialtas na hÉireann, 1977.

Ó Duinn, Sean. *Forbhais Droma Damhgháire*. Dublin: Mercier Press, 1992.

O hOgain, Daithi. *Myth, Legend and Romance: An Encylopedia of the Irish Folk Tradition*. New York: Prentice Hall, 1991.

O'Flaherty, Wendy Doniger. *Hindu Myths*. London: Penguin Books, 1975.

———. *Women, Androgynes and Other Mythical Beasts*. Chicago: University of Chicago Press, 1980.

O'Kelly, Michael J. *Newgrange*. London: Thames and Hudson, 1982.

O'Meara, John J., ed. and trans. *Gerald of Wales: The History and Topography of Ireland*. London: Penguin Books, 1982.

Osborne, Ken, ed. *Stonehenge and Neighbouring Monuments*. London: English Heritage, 1995.

Owen, Trefor M. *Welsh Folk Customs*. Llandysul, Dyfed: Gomer Press, 1987.

Patterson, Nerys. *Cattle Lords and Clansmen: The Social Structure of Early Ireland*. Notre Dame, IN: University of Notre Dame Press, 1994.

Phillips, Roger, and Nicky Foy. *Herbs*. New York: Randon House, 1990.

Piggot, Stuart. *The Druids*. New York: Thames and Hudson, 1975.

Powell, T. G. E. *The Celts*. London: Thames and Hudson, 1980.

Radford, E., and M. A. Radford. *The Encyclopedia of Superstitions*. Edited and revised by Christina Hole. New York: Barnes and Noble, 1961.

Rankin, David. *Celts and the Classical World*. New York: Routledge, 1996.

Rees, Alwyn, and Brinley Rees. *Celtic Heritage*. New York: Thames and Hudson, 1989.

Ritchie, Graham and Anna. *Scotland: Archaeology and Early History*. Edinburgh: Edinburgh University Press, 1991.

Rivet, A. L. F., and Colin Smith. *The Place-Names of Roman Britain*. London: Batsford/Cambridge University Press, 1979.

Rose, H. J. *A Handbook of Greek Mythology*. New York: E. P. Dutton, 1959.

Ross, Anne. *Pagan Celtic Britain*. Chicago: Academy Publishers, 1996.

Ryan, Michael, ed. *The Illustrated Archaeology of Ireland*. Dublin: Country House, 1991.

Sargent, Thelma. *The Homeric Hymns*. New York: W.W. Norton and Co., 1975.

Stokes, Whitley, ed. and trans. *Sanas Chormaic* (Cormac's Glossary). Calcutta: Irish Archaeological and Celtic Society, 1868.

Swire, Otta F. *Skye: The Island and Its Legends*. London: Blackie and Son Ltd., 1961.

Thorpe, Lewis, ed. and trans. *Geoffrey of Monmouth: The History of the Kings of Britain*. Middlesex, UK: Penguin, 1966.

———. *Gerald of Wales: The Journey Through Wales/The Description of Wales*. London: Penguin Books, 1988.

Tolstoy, Nicolai. *The Quest for Merlin*. Boston: Little Brown and Company, 1985.

Watkins, Calvert. *Dictionary of Indo-European Roots*. Boston: Houghton Mifflin, 2000.

Watson, W. J. *The Celtic Placenames of Scotland*. Edinburgh: Birlinn, 1993.

Wilhelm, James J. *The Romance of Arthur: An Anthology of Medieval Texts in Translation*. New York: Garland Publishing, 1994.

Willis, Roy, ed. *World Mythology*. New York: Henry Holt, 1993.

Yeats, W. B. *Fairy and Folk Tales of Ireland*. New York: Macmillan, 1983.

Young, Jean I. *The Prose Edda of Snorri Sturluson*. Berkeley: University of California Press, 1964.

Zdenek, Kopal. *The Solar System*. Oxford: Oxford University Press, 1973.

Zimmer, Heinrich. *Myths and Symbols in Indian Art and Civilization*. New York: Harper Torchbooks, 1962.

PERMISSIONS

THE AUTHOR GRATEFULLY ACKNOWLEDGES permission to excerpt from the following:

Studies in Early Celtic Nature Poetry by Kenneth Jackson, copyright © 1935, used by permission of Llanerch Press.

The Mabinogi by Patrick K. Ford, copyright © 1977, used by permission of University of California Press.

The Celtic Heroic Age by John Koch and John Carey, copyright © 2000. Published by Celtic Studies Publications and used by permission of the authors.

Every effort has been made to contact permissions holders of any copyrighted material in this book. If any required acknowledgments have been omitted, it is unintentional. If notified, the publishers will be pleased to rectify any omission in future additions.

ABOUT THE AUTHOR

SHARYNNE MACLEOD NICMHACHA is a Canadian writer, teacher, and musician of Scottish, Irish, and British ancestry. A descendant of Clan MacLeod, long recorded in oral tradition to have connections with and blood of the Sidhe, or Fairy Folk, she has a keen interest in Arthurian legends, Scottish witchcraft, and Irish and Welsh wisdom texts. She has studied Old Irish, Scottish Gaelic, and Celtic mythology through Harvard University and has presented work through the Ford Foundation's Celtic Lecture Series, the Harvard Study Group on Ancient Magic and Religion, the University of Massachusetts, the Omega Institute, and the University of Edinburgh. NicMhacha also sings and plays a number of instruments and has performed Celtic and medieval music with The Moors and, more recently, with Devandaurae. She currently lives in New England.

TO OUR READERS